Additional Praise for *The Authors of the*
Deuteronomistic History

"Brian Neil Peterson has written an important alternative to much of the literature discussing the Deuteronomistic redaction of Deuteronomy, Joshua, Judges, and 1 & 2 Samuel. Building on a strong foundation of comparative studies with the first of these books, Peterson argues his case for an early authorship from the time of David. Peterson's groundbreaking work establishes a redactional basis for the appearance of these texts in early Israel. It demands serious consideration by anyone interested in the literature of Israel's early history."

Richard S. Hess
Denver Seminary

"At last, a refreshing and provocative new look at the long-standing question of who wrote the great history of ancient Israel (Deuteronomy–2 Kings)! Instead of the 'slice and dice' approach that rules the field, Peterson offers a theory that is holistic in its approach and based on sound exegesis that demonstrates a variegated but cohesive writing created within a unified stream of tradition that had its inception during the monarchy. All future studies cannot avoid considering the proposal Peterson brings to the table."

Kenneth A. Mathews
Beeson Divinity School, Samford University

The Authors of the Deuteronomistic History

The Authors of the Deuteronomistic History

Locating a Tradition in Ancient Israel

Brian Neil Peterson

Fortress Press
Minneapolis

THE AUTHORS OF THE DEUTERONOMISTIC HISTORY

Locating a Tradition in Ancient Israel

Cover design: Laurie Ingram

Cover image: David and Nathan, Matthias Scheits, bpk, Berlin, Hamburger Kunsthalle, Elke Walford, Art Resources, NY

Library of Congress Cataloging-in-Publication Data

Print ISBN: 978-1-4514-6996-7

eBook ISBN: 978-1-4514-8746-6

Manufactured in the U.S.A.

This book was produced using PressBooks.com, and PDF rendering was done by PrinceXML.

This book is dedicated to my mother; Marion Madeline (McAffee) Peterson (1932–2012), whose life, love for God, and passion for the Bible inspired me to follow in her path of biblical study. Although she never had formal training, her astute understanding of the Word is something I strive to emulate.

Contents

Abbreviations

AASF	Annales Academiae Scientiarum Fennicae
AB	Anchor Bible
ABD	*Anchor Bible Dictionary*
ACJS	Annual of the College of Jewish Studies
AnBib	Analecta biblica
ANET	*Ancient Near Eastern Texts Relating to the Old Testament*
BA	*Biblical Archaeologist*
BAR	*Biblical Archaeology Review*
BASOR	*Bulletin of American Schools of Oriental Research*
Bib	*Biblica*
BibInt	*Biblical Interpretation*
BIS	Biblical Interpretation Series
BJS	Brown Judaic Studies

BLS	Bible and Literature Series
BibSac	*Bibliotheca Sacra*
BRev	*Bible Review*
BTB	*Biblical Theology Bulletin*
BWANT	Beiträge zur Wissenschaft vom Alten und Neuen Testament
BZAW	Beihefte zur Zeitschrift für die alttestamentliche Wissenschaft
CaE	*Cahiers évangile*
CANE	*Civilizations of the Ancient Near East*
CBC	The Cambridge Bible Commentary
CBQ	*Catholic Biblical Quarterly*
CBQMS	Catholic Biblical Quarterly Monograph Series
COT	Commentary on the Old Testament
CQR	*Church Quarterly Review*
EBC	Expositor's Bible Commentary
EncJud	Encyclopedia Judaica
ExpTim	*Expository Times*
FRLANT	Forschungen zur Religion und Literatur des Alten und Neuen Testaments
HAR	*Hebrew Annual Review*
HAT	Handbuch zum Alten Testament
HSM	Harvard Semitic Monographs
HTR	*Harvard Theological Review*
HUCA	*Hebrew Union College Annual*

Int	*Interpretation*
JBL	*Journal of Biblical Literature*
JESOT	*Journal for the Evangelical Study of the Old Testament*
JNES	*Journal of Near Eastern Studies*
JSJSup	Journal for the Study of Judaism in the Persian, Hellenistic, and Roman Periods Supplement Series
JSOT	*Journal for the Study of the Old Testament*
JSOTSup	Journal for the Study of the Old Testament: Supplement Series
JSS	*Journal of Semitic Studies*
KAT	Kommentar zum Alten Testament
KHC	Kurzer Hand-Commentar zum Alten Testament
KKHSANT	Kurzgefasster Kommentar zu den heiligen Schriften Alten und Neuen Testamentes
NAC	New American Commentary
NES	Near Eastern Studies
NICOT	New International Commentary on the Old Testament
OBO	Orbis biblicus et orientalis
OTL	Old Testament Library
PEQ	*Palestine Exploration Quarterly*
PTMS	Princeton Theological Monograph Series
QMIA	Qedem Monographs of the Institute of Archaeology
RB	Revue Biblique
SBL	Society of Biblical Literature
SBLStBl	Society of Biblical Literature Studies in Biblical Literature

SBLDS	Society of Biblical Literature Dissertation Series
SBLSS	Society of Biblical Literature Semeia Studies
SBT	Studies in Biblical Theology
SJOT	*Scandinavian Journal of the Old Testament*
TBAT	*Theologische Bücherei*, Altes Testament
Them	*Themelios*
TOTC	The Tyndale Old Testament Commentary Series
TynBul	*Tyndale Bulletin*
VT	*Vetus Testamentum*
VTSup	Supplements to Vetus Testamentum
WBC	Word Biblical Commentary
WMANT	Wissenschaftliche Monographien zum Alten und Neuen Testament
ZABR	*Zeitschrift für altorientaliche und biblische Rechtgeschichte*
ZAW	*Zeitschrift für alttestamentliche Wissenschaft*

Introduction

Deuteronomistic influence may be traced, but there is still no agreement as to who the Deuteronomists were.[1]

"Whodunit?" Everyone loves a good mystery novel or movie that highlights some persistent detective trying to get to the bottom of a prevailing conundrum. Of course, this is no less true of those seeking to solve the mystery of authorship of certain unascribed or questioned ancient texts. In the vein of "Whodunit?" inquiries, one can also find conspiracy theories galore. One need only to look at the controversies over the writings of Shakespeare—did he, or did he not, write many of his great works? A quick "online" search will reveal any number of alternate candidates such as Sir Francis Bacon, Christopher Marlowe, or Edward de Vere who have been put forward as the real genius behind the timeless and eloquent Shakespeare. Similarly, in the world of biblical studies, one could look to the long-running discussion on the authorship issues of the Pauline epistles among the non-*Hauptbriefe* texts. Furthermore, so as not to exclude my Synoptics colleagues, who is the author of the infamous "Q" source?

---

1. Richard Coggins, "What Does 'Deuteronomistic' Mean?" in *Those Elusive Deuteronomists: The Phenomenon of Pan-Deuteronomism*, ed. Linda S. Schearing and Steven L McKenzie, JSOTSup 268 (Sheffield: Sheffield Academic Press, 1999), 26.

In Old Testament (hereafter OT) studies, these same questions have been pondered literally for more than two thousand years. For example, in Jewish rabbinic tradition, which always sought to harmonize and offer solutions to plaguing questions from the text, rabbis attempted to alleviate the authorship issues of their Bible in a series of attributions found in *Baba Bathra* folios 14b and 15a. (I will address some of these in the chapters that follow.) In the world of OT/Hebrew Bible higher-critical studies, even when a text has been ascribed to a particular biblical author, scholars have spilled much ink debating the legitimacy of that attribution—Isaiah and Daniel being two of the key flashpoints in this regard over the past century.[2] Therefore, it goes without saying that OT scholars have been less than eager to offer absolute identifications of authors for particular unascribed texts.[3] Rather, scholars prefer more elastic and malleable authors such as the "Yahwist," the "Elohist," the "Priestly authors," the "school of prophet X," or, in the case of the Former Prophets, the ever-nebulous "Deuteronomist" or "Deuteronomistic Historian(s)" (Dtr).[4] Indeed, it is this latter designation that I seek to scrutinize.

2. For example, in Isaian studies, terms such as "First," "Second," and "Third Isaiah" or "Deutero-Isaiah" and "Trito-Isaiah" have become dominant monikers for blocks of Isaiah. These terms, more often than not, leave a lay audience and first-year Bible students scratching their heads and asking the question, "Who is 'Trito-Isaiah'?" In the study of the book of Daniel, scholars are split as to whether we have a sixth-century Daniel, a second-century "Daniel," or some combination of the two.
3. Some prefer to sidestep the issue entirely. See, for example, Ronald E. Clements, *Deuteronomy* (Sheffield: Sheffield Academic Press, 1993), 79. On the other hand, Rainer Albertz, in his work "In Search of the Deuteronomists: A First Solution to a Historical Riddle," in *The Future of the Deuteronomistic History*, ed. Thomas Römer (Leuven: Leuven University Press, 2000), 1–17, does posit that the Hilkiades and the "nationalistic party" wrote the DtrG (i.e., the first edition of the Deuteronomistic History [DtrH]) from Babylon. For an overview of the differing perspectives on authorship, see Albertz, 2–6, esp. the footnotes there.
4. The former grouping is used among Pentateuchal and DtrH scholars, whereas the idea of "schools of prophet X" was made popular in studies of the prophetic corpus by scholars such as Walther Zimmerli who adopted this phraseology for those who shaped and edited the book of Ezekiel. This has since become a popular phrase for labeling the ones who were responsible for the editing and compiling of a given prophet (e.g., Jeremiah, Ezekiel, Isaiah, etc.).

In this book, I will attempt to answer the query: Can one examine the text and piece together historical and textual clues to help answer the "Whodunit?" question? Much like a criminal-court setting where the preponderance of evidence decides a case, I assert that by examining the intertextual clues, possible character motives, and the historical opportunity in general, one can offer some valid suggestions and possible answers to this proposition. I will conclude that among the priestly family from the town of Anathoth, roughly three miles northeast of Jerusalem in the tribal allotment of Benjamin, may be a good place to begin this search. In particular, I will examine the likelihood that Abiathar the priest, his sons Jonathan and Ahimelech,[5] their priestly descendants, and finally Jeremiah and Baruch all may have had a key role to play in formulating what has come to be known as the "Deuteronomistic History" (hereafter the DtrH).[6] Now, to be certain, there will be those who quickly dismiss such a theory as speculative and presumptuous. Yet, is it presumptuous to assert that the DtrH may have had a number of editors or, dare I say, editions? One need only look to the numerous redactions of the DtrH suggested by scholars since the days of Martin Noth (1902–1968) to dismiss this concern (see ch. 1). Therefore,

---

5. Two sons of Abiathar are mentioned in the Bible: Jonathan (cf. 2 Sam. 15:27, 36; 17:17, 20; 1 Kgs. 1:42-43) and Ahimelech (cf. 2 Sam. 8:17; 1 Chr. 24:6, 31). Ahimelech was also the name of Abiathar's father. It was not uncommon for men to name their sons after their grandfathers.

6. I am not the first to point to a particular person as the author of the DtrH. As of the seventeenth century and earlier, scholars such as Baruch Spinoza (1632–1677) suggested that Ezra was the author/compiler. Cf. Jeffrey C. Geoghegan, *The Time, Place, and Purpose of the Deuteronomistic History: The Evidence of "Until This Day,"* BJS 347 (Providence, RI: Brown University Press, 2006), 22. Also, Richard E. Friedman, *Who Wrote the Bible?* (New York: Summit, 1987), 146–49, identifies Baruch and Jeremiah as possible authors. The discovery of the seal of Baruch, which said "belonging to Baruch son of Neriyah the scribe," gives further credence to the historicity of Baruch and his occupation. Cf. Nahman Avigad, *Hebrew Bullae from the Time of Jeremiah: Remnants of a Burnt Archive* (Jerusalem: Israel Exploration Society, 1986), 28–29; and idem, *Bullae and Seals from a Post-Exilic Judean Archive,* QMIA 4 (Jerusalem: Hebrew University Press, 1976). Of course, there is some debate as to the seal's authenticity. See Karel van der Toorn, *Scribal Culture and the Making of the Hebrew Bible* (Cambridge: Harvard University Press, 2007), 84 and nn.34–35.

what I am suggesting is that textual indicators may help focus us enough to propose a plausible theory as to when these editions were written and by whom. What better place to look than among a group of men who shared a similar occupation, locale, and perhaps even genealogy? Throughout our discussions may the following words of Rainer Albertz encourage scholars and students alike to keep an open mind about the authorship of the DtrH and may they also be our guiding principle:

> Considering the optimistic proliferation of the Dtr hypothesis on the literary level, I want to ask the simple historical question of who these enormously productive Deuteronomists could have been. Such a question seems to be totally out of fashion today, since a scholarly attitude has become prominent in recent OT research: on the one hand, it shows a surprising confidence in the reliability of literary-critical results through the most exacting investigation of the text. But, on the other hand, it demonstrates exaggerated skepticism toward any certainty on the historical level, or even a lack of interest in any historical questions. Contrary to this modern "scholarly docetism," I want to emphasize the old-fashioned opinion that a literary hypothesis can only be regarded as proved if it is possible to supply it with a plausible basis in real history.[7]

7. Albertz, "In Search," 1.

PART I

The Deuteronomistic History: An Introduction to Issues of Authorship, Date, and Influences

1

The Deuteronomistic History since Martin Noth

In this opening chapter, I want to briefly address three topics: (1) the methodological approach that I will be adopting to analyze texts; (2) the state of DtrH studies since Martin Noth; and (3) an overview of my proposed authors of the DtrH. This opening chapter is not intended to be a thoroughgoing discussion of the history of scholarship; that has been handled by other scholars elsewhere. While I will offer notes where needed for further reading, my main goal is to situate the reader in the world of the discussions as they exist today.

Methodology

Throughout this book I will adopt a canonical or a holistic approach to the text—what some people term a "synchronic" as opposed to a "diachronic" approach.[1] While higher-critical methods will be

---

1. Whereas Moshe Greenberg adopted the term *holistic* for his study of the book of Ezekiel (cf. *Ezekiel 1–20* and *21–37*, AB 22 and 22a [Garden City, NY: Doubleday, 1983, 1997]), Brevard

utilized when needed (e.g., rhetorical, form, narrative-critical theory, etc.), it is neither my desire, nor my goal, to get bogged down in the minutiae of the redaction-critical discussion. Moreover, I do not wish to enter into a "slugfest" with those who posit various strands of tradition on the micro-level, and who often bifurcate verses into subsections and sub-subsections, and so forth.[2] Rather, my purpose is to look at the Former Prophets in their canonical form and discuss possible options for who may have written or compiled these accounts, in whole, or in part, and their possible reasons for doing so. Instead of "picking at the loose threads" of the intricate DtrH tapestry until all that one has left is a pile of "threads," my goal is to draw readers into the world of the text and encourage them to ask questions of the larger narrative, and then, from the greater whole, begin to appreciate the detail and literary elegance of the final form.[3] This, I believe, will generate a greater interest in these books—books that have been the centerpiece of Sunday-school classrooms for more than a century, and seminary and university lecture halls for even longer. The methodology adopted throughout will, hopefully, foster

Childs introduced the *canonical approach* (cf. *Introduction to the Old Testament* [Philadelphia: Fortress Press, 1979], 355–72). Childs's assessment of biblical books from a canonical perspective revolutionized the way in which scholars looked at the biblical text. While Childs still embraced historical-critical tenets, in his mind, the methodology employed and conclusions often drawn by such approaches were inadequate to address the real needs of the biblical exegete. See also comments by Robert R. Wilson, "Unity and Diversity in the Book of Kings," in *'A Wise and Discerning Mind': Essays in Honor of Burke O. Long*, ed. Saul M. Olyan and Robert C. Culley, BJS 325 (Providence, RI: Brown University Press, 2000), 293–310, esp. 293.

2. In the next section, I will briefly orientate the reader into the world of the redaction discussion. For a more recent treatment of the strands and insertions of the DtrH, see Antony H. Campbell and Mark A. O'Brien, *Unfolding the Deuteronomistic History: Origins, Upgrades, Present Text* (Minneapolis: Fortress Press, 2000).

3. See Antony H. Campbell, *Of Prophets and Kings: A Late Ninth-Century Document (1 Samuel 1—2 Kings 10)*, CBQMS 17 (Washington, DC: Catholic Biblical Association of America, 1986), 205–208. Campbell notes that the sources available to Dtr "were far more extensive and already much more organized than hitherto suspected . . ." (208), yet goes on to give a somewhat intricate history of how all these sources were incorporated into the DtrH. It seems much more plausible to see an ongoing synthesis of Israel's history as opposed to a later weaving of sources and strands.

a spirit of inquiry into the biblical text that moves beyond the "trees" to view the "forest" as a whole.[4] While micro-analysis is indeed important and vital for the exegete, there is much to commend a macro-analysis of texts, which can include any number of books at one time.

The State of the Deuteronomistic "Question"

In the beginning was the Deuteronomistic History. It was not *tohu wabohu* but a well ordered creation by one author who had access to Israel's traditions. We knew not his name, though scoffers say it was Martin Noth. We called him simply "Dtr." And it was good. But as scholars multiplied on the Deuteronomistic History so did Dtrs. Soon, there arose a great division in the earth. Those in the North—of America—followed Cross while those across the Sea went after Smend. Each faction did what was right in his own eyes, and there was little interaction between them. Then in the 50th year an invitation went out from America saying, "Come, let us celebrate and let us reason together".[5]

Steven McKenzie's comment, while humorous, does in fact summarize well the state of DtrH studies as of 1993.[6] Since that

---

4. So, too, the perspective of Richard D. Nelson, "The Double Redaction of the Deuteronomistic History: The Case is Still Compelling," *JSOT* 29, no. 3 (2005): 333.

5. Steven L. McKenzie, "The Divided Kingdom in the Deuteronomistic History and in Scholarship on It," in *The Future of the Deuteronomistic History*, ed. Thomas C. Römer (Leuven: Leuven University Press, 2000), 135–45, at 135. "Cross" and "Smend" refer to the Hebrew Bible scholars Frank Moore Cross and Rudolf Smend.

6. I do not seek to be comprehensive in this summary, but only to offer a general overview of how the discussion has evolved since Noth's work. For a detailed treatment of the development of theories since Noth, see the work of Jeremy Hutton, *The Transjordanian Palimpsest: The Overwritten Texts of Personal Exile and Transformation in the Deuteronomistic History*, BZAW 396 (Berlin: de Gruyter, 2009), 79–156. Much of the summary and bibliography that follows is based upon Hutton's work. See also the works of Thomas Römer and Albert de Pury, "Deuteronomistic Historiography (DH): History of Research and Debated Issues," in *Israel Constructs Its History: Deuteronomistic Historiography in Recent Research*, ed. de Pury, Römer, and Jean-Daniel Macchi, JSOTSup 306 (Sheffield: Sheffield Academic Press, 2000), 24–141; and the compendium of essays in Steven L. McKenzie and M. Patrick Graham, eds., *The History of Israel's Traditions: The Heritage of Martin Noth*, JSOTSup 182 (Sheffield: Sheffield Academic Press, 1994).

time, a consensus on the authorship, date, purpose, scope, and so forth, of the DtrH is far from being reached. On the contrary, in the survey that follows, Jeffrey Geoghegan's assertion that "The field of Deuteronomistic studies can no longer be characterized as *refining* Noth's original hypothesis, but rather as *reconsidering* it or, in some cases, *rejecting* the whole," indeed sheds light on the true nature of DtrH studies in the first decade of the twenty-first century.[7]

Martin Noth's seminal 1943 work, *Überlieferungsgeschichtliche Studien* (*The Deuteronomistic History*), set the bar for later scholars when discussing the DtrH in its final form.[8] Noth avers that the books of Deuteronomy through 2 Kings (with the exclusion of the book of Ruth) comprise the DtrH.[9] Noth's basic assertion is that the DtrH was compiled from a variety of earlier extant sources, which may have formed a proto-, albeit segmented, history of Israel.[10] The key to understanding the theology behind these reworked extant sources is the book of the law (i.e., Deut. 4:44—30:20), which Noth links to the law book found by Hilkiah (2 Kgs. 22:8-10). These sources were brought together and edited, in some cases heavily, in the sixth century (c. 550 BCE), perhaps from somewhere within Palestine. Theologically, the Deuteronomist (hereafter Dtr) wrote with an eye

---

7. Jeffrey C. Geoghegan, *The Time, Place, and Purpose of the Deuteronomistic History: The Evidence of "Until This Day,"* BJS 347 (Providence, RI: Brown University, 2006), 119 (italics original).

8. Martin Noth, *The Deuteronomistic History*, JSOTSup 15 (Sheffield: JSOT, 1981), trans. from Noth's *Überlieferungsgeschichtliche Studien*, 2d ed. (Tübingen: Max Niemeyer, 1957), 1–110.

9. Not every scholar of Noth's era agreed with his conclusions. For example, see Otto Eissfeldt, *The Old Testament: An Introduction*, trans. Peter R. Ackroyd (New York: Harper & Row, 1965), 241–48, esp. 246–47; and Georg Fohrer, *Introduction to the Old Testament*, trans. David Green (London: SPCK, 1970), 195. Fohrer asserted that "we have a series of books Deuteronomy—Kings, each composed or edited in a different way." As cited by Gary N. Knoppers, "Is There a Future for the Deuteronomistic History?," in Römer, ed., *Future of the Deuteronomistic History*, 120.

10. Wolfgang Richter, *Die Bearbeitungen des 'Retterbuches' in der deuteronomischen Epoche* (Bonn: Peter Hanstein, 1964); and idem, *Traditionsgeschichtliche Untersuchungen sum Richterbuch* (Bonn: Peter Hanstein, 1963), argued for earlier blocks of history that were later brought into the DtrH by the Deuteronomist.

to explaining the failure of the monarchy, why the nation of Israel had lost the land, and why it found itself in exile. Generally speaking, Noth sees unity in the final form, with the author(s) presenting a clearly focused end goal.[11]

Since then, a number of scholars have proposed theories in an attempt either to explain particular redactional layers of the DtrH in an effort to improve upon Noth's theory or to do away with it totally.[12] While the scope and focus of this work does not allow me to go into a detailed discussion of the many nuanced perspectives proposed for the redaction of the DtrH, what follows will be a general overview of some of the main contributors since Noth.[13] In this vein, Frank Moore Cross, for example, takes issue with Noth's dating of the final form because of what he sees as indications of earlier material. Cross suggests that there is an earlier layer, what he calls Dtr1 (c. 620 BCE), which was written in support of Josiah's reforms and the Davidic monarchy.[14] Cross goes on to suggest that

---

11. So, too, Knoppers, "Is There a Future," 119. See also idem, *Two Nations under God: The Deuteronomistic History of Solomon and the Dual Monarchies*, HSM 53 (Atlanta: Scholars, 1994). Steven L. McKenzie, "The Books of Kings in the Deuteronomistic History," in McKenzie and Graham, eds., *History of Israel's Traditions*, 297, is no doubt correct when he muses, "Although most scholars have accepted only the first half of this proposition, I question whether it is possible to accept the unity of [the] Deuteronomistic History without acknowledging its essential unity of authorship."

12. This, of course, does not negate the numerous works that have been done on the DtrH since Noth not mentioned here. For example, Gerhard von Rad, *Studies in Deuteronomy* (London: SCM, 1953), 74–91; Hans Walter Wolff, "The Kerygma of the Deuteronomistic Historical Work," in *Reconsidering Israel and Judah: Recent Studies on the Deuteronomistic History*, ed. Gary N. Knoppers and J. Gordon McConville (Winona Lake, IN: Eisenbrauns, 2000), 66; trans. from "Das Kerygma des deuteronomistischen Geschichtswerks," *ZAW* 73, no. 2 (1961): 171–86. Some scholars argue against the idea of a DtrH and, rather, in favor of independent books with separate redactional histories. It is these separate histories that account for discrepancies in the text. See for example, Claus Westermann, *Die Geschichtsbücher des Alten Testaments: gab es ein deuteronomistisches Geschichtswerk?* (Gütersloh: Kaiser, 1994); or Artur Weiser, *Einleitung in das Alte Testament* (Göttingen: Vandenhoeck & Ruprecht, 1963), 117–66. These last two as noted by Geoghegan, *Time, Place, and Purpose*, 114–15, and n.76.

13. See, for example, the work of Geoghegan, who lists no fewer than ten categories of scholars who have "improved" or moved away from Noth's theory. Geoghegan, *Time, Place, and Purpose*, 96–118.

Dtr2 (c. 550 BCE) reworked Dtr1 in an effort to explain why the reforms of Josiah had failed to have a lasting effect and why the nation ended up in exile.[15] Cross's work does help to explain why there is a dominant theme of blessing and support for the Davidic kingship, Jerusalem, and the temple, especially in light of the eternal promises of 2 Samuel 7.[16] Cross argues that if, as Noth asserts, the material is exilic in setting, then the stressing of these motifs would be less likely, especially after the dissolution of the monarchy and the destruction of the city and temple.[17] Not surprisingly, more recently there has been a move within scholarship to highlight these positive elements within the DtrH.[18]

Others such as Rudolf Smend Jr. and his protégés, Timo Veijola and Walter Dietrich, have proposed no fewer than three redactional layers.[19] These layers included, beyond the basic DtrH, a "prophetic"

14. Frank Moore Cross, *Canaanite Myth and Hebrew Epic: Essays in the History of the Religion of Israel* (Cambridge: Harvard University Press, 1973), 274–89. This essay originally appeared as "The Structure of the Deuteronomistic History," in *Perspectives in Jewish Learning*, ed. J. M. Rosenthal, ACJS 3 (Chicago: College of Jewish Studies, 1968), 9–24. Note also the work done by Cross's students: Richard D. Nelson, *The Double Redaction of the Deuteronomistic History*, JSOTSup18 (Sheffield: JSOT Press, 1981); Richard E. Friedman, *The Exile and Biblical Narrative: The Formation of the Deuteronomistic and Priestly Works*, HSM 22 (Chico, CA: Scholars, 1981), esp. 1–43; Baruch Halpern, *The Constitution of the Monarchy in Israel*, HSM 25 (Chico, CA: Scholars, 1981). See also Steven L. McKenzie, *The Chronicler's Use of the Deuteronomistic History*, HSM 33 (Atlanta: Scholars, 1984). For a critique of the double-redaction (i.e., Dtr2) hypothesis, see Steven L. McKenzie, *The Trouble with Kings: The Composition of the Book of Kings in the Deuteronomistic History*, VTSup 42 (Leiden: Brill, 1991), 135–45. McKenzie (149–50) opts for a Josianic date for the DtrH with minor revisions at a later date.
15. For a critique of Cross's perspective, see J. Gordon McConville, "Narrative and Meaning in the Books of Kings," *Bib* 70, no. 1 (1989): 31–49.
16. Cf., for example, 2 Sam. 7:8-17; 1 Kgs. 2:4; 8:20, 25; 11:13, 32, 36; 15:4; 2 Kgs. 8:19, as cited by Hutton, *Transjordanian Palimpsest*, 93.
17. For more on the problems with this motif, see Wolff, "Kerygma," 62–78.
18. See, for example, Victor Hamilton, *Handbook on the Pentateuch*, 2d ed. (Grand Rapids: Baker Academic, 2005), 376, and those listed there.
19. Rudolf Smend, "The Law and the Nations: A Contribution to Deuteronomistic Tradition History," in Knoppers and McKenzie, eds., *Reconsidering Israel and Judah*, 95–110; for the German original, see idem, "Das Gesetz und die Völker: Ein Beitrag zur deuteronomistischen Redacktionsgeschichte," in *Probleme biblischer Theologie: Festschrift Gerhard von Rad zum 70. Geburtstag*, ed. Hans Walter Wolff (Munich: Kaiser, 1971), 494–509; Timo Veijola, *Historiographie: Eine redaktionsgeschichtliche Untersuchung*, AASF B/198 (Helsinki: Suomalainen

strand (DtrP, as per Veijola and Dietrich) and a strand focused on the law called the "nomistic" layer (DtrN, proposed by Smend)—the prophetic layer coming at a slightly earlier period than DtrN, c. 580–560 BCE.[20] Thomas Römer's caution here is important to bear in mind: "This approach risks inflating the number of redactional layers (and sigla), whose precise extent no one has yet defined in the deuteronomistic work; and the descriptions of certain 'layers' often appear quite arbitrary."[21] Moreover, Chaim Rabin has made a strong case for observable differences between prophetic speech in the DtrH from earlier periods exemplified by Moses, Nathan, Elijah, and Elisha, and the period of the classical prophets (e.g., Hosea and Amos). For example, the "Old Rhetoric" that appears in Moses' and Elijah's speeches is devoid of parallelism, which is characteristic of the later classical prophetic utterances.[22]

Another perspective that has been put forward is one that sees even earlier materials, which can be dated to the period of Hezekiah and before.[23] Those holding this perspective posit a varying number of

Tiede-akatemia, 1977); idem, *Die ewige Dynastie: David und die Entstehung seiner Dynastie nach der deuteronomistischen Darstellung*, AASF B/193 (Helsinki: Suomalainen Tiede-akatemia, 1975); and Walter Dietrich, *Prophetie und Geschichte: Eine redaktionsgeschichtliche Unterschung zum deuteronomistischen Geschichtswerk*, FRLANT 108 (Göttingen: Vandenhoeck and Ruprecht, 1972). These last three sources as noted by Hutton, *Transjordanian Palimpsest*,94–101 esp. n.63.

20. Hutton, *Transjordanian Palimpsest*, 96. See also the work of Nelson, "Double Redaction," 319–37.

21. Thomas Römer, "Deuteronomy in Search of Origins," in Knoppers and McConville, eds., *Reconsidering Israel and Judah*, 116. See further, idem, "The Book of Deuteronomy," in McKenzie and Graham, eds., *History of Israel's Traditions*, 178–212. For a concise critique of the "Smend school," see Gary Knoppers, *Two Nations under God: The Reign of Solomon and the Rise of Jeroboam*, HSM 52 (Atlanta: Scholars, 1993), 38–42.

22. Chaim Rabin, "Discourse Analysis and the Dating of Deuteronomy," in *Interpreting the Hebrew Bible: Essays in Honour of E. I. J. Rosenthal*, ed. J. A. Emerton and Stefan C. Reif (Cambridge: Cambridge University Press, 1982), 176–77.

23. For example, those who see an earlier strand dating to the period of Hezekiah include Norbert Lohfink, "Culture Shock and Theology," *BTB* 7, no. 1 (1977): 12–22, esp. 13; Moshe Weinfeld, *Deuteronomy 1–11*, AB 5 (New York: Doubleday, 1991), 44–54; Ronald E. Clements, "Jeremiah 1–25 and the Deuteronomistic History," in *Understanding Poets and Prophets: Essays in Honour of George Wishart Anderson*, ed. A. Graeme Auld, JSOTSup 152 Sheffield: Sheffield Academic

sources, which were at the disposal of the final Dtr. Helga Weippert, Baruch Halpern, Iain Provan, and Andrew D. H. Mayes offer varying perspectives of this theory.[24] One of the basic premises is that 2 Kgs. 18:5 points to a culmination of an earlier version of the DtrH composed in Hezekiah's day. The text reads, "He [Hezekiah] trusted in YHWH the God of Israel and after him there has not been one like him among all the kings of Judah or among those who lived before him." I will address this concept in more detail in chapter 10 below.

Another theory which in some ways reflects the thesis I am proposing is the idea that the DtrH was the product of a "school" or "circle" of scribes over a period of time. The main proponents of this line of inquiry include Ernest Nicholson, Moshe Weinfeld, and Raymond F. Person.[25] Now, to be sure, the major differences between the variations of this proposed theory and what I am presenting in this work are the dating, motives, location of this "school," and the scope of their works. Nevertheless, the position that

Press, 1993), 108; F. García López, *Le Deutéronome: Une Loi prêchée*, CaE 63 (Paris: Cerf, 1988), 9–13, esp. 10.

24. See Helga Weippert, "Die 'deuteronomistischen' Beurteilungen der Könige von Israel und Juda und das Problem der Redaktion der Königsbücher," *Bib* 53, no. 3 (1972): 301–39; idem, "Die Ätiologie des Nordreiches und seines Königshauses (I Reg 11 29–40)," *ZAW* 95, no. 3 (1983): 344–75; Baruch Halpern, "Sacred History and Ideology: Chronicles' Thematic Structure—Indications of an Earlier Source," in *The Creation of Sacred Literature: Composition and Redaction of the Biblical Text*, ed. Richard E. Friedman, NES 22 (Berkeley: University of California Press, 1981), 35–54, esp. 54; Baruch Halpern and D. S. Vanderhooft, "The Editions of Kings in the 7th–6th Centuries B.C.E.," *HUCA* 62 (1991): 179–244, esp. 182, 239; Iain Provan, *Hezekiah and the Books of Kings: A Contribution to the Debate about the Composition of the Deuteronomistic History*, BZAW 172 (Berlin: de Gruyter, 1988); A. D. H. Mayes, *The Story of Israel Between Settlement and Exile: A Redactional Study of the Deuteronomistic History* (London: SCM, 1983). Cf. also comments by Geoghegan, *Time, Place, and Purpose*, 105–108.

25. Ernest W. Nicholson, *Deuteronomy and Tradition* (Philadelphia: Fortress Press, 1967), esp. 123–24; Moshe Weinfeld, *Deuteronomy and the Deuteronomistic School* (Oxford: Clarendon Press, 1972), 7–9, esp. 9; and Raymond F. Person Jr., *The Deuteronomistic School: History, Social Setting, and Literature*, SBLStBl 2 (Atlanta: SBL, 2002), 7. Person sees this group at work in the exilic or Persian periods. On these works, see the comments by Geoghegan, *Time, Place, and Purpose*, 108–109; and Römer, "Deuteronomy in Search of Origins," 117. Even though my dating would be vastly different, even Smend concluded that there must have been a "school" of sorts that existed for generations. Cf. Rudolf Smend, *Die Entstehung des Alten Testaments* (Stuttgart: Kohlhammer, 1978).

the DtrH was the product of an amalgamation of works over time has much to commend it and, in all reality, appears to make the most sense of the biblical material as we have it.

Now, while all of these theories have been met with varying degrees of acceptance and/or rejection, there may be a more simplistic answer as to why, for example, prophetic and nomistic aspects find expression in the DtrH. If my proposal is correct, the priestly line of Abiathar and especially Jeremiah would have been extremely interested in both of these facets as the history of Israel was being brought together and reworked.[26] Furthermore, what has tended to be the case since Noth's theory was proposed, especially as of late, is a desire to know how much of Dtr1 may be attributed to the earlier period and what that strand may have looked like.[27] It is precisely in response to such queries that I move the discussion forward and propose a theory of what this earlier strand may have entailed, at least coming from the hands of those at Anathoth.[28]

Closely connected to this discussion is the problem of identifying, specifically, the individual(s) responsible for writing the DtrH. Robert Wilson notes that in a not-so-distant period most scholars accepted a narrowly focused corpus of Dtr influence. He avers,

> Traditionally scholars have seen the hand of the Deuteronomists in an impressive amount of biblical literature, but their influence was still confined to a relatively small portion of the biblical corpus. They were responsible for Deuteronomy, of course, and for most of the so-called Deuteronomistic History—Joshua, Judges, Samuel and Kings.

26. So, too, the conclusion of Geoghegan, *Time, Place, and Purpose*, 139, 152–53. I will deal with this in more detail in subsequent chapters. P. Kyle McCarter, *I Samuel: A New Translation with Introduction: Notes and Commentary*, AB 8 (Garden City, NY: Doubleday, 1980), 18–23; idem, *II Samuel: A New Translation with Introduction: Notes and Commentary*, AB 9 (Garden City, NY: Doubleday, 1984), 7–8; and Campbell, *Of Prophets and Kings*, offer variations of the prophetic redaction of the DtrH.

27. Hutton, *Transjordanian Palimpsest*, 94.

28. See Baruch Halpern, "Shiloh," *ABD* 5:1213–15, for connections between Shiloh, Anathoth, and the DtrH.

Outside of these obviously Deuteronomistic books, the Deuteronomists were usually thought to be responsible primarily for the non-narrative prose in Jeremiah, for Isaiah 36–39 (paralleled almost verbatim in 2 Kgs 18–20), and for small units in Amos and Hosea.[29]

Unfortunately, within OT studies, authorship attributed to the nebulous, and all-pervasive, Deuteronomists has reached a level of incredulity. When faced with the need for a new dissertation, book, or paper topic, scholars cast a suspicious eye to almost any book of the OT and, in an accusatory tone, deconstruct traditional authorship attributions, often propounding later authorship to these ever-elusive Deuteronomists. As of 1999, Wilson summed up this "pan-Deuteronomism" madness by noting,

> Modern Pentateuchal studies seem to find the Deuteronomists represented in most of the books of the Torah, and some scholars have even gone so far as to suggest that the Deuteronomists were in fact the compilers, if not the authors, of the Torah as we now have it. In the Deuteronomistic History itself the Deuteronomists are being given credit for creating most of their material out of whole cloth, and, in some extreme circles, they are being credited with shaping virtually all of the prophetic books, not to mention a number of the Psalms. Indeed, even a casual reading of recent scholarly literature suggests that we are rapidly entering an era of pan-Deuteronomism. Whenever the authorship of a particular piece of biblical literature is investigated, the identity of the author(s) always turns out to be the same: the Deuteronomists.[30]

29. Robert R. Wilson, "Who Was the Deuteronomist? (Who Was Not the Deuteronomist?): Reflections on Pan-Deuteronomism," in *Those Elusive Deuteronomists: The Phenomenon of Pan-Deuteronomism*, ed. Linda S. Schearing and Steven L. McKenzie, JSOTSup 268 (Sheffield: Sheffield Academic Press, 1999), 68. Wilson notes the work of Bernhard Duhm, *Das Buch Jeremia*, KHC 11 (Tübingen: J. C. B. Mohr, 1901).

30. Wilson, "Who Was the Deuteronomist?" 68. Wilson notes the influential work of Lothar Perlitt, *Bundestheologie im Alien Testament*, WMANT 36 (Neukirchen-Vluyn: Neukirchener, 1969), as key in opening the floodgates for theories of Deuteronomistic influence on the Torah. He goes on to cite H. H. Schmid's book, *Der sogenannte Jahwist: Beobachtungen und Fragen zur Pentateuchforschung* (Zurich: Theologischer, 1976) as one example of this extreme. See, further, his short bibliography on advancements of Schmid's theory in Wilson's article on p. 70 nn.4–6. In the discussion that follows, I will be relying heavily on Wilson's brief, but concise,

Of course, the main problem with most of these theories is that they place the dating of the Deuteronomists, almost exclusively, in the Josianic period or later. Little room is left for the possibility of earlier writings with only minor editing at a later period. To be fair, at least Noth, and many from his era, were willing to see older sources in the DtrH (e.g., The Deuteronomic Law Code: Deuteronomy 12–26; The Ark Narrative: 1 Samuel 4–6; The History of David's Rise: 1 Samuel 15—2 Samuel 8; and Solomon's Succession Narrative: 2 Samuel 9–20; 1 Kings 1–2).[31] Indeed, one can look to the text itself and find references to what Wilson calls, "a sort of scholarly reference for the reader," which reflects extant sources used by the author(s) of the DtrH.[32] These sources include, for example, the book of Jashar (Josh. 10:13; 2 Sam. 1:18), the book of the Acts of Solomon (1 Kgs. 11:41);[33] and the book of the Chronicles of the Kings of Israel (1 Kgs. 14:19; 15:31; 16:5, 14, 20, 27; 22:39; 2 Kgs. 1:18; 10:34; 13:8, 12; 14:15, 28; 15:11, 15, 21, 26, 31); and Judah (1 Kgs. 14:29; 15:7, 23; 22:45; 2 Kgs. 8:23; 12:19; 14:18; 15:6, 36; 16:19; 20:20; 21:17,

analysis of the state of the problem. In the past decade, not much has changed in rectifying the pan-Deuteronomism prevalent throughout OT scholarship. See, for example, the discussion by Thomas Römer, "L'école deutéronomiste et la formation de la Bible hébraïque," in idem, ed., *Future of the Deuteronomistic History*, 179–93; and the final footnote of P. Kyle McCarter in "The Books of Samuel," in McKenzie and Graham, eds., *History of Israel's Traditions*, 280. See also cautions by Rob Barrett, "The Book of Deuteronomy," in *A Theological Introduction to the Pentateuch: Interpreting the Torah as Christian Scripture*, ed. Richard S. Briggs and Joel N. Lohr (Grand Rapids: Baker Academic, 2012), 148–50; and Richard Coggins, "What Does 'Deuteronomistic' Mean?" in Schearing and McKenzie, eds., *Those Elusive Deuteronomists*, 22–23. For a rebuttal of Coggins and a defense of "pan-Deuteronomism" as a concept, see Person, *Deuteronomistic School*, 13–16.

31. This list appears in Marsha White, "'The History of Saul's Rise': Saulide State Propaganda in 1 Samuel 1–14," in Olyan and Culley, eds., *'A Wise and Discerning Mind,'*, 271–92, at 272.

32. Wilson, "Who Was the Deuteronomist?" 72. See also the list of possible blocks of material that served as sources for Dtr in Douglas A. Knight, "Deuteronomy and the Deuteronomists," in *Old Testament Interpretation Past, Present, and Future: Essays in Honour of Gene M. Tucker*, ed. James Luther Mays, David L. Petersen, and Kent Harold Richards (Edinburgh: T&T Clark, 1995), 61–79, at 66–67.

33. The Chronicler adds the following to the sources for the period of Solomon and Rehoboam: the records/prophecies of Nathan, Ahijah, Shemaiah, Iddo the seer (cf. 2 Chr. 9:29; 12:15). He also notes the acts of Abijah, the son of Rehoboam, which were recorded by Iddo (2 Chr. 13:22).

25; 23:28; 24:5). On a side note, one could easily argue, as I do below, that the earliest "Deuteronomist" may have been someone much earlier than the sixth century, especially in light of the absence of the book of Jashar after 2 Sam. 1:18. This source was extant at the time of the early monarchy but appears to have been lost by the time of the recording of the book of Kings.

Next, within the last thirty years or so, attempts have been made to push the theory that the entire history of Israel was either written in the postexilic period or that good portions of it are nothing more than a fabrication, which were authored predominantly by one person.[34] In the former case, Brian Peckham argues for a postexilic writing of the DtrH whereby "Dtr2" (Peckham's designation) had at his disposal sources (in this order "J," "Dtr1," "P," "E"), which had been complied over generations and commented on along the way.[35] For Peckham, the writing of Israel's history was one that took place over centuries with each subsequent author/editor reworking that history so as to make earlier layers undetectable.[36] On the other hand, John Van Seters postulates that the bulk of the DtrH was written in the exilic or postexilic period to offer the nation of Israel hope in the midst of suffering an ignominious exile—a people without a past, unlike, for example, the Greeks.[37] In this regard, Steven L.

---

34. Noth, *Deuteronomistic History*, 84, asserts that Dtr was not interested in "fabricating the history of the Israelite people."

35. Brian Peckham, *The Composition of the Deuteronomistic History*, HSM 35 (Atlanta: Scholars, 1985), 1, 73. Peckham's model in ways parallels what I am proposing here, although he would not date the larger blocks of material as early as I do.

36. So McKenzie, *Trouble with Kings*, 16.

37. John Van Seters, *In the Search of History: Historiography in the Ancient World and the Origins of Biblical History* (New Haven: Yale University Press, 1983) and idem, *The Biblical Saga of King David* (Winona Lake, IN: Eisenbrauns, 2009). So, too, Wilson, "Who Was the Deuteronomist?" 72. For a concise example of Van Seters's methodological approach to the text, see idem, "The Deuteronomistic History: Can It Avoid Death by Redaction?," in Römer, ed., *Future of the Deuteronomistic History*, 213–22. For a concise, but accurate, critique of Van Seters's methodology, see Robert Polzin, *Samuel and the Deuteronomist: A Literary Study of the Deuteronomistic History Part II: 1 Samuel* (San Francisco: Harper & Row, 1989), 13–17; or Tomoo Ishida, "Adonijah the Son of Haggith and His Supporters: An Inquiry into Problems

McKenzie's query concerning the postexilic theory, while not profound, does bear weight on the discussion. He posits, *If* Dtr wrote in the postexilic period, why does the history stop where it does c. 560 BCE?[38]

Recently, Kurt L. Noll has proposed that Noth's theory of a sixth-century Dtr should be abandoned totally for a much later text and compilation in the Persian or Greek period.[39] Elsewhere, Noll goes on to propound, "The notion that the Former Prophets add up either to an interpretation of the past or to a coherent theological message derives from a mistake. It derives from the Bible's 2,000-year status as a revealed 'Word of God,' an artificial status that has nothing to do with the text but has nevertheless motivated religious readers to find history or theology, or both, where none exists."[40] Holding variations of this type of thinking are scholars such as Philip R. Davies, Niels P. Lemche, and Thomas L. Thompson.[41] In most cases, those proposing minimalistic theories decry the long-running scholarly "marriage"

about History and Historiography," in *The Future of Biblical Studies—The Hebrew Scriptures*, ed. Richard E. Friedman and H. G. M. Williamson (Atlanta: Scholars, 1987), 167–68.

38. McKenzie, "The Books of Kings," 303.

39. Kurt L. Noll, "Deuteronomistic History or Deuteronomic Debate? (A Thought Experiment)," *JSOT* 31, no. 3 (2007): 316. See also competing comments by Walter Dietrich, "Martin Noth and the Future of the Deuteronomistic History," in McKenzie and Graham, eds., *History of Israel's Traditions*, 159. Here Dietrich rightly notes, "Even before Chronicles, the language and thought of the Persian period as a whole represents a *terminus ad quem* for the Deuteronomistic historical writing."

40. Kurt L. Noll, "Presumptuous Prophets Participating in a Deuteronomic Debate," in *Prophets, Prophecy, and Ancient Israelite Historiography*, ed. Mark J. Boda and Lissa M. Wray Beal (Winona Lake, IN: Eisenbrauns, 2013), 125–42, at 142.

41. Cf. Philip R. Davies, *In Search of "Ancient Israel,"* JSOTSup 148 (Sheffield: JSOT, 1992), 57–71, esp. 57, 155; Niels Peter Lemche, *The Israelites in History and Tradition* (Louisville: Westminster John Knox, 1998), 65–85, 163–67; idem, "The Old Testament—A Hellenistic Book?" *SJOT* 7, no. 2 (1993): 163–93; Thomas Thompson, *The Early History of the Israelite People: From the Written and Archaeological Sources* (Leiden: Brill, 1994), 127. In his essay in "tribute" to the work of Martin Noth at fifty years, Thompson gives a scathing critique of Noth's theory and the work of biblical archaeologists while praising the work of Lemche, Heike Friis, Van Seters, and himself. Cf. idem, "Martin Noth and the History of Israel," in McKenzie and Graham, eds., *History of Israel's Traditions*, 81–90, esp. 81–83. One can sense the jaded perspective of the author on page 82 n.2.

between archaeological findings/historical realities and the biblical perspective—a "marriage" they see as needing a "divorce."[42] Of course, these extreme positions force the assumption that virtually nothing from the Bible prior to the postexilic period has any historical value—a position that is untenable for many DtrH scholars.

Deuteronomistic Language and Style

Another major hurdle facing DtrH studies has been the discussion of what actually makes something "Deuteronomistic." Wilson rightly points out that the pervasive problem within DtrH studies is that there really is no consensus in this regard, perhaps with the exception of language.[43] And even here, the criteria for determining what writing style and language peculiarities conclusively demonstrate Deuteronomistic style is questioned.[44] On this, Dietrich avers, "Their

42. The subjective nature of archaeological interpretation in relationship to the Bible cannot be overstated. Having worked in the field of archaeology for several seasons, I am all too familiar with the subjectivity that often accompanies the interpretation of the data collected. If one approaches the data with presuppositions hostile to the Bible as "history" or vice versa, two completely different perspectives can emerge. Of course, few would admit that they are "hostile" toward the Bible because, in their opinion, it is not "history" to begin with. Thus, a circular argument develops. For them, archaeology is "scientific," whereas the Bible is "myth." When archaeology appears to compliment the Bible, it is either a mere coincidence or the data is interpreted in such a way to prove the Bible "wrong" and to perpetuate their own theories. This is exemplified in the somewhat recent discovery of the Tel Dan Stele in 1993. When faced with the presence of the "house of David" inscribed in stone, a segment of scholarship, which holds that David either did not exist or was a petty chieftain, argued that the text should be interpreted as the "house of the beloved" or of a god, or "uncle," or "kettle," etc. This interpretation, of course, flies in the face of the actual military context of the stele. Cf., for example, Lemche, *Israelites in History and Tradition*, 38–43; Philip R. Davies, "'House of David' Built on Sand," *BAR* 20, no. 4 (July/August 1994): 54–55; Frederick H. Cryer, "On the Recently-discovered 'House of David' Inscription, *SJOT* 8, no. 1 (1994): 3–19, esp. 14–15. For a scathing refutation of these claims, see Baruch Halpern, "Erasing History: The Minimalist Assault on Ancient Israel," *BRev* 11, no. 6 (1995): 26–35, 47, esp. 35.

43. Wilson, "Who Was the Deuteronomist?" 78–79. See, too, Römer, "Deuteronomy in Search of Origins," 116 and n.17. For a comprehensive listing of proposed Dtr language, see Weinfeld, *Deuteronomy and the Deuteronomic School*, 320–65.

44. Wilson, "Who Was the Deuteronomist?" 79; idem, "Unity and Diversity," 303; and J. Gordon McConville, "The Old Testament Historical Books in Modern Scholarship," in *Them* 22, no. 3 (1997): 3–13, esp. 6.

[Dtrs'] vocabulary may have been much richer than has generally—and somewhat condescendingly—been conceded. They could speak the language of others, specifically that of their sources. In fact, given that they reproduced these sources, was it not ultimately necessary for them to adopt the language (and the thought) contained in them?"[45] Here I must wholeheartedly agree with Dietrich's assumption. As a matter of fact, as I move forward with my evaluation of the DtrH and the language and rhetoric of Dtr, in many places I will appeal to specific phrases that seem to reflect a particular period. However, in doing this, I do try to remain open to the number of possibilities for when and who may have used such language. It is only when I can clearly isolate a term or a phrase to a given period and author that conclusions will be drawn.

Closely related to the identification of what makes something Deuteronomic is the theology of Dtr. In this regard, Noll correctly asks, "[I]s this writer pro- or antimonarchic, does this writer hope for restoration or acknowledge an utter end to the covenant, is the writer monolatrous or monotheistic, does the writer handle prophetic and nomistic concerns or are these later additions, etc.?"[46] As for linguistic concerns, Wilson avers that if more was known of biblical-era Hebrew then perhaps we could understand the writing style of a given period. At this juncture, I must offer a word of caution. Dtr does not have a monopoly on "Deuteronomistic" language per se. Other ancient Near Eastern (hereafter ANE) texts share similar themes.[47] For example, the Moabite Stele from the mid-ninth century BCE, which was discovered in 1868, has many "Deuteronomistic" themes written in ancient Moabite![48] Will the pan-Deuteronomists

---

45. Dietrich, "Martin Noth," 161.
46. Noll, "Deuteronomistic History," 317. Cf. also Dietrich, "Martin Noth," 167.
47. So, too, Hamilton, *Handbook*, 377.
48. These themes include: losing the land to your enemy (here Israel) because you angered your god (here Chemosh); one's god having mercy on the land and his people; and the idea of

argue that the Deuteronomists wrote this text as well? Furthermore, in some cases many of these ANE texts predate the traditionally "accepted" date of the DtrH by centuries. Are we to assume that Dtr could only introduce these ideas at such a late date?[49] Of course, if one is honest, the answer must be a resounding "No!" In this vein, Wilson correctly notes the tenuousness of asserting Deuteronomistic links between texts by appealing only to tangential connections to motifs and themes of retribution and prophetic interests—something in which any author from almost any period could have been interested.[50]

Furthermore, there is the problem of dating the material (either early or late), which compounds the problem of identifying an author(s). When did these authors first begin their writing? Was it during David's, Hezekiah's, or Josiah's period—or later? Is the final form entirely exilic or postexilic, or are there clear indications of earlier compiling? Again, Wilson warns, "it is always necessary to keep open the possibility that all of these suggestions may be correct and that the Deuteronomists were active over a long period of time . . ."[51]

Now, to be sure, I can appreciate the borderline fatalistic perspective of Wilson when he opines that perhaps one should cease speaking in terms of Deuteronomistic influence because "the concept of Deuteronomism has become so amorphous that it no longer has

kherem. See also comments by Alexander Rofé, "Ephraimite Versus Deuteronomistic History," in Knoppers and McConville, ed., *Reconsidering Israel and Judah*, 471.

49. Hamilton, *Handbook*, 377. Noll, "Deuteronomistic History," 317, posits, "If words and phrases that are identical to passages of Deuteronomy do not seem to affirm a Deuteronomic worldview, these words and phrases are not necessarily deuteronomistic. Likewise, when we encounter words and phrases that parallel Deuteronomy, but we are not able to demonstrate the direction of influence, the passages are, once again, not necessarily Deuteronomic." While Noll's assertion is in support of a much later date for much of the DtrH, he is still nonetheless correct in his assessment concerning the ambiguity on the direction of influence.

50. Wilson, "Who Was the Deuteronomist?" 80.

51. Ibid., 81.

any analytical precision and so ought to be abandoned."[52] However, while Wilson may not be ready to make such a leap, it is possible that many scholars are in just such a place. It is for this reason that I insist that it may be best to view this material from the perspective of having historical and rhetorical value for a given *earlier* period. It was only later that this history was reworked for secondary purposes. Of course, it is indeed possible that Dtr simply sought to preserve Israel's fragile history in a foreign land—a history that could easily be lost in a generation or two once Israel was removed from its homeland. Nevertheless, who would have had motive and opportunity even to begin the process of recording the earliest sources/history? It is to this I now turn as I consider the authors from the city of Anathoth.

The Priestly Authors from Anathoth

The evidence . . . strongly suggests that Dtr was a Levite or, at a minimum, sought to represent the interests of the Levites. . . . The repeated use of "until this day" with reference to the rights and responsibilities of the Levites demonstrates that they were much more than an antiquarian interest for Dtr, or a faction he had to accommodate when compiling his history. Rather, the "Levitical priests," as Dtr makes plain in redactional material accompanying our phrase, played a central role in many of Israel's past success and held the key—quite literally in the "torah of Moses"—to Israel's future success.[53]

These poignant words by Jeffrey Geoghegan make it clear that the priests were more than an afterthought in the mind of Dtr. Indeed, Geoghegan rightly goes on to conclude that Dtr was from the tribe of Levi![54] Of course, for Geoghegan, Dtr was from a much later

---

52. Ibid., 82.

53. Geoghegan, *Time, Place, and Purpose*, 138, 148.

54. Ibid., 149. Gerhard von Rad also posited this theory for the book of Deuteronomy in *Studies in Deuteronomy*, 66–69. Richard D. Nelson, "The Role of the Priesthood in the Deuteronomistic History," in Knoppers and Gordon, eds., *Reconsidering Israel and Judah*, 191–93, is incorrect in his assessment that because priests appear as secondary "redactional tools" then the Dtr was not interested in them. Are we to conclude that if the author was a priest he would only focus

period than the eleventh or tenth centuries. For many, the problem of an "early" priestly author is rooted not only in rhetorical concerns but also in the more practical aspects of literacy in ancient societies. Therefore, before entering into a discussion about the Anathothian priests as "authors," one must first consider the likelihood that this segment of ancient Israel was actually literate.

Literacy in Ancient Israel

For decades, scholars considered literacy rates in Israel to be very low, only rising toward the end of the seventh century.[55] However, writing is attested in Canaan from an early period (e.g., the Amarna Tablets; cf. also Judg. 8:14) and, indeed, finds a long history among the leadership of Israel, the priests and Levites obviously falling within this category (cf. Num. 5:23; Deut. 17:18; 31:24-26; Josh. 8:32-35; 24:26; Ezra 7:11, 12, 21; Neh. 8:8, 9; Isa. 8:1; 30:8; Jer. 30:2; Ezek. 24:2; 37:16, 20; 43:11).[56] Furthermore, one does not need to

---

on priests and himself? While it is clear that the DtrH contains biases and interests reflecting Abiathar and the priests of Anathoth, that does not mean that he/they placed it upon every written page. Diversity of content is what makes the DtrH so rich.

55. For an excellent overview on the history of writing in Iron Age Israel, see Hutton, *Transjordanian Palimpsest*, 168–73. Many of the sources listed below are as noted by Hutton. David W. Jamieson-Drake, *Scribes and Schools in Monarchic Judah: A Socio-Archaeological Approach*, JSOTSup 109 (Sheffield: Almond, 1991), 11–15; Karel van der Toorn, *Scribal Culture and the Making of the Hebrew Bible* (Cambridge: Harvard University Press, 2007), 75–108; Aaron Demsky, "Literacy in Israel and Among Neighboring People in the Biblical Period," PhD diss. (Jerusalem: Hebrew University, 1976), 117–32; and idem, *Literacy in Ancient Israel* [Heb], The Biblical Encyclopaedia Library (Jerusalem: Bialik Institute, 2012). These last two as cited by Ellen F. Davis, *Swallowing the Scroll*, BLS 21 (Sheffield: Sheffield Academic Press, 1989), 42–43. See also Joseph Naveh, "A Paleographic Note on the Distribution of the Hebrew Script," *HTR* 61, no. 1 (1968): 68–74. Naveh postulates that, based upon "recent" (as of 1968) archaeological finds, there seems to be clear evidence that Judah was a literate society as of the late seventh and early sixth centuries BCE. See also Halpern, "Erasing History," 26–35, 47; Ryan Byrne, "The Refuge of Scribalism in Iron I Palestine," *BASOR* 345 (2007): 1–31; Seth L. Sanders, "Writing and Early Iron Age Israel: Before National Scripts, Beyond Nations and States," in *Literate Culture and Tenth-Century Canaan: The Tel Zayit Abecedary in Context,* ed. Ron E. Tappy and P. Kyle McCarter Jr. (Winona Lake, IN: Eisenbrauns, 2008), 97–112; Christopher A. Rollston, "Scribal Education in Ancient Israel: The Old Hebrew Epigraphic Evidence," *BASOR* 344 (2006): 47–74.

look immediately to royal court scribes as the writers of the Bible. On the contrary, priestly/temple scribes were most likely the ones responsible for writing the Bible.[57] The role of the priesthood as preservers and teachers of the law seems to lead one to the foregone conclusion that priests, especially those at the highest levels, of which Abiathar and Jeremiah were a part, needed to be literate. Interestingly, Aaron Demsky posits that the seemingly late ages of twenty-five for Levites and thirty for priests to enter cultic service may be due in large part to their extended period of education and apprenticeship.[58]

At the same time, archaeological finds are helping to shed light on early literacy in Israel and the surrounding regions. For example, the Gezer Calendar, the Moabite Stone, the Tel Zayit Abecedary (2005),[59] and the 2008 inscriptional find at Khirbet Qeiyafa in the Elah Valley show evidence of early literacy in Israel.[60] The latter case alone makes it clear that as early as the united monarchy, scribes were at work in Israel.[61] No longer is it necessary to conclude that priests and scribes were merely memorizing and reciting texts at these early

56. So, too, van der Toorn, *Scribal Culture*, 80, 85. See further the lists of texts and the identification of those who were literate in ancient Israel in David M. Carr, *Writing on the Tablet of the Heart: Origins of Scripture and Literature* (New York: Oxford University Press, 2005), 112 nn.2–4; 116–21. For a discussion on the literacy of preexilic Israel, see Davis, *Swallowing the Scroll*, 41–45.

57. Van der Toorn, *Scribal Culture*, 82, 89.

58. Aaron Demsky, "Education," *EncJud* 6:381–98 (esp. 383, 391–97), at 396.

59. Tappy and McCarter, eds., *Literate Culture*.

60. So, too, the conclusion of Carr, *Writing on the Tablet of the Heart*, 114–15. Note also the discovery of the Tel Dan Stele in the 1990s, which dates to the ninth century BCE and the Kuntillet Ajrud inscriptions found in the mid-1970s, which date to the ninth or eighth centuries. For notes on the Kuntillet Ajrud inscriptions, see Richard Hess, *Israelite Religions: An Archaeological and Biblical Survey* (Grand Rapids: Baker Academic, 2007), 283–89; and Mark Smith, *The Early History of God*, 2d ed. (Grand Rapids: Eerdmans, 2002), 118–25. See esp. Smith's bibliography on p. 118 n.46. For a concise analysis of Iron I inscriptions, see Byrne, "Refuge of Scribalism," 17–22.

61. One must keep in mind that "the absence of evidence does not constitute evidence of absence." The sparseness of inscriptional evidence from the Iron Age I may have more to do with the accident of discovery or the perishable nature of the writing media. So Byrne, "Refuge of Scribalism," 22.

stages, but they no doubt were recording them, too. To this end, Jeremy Hutton concludes, "It is, I suggest, within this confluence of the oral-textual milieu and the emergent monarchy in Israel that the apologetic texts of Saul's and David's reigns would have first been composed."[62] I would add that it is just as possible to assume that at least select members of the priestly guild were among this scribal class.[63]

In this regard, one should remember that Ezra was both priest and scribe (Ezra 7:11, 12, 21). Whether the scribal training was in formal schools or whether it was homegrown is up for debate.[64] It is indeed possible that the family of Abiathar, living during the Iron Age II period, may have passed their training from one generation to the next,[65] which would align with epigraphic exemplars from this period; exemplars that show relative consistency over periods of time.[66] And even though Jeremiah may have employed Baruch to write many of his oracles does not mean that he was illiterate.[67] The apostle Paul certainly was literate, yet he often used an amanuensis (e.g., Rom. 16:22; 1 Cor. 16:21; Gal. 6:11). Therefore, to move forward under the assumption that the priestly family at Anathoth could very well have been the literate preservers of Israel's tradition is not merely an a priori conclusion but also has ANE empirical evidence that supports this conclusion.

---

62. Hutton, *Transjordanian Palimpsest*, 173.

63. So, too, van der Toorn, *Scribal Culture*, 85.

64. See discussion by Jamieson-Drake, *Scribes and Schools*, 149–57.

65. On this type of educational model, see Carr, *Writing on the Tablet of the Heart*, 113, and van der Toorn, *Scribal Culture*, 97.

66. Rollston, "Scribal Education," 48–50, 67–68.

67. Whether the authorship of the final form is from either Jeremiah or Baruch is not as important to our discussion as is our focus on the tradition stemming from Anathoth. In reality, the work of these two authors is so intertwined it is impossible to determine one from the other. The theory that Jeremiah is responsible for the poetic sections of his book, while Baruch is responsible for the narrative portions (or vice versa), is impossible to prove.

The Priests of Anathoth

Anathoth was a Levitical city in the tribal allotment of Benjamin (Josh. 21:18), situated approximately two to three miles northeast of Jerusalem. Abiathar's family were from this town, as was Jeremiah (cf. 1 Kgs. 2:26; Jer. 1:1; 29:27; 32:7-9).[68] As one of the closest priestly cities to Jerusalem, Anathoth would have served as an excellent base from which to collect, write, and edit a biblical history, especially its final form in the days of Jeremiah. It is obvious that during the early days of the Babylonian invasion, Anathoth was not destroyed (Jeremiah 32, 37). Many of the copies of the biblical books and noncanonical works (e.g., the book of Jashar) no doubt were destroyed during the destruction of Jerusalem and the temple.[69] Yet, it is possible that Jeremiah may have saved copies of his work, along with priestly and canonical sources, by sending them out of Jerusalem to Anathoth with either his cousin Hanamel (cf. Jer. 32:7-12) or during one of his trips out of the city (cf. Jer. 20:3).[70] Interestingly, Jeremiah actually warns his fellow Benjaminites to flee Jerusalem (Jer. 6:1). Knowing that Jeremiah sent letters out of the city by couriers opens the door for the possible removal of important copies of texts from the doomed city (cf. Jeremiah 29). Moreover, Jeremiah's fame with the Babylonians may have saved Anathoth for a time. This may explain how Hanamel had access to Jeremiah inside the besieged city. In this vein, the text makes it clear that Jeremiah received favorable treatment from Nebuzaradan (Jer. 40:1-4). Whatever the case, Anathoth appears to be a valid location from which a history of

68. It appears that by the time of Jeremiah the men of Anathoth, whether priestly or not the text does not say, rose up against Jeremiah. Thus Jeremiah may have been the last of the Deuteronomists of Anathoth (cf. Jer. 11:21, 23).

69. The book of Jashar does not appear after 2 Samuel 1 and was therefore not available to the Chronicler in the postexilic period. Of course, it is speculation that it was destroyed in the destruction of Jerusalem, but one cannot rule it out either.

70. Note also the lifting of the siege when Egypt came to fight Assyria (Jeremiah 37).

Israel may have been recorded in its final form (see more on this in the following chapters). Nowhere is this more evident than during the earlier history of Israel, in the lifetime of Abiathar and his sons Jonathan and Ahimelech.

Abiathar, Jonathan, and Ahimelech

Abiathar was the high priest of David. Abiathar's descent may be traced through Eli, who in turn was descended from Ithamar, Aaron's son. As a part of the educated class, Abiathar had not only the ability, but both motive and opportunity to write good portions of the DtrH, especially when one considers the numerous eyewitness-like accounts throughout 1 and 2 Samuel and 1 Kings 1–2. Abiathar was David's "right-hand man" when it came to inquiring of the Lord and in serving as a spy during the revolt of Absalom. Sadly, because Abiathar sided with Adonijah in the latter's bid for the throne of David, Solomon exiled Abiathar (1 Kgs. 2:26-27). It is possible that Abiathar, once exiled to Anathoth, updated the history of Israel at least up until the period of Solomon. Breaks in the narrative flow and writing style in the DtrH, evidenced in the record of Solomon's reign, betray a change of author at this strategic period (see ch. 10 below).

It is at this time that one of Abiathar's sons, Jonathan or Ahimelech, could have recorded the account of Solomon's life and perhaps started the practice of preservation and updating Israel's history. As I will demonstrate in chapter 10, Jonathan appears to be a prime candidate for the recording of Solomon's early reign, perhaps with input from his brother, Ahimelech. Both had access to the inner circles of the Davidic and Solomonic administrations as well as the priestly guild. As such, their part in the preservation of the DtrH would have been a fitting tribute to their father's work. Over the next 360 years or so, the priestly family of Anathoth could easily have continued to record

Israel's history while preserving the work of Abiathar, the greatest ancestor of their city. This would have continued in some form until Jeremiah, the last notable priest from Anathoth, picked up where his predecessors left off. It is likely that this was how the "proto-DtrH" survived the conflagration of Jerusalem in 586 BCE.

Jeremiah and Baruch

That Jeremiah was responsible for portions of the DtrH is not at all a new assertion.[71] For example, whereas Jewish tradition did not suggest a moniker such as the "DtrH" or "Dtr," it does assign the book of Kings to Jeremiah (*Baba Bathra* 15a). As I will cover in chapter 10, many parallels between the books of Jeremiah and Kings are evident, which, despite popular scholarly opinion, supports the Jewish tradition.[72] Interestingly, Thomas Römer posits, "In this edition [i.e., Jeremiah 7–35] Jeremiah speaks as if he were a member of the dtr party."[73] Of course, scholars are quick to assume a borrowing in the opposite direction. On this, Wilson notes that

> [Sigmund] Mowinckel's analysis, involving the prose passages [of Jeremiah] in 3.6-13; 7.1-8.3; 11.1-5, 9-14; 18.1-12; 21.1-10; 22.1-5; 25.1-11a; 27.1-22; 29.1-23; 32.1-2, 6-16, 24-44; 34.1-7, 8-22; 35.1-19; 39.15-18; 44.1-14; and 45.1-5, has been accepted by most scholars as proof of a Deuteronomistic layer in Jeremiah, although there remains a great deal of debate concerning the relation of this material to the book's biographical prose and to the prophet's poetic oracles.[74]

71. A. Graeme Auld, *Kings without Privilege: David and Moses in the Story of the Bible's Kings* (Edinburgh: T&T Clark, 1994), 167–70, suggests that Jeremiah was responsible for writing Kings.

72. For a concise presentation of the somewhat convoluted editorial history of the book of Jeremiah, see Person, *Deuteronomistic School*, 9–13.

73. Thomas Römer, "How Did Jeremiah Become a Convert to Deuteronomistic Ideology?," in Schearing and McKenzie, eds., *Those Elusive Deuteronomists*, 197. Römer argues for no less than two Dtr editings of Jeremiah—the latest one in the Babylonian exile after 582 BCE.

74. Wilson, "Who Was the Deuteronomist?" 74, citing the work of Sigmund Mowinckel, *Zur Komposition des Buches Jeremia* (Kristiania: Jacob Dybwad, 1914). See further Wilson's list, which includes: Clements, "Jeremiah 1–25 and the Deuteronomistic History," 93–113; and

Rarely do scholars today actually consider the possibility that Jeremiah may be one and the same with the "Deuteronomistic school," or Dtr, for that matter.[75] Moreover, many within the scholarly community refuse to allow for the possibility that Jeremiah may be responsible for the final form of his own work, let alone the DtrH.

Textually, we do know that Jeremiah was free to stay in Israel after the destruction of Jerusalem. Indeed, Jeremiah actually went home and then on to Mizpah after Jerusalem was destroyed (Jer. 39:14; 40:6, 12; 41:4-8).[76] Scholars are also aware of the possible links between the final editorial work on the DtrH and the location of Mizpah.[77] In this vein, Rainer Albertz suggests that two groups, once holding similar views during the seventh century, adopted competing agendas after the death of Josiah in 609 BCE.[78] The first was the "Shaphanide,"

Robert P. Carroll, *Jeremiah*, OTL (Philadelphia: Westminster, 1986). See also the similar conclusion of Steven L. McKenzie, "Postscript: The Laws of Physics and Pan-Deuteronomism," in Schearing and McKenzie, eds., *Those Elusive Deuteronomists*, 270.

75. See, for example, the cautious approach of Patricia Dutcher-Walls, "The Social Location of the Deuteronomists: A Sociological Study of Factional Politics in Late Pre-Exilic Judah," *JSOT* 52 (1991): 92. Here she refuses to draw a direct connection between the Deuteronomists and Jeremiah even though she asserts that they have a "kindred spirit."

76. Jer. 40:6 and 12 note that Jeremiah and the remaining people lived in Mizpah, but this does not preclude Jeremiah's editorial work there or at Anathoth (cf. Jer. 41:4-8).

77. E.g., Dietrich, "Martin Noth," 169-70; Timo Veijola, *Verheissung in der Krise: Studien zur Literatur und Theologie der Exilszeit anhand des 89. Psalms*, AASF B/220 (Helsinki: Suomalainen Tiede-akatemia, 1982), 190-97; and McCarter, "Books of Samuel," 278-80. Steven L. McKenzie, "Trouble with Kingship," in De Pury, Römer, and Macchi, eds., *Israel Constructs Its History*, 312-14. McKenzie, "Divided Kingdom," 138, rejects the Mizpah material in 1 Samuel 8-12 and Judges 19-21 as anachronistic because Mizpah "was nothing more than a border fortress until 586 B.C.E., when it replaced Jerusalem as Judah's administrative and cultic center." (So, too, Patrick M. Arnold, "Mizpah," *ABD* 4:879-80.) McKenzie dates these additions to the exilic period. While McKenzie's conclusions are correct to a degree, he fails to consider the cultic nature of a region without the need for a major city to be directly connected to it. Indeed, to this day the sites of Bethel and especially Gilgal (Khirbet el-Mefjir?) are debated; the latter mainly because of the lack of ruins of a major city in the proposed region. There is no textual or archaeological reason why Mizpah (tell en-Naṣbeh?) could not have been a major cultic center in the eleventh century (cf. A. F. Rainey, "Mizpah," *ISBE* 3:387-88). On the problems associated with identifying Mizpah today, see Arnold, "Mizpah," *ABD* 4:880. For a perspective on its historicity, see J. Maxwell Miller and John H. Hayes, *A History of Ancient Israel and Judah* (Great Britain: SCM, 1986), 121.

pro-Babylonian and pro-Jeremian, "reform party" living in Mizpah after the fall of Jerusalem (cf. Jeremiah 36; 40). Here they completed a "Deuteronomistic" editing of the book of Jeremiah (what Albertz called JerD).[79] The other group was the "nationalistic party" (pro-Davidic kingship—namely, Jehoiakim and Zedekiah), succeeded by Hilkiah's family who were anti-Babylonian and anti-Jeremian (in this camp were the priest Pashhur [Jer. 20:1-6] and prophet Hananiah [Jeremiah 28]). According to Albertz, the latter group edited the DtrH during the Babylonian exile and looked forward to the return of the offspring of David to the throne (hence the notation on Jehoiachin in 2 Kgs. 25:27-30).[80]

Albertz's theory does allow for editorial work at a later date but it does not take into account the numerous parallels with the book of Jeremiah in the DtrH. If the final editors were from the line of Hilkiah and were anti-Jeremian, why would they allow these parallels to stand? Furthermore, is it not possible that Jeremiah evolved in his thinking concerning certain entities and people in light of God's plans (cf. Jer. 18:1-10)? Just because Jeremiah pronounced judgment against the kingly descendants of Josiah does not make him anti-Davidic. In this vein, the book (or tradition) of Jeremiah also ends up denouncing even Babylon, which at one time Jeremiah promoted as the instrument of God's judgment (cf. Jer. 25:9; 27:6, 9-14; 29:10; 43:10; chs. 50; 51).

These concerns aside, it is possible that Jeremiah's amanuensis, Baruch, also played a key role in the editing process (Jer. 36:4, 18,

---

78. See also Dutcher-Walls, "Social Location," 77–94.

79. JerD = Deuteronomistic editing of Jeremiah. See also the comments by James Muilenburg, "Baruch the Scribe," in *Proclamation and Presence: Essays in Honour of G. Henton Davies*, ed. John I. Durham and J. R. Porter (Richmond: John Knox, 1970), 215–38, who argues that the "Deuteronomic" aspects of Jeremiah may be from Baruch.

80. Rainer Albertz, "In Search of the Deuteronomists: A First Solution to a Historical Riddle," in Römer, ed., *Future of the Deuteronomistic History*, 10–17. For a competing position that the house of Shaphan wrote the DtrH, see Muilenburg, "Baruch the Scribe," 215–38, esp. 220–21.

27),[81] even being told to add to the words of Jeremiah (Jer. 36:32).[82] Furthermore, while the rebellion that came in the days of Gedaliah was seven months after the destruction of the city (Jer. 41:1), Jeremiah would have had plenty of time to record much of the last portions of Israel's history during this period, especially if much of it had already been outlined at an earlier period by the priestly family at Anathoth. Interestingly, Noth's last comments in his footnotes/endnotes point to the high degree of probability that the author(s) of the DtrH was someone who remained in the land and was not deported by Nebuchadnezzar: the same person had access to sources not destroyed by the Babylonian siege.[83] Thus, despite scholarly opinions, Jewish tradition may "know better" than modernity has allowed. Jeremiah is a fitting candidate to play a key role in bringing the DtrH to its final form.

Another striking fact that helps draw Jeremiah into the Deuteronomists' circle is how Jeremiah introduces himself in his own book. He begins his prophecy by actually identifying himself not only by his immediate family connections (i.e., the son of Hilkiah) but also as being from the priests of Anathoth who were from the land of Benjamin (Jer. 1:1)! This is indeed a strange connection, seeing how no other Old Testament prophet makes a connection to a group of individuals from a particular tribe.[84] In light of this, it appears that Jeremiah may have been in the direct lineage of Abiathar

---

81. Noth, *Deuteronomistic History*, 74. In noting the parallels between 2 Kings and Jeremiah, Noth suggests that Baruch's work in Jeremiah may have been the source. Of course, Noth assumes that Dtr adopted it as opposed to identifying Baruch as a possible final editor of the DtrH along with Jeremiah the prophet.

82. For the role of Baruch in the writing of Jeremiah, see Muilenburg, "Baruch the Scribe," 215–38.

83. Noth, *Deuteronomistic History*, 142 n.10. See similar comments on 141 n.9.

84. Amos does connect himself with the sheepherders of Tekoa, whereas Micah and Nahum both identify their home regions (Moresheth and Elkoshite respectively). Most of the prophets also give at least their father's/ancestor's name. However, here Jeremiah actually gives three pieces of identifying information: (1) his father's name; (2) his home region; and (3) his association with the priests of Anathoth.

and the priestly family at Anathoth.[85] These data help draw a direct connection to the traditions started by Abiathar, which continued for over 360 years until Jeremiah, or Baruch, finished them. What is more, if Jeremiah's father, Hilkiah, is the same Hilkiah who found the temple scroll, then this further explains the "Deuteronomic" connections for both Jeremiah and the DtrH![86] This may also explain why Hilkiah sought out Huldah the prophetess, as opposed to Jeremiah, to give a word from the Lord after the discovery of the law book (2 Kgs. 22:14). Did Hilkiah not want to appear biased by going to his son for a "word from the Lord" about the discovered law book, which would help fuel the reforms? Or is it possible that Hilkiah needed an immediate word from the Lord and therefore went to someone within Jerusalem proper? In this vein, in 2 Kgs. 22:14, Dtr goes out of his way to note where Huldah lived, namely, the "second quarter in Jerusalem." At the same time, Dtr also takes the opportunity to record Huldah's problematic prophecy about Josiah's death, which could be construed in a negative light (2 Kgs. 22:20). Could this be Jeremiah's subtle jab at the prophetess?

It also appears that when Solomon exiled Abiathar to Anathoth, this priestly family was somewhat blacklisted and replaced by the line of Zadok (1 Kgs. 2:35)—even though they still may have performed some services in the temple (i.e., 1 Chronicles 24 and Hilkiah's high

---

85. So, too, Roger W. Uitti, "Hilkiah," *ABD* 3:201; and Baruch Halpern, "Shiloh," *ABD* 5:1215. H. Wallace, "Hilkiah," *ISBE* 4:713, points up that "According to tradition he [Hilkiah] was the brother of Jeremiah."

86. So, too, Richard E. Friedman, *Who Wrote the Bible?* (New York: Summit, 1987), 146, 149. Ernest W. Nicholson, *Jeremiah 1–25*, CBC (Cambridge: Cambridge University Press, 1973), 20, concludes that even though it is "improbable" that Hilkiah is Jeremiah's father, at the same time "we cannot be certain."

priestly activities).[87] This could further explain why Jeremiah's prophetic message was not accepted by those of Jerusalem.

Finally, I want to make it clear that these priests were more than compilers of older traditions. They were in fact authors who used their sources judiciously and with rhetorical intent to fashion an ongoing history of Israel and Judah. They were not the "inventors" of history they were the recorders of it. Here Gary Knoppers's conclusion seems fitting:

> . . . I wish to avoid, however, the impression that the Deuteronomist was simply a grand inventor, someone who created his work out of whole cloth. To reduce the tremendous diversity of vocabulary, styles, forms, and idiomatic expressions within this extensive corpus to a single author is reductive. By the same token, the Deuteronomist was more than simply an editor, someone who simply gathered pre-assembled materials and slightly altered them, according to a particular purpose. In short, the Deuteronomist, was both editor and an author—someone who selected and reworked sources, but also someone who created his own material and arranged the whole into a broadly sequential and connected work.[88]

Whereas Knoppers appears to identify Dtr as a single person from a later period using a series of sources from antiquity, I will argue that it may be best to see a series of authors who are subsumed under the final "Dtr" editing of Jeremiah or Baruch—this is how one avoids the "reductive" nature of many DtrH theories. Indeed, when the material is viewed from this perspective, the complexity and diversity in language and idioms makes the most sense.

This brief overview of the authors at Anathoth is not intended to be encumbered with details and textual support; those will appear in the chapters that follow. As we move forward, I will unpack the

---

87. On the one hand, it is possible that the priestly lines of Zadok and Abiathar may have lived together in Anathoth and, as such, Hilkiah may have been from the accepted priestly line of the Zadokites. On the other hand, Abiathar's family may have returned to a prominent position in the temple three-and-a-half centuries after Abiathar's death.
88. Knoppers, "Is There a Future," 133–34.

implications that this authorship theory has on the DtrH narrative. It hopefully will become clear that this perspective has much to commend it when viewed in the light of the special interests of a given author that are reflected in the recorded text. While I will certainly not convince everyone of the merits of this thesis, I do hope that many will begin to ask questions about the texts that heretofore have been glossed over by the supposition that the nebulous Dtr of the seventh or sixth centuries (or later) is in fact the author of the *entire* DtrH. At this juncture, it seems only fitting to assess Noth's assertions about this late Dtr. It is to this that we now turn.

2

The Deuteronomist(s) according to Martin Noth: An Assessment

In this chapter I will consider the impact that several of Noth's suppositions, found in his seminal work *The Deuteronomistic History*, have had not only on this present work but also on DtrH scholarship in general. Scholars are quick to assert that one cannot begin a discussion of the DtrH without considering, and engaging with, Noth's work on these books.[1] Rarely will an OT introduction or survey begin a discussion on the Former Prophets, Historical Books, or the DtrH (such designations depending on one's perspective) without addressing Noth's theory.[2] While the scope and limitations of this present work will not allow me to execute a detailed assessment of Noth's thesis in toto, I will attempt to tease out some

---

1. See, for example, the remarks of Jeremy Hutton, *The Transjordanian Palimpsest: The Overwritten Texts of Personal Exile and Transformation in the Deuteronomistic History*, BZAW 396 (Berlin: de Gruyter, 2009), 81.
2. See, for example, William LaSor, et al., *Old Testament Survey: The Message, Form, and Background of the Old Testament*, 2d ed. (Grand Rapids: Eerdmans, 1996), 134.

of Noth's assertions to their natural conclusions.[3] Moreover, I will examine a number of Noth's propositions, which have become axiomatic throughout DtrH studies.

Even though there have been a number of "advancements" in DtrH theories over the past seven decades (see the discussion in ch. 1), this has not negated many of Noth's assumptions that hold sway over the discussion of the DtrH even today. Furthermore, it is readily apparent that several of the suppositions Noth put forward do not negate the thesis proposed here in this work. On the contrary, my proposal actually meshes in many ways with Noth's assertions, especially when one teases them out to their natural conclusions.

Noth's propositions about the DtrH and Dtr can be categorized into two main groups: (1) queries or musings peculiar to Noth, which, in some cases, have remained unanswered—these generally focus on the personal qualifications of the author; and (2) suppositions that have become axioms among the broader field of DtrH studies—these tend to focus on the writing style peculiar to Dtr, the influences on said writing style, and the date of the bulk of the DtrH. Now, while it is impossible to handle every pondering of Noth, several deserve closer attention. I will begin by looking at category one: those comments and musings of Noth that in some cases he left unanswered. Interestingly, many of these conjectures are directly related to authorship issues—concerns that may aid us in our discussion throughout.

Queries or Musings Peculiar to Noth

On the first page of his second chapter, Noth posits that the DtrH had one author/editor, the generally accepted position of Noth's day.[4] He continues by asserting that, if there was more than one DtrH

---

3. I will interact with Noth's work at select points in my discussion in the following chapters as I deal with the composition of particular books.

editor, they "closely resemble one another in their style, and that the nature of their work was to adapt, to some extent, something which had already come into being as a comprehensive narrative complex or as various lengthy narrative complexes."[5] To begin with, it seems plausible that these similarities in style may be best explained by the similarities in focus and motives that one priestly family from a given region may have had. Is it not logical that a writing style would have been emulated by a son or a grandson or some other family member? Furthermore, Noth's proposition is in keeping with my thesis that the DtrH was fashioned and shaped over a period of time within one family or town of priests who shared many of the same understandings and presuppositions about the law and YHWH's plans for his nation.[6] Now, it is possible that the structural and literary unity that the DtrH exhibits could have come from the work of the final compiler (Noth's Dtr and my Jeremiah or Baruch), but that does not de facto eliminate the possibility of earlier unified compilations of material. In essence, this is what Noth was suggesting by the above-noted excerpt. As such, similarities in writing style could just have easily been copied over time within one family or community.[7] In this vein, Jeffrey H. Tigay has pointed up that authors of the ANE formulated their literary works many times in uniform ways:

> . . . this involved the use of standard formulas, similes, epithets, and the like. But beyond this, ancient writers drew extensively upon larger

---

4. I use the page numbers and chapter divisions as they appear in the 1981 English version of Noth's *The Deuteronomistic History*, JSOTSup 15 (Sheffield: JSOT Press, 1981).

5. Ibid., 4.

6. This is what one would expect from Abiathar's family line, a family who later served in the temple as priests; cf. Eugene Merrill, *Kingdom of Priests: A History of Old Testament Israel*, 2d ed. (Grand Rapids: Baker Academic, 2008), 156, 301.

7. See comments by Walter Dietrich, "Martin Noth and the Future of the Deuteronomistic History," in *The History of Israel's Traditions: The Heritage of Martin Noth*, ed. Steven L. McKenzie and M. Patrick Graham, JSOTSup 182 (Sheffield: Sheffield Academic Press, 1994), 161–63. Dietrich comments, "The Deuteronomistic History did not flow from a single pen but grew over time" (163).

components, such as topoi, motifs, groups of lines, and episodes, which had their original settings in other compositions. Sometimes they composed passages imitating such elements, and at other times they simply transferred such elements verbatim into their own compositions. . . . by the standards of the ancient Near East, these phenomena reflected a highly valued reliance on tradition . . .[8]

We find examples of this tendency to imitate within the prophetic corpus and, as already noted above, among the parallels of Jeremiah and 2 Kings. One need only to peruse portions of Micah and Isaiah to find texts lifted from one author and placed upon the pen of another.[9] As such, catchphrases and themes could very easily have been copied from one generation to the next, thus eliminating the need for one, all-encompassing author at a later period.

Noth also asks the question, "Do we in fact have here a comprehensive framework indicating a large literary unit which has adopted much traditional material?" Noth answers his own query in the affirmative.[10] Again, Noth's perspective that Dtr "adopted much traditional material" makes sense in light of the number of "hands" that may have had a part in the compiling process throughout the extended period handled in the DtrH. This framework, namely a history of YHWH's people and the Davidic kingship, most likely was already set in place by the first and second generations of the DtrH authors: Abiathar, Jonathan, and/or Ahimelech.

Next, Noth suggests that the DtrH was written by someone who was not from the ruling/governing class.[11] This, he asserts, is evident

8. Jeffrey Tigay, *The Evolution of the Gilgamesh Epic* (Philadelphia: University of Pennsylvania Press, 1982), 162.
9. Compare Isa. 2:2-4 to Mic. 4:1-3 and portions of Isaiah 36–39 to 2 Kings 19–20. One can also note Psalm 29 and the parallel motifs attributed to Baal and the motif of the Divine Warrior present throughout the OT and the ANE literature. Cf. also, Frank Moore Cross, "Divine Warrior in Israel's Early Cult," in *Biblical Motifs: Origins and Transformations*, ed. Alexander Altmann (Cambridge: Harvard University Press, 1966), 11–30.
10. Noth, *Deuteronomistic History*, 3.
11. Ibid., 99.

from Dtr's harsh assessment of the majority of the kings, especially those of the Northern Kingdom, and the elite of society. The role of the priests and prophets as law and covenant "enforcers" respectively meshes well with Noth's conclusion—a conclusion with which I unreservedly agree.[12] As enforcers of law and covenant, the groups generally in the crosshairs of the priests and prophets were in fact the kings and elite of society—those who had the ability to abuse their power and oppress the underclass. On the other hand, while Noth is correct in pointing up the anonymous nature of the DtrH,[13] he is too quick to rule out the possibility that the DtrH came from the "priestly sphere." He comes to this conclusion based upon his assertion that the author lacks an interest in the cult.[14] However, Noth's assessment is unfounded when one considers the rhetorical purposes of the DtrH and the evidence itself. Even though cultic themes and motifs may not appear with the frequency of, say, Leviticus, they do, nonetheless, appear frequently with various foci (e.g., normal cultic observances and sacrifices; covenant ceremonies; dedication rituals; or warnings against rival cults and cult sites such as the high places).[15]

---

12. In some cases, one individual played both roles (e.g., Ezekiel and Jeremiah).

13. Ibid., 4.

14. Ibid., 99. This same perspective has been perpetuated by others. For example, see Richard D. Nelson, "The Role of the Priesthood in the Deuteronomistic History," in *Reconsidering Israel and Judah: Recent Studies on the Deuteronomistic History*, ed. Gary N. Knoppers and J. Gordon McConville (Winona Lake, IN: Eisenbrauns, 2000), 179–93. Here Nelson sees the priesthood as ancillary to the purposes of Dtr, only using them when Dtr needed to "make a theological point" (193). However, see the opposite comments by Rainer Albertz, in his work "In Search of the Deuteronomists: A First Solution to a Historical Riddle," in *The Future of the Deuteronomistic History*, ed. Thomas Römer (Leuven: Leuven University Press, 2000), 8–9.

15. The terms "sacrifice" and "altar" (including their derivates) appear throughout the DtrH. First, "sacrifice" appears in: Josh. 8:31; 22:23, 26–29; Judg. 2:5; 1 Sam. 1:3, 4, 21; 2:13, 15, 19, 29; 3:14; 6:15; 9:12, 13; 10:8; 11:15; 15:15, 21, 22; 16:2, 3, 5; 20:6, 29; 2 Sam. 6:13; 1 Kgs. 1:9, 19, 25; 3:3, 4; 8:15, 62, 63; 12:27; 13:2; 15:12; 18:29, 36; 19:21; 2 Kgs. 3:20; 5:17; 10:24; 14:4; 15:4, 35; 16:4, 15; 17:35, 36. Second, "altar" appears in: Josh. 8:30, 31; 9:27; 22:10, 11, 16, 19, 23, 26, 28, 29, 34; Judg. 6:24, 25, 26, 28, 30, 31, 32; 13:20; 21:4; 1 Sam. 2:28, 33; 7:17; 14:35; 2 Sam. 24:18, 21, 25; 1 Kgs. 1:50–53; 2:28, 29; 3:4; 6:20, 22; 7:48; 8:22, 31, 54, 64; 9:25; 12:32, 33; 13:1–5, 32 (those in chs. 12 and 13 refer to Jeroboam's altars); 18:30, 32, 35; 2 Kgs. 11:11; 12:9; 16:10–15; 18:22; 23:9, 15, 16, 17 (ch. 23 refers to the altars destroyed by Josiah). This basic search reveals

Moreover, there are a number of possible reasons why priestly writers may have allowed this apparent lacuna in their cultic bent—reasons Noth does not address. First, it seems evident that the author(s) was in fact more interested in recording a history and apologetic literature as opposed to formulating a cultic "how-to" guide. Must priests be so myopic that they can only focus on the cult, as per Noth? Even prophet-priests like Ezekiel and Jeremiah are not as concerned with cultic matters as one would expect, especially in light of their greater goal of addressing the breach of the covenant or the rebelliousness of Israel.[16] On these latter two points, Noth himself acknowledges Dtr's focus on the people's apostasy (i.e., the broken covenant).[17]

Second, the priestly authors may have had other reasons for not focusing on cultic matters for large portions of the material, especially the earliest strands/blocks. For example, Abiathar, as a fugitive with David, would have been separated from the cult sites and his role as an officiating priest—something clearly evidenced by the scarcity of cultic references in 1 Samuel 21 through 2 Samuel 5—the exact period of Abiathar's fugitive status and David's early kingship from Hebron.[18]

Third, as we will see in our discussion in chapters 7–9 below, even though priestly leanings may still appear in places, some of the "traditional material" integrated into the DtrH may have had other

---

no fewer than 120 occurrences of just these two terms alone. A wider search of cultic terms is sure to reveal many more references.

16. For more on the prophet-priest motif in Ezekiel, see Brian Peterson, *Ezekiel in Context: Ezekiel's Message Understood in its Historical Setting of Covenant Curses and Ancient Near Eastern Mythological Motifs*,PTMS 182 (Eugene, OR: Pickwick, 2012).

17. Noth, *Deuteronomistic History*, 76, 89.

18. The only references to sacrifices/offerings appear in 1 Sam. 26:29 (here it is not referring to an actual sacrifice but, rather, is a tangential reference in David's speech to Saul) and 2 Sam. 6:13, 17, 18 (references to the festivities of bringing the Ark to Jerusalem). There is one reference to Ahithophel's offering of sacrifice in 2 Sam. 15:12, but not in connection with Abiathar. Not surprisingly, David does inquire of the Lord for direction with the aid of Abiathar (cf. 1 Sam. 23:2, 4; 30:8; 2 Sam. 2:1; 5:19, 23).

rhetorical purposes (i.e., as an apologia for David's rule), which in turn eliminated the need and purpose of a dominant cultic focus.

Fourth, despite Noth's assertions that there is heavy sixth-century editing in the early books of the DtrH, it is very likely that the bulk of the DtrH (at least up until 1 Kings 4) was written *before* the temple was even constructed. If this is the case, organized sacrifice in the temple would not even have been a part of the author's knowledge, let alone his purview.[19] In this vein, if one looks at the actual recorded accounts of sacrifice at cult sites prior to the temple's construction, one sees exactly what Abiathar would have been all too familiar with: a number of cult sites used over particular periods of time (cf. 1 Sam. 7:15; 10:3, 17; 1 Kgs. 3:4, 5, etc.).[20] Further, the status of the priesthood and the cult was anything but prolific in the period after Joshua until the temple was constructed—one need only look at the apostasy of the judges' period (Eli's family included) to draw this conclusion. Therefore, one of Noth's main assertions that Dtr was not a priest because of Dtr's leniency toward numerous cult sites outside of Jerusalem may have another explanation. The reason for Dtr's willingness to include/allow within his work accounts concerning numerous sacrificial sites prior to the temple's construction was due to the historical veracity of such a reality and due to sheer necessity—something even Abiathar was a part of at Nob.[21]

---

19. That is not to say that the priests were not involved or interested in cultic activity at the shrines or at the mobile tabernacle (e.g., at Shiloh) up until this point; rather, I am merely making the point that it was in fact the construction of the temple, which served as the impetus for a more organized and centralized form of worship and sacrifice. Sadly, even this centralization did little to entrench, in any meaningful way, cultic legislation and praxis in the lives of Israel's kings, let alone the people. One need only look to the judges' period to see the beginning of the move away from the systematic sacrificial system as Moses instituted in the wilderness. A number of reformers over several centuries attempted to correct the spiritual repercussions of this hiatus from the cult during the judges' era, a hiatus that was never fully rectified until the postexilic period.

20. Noth, *Deuteronomistic History*, 87, proposes that Dtr actually wrote the temple-construction narrative at a later date. But there is no conclusive evidence for this assertion, nor does this need be the case if one of Abiathar's sons recorded the majority of this account.

In this regard, Noth is on the right track when he suggests that the temple construction event and the much-debated 480 years of 1 Kgs. 6:1 must have had special significance for Dtr.[22] Now, while I do not seek to enter into a debate of what this date means for an early or late exodus/conquest, suffice it to say that if Abiathar and his sons are the first of the authors of the DtrH, then the presence of this date as "significant," according to Noth, makes perfect sense. The event of the temple construction would not only have been a benchmark in Israel's recorded history, but would also be a major milestone in the life of any priest who had seen the fulfillment of the promise made to David in 2 Samuel 7. Moreover, the fulfillment of Deuteronomy 12 would have afforded any priest a level of joy. The fulfillment of the Mosaic promise may have sparked one of these priests to connect the temple construction event to the exodus generation—the generation that witnessed the recording of the great promise!

Finally, and perhaps some of the most interesting notations by Noth thus far, are his comments about the perspective of the authors and where the author(s) of the DtrH may have lived. On the former point, Noth suggests that the authorial perspective is "Judaean."[23] This, of course, is reflected in the author's pro-Davidic sympathies. Yet, this is not at all surprising coming from the pen of Abiathar (and the priests of Anathoth), even though he lived in the tribal region of Benjamin. Abiathar was fiercely loyal to David, owing David his very life (see more in ch. 7 below). Moreover, Abiathar lived with David for the majority of his life within the tribal region of Judah; his second home. It only stands to reason that those who followed in the literary footsteps of Abiathar from the town of Anathoth no doubt

---

21. Ibid., 96. Noth asserts that the later Dtr was being "lenient" toward his predecessors in this regard. However, he may have been remaining faithful to a long history that started with Abiathar's version of Israel's history.
22. Ibid., 19, 60.
23. Ibid., 64.

also respected David due to his treatment of their forefather, Abiathar. The proximity of Anathoth to the capital city would have forced them to have a vested interest in the Davidic lineage and Judah—as goes Jerusalem so goes Anathoth!

The second point Noth brings up actually appears toward the end of his book. Here, tucked away in an endnote that few perhaps have read, Noth suggests that Dtr may have lived in or near Mizpah or Bethel.[24] Noth makes this assertion because Dtr had knowledge of these local shrines, and because it appears that he had access to local sources and traditions from these cult sites (e.g., 1 Kgs. 12:32—13:32; 2 Kgs. 17:25-28; 23:16-18).[25] Indeed, Noth even posits, albeit again in an endnote, that "It is tempting to conclude that this is where Dtr. himself lived and wrote—it is perfectly possible."[26] Interestingly, these sites are all within a ten-mile radius of Anathoth! Did Noth speak better than he knew? A close evaluation of the books may answer this question in the affirmative—an undertaking that we will address further in part 2 below.

Noth's Suppositions That Have Become Axiomatic

The second category of suppositions Noth proposed focuses on his proposals that have become axiomatic for a majority of DtrH scholars. These axioms deal with the writing style, influences, date, and setting of Dtr. These "sacred" axioms have so shaped and driven the discussion on the DtrH and Dtr that many within scholarship will

24. See similar comments concerning Mizpah by Steven L. McKenzie, "The Trouble with Kingship," in *Israel Constructs Its History: Deuteronomistic Historiography in Recent Research*, ed. Albert de Pury, Thomas Römer, and Jean-Daniel Macchi, JSOTSup 306 (Sheffield: JSOT, 1994), 312–14; and P. Kyle McCarter, "The Books of Samuel," in McKenzie and Graham, eds., *History of Israel's Traditions*, 278–80. McCarter sees the Mizpah material in the DtrH as perhaps only an "exilic revision from a prophetic perspective" (280), as opposed to its own redactional layer.

25. Noth, *Deuteronomistic History*, 85.

26. Ibid., 141 n.9. Cf. also his similar comments on 142 n.10.

have a hard time entertaining, let alone accepting, anything different. Now, while many of these entrenched beliefs do not do irreparable damage to my thesis, some do need to be reexamined in light of proposed earlier dates for blocks of the DtrH. However, an honest discussion of the authorship possibilities, setting, intent, and so forth will perhaps move the "goalposts" beyond where they have been set for the past seventy years.

To begin, Noth concludes his opening chapter by stating that the DtrH is "independent and unified"—a point with which I wholeheartedly agree.[27] As a matter of fact, most DtrH scholars would agree that there is a degree of unity in the DtrH.[28] For example, when considering the criteria for isolating Dtr material in the DtrH, Steven L. McKenzie concludes ". . . that one writer, Dtr, had a greater hand in shaping, revising and organizing his source material than scholarship as a whole, with its preoccupation with redactions, has credited him."[29] Of course, one should expect nothing less than a somewhat unified text coming from one group/family of priests, especially if the author of the final editing sought to pull what may have been diverse traditions together. I say "somewhat unified" and "diverse" because total unity of thought is next to impossible even for *one* author, let alone perhaps a dozen or more over such a span of time.[30]

27. Ibid., 3. So, too, Thomas Römer, "Deuteronomy in Search of Origins," in Knoppers and McConville, eds., *Reconsidering Israel and Judah*, 117.
28. I am fully aware that this is a broad statement. Of course, there will be those who would argue otherwise. There has been a move within certain branches of minimalist scholarship to push not only the date of the material to a much later period, but also to argue for the conflicting nature of the work (see ch. 1).
29. Steven L. McKenzie, "The Books of Kings in the Deuteronomistic History," in McKenzie and Graham, eds., *History of Israel's Traditions*, 302.
30. Even as I write this book over a period of months my ideas tend to fluctuate at key junctures, even though my overall thesis remains intact. That authors from a period before computers with cut-and-paste functions and delete keys should include what later may appear as "conflicting" ideas need not dissuade us from the unity and purpose of the overall DtrH.

It goes without saying that if the "traditional material" was the product of a number of hands over centuries, even though they were from the same family or group, then different motives may have driven select authors in different eras. It therefore should not be surprising to find what scholars call pro-monarchical accounts side-by-side with apparent anti-kingship statements.[31] There can be no question that someone living in Asa's, Hezekiah's, or Josiah's day may have been more amenable to the monarchy, whereas someone from Ahaz's, Manasseh's, Jehoiakim's, or Zedekiah's day would have had the opposite sentiment. In this regard, Walter Dietrich comments, "Perhaps Dtr did not reject the monarchy *per se*, but only a specific form of monarchy considered to be irreconcilable with the Torah."[32] If this is the case, which I would argue seems most likely, then would the next author erase the history that had been handed down to him from previous generations just because there may be a conflict in opinion? I think not! And this is even more apparent with the final editor, who did not seek to undermine the long tradition handed down to him.[33] On the contrary, he sought to amalgamate it and add commentary along the way, perhaps for the purpose of showing

---

31. See, for example, the comments of Römer, "Deuteronomy in Search of Origins," 115. The classic example of this is the apparent conflicting accounts of Samuel in the early monarchical period; cf. 1 Sam. 8:1-22; 9:1—10:16; 10:17-27; 11:1-15; 12:1-25—these texts oscillate between what scholars say are anti-monarchic and pro-monarchic traditions. Was Samuel pro-monarchy or not? Or was Samuel merely presenting his internal struggle with the new form of leadership in Israel and his loss of position? Or is it possible to see Samuel recording portions of the account and someone later, like Abiathar, recording events from his perspective? See further comments in ch. 8 below.

32. Dietrich, "Martin Noth," 157. Note that this is only a postulation and not a position Dietrich held. See further comments by Lyle Eslinger, "Viewpoints and Points of View in Samuel 8–12," *JSOT* 26 (1983): 61–76; and idem, *Kingship of God in Crisis: A Close Reading of 1 Samuel 1–12*, BLS 10 (Sheffield: Almond, 1985), 55–62.

33. Contra Albertz, in his work "In Search of the Deuteronomists," 10–11, who suggests that any discontinuity proves that two separate groups were at work with competing agendas after the death of Josiah in 609. Albertz suggests that one was the "Shaphanide" group—the pro-Babylonian and pro-Jeremian "reform party" working from Mizpah after the fall of Jerusalem (cf. Jeremiah 36; 40)—and the other was the "nationalistic party" from Hilkiah's family who were anti-Babylonian and anti-Jeremian.

why the nation went into exile—a motivation not apparent for earlier authors. The final editor's end goal or motivation need not be the driving force to expunge every apparent contradictory statement or pericope that may not adhere to this final theme.[34] In this vein, S. L. Richter says it well when he concludes,

> In the mind of the present author, the current state of confusion in Deuteronomistic studies ultimately is the result of an overly optimistic opinion of how much redactional activity might be isolated within a finished piece, augmented by the atomistic tendencies that seem to be inherent to the critical methodologies of OT exegesis. Too often this atomistic optimism has been further exacerbated by a lack of respect for the ancient historian—the apparent assumption that an ancient historian would be incapable of maintaining a complex perspective on the subject matter, or unable to hold conflicting views in tension.[35]

Indeed, it is arrogant to assume that we know better about how the ancients would or would not incorporate earlier traditions. Thus, despite apparent contradictions, I will demonstrate below that this particular axiom of Noth concerning the unity of the final form of the DtrH is valid.

Next, Noth, in his closing chapter, points out how Dtr was faithful to his sources and honored what they had to say, especially those sources associated with the prophet Samuel.[36] While I will address this more fully in chapter 7, suffice it to say that Abiathar respected Samuel on several levels. Among other things, the aged prophet

---

34. So, too, the conclusion of Mark A. O'Brien, "Judges and the Deuteronomistic History," in McKenzie and Graham, eds., *History of Israel's Traditions*, 256–57.
35. S. L. Richter, "Deuteronomistic History," in *Dictionary of the Old Testament: Historical Books*, ed. Bill T. Arnold and H. G. M. Williamson (Downers Grove, IL: InterVarsity, 2005), 227–28.
36. Noth, *Deuteronomistic History*, 96. So, too, Baruch Halpern, "Sacred History and Ideology: Chronicles' Thematic Structure—Indications of an Earlier Source," in *The Creation of Sacred Literature: Composition and Redaction of the Biblical Text*, ed. Richard E. Friedman, NES 22 (Berkeley: University of California Press, 1981), 53; and Richard D. Nelson, "The Double Redaction of the Deuteronomistic History: The Case is Still Compelling," *JSOT* 29, no. 3 (2005): 333.

anointed Abiathar's friend, David (1 Samuel 16) and was like a son to Abiathar's descendant, Eli. As such, source material attributed to Samuel would have held weight with the young priest. This would explain why Dtr (i.e., Abiathar) did not criticize Samuel's sacrificial activities. Furthermore, one should not be surprised to find minimal concern from the author regarding the numerous cult sites until after the temple is constructed—these earlier portions of the DtrH would have come from the hand of Abiathar before the building of the temple (see the discussion above). It is only after this watershed event that a direct connection between Jerusalem and the place where YHWH will place his name becomes dominant (2 Kgs. 18:16; 21:4; 23:4, 27; 24:13; 25:14, 18).[37] This later portion of the DtrH, of course, may be attributed to later priests from Anathoth, or even Jeremiah himself.

Closely related to our discussion immediately above is another of Noth's prominent axioms, also related to Dtr's use of source materials, namely, Noth's insistence on the presence of early traditions within the larger work, especially those found within the books of Deuteronomy, Joshua, and Samuel. Noth asserts that Dtr organized his history according to eras or defining periods in the history of Israel. These included the Mosaic era; the occupation of the land (west of the Jordan) under Joshua; the judges' era; the periods of Saul, David, and Solomon; and, finally, the period of the kings of Israel and Judah.[38] Dtr recorded his history using these traditions as a framework for his history. Noth avers that Dtr had at his disposal large portions of the early history of Israel, to which he remained faithful as he wove them into his work. It is worth noting that

---

37. The common refrain of a "house for my name/the name of the Lord" or the "place where my name is" appears in the temple-construction narrative (1 Kgs. 5:3, 5; 8:16-20; 8:29, 33, 35, 42, 43, 44, 48; 9:3, 7) and sporadically in the remaining narratives of 1 and 2 Kings (1 Kgs. 11:36; 14:21; 2 Kgs. 21:4, 7; 23:27).
38. Cf. Noth, *Deuteronomistic History*, 26–74.

these blocks make up the majority of the DtrH (I will return to this below). Noth continues by pointing up that Dtr had "to construct and compose by himself the account of the monarchy from Solomon onwards" using sources such as the Chronicles of the kings.[39] Not surprisingly, this meshes with my theory that Abiathar could have easily written much of this early material found in the DtrH before his death. This would be sometime during the early reign of Solomon when the style of the DtrH changes—perhaps due to one of Abiathar's sons taking over the recording of the DtrH. Thus, the reason that the material from 1 Kings 10 through 2 Kings 25 appears more annalistic is due to the fact that this would be from the period *after* Abiathar's death. As for the earlier source material, which dominates the DtrH, Abiathar, as a court priest, would have had access to much of the material of Joshua, Judges, and the first half of 1 Samuel and would have actually lived through the period covering the last half of 1 Samuel, all of 2 Samuel, and part of 1 Kings. Thus, one need not look to a later author for the majority of the DtrH—a common trend among DtrH scholars since the time of Noth.

Moreover, Abiathar was not only from the line of Eli, the priestly class who were the most likely to be the recorders and preservers of history (see ch. 1), but he would have had access to the written and oral accounts, in whole or in part, from his own family history, Samuel, Nathan, and Gad (1 Chr. 29:29), as well as direct access to these court prophets themselves (see further comments on this in ch. 7). As a contemporary with Saul and David, Abiathar could easily have fashioned many of what Noth calls the "existing traditional sources."[40] Further, David, at least under the cultic tutelage of Abiathar (and perhaps Zadok), centralized the political structure of Israel in Jerusalem (2 Samuel 5) where historical sources would have

---

39. Ibid., 77. Note also comments on p. 12.
40. Ibid., 77.

been recorded and stored. The text makes it clear that David hired scribes/secretaries and recorders once Jerusalem was conquered (2 Sam. 8:16, 17; 20:24, 25). Some time later, David began the centralization process of the cult (cf. 2 Samuel 6).

In this vein, the presence of a centralized cult in the final form of the DtrH also has become one of the fundamental tenets among DtrH scholarship. This concept is often marshaled as evidence of the work/hand of Dtr.[41] This is often attributed to the period of Josiah's reforms because of the discovery of the law book at that time (2 Kings 22) and the king's desire for centralization of worship. However, if one sets aside the theory Wilhelm M. L. de Wette propounded[42] just for a moment, and supposes that the bulk of Deuteronomy was in fact written by Moses, could this change the possible focus of hypothesized earlier authors? Indeed, it would! Thus, there may be another way of looking at this and similar motifs—motifs that may have played a key role at a much earlier period than the late seventh or early sixth century. As early as the tenth century, the stressing of cultic centralization and temple construction should be of no surprise if Abiathar (and later his family) was instrumental in effecting this program in Jerusalem (cf. 2 Samuel 6). He and the priests of Anathoth would have indeed been interested in how the

---

41. For recent arguments against the author of Deuteronomy's choice of Jerusalem as the place that YHWH chose, cf. Nadav Na'aman, "The Law of the Altar in Deuteronomy and the Cultic Site Near Shechem," in *Rethinking the Foundations: Historiography in the Ancient World and in the Bible: Essays in Honour of John Van Seters,* ed. Steven L. McKenzie, Thomas Römer, and Hans Heinrich Schmid (Berlin: Walter de Gruyter, 2000), 141–61, esp. 143–44; J. Gordon McConville, "Restoration in Deuteronomy and the Deuteronomic Literature," in *Restoration: Old Testament, Jewish, and Christian Perspectives,* ed. James M. Scott, JSJSup 72 (Leiden: Brill, 2001), 11–40, esp. 33–34. Here McConville correctly points out that the "place" where YHWH chooses is "a way of referring to all places at which Israel might meet Yahweh" (33), i.e., Horeb (Deuteronomy 4–5), Shechem (Deuteronomy 27; Josh. 8:30–35; ch. 24), or Shiloh (Jer. 7:12).
42. De Wette postulated that the "law book" of Josiah's day was to be equated with the book of Deuteronomy. De Wette postulated that the priests of Josiah's day actually wrote Deuteronomy—and assigned it to Moses—as a means of supporting their reforms (note specifically Deut. 12). See more on this in ch. 3.

temple and YHWH's presence were hallowed in light of the sinful practices of the kings. Further, this interest would account for the texts that develop the positive outcomes of kingships that held the law and the tabernacle/temple in high regard (i.e., David, Solomon [to a degree], Asa, Jehoshaphat, Hezekiah, and Josiah). If Abiathar and his family were proponents of cultic centralization, they would have had a vested interest in effecting such a change and propagating its continuation. (This would have placed Anathoth, which was so close to Jerusalem, in an enviable and powerful position among the priestly class.) There is also the reality that Abiathar's family had lost the Ark and had witnessed the destruction of the tabernacle at Shiloh (cf. 1 Samuel 4–7). A centralized cult and tabernacle/temple under the protection of the king and in the stronghold of Jerusalem would have been appealing to this priestly family indeed. Thus, this centralizing bent need not rest solely in the period of Josiah, even though Josiah may have been the most forceful in this regard.

According to most scholarly assertions—Noth included—this Dtr program of centralization is rooted in the Mosaic promise found in Deuteronomy 12. It is here that one first encounters what appears to be the prophetic basis for identifying Jerusalem as the site where YHWH will place YHWH's name (cf. 1 Kgs. 11:13, 32, 34, 36; 14:21; 2 Kgs. 21:7; 23:27).[43] However, Noth goes on to suggest that Dtr was ambivalent toward the sacrificial system in the temple at Jerusalem (see the above discussion).[44] In this regard, Noth posits that after the temple is constructed, the major sin of the kings and the people, which is addressed by Dtr, is not improper ritual in the temple per se but, rather, sacrifices offered on the high places outside of Jerusalem.[45] (This concept is really only applicable to the

---

43. Of course, the Samaritan Pentateuch identifies this site as Mt. Gerizim.
44. Noth, *Deuteronomistic History*, 95.
45. Ibid., 97.

period after the temple's construction, as I noted above.) The one exception Noth puts forward is the Mt. Carmel event (1 Kings 18). Here Noth proposes that due to the fact that Elijah's sacrifice on Mt. Carmel happens *after* the construction of the temple, Dtr had to make an extraordinary "concession" to the sacrificial rules of a centralized cult.[46] While I will touch more on the rhetorical purposes for Dtr's inclusion of the Elijah and Elisha narratives in chapter 10, one important fact needs to be considered that will hopefully ameliorate Noth's contention (and perhaps those of other scholars).[47] Even though, as Noth points out, it is true that this is an exceptional case, it is really not that problematic. Furthermore, it does not require a "concession" from Dtr. Elijah did not "perform" the sacrifice in toto; YHWH himself was responsible for this event when YHWH consumed the sacrifice by lightning as evidence of who YHWH was. Richard Nelson makes the same mistake as Noth by noting Dtr's ambivalence on sacrifice, not only about the Elijah event but also concerning Gideon's and Samuel's sacrifices (Judg. 6:19-24; 1 Sam. 7:9).[48] Much like Elijah, Gideon did not offer a sacrifice; it was performed by the heavenly being (Judg. 6:21). And, in Samuel's case, he was in fact from a priestly lineage (cf. 1 Chronicles 6) operating at a time *before* centralization. In many of the other cases Nelson notes (e.g., 1 Sam. 7:1b; 2 Sam. 6:3; 20:26; 1 Kgs. 4:5), an alternate explanation can be offered that is in keeping with Dtr's respect for the priestly office.[49] Indeed, even Nelson himself clarifies some of the supposed problems in the text.[50] Moreover, if my contention is

---

46. Ibid., 142 n.6.
47. For example, Nelson, "Role of the Priesthood," 183.
48. Ibid., 183. See also Jon D. Levenson, "Who Inserted the Book of the Torah?," *HTR* 68, no. 3 (1975): 203–33, esp. 228–29.
49. Nelson, "Role of the Priesthood," 183.
50. Ibid., 183 n.12. In other cases where Nelson argues that Dtr was ambivalent toward the kings offering sacrifices, the texts are either unclear or descriptive not prescriptive. In 2 Samuel 6, David wears a linen ephod but it is not clear who actually offered the sacrifices—obviously there were priests present. In 2 Kgs. 16:12, Ahaz's offering of the sacrifice on his new altar appears

correct that Jeremiah, or someone close to him, was in fact the final editor of the DtrH, then he would have been all too familiar with the similar situation developing in his own day as that witnessed on Mt. Carmel. YHWH could easily work outside of the temple precincts to prove who YHWH was, especially apart from a corrupted cult (cf. Jer. 7:1-14, esp. v. 4).

Scholars are also rightly beginning to ask the important question, that if in fact Deuteronomy 12 was a later addition by Dtr as a pseudo-Mosaic prophecy to legitimize Jerusalem, why wouldn't Dtr have made it clearer in the text of Deuteronomy?[51] And why would Dtr muddy the water by including Shechem as a central cult site for Israel (cf. Deut. 11:26-30; 27:11-13)?[52] Moreover, if Jerusalem is such an important feature for Dtr, why is it only mentioned in passing in the books of Joshua, Judges, and 1 Samuel (cf. Joshua 10; 15:63;

descriptive not prescriptive. And contra ibid., 191, and idem, "The Altar of Ahaz: A Revisionist View," *HAR* 10 (1986): 267–76, Dtr appears to be showing the malfeasance of Ahaz's reign, which was marked with cultic and spiritual rebellion (2 Kgs. 16:2-4, 17-18)—so, too, Norbert Lohfink, "Culture Shock and Theology," *BTB* 7, no. 1 (1977): 19. Moreover, Dtr's language of a king "offering a sacrifice" may be more reflective of the king's overseeing of those sacrifices as a titular head of the nation. This is apparent in Solomon's "offering" of sacrifices. They certainly were not done by the king (1 Kgs. 3:15; 8:63-64) unless we are also to believe that Solomon personally sacrificed 22,000 oxen and 120,000 sheep (1 Kgs. 8:63)!

51. Gordon Wenham notes that scholars who hold to the late date of Deuteronomy answer this query by stating, "This, it is argued, is quite understandable: the author of Deuteronomy realized that it would be anachronistic to have Moses specify Jerusalem as the central shrine when it was not captured by Israel till the time of David. He preferred to use the discreet code name 'the place which the LORD will choose', which was perfectly clear to the men of Josiah's time and did not make it so obvious that Moses was not the real author of Deuteronomy." Cf. Gordon Wenham, "The Date of Deuteronomy: Linch-pin of Old Testament Criticism. Part One," *Them* 10, no. 3 (1985): 17. However, even this response is not persuasive in light of scholars' proposals of other glaring "anachronisms." For example, scholars are quick to point up the "late" gloss of Josiah's name in 1 Kgs. 13:2 and the appearance of Cyrus' name in Isa. 44:28 and 45:1. Thus the question of why this later author did not just insert Jerusalem in Deuteronomy 12 and thus end the ambiguity altogether does not have an adequate answer. See also responses by Steven L. McKenzie, *The Chronicler's Use of the Deuteronomistic History*, HSM 33 (Atlanta: Scholars, 1984), 9; or Na'aman, "Law of the Altar," 143. McConville's astute comments do come close in helping to alleviate the tension; see his "Restoration in Deuteronomy," 33.

52. Of course, redaction critics get around this dilemma by going through a series of redactional gymnastics, or they excise these texts as later additions. See, for example, Na'aman, "Law of the Altar," 143–61.

Judg. 1:7, 8, 21; 19:10; 1 Sam. 17:54)?[53] Is it not just as likely that the author of this material may have held centralization as an important concept, but not held it as the "end-all" of his goals in writing his history? And is it not also possible that the author(s) may have in fact already been familiar with the Mosaic legislation long before the hypothesized seventh or sixth centuries, and have been writing with this "Deuteronomic law" in mind all along?[54]

In seeking answers to these questions, this leads us naturally to another dominant axiom that Noth (as well as many scholars today) asserts, namely, that the DtrH was written by Dtr who utilized the recently rediscovered Deuteronomic law—hence the very name of the DtrH. This certainly does not discredit a priestly origin (see above)—what priest would not be interested in the Deuteronomic laws?[55] Therefore, it is not farfetched to assume that the priests of Anathoth would have been familiar with the laws of Deuteronomy (in whatever form they took at an earlier or later date). On the other hand, and here I am merely playing the proverbial "devil's advocate," there has been a long-held assumption that the book of Deuteronomy was actually the product of northern *priests* who escaped the Assyrian oppression of the eighth century.[56] Where would those refugee

---

53. So, too, Gordon J. Wenham, "The Deuteronomic Theology of the Book of Joshua," *JBL* 90, no. 2 (1971): 148; and Yehezkel Kaufmann, *The Biblical Account of the Conquest of Palestine* (Jerusalem: Magnes, 1953), 24.

54. Interestingly, Wenham asserts that, "On balance then it seems likely that the deuteronomic language was not a phenomenon restricted to the late seventh/early sixth centuries BC, but that it persisted much longer. It could indeed have been the preferred style of explicitly religious texts for a long while in Israel. Certainly the evidence of the prophets Amos and Hosea is most easily explained on the basis of at least some form of Deuteronomy antedating their preaching and being known to them." Cf. Wenham, "Date of Deuteronomy," 19. See further comments by Römer, "Deuteronomy in Search of Origins," 116 n.17.

55. Note also a similar conclusion, or dare I say frustration, presented by Richter in the conclusion to his article, "Deuteronomistic History," 219–30, at 227–28.

56. See, for example, the comments of Jeffrey C. Geoghegan, *The Time, Place, and Purpose of the Deuteronomistic History: The Evidence of "Until This Day,"* BJS 347 (Providence, RI: Brown University Press, 2006), 149; Mark Leuchter, *Samuel and the Shaping of Tradition* (New York: Oxford University Press, 2013), 16–17; and Douglas A. Knight, "Deuteronomy and the

priests have settled? The priestly cities of Anathoth, Jerusalem, and Hebron (among others) immediately come to mind. If this theory is true, is it not possible to assert that the priests of these cities would have been familiar with this body of legal material? Of course, once again this poses the problem of dating the authorship of the earlier traditions—when was the "Deuteronomic layer" applied? Either way, Dtr's interest in "Deuteronomic" legislation makes sense at any period throughout the work. What the discussion really boils down to is one's presuppositional stances—early vs. late influences.

Turning our discussion to the dating of the final form, Noth avers that based upon the notations of 2 Kgs. 25:27-30, the final form of the DtrH was written in the mid-sixth century.[57] Sadly, this *terminus ad quem* has been the axiomatic basis for dating not just the final form, but the majority of the writing of the DtrH—a position Noth held as well.[58] The problem with this portion of Noth's theory, even though it is obvious that final notations were made some time after 561 BCE, is that it detracts from the probability that the beginning to the work (i.e., a proto-DtrH) was very early—a work that may have been ongoing over several centuries. To be fair, Noth does point out the interest that Dtr had in the "traditions concerning the history of the centuries before his time."[59] However, it is again my contention that this "interest" can best be explained by an ongoing tradition within a given area/family whereby more, not less, of the material was fashioned. The strength of this assertion is that it not only allows

Deuteronomists," in *Old Testament Interpretation Past, Present, and Future: Essays in Honour of Gene M. Tucker*, ed. James Luther Mays, David L. Petersen, and Kent Harold Richards (Edinburgh: T&T Clark, 1995), 70.

57. Noth, *Deuteronomistic History*, 79. See idem, "The Jerusalem Catastrophe of 587 B.C. and Its Significance for Israel," in *The Laws in the Pentateuch and Other Studies*, trans. D. R. Ap-Thomas (London: Oliver & Boyd, 1966), 260–80, esp. 280.

58. For a discussion on the theological issues surrounding 2 Kgs. 25:27-30, see Hans Walter Wolff, "The Kerygma of the Deuteronomistic Historical Work," in Knoppers and McConville, *Reconsidering Israel and Judah*, 65–66.

59. Noth, *Deuteronomistic History*, 83.

room for the involvement of the priests at Anathoth as compilers and writers in the earlier portions of the DtrH, but also opens the door for Jeremiah and Baruch to play a dominant role in the bulk of the final editing. Noth himself correctly notes the Jeremian language present in the closing notations of the DtrH.[60] Thus, the devastation of Jerusalem and Judah that Baruch and Jeremiah witnessed may have been the very reason why the DtrH ends in a very pessimistic way, especially if Jeremiah had already made note of the hope of a future return in his own prophetic work.

This finds poignancy in the way 2 Kings ends by quoting from Jeremiah as a means of "carrying forward" the story. If this is the case, then 2 Kgs. 25:27-30's connection to Jeremiah makes sense. Jewish tradition therefore finds legitimacy in this connection. This will become more apparent in light of my analysis of the parallels between 2 Kings 23–25, Jeremiah 39–41 and 50:31-34 in chapter 10 below.[61]

In a similar vein, the central focus of Dtr on apostasy and rebellion, which dominates 1 Kings 11 through 2 Kings 25, could easily have been in keeping with Jeremiah's ideals. It goes without saying that Dtr is interested in prophetic motifs.[62] This element reaches back to the life of Samuel, Nathan, and Gad, but is brought to the fore in the period after Solomon's rule. Here again, it is very possible that Jeremiah may have included this heavy prophetic element in the final form for a particular rhetorical purpose.

Finally, and one could go on with a number of axioms, Noth points up Dtr's literary technique of having dominant characters give speeches at key junctures in his history (e.g., Josh. 1:11-15; ch. 23; 1 Sam. 12:1-25; 1 Kgs. 8:12-51)—a literary feature glaringly

60. Ibid., 74.
61. Ibid.
62. Ibid., 68–72.

absent after Solomon's speech of 1 Kings 8.[63] What is more, Chaim Rabin has noted that even the style of speeches from Deuteronomy until the time of Elijah differs from later prophetic utterances in the period of the DtrH. Scholars have tried to explain away this anomaly with little success.[64] Similarly, Otto Plöger questions why no great speech appears at other key junctures such as the division of the kingdom under Rehoboam. Instead of considering the possibility that the DtrH may have earlier layers or contributors, Plöger suggests that the "Deuteronomist was probably satisfied with the prophetic proclamations, such as the ones put in the mouths of the prophet Ahijah of Shiloh in 1 Kgs. 11:29ff. and the man of God Shemaiah in 1 Kgs. 12:22ff."[65] This is hardly a satisfying solution unless one considers the possibility that the early "Dtr" and Abiathar are one in the same and that after his death, those who followed altered their style. Of course, if Jeremiah, a prophet, in fact edited and compiled this last portion of the DtrH—a position I argue throughout—then the change to a more prophetic style would make sense.[66]

---

63. Ibid., 6, 77. Kurt L. Noll, "Deuteronomistic History or Deuteronomic Debate? (A Thought Experiment)," *JSOT* 31, no. 3 (2007): 313 n.7, suggests that these speeches (i.e., 1 Samuel 12; 1 Kings 8; *and* 2 Samuel 7—Noll's addition) should not be assigned to a Deuteronomistic editor but, rather, he suggests they serve the personal agendas of the characters in question. McKenzie, *Chronicler's Use of the Deuteronomistic History*, 1, adds to the list the proposed *narrative* comments of Dtr (i.e., Joshua 12; Judg. 2:11-22; 2 Kgs. 17:7-18, 20-23). For a detailed discussion on these and other speeches in the DtrH, see Hartmut N. Rösel, "Does a Comprehensive 'Leitmotiv' Exist in the Deuteronomistic History?," in Römer, ed., *Future of the Deuteronomistic History*, 195–211.

64. Chaim Rabin, "Discourse Analysis and the Dating of Deuteronomy," in *Interpreting the Hebrew Bible: Essays in Honour of E. I. J. Rosenthal*, ed. J. A. Emerton and Stefan C. Reif (Cambridge: Cambridge University Press, 1982), 171–77. Rabin calls the language and rhetorical style of Moses, Nathan, Elijah, and Elisha "Old Rhetoric," whereas the later prophets used "New Rhetoric" styles that incorporated parallelism (176).

65. Otto Plöger, "Speech and Prayer in the Deuteronomistic and the Chronicler's Histories," in Knoppers and McConville, eds., *Reconsidering Israel and Judah*, 31–46, at 34. Originally published in German as "Reden und Gebete im deuteronomistischen und chronistischen Geschichtswerk," in *Festschrift für Günther Dehn zum 75. Geburtstag*, ed. W. Schneemelcher (Neukirchen-Vluyn: Neukirchener, 1957), 35–49.

66. Richard D. Nelson, *The Double Redaction of the Deuteronomistic History*, JSOTSup18 (Sheffield: JSOT, 1981), 27, also suggests the work of a later hand after the formulaic speeches end.

As for the issue of the speeches prior to the death of Solomon, it is very likely that Abiathar, even though he was an old man when he was forced into exile, lived at least until after the dedication of the temple (c. 959 BCE). As such, Abiathar could easily have been responsible for this literary peculiarity, which just so happens to disappear after Solomon's reign. I would even expand upon this aforementioned literary device and include Dtr's propensity to conclude each of the great leaders' era/life with final words or collections (Saul excluded).[67] This is evidenced for Moses (Deuteronomy 32–33), Joshua (Joshua 23–24), Samuel (1 Samuel 12), David (2 Samuel 22–23), and Solomon (1 Kings 8). Not surprisingly, these are the great rulers throughout Israel's history before the kingdom divides—a period in concert with Abiathar's lifetime.[68] In this regard, it is telling of the author's time period when the speech of Solomon actually comes early in Solomon's life as opposed to the expected endpoint so common with the other rulers. Did the author realize he would not see the end of Solomon's life? Or did he in some way see David as the last of the great rulers?—something one would expect from Abiathar, who was a friend of David. Not surprisingly, the absence of a final speech for Solomon may reflect the fact that Abiathar had long since died and his sons or the priests of Anathoth altered the "Dtr" style in this regard. Again, one is left considering the possibility that the literary style of Dtr may best match an earlier, as opposed to a later, author.

---

67. As will be argued in ch. 7, Abiathar's complete loathing for Saul would explain the omission of this "courtesy" for Saul.
68. Of course, Jonathan or Ahimelech, Abiathar's sons, may have had a hand in recording Solomon's words.

Conclusion

The purpose for this brief analysis of Noth's work has not been to offer a thoroughgoing assessment of his theory but, rather, to highlight authorial possibilities that have been long overlooked. Literary style, date, influences, and the like need not fall exclusively within a seventh- or sixth-century setting. On the contrary, there is just as much merit in considering earlier authorship for more, not less, of the DtrH. It is high time for axioms that have become "sacred cows" to be reevaluated in light of the merits of the canonical work that we have before us. One "sacred cow" of DtrH scholars that needs further evaluation is the presupposition that the book of Deuteronomy is a late seventh-century construct, which formed the introduction to the DtrH. It is to this we now turn.

3

Deuteronomy as the Linchpin to the Deuteronomistic History

The book of Deuteronomy occupies a unique position in the Hebrew Bible. First, it concludes the first portion of the Bible, the Torah or Pentateuch. But at the same time it serves as a prologue to the books that are called the "historical" books (Joshua to 2 Kings) and thus constitutes the opening of what since Martin Noth has been called the "Deuteronomistic History."[1]

To be sure, according to many DtrH scholars, no one book holds as much importance to the scholarly discussion on the DtrH as does the book of Deuteronomy. The very name "Deuteronomistic History" was birthed from Martin Noth's belief that Deuteronomy was fundamental in the theological shaping of the final form of the DtrH. Noth severed the book of Deuteronomy from the Pentateuch and renamed the truncated introduction to the Hebrew canon the

---

1. Thomas Römer, "Deuteronomy in Search of Origins," in *Reconsidering Israel and Judah: Recent Studies on the Deuteronomistic History*, ed. Gary N. Knoppers and J. Gordon McConville (Winona Lake, IN: Eisenbrauns, 2000), 112–38, at 113.

"Tetrateuch" (i.e., Genesis through Numbers).[2] Noth then propounded that Dtr took a "proto" form of the book of Deuteronomy and attached it as an introductory tome to the "Deuteronomistic History." As an introduction to the DtrH, Deuteronomy set the theological parameters for Dtr's history of Israel.[3] Thus for Noth (and many since), the issue was what portions of Deuteronomy were in fact part of this "proto" Deuteronomy (whether Mosaic or not is another question completely) and what portions were from the hand of Dtr.

Now, while I do not seek to enter into a detailed discussion concerning the editing process of the book of Deuteronomy—for, as I noted in my methodological introduction in chapter 1 above, that would be far from the scope of this work—a few fundamental issues need to be clarified as I move forward.[4] Therefore, my goal in giving this brief overview on the "question" of Deuteronomy is to situate the reader in the world of the discussion on Deuteronomy's

2. Not surprisingly, others have asserted variations of this ordering. Gerhard von Rad, for example, proposed a "Hexateuch," whereby the book of Joshua served as an appropriate conclusion to the promises to Abraham found in Genesis 12:1-3. For von Rad, the settlement of the land allowed the people of Israel finally to be at rest in their own land in fulfillment of all that YHWH had promised to the Patriarchs and as a means of completing the "incomplete" picture of Deuteronomy and Numbers—a stateless people on the Plains of Moab awaiting the final fulfillment of YHWH's good word. A similar "Hexateuchal" perspective is proposed by Reinhard G. Kratz, *The Composition of the Narrative Books of the Old Testament*, trans. John Bowden (London: T&T Clark, 2005), 126, 209. Von Rad's perspective was in no way novel. In the late eighteenth and early nineteenth centuries, Scottish scholar Alexander Geddes (1737–1802) proposed a similar theory in his works *The Holy Bible, or the Books accounted Sacred by Jews and Christians, Otherwise Called the Books of the Old and New Covenants, with Various Readings, Explanatory Notes and Critical Remarks* (1792) and *Critical Remarks on the Hebrew Corresponding with a New Translation of the Bible* (1800). For a further discussion of these latter works, cf. T. Desmond Alexander, *From Paradise to the Promised Land: An Introduction to the Pentateuch*, 3d ed. (Grand Rapids: Baker Academic, 2012), 12, 13.

3. Römer, "Deuteronomy in Search of Origins," 136, suggests that the book of Deuteronomy was originally part of the DtrH and only later (in the Persian period) was removed and placed with the Torah as its conclusion. See further, Frank Crüsemann, "Le Pentateuque, une Torah: Prolégomènes à l'interprétation de sa forme finale," in *La Pentateuque en question*, ed. Albert de Pury, Le Monde de la Bible (Geneva: Labor et Fides, 1991), 339–60.

4. I will address authorship issues in ch. 5.

role in influencing the DtrH. By engaging in this exercise, my hope is to introduce the reader to the vastly different perspectives of both ends of the interpretive spectrum.[5] Nevertheless, in an effort for full disclosure, I do want my readers to be aware of the presuppositions that I hold regarding the authorship of Deuteronomy. I tend to agree with the arguments for an early authorship of Deuteronomy. However, I do allow for the possibility of later editing, though not to the degree that Noth and others posit. For example, notations such as those found in Deut. 1:1; 3:6; 4:46; 34:6, 10, clearly appear as later additions; the issue at stake is how much later. For me, it seems very unlikely that the first four chapters of the book would have been written by Dtr (contra Noth and others) if the book of Deuteronomy follows a second-millennium Hittite-treaty format. Without this introductory material, the unity and structure of the treaty/Deuteronomy would be destroyed.[6] Furthermore, is it not just as plausible that Joshua, or someone close to him, may have added the appendixes of chapters 33–34?[7] While this presuppositional revelation may turn off some readers, I trust that the merits and strength of my arguments that follow will speak for themselves. Again, it is my desire to get people asking questions of the text as we have it; after all, until a better one is found, this is all we have.[8]

5. For an excellent up-to-date essay on the state of the "argument" concerning the composition of the book of Deuteronomy along with valid cautions in this regard, see James Robson, "The Literary Composition of Deuteronomy," in *Interpreting Deuteronomy: Issues and Approaches*, ed. David G. Firth and Philip S. Johnston (Downers Grove, IL: IVP Academic, 2012), 19–59.

6. So, too, Victor Hamilton, *Handbook on the Pentateuch*, 2d ed. (Grand Rapids: Baker Academic, 2005), 377. Similarly, the sermonic structure would be destroyed as well (cf. 1:6-4:40; 5:1-28:68; 29:2 [29:1 MT]—30:20). See comments by Rob Barrett, "The Book of Deuteronomy," in *A Theological Introduction to the Pentateuch: Interpreting the Torah as Christian Scripture*, ed. Richard S. Briggs and Joel N. Lohr (Grand Rapids: Baker Academic, 2012), 146.

7. One could narrow this even further to just ch. 34 and the introductory notations of 33:1-2a.

8. I am not attempting to venture into the realm of naïveté, as some may wish to assert. I am familiar with the types of conclusions and the detailed and painstaking source, form, redaction, and text-critical work done by scholars both past and present. The problem with these approaches, as with any theory, is that a theory is only valid until the next theory displaces it. What I am attempting to do here is offer an alternative to this theory, which in many cases

This being noted, there are basically two camps regarding the dating, authorship, and editing process of Deuteronomy: (1) Deuteronomy is a late literary construction of the first millennium;[9] and (2) Deuteronomy is a Mosaic-authored text from the second millennium.

The first camp proposes that Deuteronomy is an amalgam of legal and cultic material assembled over time that was used to influence many of the writers of the Hebrew Bible, none more than the author of the DtrH. Paradigmatic of this line of reasoning is Steven L. McKenzie, who notes, "Its [Deuteronomy's] influence on the literati may have been enhanced by its having been composed by a coalition of upper-class groups (prophets, priests, sages, scribes, members of the royal court) . . ."[10] Whereas in years past scholars have taken such a belief and postulated a "Pan-Deuteronomism," which suggests that Deuteronomy basically influenced every writer of the OT, today some scholars are moving away from that stance as being too extreme.[11] Nevertheless, those in this first group generally reject

has devolved into a splitting of "hairs" as to what word or phrase or block of material may have been written or redacted by Dtr 1, 2, 3, 4, etc.

9. I realize that this may appear to some people as an oversimplified assertion due to the number of variations of this first grouping. For example, some scholars are willing to concede that Moses may have written portions of "proto" Deuteronomy, while others would argue that the entire work of Deuteronomy was a much later construction (e.g., Steven L. McKenzie). Because both of these camps insist that Dtr or some other nebulous author or group of authors formulated at least portions of Deuteronomy, for the sake of conciseness I have grouped them together under this one heading.

10. Steven L. McKenzie, "Postscript: The Laws of Physics and Pan-Deuteronomism," in *Those Elusive Deuteronomists: The Phenomenon of Pan-Deuteronomism*, ed. Linda S. Schearing and Steven L McKenzie, JSOTSup 268 (Sheffield: Sheffield Academic Press, 1999), 267. See also Robert R. Wilson, "Who Was the Deuteronomist? (Who Was Not the Deuteronomist?): Reflections on Pan-Deuteronomism," in ibid., 68; Patrick D. Miller Jr., *Deuteronomy*, Interpretation (Louisville: John Knox, 1990).

11. On this see McKenzie, "Postscript," 262–71. Richard Coggins, "Prophecy—True and False," in *Of Prophets' Visions and the Wisdom of Sages: Festschrift for R. N. Whybray*, ed. Heather A. McKay and David J. A. Clines, JSOTSup 162 (Sheffield: JSOT, 1993), 80–94, esp. 85–86. On the far extreme the other way is Kurt L. Noll, "Deuteronomistic History or Deuteronomic Debate? (A Thought Experiment)," *JSOT* 31, no. 3 (2007): 311–45, who concludes that there is no "deuteronomism" or "Deuteronomistic Historian" as proposed by Noth and those after him. Instead, he argues that the "Former Prophets are [in] a conversation with the book of

Mosaic authorship of the material and posit that Deuteronomy is to be dated c. 622/21 BCE.[12]

A late date for the book of Deuteronomy was first considered by scholars such as Georg Lorenz Bauer (1755–1806)[13] and Johann Severin Vater (1771–1826).[14] However, it was later made popular by Wilhelm M. L. de Wette (1780–1849) in his dissertation from 1805,[15] which was followed by the work of Eduard Riehm.[16] Of course, these scholars had different reasons for drawing such a conclusion. De Wette, for example, "was convinced that the books of Joshua to Kings displayed no knowledge of Deuteronomic legislation before the time of Josiah,"[17] whereas Bauer propounded "that much of

Deuteronomy" (344). Noll sees the entire corpus of the Former Prophets reaching their final form after a slow process that culminated c. 200 BCE.

12. Julius Wellhausen, *Prolegomena to the History of Ancient Israel* (Gloucester, MA: Peter Smith, 1973 [German: 1885]), appears to be the first to posit this date as the date around which the rest of the sources of the JEDP theory are built. This is axiomatic for many scholars today. E.g., Alexander Rofé, *Deuteronomy: Issues and Interpretation* (London: T&T Clark, 2002), 5. Cf. Hamilton, *Handbook*, 370, for a concise discussion of this issue.

13. G. L. Bauer, *The Theology of the Old Testament: Or, a Biblical Sketch of the Religious Opinions of the Ancient Hebrews*, trans. P. Harwood (London: Charles Fox, 1838), 36.

14. Johann Severin Vater, *Commentar über den Pentateuch*, 3 vols. (Halle: Waisenhaus Buchhandlung, 1802–1805), suggested that at least part of the book of Deuteronomy is to be "equated" with the law book of Josiah. As cited by Alexander, *From Paradise to the Promised Land*, 12.

15. Originally, this idea was posited in a footnote in a thesis presented to the University of Jena in 1805 with the full title "Dissertatio critic-exegetica qua Deuteronomium a priorbus Pentateuchi Libris diversum, alius cuiusdam recentioris opus esse monstratur." ["A critical-exegetical discussion which shows that Deuteronomy is a work that differs from the first books of the Pentateuch, and is the work of another, later author."]. As cited by Eugene Merrill, "Deuteronomy and de Wette: A Fresh Look at a Fallacious Premise," *JESOT* 1, no. 1 (2012): 26. See further discussion by Paul B. Harvey Jr. and Baruch Halpern, "W. M. L. de Wette's 'Dissertatio Critica . . .': Context and Translation," *ZABR* 14 (2008): 47–85. Note also that British scholars at the end of the nineteenth century were adopting de Wette's views as well. Cf. S. R. Driver, *An Introduction to the Literature of the OT* (Edinburgh: Clark, 1891); idem., *A Critical and Exegetical Commentary on Deuteronomy* (Edinburgh: Clark, 1895). Wellhausen merely adopted de Wette's dating of Deuteronomy in his Documentary Hypothesis theory.

16. Eduard Riehm, *Die Gesetzgebung Mosis im Lande Moab* (Gotha: Friedrich Andreas Perthes, 1854). Note also a similar conclusion of Karl Heinrich Graf, *Die geschichtlichen Bücher des Alten Testaments: Zwei historisch-kritische Untersuchungen* (Leipzig: Weigel, 1866). As cited by Alexander, *From Paradise to the Promised Land*, 15–16.

17. Alexander, *From Paradise to the Promised Land*, 13.

Deuteronomy must have been written after the time of Moses, because it reflects a view of God superior to that found in Exodus to Numbers."[18] Many go on to argue that Deuteronomy may have been written by northern priests during the reign of Manasseh (c. 696–642 BCE) and was then held in safe keeping for the opportune time when reformation would be politically suitable.[19] This opportune time came with the young, reforming king, Josiah. It was during this king's reforms of 621 BCE that Deuteronomy was "found" by the priests (i.e., Hilkiah; cf. 2 Kgs. 22:8) and then "dusted off" and presented to the gullible king as the work of Moses.[20] This further fueled the ongoing cultic and priestly reforms of the late seventh century.[21] This book then became the theological inspiration behind the work of Dtr as he began to record his history of Israel during the late seventh or mid-sixth century—the latter time period being the most widely accepted date for a "final form" of the DtrH.

The two central tenets of this camp are: (1) that the parallels between the language of Deuteronomy and that found in other sixth-century works (e.g., 2 Kings, Jeremiah, and Ezekiel) points to a late date; and (2) a program of centralization in both Deuteronomy and the rest of the DtrH point to the era of Josiah's reforms (see the above discussion in ch. 2).[22] On the language issue, Gordon Wenham has concisely presented key arguments from both ANE cultic literary norms and the prophetic corpus, which militate against

18. Ibid., 11.
19. E.g., Ernest W. Nicholson, *Deuteronomy and Tradition* (Philadelphia: Fortress Press, 1967), 1, 2 n.2.
20. Harvey and Halpern, "W. M. L. de Wette's '*Dissertatio Critica* . . . ,'" 65, posit the possibility that either Hilkiah, Shaphan, or Huldah *may* have been involved in the forgery. The biblical authors note that the discovery of the law book took place in Josiah's eighteenth year, which corresponds to c. 622/1 (cf. 2 Kgs. 22:3, 8; 2 Chr. 34:8).
21. De Wette later called it a "pious forgery," cf. *Beiträger zur Einleitung in das Alte Testament*, 2 vols. (Halle: Schimmelpfennig, 1806–1807), 1:179. As cited by Merrill, "Deuteronomy and de Wette," 28 n.10. A .G. Auld, *Kings without Privilege: David and Moses in the Story of the Bible's Kings* (Edinburgh: T&T Clark, 1994), viii, pushes the date even later than 621.
22. Wenham, "Date of Deuteronomy," 17.

the supposition that similarities in language necessitates that Deuteronomy must be contemporaneous with these late works.[23] First, he notes the pervasive use of Old Babylonian and Middle Egyptian, which were used as the written language of Babylon and Egypt over centuries, long after both languages ceased to be spoken.[24] This alone shows the possibility that older "Deuteronomic" language may have remained in use long after the recording of the book of Deuteronomy. Second, Wenham points up that the earliest writing prophets from the eighth century—Hosea and Amos—clearly used "Deuteronomistic" language. Even though there have been attempts to assign these portions to the later Dtr, the arguments are unconvincing.[25]

On the other side of the debate we find a camp that holds just as adamantly to an earlier dating for Deuteronomy, namely, the Mosaic period.[26] Those in this second camp argue that it only stands

---

23. Ibid., 19. Wenham aptly notes the work on discourse analysis done by Chaim Rabin. Rabin concludes that the lack of parallelism in the sermons in Deuteronomy aligns best with the earlier periods of Samuel and Elijah. Cf. Chaim Rabin, "Discourse Analysis and the Dating of Deuteronomy," in *Interpreting the Hebrew Bible: Essays in Honour of E. I. J. Rosenthal*, ed. J. A. Emerton and Stefan C. Reif (Cambridge: Cambridge University Press, 1982), 171–77. Wenham goes on to note the philological work of Gary Rendsburg, who concludes that the presence of archaic language in the Pentateuch pushes for an earlier, not later, date for the Pentateuch. Cf. Gary A. Rendsburg, "A New Look at Pentateuchal *HW*," *Bib* 63, no. 3 (1982): 351–69.

24. Wenham, "Date of Deuteronomy," 18.

25. Ibid., 18–19. Wenham notes the work of F. I. Andersen and D. N. Freedman, *Hosea*, AB 24 (Garden City, NY: Doubleday, 1980), 75; E. W. Hengstenberg, *Dissertations on the Genuineness of the Pentateuch* I (Edinburgh: 1847), 1–3; 107–35; E. W. Pusey, *The Minor Prophets with a Commentary* (London: Smith, 1883), 6; and Douglas K. Stuart, "The Old Testament Prophets' Self Understanding of Their Prophecy," *Them* 6, no. 1 (1980): 9–14, as examples of those holding to an earlier form of Deuteronomy influencing the writing prophets.

26. E.g., Merrill, "Deuteronomy and de Wette," 25–42; K. A. Kitchen, *On the Reliability of the Old Testament* (Grand Rapids: Eerdmans, 2003), 283–307; Alfred J. Hoerth, *Archaeology and the Old Testament* (Grand Rapids: Baker Academic, 1998), 176. For the structure of the treaty as compared to Deuteronomy, see Alexander, *From Paradise to the Promised Land*, 289; or Gary Edward Schnittjer, *The Torah Story: An Apprenticeship on the Pentateuch* (Grand Rapids: Zondervan, 2006), 254. For examples of those who adhere to Hittite parallels for Deuteronomy, see Peter Craigie, *Deuteronomy*, NICOT (Grand Rapids: Eerdmans, 1976); and Earl S. Kalland, *Deuteronomy*, EBC 3 (Grand Rapids: Zondervan, 1992). For those who hold to

to reason that the DtrH reflects Deuteronomy because the priests and prophets, especially, would have been familiar with the law of Moses.[27] Recently, in an article dealing with the present status of the Documentary Hypothesis, which is still widely adhered to in Pentateuchal studies, Eugene Merrill has presented a scathing denunciation of the long-standing late dating for Deuteronomy, calling it a "fallacious premise." He does a concise analysis of the literary, political, and historical propositions of the theory and systematically shows how an early date for the book is just as plausible. Part of his conclusion merits inclusion here:

> Close examination of the actual biblical data themselves reveals quite a different alternative and that is a return to the ancient Jewish, New Testament, and Christian traditions of Mosaic provenance and authorship. Only a mindset willing to bend to critical consensus or oblivious to the issues involved and their damaging implications for young Christian scholars and the Church can, it seems, continue to ignore the tradition in favor of unproven and unprovable hypotheses to the contrary.[28]

In similar critical fashion, Wenham has noted that proponents of the late dating of Deuteronomy put forward the theory without even offering a defense of it.[29] Rarely do "liberal" scholars interact with the "conservative" position, choosing, rather, to move forward under the assumption, passed on from generation to generation,

---

Mosaic authorship of Deuteronomy, see R. K. Harrison, *Introduction to the Old Testament* (Grand Rapids: Eerdmans, 1969); Meredith G. Kline, *Treaty of the Great King: The Covenant Structure of Deuteronomy* (Grand Rapids: Eerdmans, 1963); J. A. Thompson, *Deuteronomy: An Introduction and Commentary*, TOTC (Downers Grove, IL: InterVarsity, 1978); G. T. Manley, *The Book of the Law: Studies in the Date of Deuteronomy* (Grand Rapids: Eerdmans, 1957); and Samuel J. Schultz, *Deuteronomy*, Everyman's Bible Commentary (Chicago: Moody, 1971). These last five as noted by Hamilton, *Handbook on the Pentateuch*, 368. Note also Hamilton's early-date position (373–75).

27. Stuart, "Old Testament Prophets' Self Understanding," 11–12, points to the numerous quotations/allusions to Deuteronomy in Hosea.

28. Merrill, "Deuteronomy and de Wette," 39–40.

29. Wenham, "The Date of Deuteronomy," 15.

that early-date advocates have gotten it wrong. Wenham goes on to suggest that much of the ambivalence toward the "conservative" dating of Deuteronomy rests in mainline scholarship's rejection of the inspiration of Scripture.[30] Once this attribute has been stripped away, the argument for Mosaic authorship of the Pentateuch, in whole or in part, easily falls by the wayside.

Next, arguments based upon the structure of Deuteronomy remain among the most persuasive for many conservative scholars, especially in light of the entrenched seventh-century date for Deuteronomy. Some argue that the book, almost in its entirety, shows evidence of earlier shaping and thought, perhaps as early as the Late Bronze Age (1550–1200 BCE).[31] The argument is put forward that Moses fashioned Deuteronomy after the format of Hittite treaties of the period—something with which he would have been familiar, having been raised in the court of Pharaoh.[32] The book of Deuteronomy thus served not only as a "second law book" (hence the name *deutero* [second] *nomos* [law]) for the generation entering the promised land, but also as a written covenant and witness against the people if they broke the law (cf. Deut. 28:58; 29:20, 21, 27; 30:10; esp. 31:26). Chart 3.1 highlights the parallels.

---

30. Ibid., 16. Wenham does qualify this statement by noting that many in this camp would argue for the "inspired imagination of a later writer addressing the problem of his own generation."

31. Within this group there are also two perspectives on the dating of the exodus/conquest; often labeled the "early" or "late" date: 1446–1406 BCE and c. 1260–1220 BCE.

32. E.g., Kitchen, *On the Reliability*, 283–307; Kline, *Treaty of the Great King*. While Hittite and Egyptian interaction was most prevalent during the thirteenth century, there can be no question that these two superpowers would have been familiar with each other's treaty formats from a much earlier period. The power of the Hittite Empire ebbed and flowed for several centuries but the sixteenth to thirteenth centuries were marked as the highpoint of their power. For those suggesting Neo-Assyrian treaty influence on Deuteronomy, see, for example, Dennis J. McCarthy, *Treaty and Covenant* (Rome: Pontifical Biblical Institute, 1963), esp. 80–140; and idem, *Old Testament Covenant: A Survey of Opinions* (Richmond: John Knox, 1972), 24–30; Ronald E. Clements, *Prophecy and Covenant*, SBT 43 (London: SCM, 1965); Nicholson, *Deuteronomy and Tradition*; Klaus Baltzer, *The Covenant Formulary*, trans. David E. Green (Philadelphia: Fortress Press, 1971); Moshe Weinfeld, *Deuteronomy and the Deuteronomistic School* (Oxford: Clarendon, 1972), esp. 146–57; Rofé, *Deuteronomy*, 5.

Chart 3.1

Early (Hittite) treaty (c. 2d mil)	Deuteronomy	Late (Assyrian) treaty (c. 1st mil)
1. Preamble	1. Preamble 1:1-4	1. Preamble
2. Historical introduction	2. History 1:5—3:29	2. God list
3. Stipulations	3. Stipulations chs. 4–26	3. Stipulations
4. Document clause 5. God list	4. Document clause ch. 27	
6. Curses/blessings	5.Blessings/curses ch. 28	4. Curses (Blessings)[33]

As is evident from chart 3.1, there are a number of convincing parallels between the Hittite treaty format and the book of Deuteronomy. Not surprisingly, however, the "gods list" is glaringly absent from Deuteronomy because of the monotheistic thrust of the work. Normally, the gods served as witnesses to the treaty between the two parties; in Deuteronomy, however, YHWH, heaven and earth, and the book itself served that function (4:26; 30:19; 31:26).

Beyond the clearly different ordering of their format, in the late Assyrian treaties the pompous Assyrians offered no "history" of service and amicable relations with a vassal; instead, a vassal was to serve the "Great King" of Assyria simply because to fail to do so meant certain death and destruction. Indeed, the biblical account of Sennacherib's words to Hezekiah and his men through the Assyrian king's spokesman, the Rabshakeh, intimates as much (cf. 2 Kgs. 18:19, 28; Isa. 36:4, 13).[34] Good will toward a vassal, something prevalent

33. Chart modified from Wenham, "Date of Deuteronomy," 19. For variations of this chart, see Kitchen, *On the Reliability of the Old Testament*, 284, 288.
34. YHWH is also referred to as the "Great King" in poetic texts of the OT (cf. Pss. 47:2; 48:2; 95:3; Mal. 1:14).

in Hittite treaties, is almost nonexistent in the later Assyrian treaties. Moreover, if you failed to keep the stipulations of the treaty, curses awaited you. The "blessings" or "benefits" that the Assyrians offered their vassals was not to annihilate them. Therefore, curses abounded, whereas "blessings" found little room in their treaties.[35]

Wenham also notes the work done by Moshe Weinfeld on second-millennium legal codes as they relate to the format of Deuteronomy. Weinfeld plays down these parallels, suggesting that if more treaties and legal codes from the seventh century had been/were discovered then, these parallels may be less persuasive.[36]

Chart 3.2

Early (Hittite) treaty	Law collection e.g., Laws of Hammurapi c. 1750 BCE	Deuteronomy
1. Preamble		
2. History	1. History	1. History chs. 1–3
3. Stipulations	2. Laws	2. Laws chs. 4–26
4. Document clause 5. God list	3. Document clause	3. Document clause ch. 27
6. Curses/blessings	4. Blessings/curses	4. Blessings/curses ch. 28[37]

35. So, too, Weinfeld, *Deuteronomy and the Deuteronomic School*, 68–69. Interestingly, Weinfeld goes to great lengths (pp. 68–81) to show the parallels between the Hittite prologue and the biblical texts, especially the introduction to Deuteronomy, but he still moves away from the early date, choosing, rather, to conclude that the reason the Assyrians did not use the historical prologues, even though they knew of them, was a matter of "principle." Namely, it was beneath the Assyrian rulers to offer "any sign of affection from a sovereign to a vassal" (69).

36. Wenham, "Date of Deuteronomy," 19. See specifically, Weinfeld, *Deuteronomy and the Deuteronomic School*, 67.

The parallels here are just as convincing as the Hittite treaty parallels, especially the ordering of the law code of Hammurabi whereby the blessings and curses appear in the same order. Again, those arguing for a seventh-century parallel downplay these connections, offering instead a number of close connections between the curse lists of Esarhaddon's treaties and those found in the curse list of Deuteronomy 28. Again, however, Wenham has correctly noted that it is just as likely that these curses came from stock lists that were used over a period of time or that some of the later Assyrian curses may have been added to the book of Deuteronomy at a later date.[38] Scholars within the late-date camp are quick to note the fluid nature of the biblical texts when it comes to additions, so why not in this case?

For many in the second camp, these parallels are not only instructive, but also conclusive in helping to date the book of Deuteronomy to the second millennium and to Moses himself. Indeed, if one is to set aside the presupposition of a seventh-century date and just look at the facts, then Deuteronomy does appear closer to the date its internal indicators suggest. Yet, is it still possible that the ordering/structuring of the work into a Hittite treaty or legal code may in fact be from a later hand, and not from Moses?

When faced with the overwhelming evidence of the Hittite treaty parallels, some scholars, unwilling to retreat from a seventh-century date, have actually posited that the author of Deuteronomy anachronistically organized the material after this ancient treaty format.[39] Of course, the major problem with this theory is answering

37. Chart modified from Wenham, "Date of Deuteronomy," 19. Cf. Weinfeld, *Deuteronomy and the Deuteronomic School,* 66.

38. Wenham, "Date of Deuteronomy," 19. Cf. further the work of D. J. Wiseman, "The Vassal Treaties of Esarhaddon," *Iraq* 20, no. 1 (1958): 26–28.

39. See, for example, Weinfeld, *Deuteronomy and the Deuteronomic School,* 61, here 157. While Weinfeld does not name the Hittite treaty per se, he does say of the later author of Deuteronomy, "He enriched the covenant theme by introducing all the elements of the

the question of how and where someone in the seventh century could acquire this format at such a late date.[40] I suggest that if one is willing to posit such a theory, why not consider the possibility that Abiathar may have in fact been that organizer? This would not only leave intact most of the words of Moses in Deuteronomy but would also answer questions concerning the editing of the text as well. Now again, I must make it clear that I am only musing here, for Moses could very easily have done the organizing himself. However, let us stop and consider who actually would have had access to Hittite covenant forms after the time of Moses and who would have had the desire for the nation to keep covenant with YHWH. Of course, Abiathar and the priestly class immediately come to mind. Moreover, when one compares the numerous parallels between the curse lists of Leviticus 26 and Deuteronomy 28, such a conclusion does not appear so far-fetched—Leviticus, of course, being the priestly book par excellence.

David's use of mercenaries from foreign nations is obvious; the most famous of these being Uriah the *Hittite* (note also Ahimelech the Hittite in 1 Sam. 26:6).[41] Now, why does the author of Samuel stress

vassal treaty . . ." Note also the work of McCarthy, *Treaty and Covenant* (1963); and idem, *Old Testament Covenant* (1972). This theory is propagated even today. See Christine Hayes, *Introduction to the Bible* (New Haven: Yale University Press, 2012), 179.

40. George Mendenhall, "Covenant Forms in Israelite Tradition," *BA* 17, no. 3 (1954): 50–76, esp. 56–57, 61. Even though Mendenhall does not compare the Hittite treaties with the covenant on the plains of Moab, he still suggested that the Hittite forms were not known by the first millennium. Of course since his article was published other treaties have surfaced, which scholars say reflect an ongoing pattern of treaty writing between the first and second millenniums. Cf., for example, McCarthy, *Treaty and Covenant*, 80–140; or Weinfeld, *Deuteronomy and the Deuteronomic School*, 60. As such, a debate has continued concerning how these later treaties parallel the book of Deuteronomy. Kitchen, *On the Reliability of the Old Testament*, 283–94, is adamant that the treaty formats changed with time and that the resemblance of Deuteronomy best fit the earlier Hittite forms.

41. Beyond Uriah and Ahimelech it is also clear that Ittai the Gittite was a foreigner from Gath (2 Sam. 18:2, 5, 12). Also, Cherethites and Pelethites (2 Sam. 8:18; 15:18; 20:7, 23; 1 Kgs. 1:38, 44), Ammonites (1 Chr. 11:39), and Moabites (1 Chr. 11:46) were a part of David's army. So, too, R. Norman Whybray, *The Succession Narrative: A Study of II Samuel 9–20; I Kings 1 and 2*, SBT 9 (London: SCM, 1968), 3.

this fact? It is likely that Abiathar knew Uriah very well, especially if Uriah had joined David while he was on the run from Saul or after David had conquered Jerusalem (cf. 2 Samuel 5). Even if there was not a close connection, Abiathar would have been familiar with the numerous treaties that David had made with surrounding nations.[42] Nevertheless, with such a close connection to a Hittite, and one in the military at that (see more on this in ch. 4), one could just as soundly argue that the "later" editor was none other than Abiathar. After all, he would have had direct access to Uriah (or Ahimelech) and his knowledge of the Hittite treaty formats. What is more, even the prophet Ezekiel points out the close affinity that Jerusalem had with the Hittite empire when he says that metaphorical Jerusalem had a "Hittite mother and an Amorite father" (cf. Ezek. 16:3, 45).

Now, while it may be concluded that both sides of the debate have commendable arguments, neither position causes my thesis to rise or fall. Even though, according to Noth's perspective, and of many others as well, the DtrH by its very name and style must include Deuteronomy, what I am primarily seeking to demonstrate is the identification of the earlier source material in Joshua to Kings. Therefore, in my discussion in chapter 5 below I will only make brief notations concerning the arguments for later insertions in Deuteronomy where needed. Before such a discussion can be undertaken, however, I think it only fitting to examine specific grammatical constructions that may help identify eras of compilation or editing of the DtrH.

---

42. David not only made treaties with Phoenicia and Ammon but also may have made treaties with the Hittites themselves (2 Sam. 10:2; note that Hiram "loved David all his days," which is treaty language cf. 1 Kgs. 5:1). It appears that Solomon at least had done so in his trading enterprises with them (1 Kgs. 10:29; 2 Chr. 1:17). David seems to have entered treaties through marriage as well (Absalom's grandfather was the *king* of Geshur; cf. 2 Sam. 3:3; 13:37). Many of Solomon's marriages no doubt were for treaty purposes too (e.g., Egypt; cf. 1 Kings 3).

4

Grammatical Constructions Showing Later Editing in the Deuteronomistic History

Those who seriously study the DtrH must take into account the presence of key phrases that point to periods of later editing of this material. Of particular note are two phrases that serve as editorial comments on the earlier days in the Transjordan or attempt to situate the reader in past events by noting their relevance to a later time period. The first of these notations is the phrase "across/beyond the Jordan" (בעבר הירדן—$b^e\dot{e}ber\ hayyard\bar{e}n$); the second is "unto this day" (עד היום הזה— '$ad\ hayy\hat{o}m\ hazzeh$). I will handle these *in seriatim*. However, I must stress from the outset that the presence of these phrases in select books of the DtrH, especially the book of Deuteronomy, in no way diminishes the possibility that Moses, Joshua, or even Samuel (to a degree) could have authored large portions of material germane to their eras. On the contrary, what these editorial phrases show, at best, is that the material was edited—whether heavily or not one may never know—at a later date.

"Across/Beyond the Jordan"

Two nouns side by side—ēber ("the region across") and yardēn ("Jordan")—with the first word having a ב (bet) preposition attached (denoting location) comprise the first phrase: "beyond the Jordan." This particular phrase appears nine times in Deuteronomy,[1] two other times in the Pentateuch (cf. Gen. 50:10, 11),[2] and eighteen times throughout the DtrH. Interestingly, the use of the phrase does not appear after the death of Saul.[3] After the last occurrence in 1 Sam. 31:7, the phrase of choice used to denote the Transjordan, or movement across the Jordan, in the rest of the DtrH changes to the noun "Jordan" with some form of the verb 'abar ("to cross").[4] What this tells us is that the editor of these earlier blocks of material (i.e., the Mosaic period, the conquest and settlement eras, and Saul's reign) may have lived sometime during Saul's lifetime, at least the latter portion of it. One could draw the initial conclusion that Abiathar, as editor/author, meets the timeframe criteria. Now, to be sure, the person or persons who edited the DtrH may have also edited portions of the Pentateuch.[5] However, one should not place too much weight upon such an assumption when there are only two occurrences of the phrase in the Tetrateuch—both in Genesis 50.

---

1. Deut. 1:1, 5; 3:8, 20, 25; 4:41, 46, 47; 11:30. However, three of these actually refer to the Cisjordan and appear to have come from the mouth of Moses (3:20, 25; 11:30).
2. A variation of the phrase appears in Num. 22:1.
3. Cf. Josh. 1:14, 15; 2:10; 5:1; 7:7; 9:1, 10; 12:1, 7; 13:8; 22:4; 24:8; Judg. 5:17; 10:8; 1 Sam. 31:7. A variation of the phrase appears once after 1 Sam. 31:7 in Isa. 8:23, but here it is without the ב preposition.
4. See, for example, 2 Sam. 2:29; 10:17; 17:22, 24; 19:16, etc.
5. There is an ongoing debate as to who edited/compiled the Pentateuch and when this was done. Pre-Noth scholars tended to see a Hexateuch with sources from these books (e.g., J or E) continuing into the DtrH.

At the same time, it is intriguing that the phrase is concentrated in the first four chapters of Deuteronomy and in the book of Joshua. Three conclusions could be drawn from this anomaly: (1) Joshua was in fact the editor of Deuteronomy; however, this does not explain the presence of the phrase twice in Judges and twice in 1 Samuel (Judg. 5:17; 10:8; 1 Sam. 31:7 [2x]); (2) someone such as Abiathar edited the early material and then for some reason changed his literary usage of the phrase for later works; or (3) Joshua used the phrase and someone later borrowed it for the books of Samuel and Judges. To be sure, any of these three scenarios is possible, or some totally different combination cannot be ruled out. Notwithstanding, options 2 and 3 become even more plausible, especially if Abiathar may have organized the book of Deuteronomy as a Hittite treaty (see the discussion in ch. 3 above). This latter idea is particularly poignant in light of the recurring phrase "beyond the Jordan" in the first four chapters of the book of Deuteronomy, which deal with the historical recitation of Israel (chs. 1–3) and the introduction to the laws (chs. 4–26), the sections aligning with blocks two and three in the Hittite treaties.[6]

Another reason that Abiathar may be an editor of this earlier material is due to the absence of the phrase after the death of Saul in 1 Samuel 31. By 2 Samuel 1–4, David is embroiled in a civil war with the northern and Transjordan tribes loyal to Saul's family (i.e., Ishbosheth). Whoever was recording this portion of Samuel and the remainder of the book focused heavily on the uniting of the nation, the aftermath of the civil war, and David's centralizing of the government. In this case, the reason the phrase disappears may have more to do with the author's focus on David's kingship and administration as opposed to a recitation of earlier history of the Transjordan tribes and region. Finally, it is noteworthy that some

6. See Chart 3:1 p. 70.

of Saul's staunchest allies (e.g., the people of Jabesh-gilead; cf. 1 Samuel 31) lived in the Transjordan. It is no coincidence that the last appearance of the phrase "beyond the Jordan" is in reference to those allies and Israelites deserting Saul, who were from this very region! Could this again betray the rhetorical motives of the author/ compiler?

"Unto this Day"

The second phrase, "unto this day" (עד היום הזה, *'ad̲ hayyôm hazzeh*), has been scrutinized for centuries by a vast number of scholars from all traditions.[7] It appears in every book of the DtrH, and even though it may be more problematic than the above phrase to pinpoint to a particular era in any given book, its importance to our discussion on authorship cannot be overstated.[8] In his extensive study of this phrase, Jeffrey Geoghegan summarizes this idea well when he notes, "the evidence of 'until this day' addresses some of the most pressing questions related to Israelite historiography: When was Israel's history first compiled and by whom? What was the original scope of this history? And, perhaps most important, *why* was this history compiled?"[9] Some of the earliest rabbinic interpreters struggled to answer these questions, especially while trying to remain faithful to traditional authorship attributions. Three options

---

7. For a detailed history of research on this phrase starting with the early rabbis and continuing up "until this day," see Jeffrey C. Geoghegan, *The Time, Place, and Purpose of the Deuteronomistic History: The Evidence of "Until This Day,"* BJS 347 (Providence, RI: Brown University Press, 2006), 9–41. See also idem, "'Unto this Day' and the Preexilic Redaction of the Deuteronomistic History," *JBL* 122, no. 2 (2003): 201–27; Brevard S. Childs, "A Study of the Formula, 'Until this Day,'" *JBL* 82, no. 3 (1963): 279–92; and J. A. Montgomery, "Archival Data in the Book of Kings," *JBL* 53, no. 1 (1934): 46–52.

8. Frank Moore Cross, *Canaanite Myth and Hebrew Epic: Essays in the History of the Religion of Israel* (Cambridge: Harvard University Press, 1973), 275. On the other hand, Richard D. Nelson, *The Double Redaction of the Deuteronomistic History,* JSOTSup18 (Sheffield: JSOT, 1981), 23–25, suggests that one cannot separate the phrase from earlier source material used by Dtr1 or Dtr2.

9. Geoghegan, *Time, Place, and Purpose,* 6.

dominated the discussion. "Unto this day" "could mean: 1) 'forever' . . . , 2) anytime before the said entity ceased to exist . . . , or 3) the biblical author's own day . . ."[10] Moreover, numerous scholars have pointed up the importance of the phrase in assigning portions of the DtrH to a wide range of earlier periods.[11] And not just to a wide range of periods, but also to a number of unknown authors/sources. Richard Nelson says it well when he posits, "In fact, in most cases, the phrase belongs without question to the historian's narrative sources ..."[12] It is to these "sources" that we now turn.

At first glance, this phrase seems to have been used by several authors/editors over a period of centuries. The phrase appears no less than ninety-four times throughout a range of OT books.[13] Nine of these occurrences appear in the Tetrateuch,[14] sixteen appear in various other prophetic and postexilic works (i.e., once in Ezra, twice in Nehemiah, once in Isaiah, nine times in Jeremiah,[15] and three times in Ezekiel),[16] while the remaining sixty-nine appearances fall within the DtrH and Chronicles.[17] Not surprisingly, six of the eleven occurrences of the phrase in Chronicles appear in almost verbatim quotations from the books of Samuel and Kings. Thus, the concentration of this phrase (fifty-eight appearances) falls within the

---

10. Ibid., 14.
11. Ibid., 39–40. See, for example, Cross, *Canaanite Myth*, 275.
12. Nelson, *Double Redaction*, 24.
13. There are actually ninety-five occurrences if one counts both appearances of the phrase in Josh. 7:26.
14. Gen. 19:38; 26:33; 32:33; 35:20; 47:26; 48:15; Exod. 10:6; Lev. 23:14; Num. 22:30. The passage in Leviticus has a variation of the phrase, namely, עד עצם היום הזה, 'aḍa'eṣem hayyôm hazzeh ("unto this very day"). For a discussion on the use of "unto this day" in relation to the redactional unity of the DtrH and the Tetrateuch, see Geoghegan, *Time, Place, and Purpose*, 153–57; and idem, "Additional Evidence for a Deuteronomistic Redaction of the Tetrateuch," *CBQ* 67, no. 3 (2005): 405–21.
15. The frequency of the phrase in Jeremiah may be telling of his possible involvement in the final editing of the DtrH.
16. Ezra 9:7; Neh. 8:17; 9:32; Isa. 39:9; Jer. 3:25; 7:25; 11:7; 25:3; 32:20; 32:31; 35:14; 36:2; 44:10; Ezek. 2:3; 20:29, 31. Ezek. 2:3 has a variation of the phrase and follows the infrequent pattern noted in Lev. 23:14 above.
17. Those appearing only in Chronicles include: 1 Chr. 4:41, 43; 5:26; 2 Chr. 20:26; 35:25.

DtrH. The chart that follows summarizes these fifty-eight occurrences. I will offer an assessment of the chart in the discussion that follows. What will become apparent is that the use of the phrase "unto this day" throughout the DtrH pushes against a single editing of the material in the seventh or sixth century. From an editorial standpoint, many of the appearances of this notation, especially from Deuteronomy to 1 Kings 9, fit best in the period prior to Solomon's reign.

These entries can be broken into five categories: (1) geographic, (2) demographic, (3) political policies, (4) cultic, and (5) quoted speech.[18] While I will not attempt to scrutinize each one individually, I do want my reader to be aware of the categories within which each may fall.

---

18. This list is revised from Geoghegan, *Time, Place, and Purpose*, 43. Geoghegan does note in passing the quoted speech grouping, but does not address the connection to Jeremiah's use of the phrase until his concluding remarks on pp. 158–64.

The Frequency of the Phrase "unto this day" in the DtrH			
Verse Location	**Content**	**Era of Reference**	**Era of Writing**
Deut. 2:22	Edom's settlement in the land of the Horites	Patriarchal	Uncertain (any time from Moses onward)
Deut. 3:14 =Judg.10:4; Num. 32:39-41; 1 Chr. 2:22-23	Hawoth-jair named after Jair, son of Manasseh[19]	Judges	Anytime from the Judges' period but before the ninth century (cf. 1 Kgs. 22:3; 2 Kgs. 10:32-33)
Deut. 10:8	Levi chosen to serve before God	Wilderness period	Any time after the wilderness period
Deut. 11:4; 29:3 [Heb]	**Quoted speech of Moses (2x)**	Wilderness period	Wilderness period
Deut. 34:6	Moses burial place unknown	End of Mosaic period	Anytime after Moses' death
Josh. 4:9	Joshua's stones of memorial	Conquest period	Any time after the conquest
Josh. 5:9	Gilgal named	Conquest period	Any time after the conquest

19. Herbert Wolf, *Judges*, EBC 3 (Grand Rapids: Zondervan, 1992), 37, suggests that there were two Jairs and that the one mentioned in Judges is a later descendant by the same name. Based upon Josh. 13:30, this is possible. Nevertheless, because the book of Judges does not present the judges in a chronological fashion, the Jair of Judges may in fact be part of an earlier generation close to the time of the death of Joshua (cf. Num. 32:41; 1 Kgs. 4:13).

Josh. 6:25	Rahab lives among Israel	Conquest period	Any time after the conquest
Josh. 7:26 (2x)	A heap of stones over Achan	Conquest period	Any time after the conquest
Josh. 8:28, 29	Ai is destroyed and their king is buried in the city gate	Conquest period	Any time after the conquest perhaps by someone who lived near Ai
Josh. 9:27	Gibeonites are slaves to Israel	Conquest period	Any time after the conquest but before 586 BCE
Josh. 10:27	Stones over the burial site of the five kings of the southern coalition	Conquest period	Any time after the conquest
Josh. 13:13	Geshur and Maacath live with Israel	Conquest period	Any time after the conquest but perhaps before 1 Sam. 27:8 (c. 1012 BCE)
Josh. 14:14	Hebron owned by Caleb	Conquest period	Anytime after the conquest period
Josh. 15:63	Jebusites live in Jerusalem	Conquest period	Before c. 1004 BCE
Josh. 16:10	Canaanites in Gezer	Conquest period	Before 1 Kgs. 3; 9:15, 16, c. 965 BCE
Josh. 22:3, 17; 23:8, 9	**Quoted speech by Joshua (4x)**	Conquest period	Conquest period
Judg. 1:21	Jebusites live in Jerusalem	Judges' period	Before c. 1004 BCE

Judg. 1:26	The capture of Bethel and naming of Luz in the land of the Hittites	Judges' period	Sometime after the Judges' period
Judg. 6:24	Gideon's altar in Ophrah	Judges' period	Sometime after the Judges' period
Judg. 10:4=Deut. 3:14	Thirty cities called Hawoth-jair	Judges' period	Sometime after the Judges' period
Judg. 15:19	Samson named water source En-hakkore	Judges' period	Sometime after the Judges' period
Judg. 18:1	Danites have no inheritance	Judges' period	Sometime after the Judges' period
Judg. 18:12	Danites name site west of Kiriath-jearim, Mahaneh-dan	Judges' period	Sometime after the Judges' period
Judg. 19:30	**Quoted speech by the populace:** Levite's concubine divided into twelve pieces	Judges' period	Judges' period
1 Sam. 5:5	Priests will not step on the threshold of Dagon's temple	Period of Samuel and Eli	After Eli and Samuel
1 Sam. 6:18	Monument to the return of the Ark	Period of the Ark narratives/ Samuel and Eli	After Eli and Samuel
1 Sam. 8:8	**Quoted speech by YHWH**	Samuel's day	Samuel's period

1 Sam. 12:2	**Quoted speech by Samuel**	Samuel's day	Samuel's period
1 Sam. 27:6	Ziklag belongs to the kings of Judah	David's day	Post-930 BCE
1 Sam. 29:3, 6, 8	**Quoted speech from Achish (2x) and David**	David's day	David's era
1 Sam. 30:25	The law of sharing the spoils of war	David's day	Sometime after David's era
2 Sam. 4:3	Beerothites sojourners in Gittaim	David's day	Sometime after David's era but before the exile of 586 BCE
2 Sam. 6:8 = 1 Chr. 13:11	Name of site of Uzzah's death	David's day	Sometime after David's era
2 Sam. 7:6 = 1 Chr. 17:5	**Quoted speech by YHWH**	David's day	David's era
2 Sam. 18:18	Absalom's monument	Absalom's day	Sometime after Absalom
1 Kgs. 8:8 = 2 Chr. 5:9	Ark poles in inner sanctuary	Solomon's day	Sometime after 960 BCE but before 586 BCE
1 Kgs. 9:13	Hiram calls the cities Solomon gives him, Kabul	Solomon's day	Sometime after c. 947 BCE
1 Kgs. 9:21 = 2 Chr. 8:8	Foreigners enslaved	Solomon's day	Sometime after Solomon but before 930 BCE
1 Kgs. 10:12	Abundant almug trees in Jerusalem	Solomon's day	Sometime after Solomon

1 Kgs. 12:19 = 2 Chr. 10:19	Israel rebels against Judah	Rehoboam's day	Sometime after c. 930 BCE but before 722 BCE
2 Kgs. 2:22	Elisha heals the waters	Elisha's day	Sometime after Elisha
2 Kgs. 8:22 = 2 Chr. 21:10	Edom revolted in the days of Jehoram	Jehoram's day	Sometime after Jehoram but before c. 782 BCE
2 Kgs. 10:27	House of Baal made into a latrine	Jehu's day	Sometime during or after the time of Jehu but before 722 BCE
2 Kgs. 14:7	Sela renamed Joktheel	Amaziah's day	Sometime after Amaziah
2 Kgs. 16:6	Judah driven from Elath	Ahaz's day	Sometime after Ahaz perhaps in the period of Hezekiah
2 Kgs. 17:23	Israel captive in Assyria	Ahaz's day	Sometime after Ahaz but prior to 605 BCE
2 Kgs. 17:34, 41	Sin of post-722 BCE Samaria	Hezekiah's day	Sometime after 722 BCE
2 Kgs. 20:17	**Quoted speech from Isaiah**	Hezekiah's day	Hezekiah's era
2 Kgs. 21:15	**Quoted speech from YHWH**	Manasseh's day	Manasseh's era

I will begin my assessment by noting the use of the phrase in quoted speech (see boldface font in chart above). In the fifteen verses where the phrase is used (cf. Deut. 11:4; 29:3 [Heb]; Josh. 22:3, 17; 23:8, 9; Judg. 19:30; 1 Sam. 8:8; 12:2; 29:3, 6, 8; 2 Sam. 7:6; 2 Kgs. 20:17; 21:15) it appears on the lips of eight different speakers (i.e., Moses

[2x], Joshua [4x], the people [1x], Samuel [1x], Achish [2x], David [1x], Isaiah [1x] and YHWH [3x]). Now, while it is indeed possible that this phrase was used by a variety of speakers (including YHWH), it seems more likely that it was used by the editor of the material. In this regard, Gary Knoppers comments, "The Deuteronomist ordered these sources, shaped them, introduced his own distinct chronology, and inserted his own comments (often in the mouths of major characters) at critical junctures in his history."[20] Interestingly, six of the appearances of the phrase in quoted speech come from the period of Samuel and David—Abiathar's period as well.

On the other hand, the dominant use of the phrase by the prophet Jeremiah (nine times) and its infrequency elsewhere in the prophets may also be indicative of his work as the editor of the final form (cf. Jer. 3:25; 7:25; 11:7; 32:31; 35:14; 36:2; 44:10 [quoted speech from YHWH]; 25:3; 32:20 [quoted speech from Jeremiah]). What is more, seven of the nine uses of the phrase in Jeremiah appear in quoted speech from YHWH![21] As noted in the chart above, three of the fourteen occurrences of the phrase appear on the lips of YHWH. These parallels beg the question: Are these similarities coincidental or do they reflect a much deeper connection? Based upon these preliminary findings alone, one could argue that Jeremiah, a priest from Anathoth, may have had a hand in editing the final form of the DtrH.[22]

---

20. Gary N. Knoppers, "Is There a Future for the Deuteronomistic History?," in *The Future of the Deuteronomistic History*, ed. Thomas C. Römer (Leuven: Leuven University Press, 2000), 119.

21. I am not suggesting that YHWH could not have spoken to a number of authors over a period of time using the phrase "unto this day" but, rather, that it is interesting that it is Jeremiah, a priest from Anathoth, who uses it predominantly in this manner. It is possible that either Jeremiah picked up on this phrase from these earlier sources and used it in a similar manner or was the one who used it and then projected it back in earlier quoted speech from YHWH and DtrH characters. For a similar view, see Moshe Weinfeld, *Deuteronomy and the Deuteronomistic School* (Oxford: Clarendon, 1972), 51–53, at 53. While Weinfeld calls the speeches of Deuteronomy the "product of speculative thought," I believe that the general content of the speeches of the great men and women of the past was in fact already recorded and was only later supplemented to reflect a particular compiler's agenda.

Nevertheless, this does not preclude the fact that Abiathar, or someone close to him, may have initiated the use of the phraseology, which in turn was used over a long period of time by his successors. This conclusion is bolstered by the use of this same phrase during a very narrow window of time in the history of Israel where a *terminus ad quem* can easily be determined. Indeed, many occurrences of the phrase fit only a narrow span of time, none more telling, for example, than its appearance in Judg. 1:21.

In the opening chapter of Judges, the author situates his reader in the world of the judges' period by identifying the nonliberated status of Jerusalem. In 1:21, we find the following statement: "Now the Jebusites (the ones inhabiting Jerusalem), the sons of Benjamin could not dispossess, therefore the Jebusites dwell with the sons of Benjamin in Jerusalem unto this day."[23] From this statement we can determine that the city of Jerusalem had not yet been conquered by David and the tribe of Judah at the time of the recording of the text (cf. 2 Sam. 5:6-9).[24] Historically, we know that David's subjugation of the Canaanite city took place c. 1004–1000 BCE.[25]

Thus, the *terminus ad quem* for this portion of Judges fits the time period of Abiathar and, based upon the rhetorical message of Judges, fits his *Sitz im Leben* as well (on this latter point, see more in ch. 7 below). Therefore, in this paradigmatic passage we see the likelihood that the phrase was used earlier than the time of Jeremiah. This being noted, is it possible to see clear evidence of the use of the phrase

---

22. See a similar conclusion by Geoghegan, *Time, Place, and Purpose*, 158–64.

23. All translations are mine unless otherwise noted.

24. Some argue that because some Jebusites remained in Jerusalem even after David defeated them (e.g., 2 Sam. 24:16) proves that this notation cannot be taken as evidence of an earlier author. However, the phrase in the context of Judges 1 is not about noting the presence of a few remaining Jebusites in Jerusalem, it is clearly dealing with conquest and conquering, something only David did. For the former position, see comments by ibid., 26.

25. Eugene Merrill, *Kingdom of Priests: A History of Old Testament Israel*, 2d ed. (Grand Rapids: Baker Academic, 2008), 259. Merrill narrows this date to 1004 BCE.

even earlier by Joshua or Moses, or can these earlier occurrences of the phrase likewise be attributed to someone later such as Abiathar, Jeremiah, or Baruch? It is to this investigation we now turn.

Deuteronomy

The phrase "unto this day" is used six times in Deuteronomy (the fewest of the DtrH books) and sixteen times in Joshua.[26] The book of Joshua thus has the highest frequency of the phrase, with the books of Kings and Samuel following a close second and third with fifteen and thirteen appearances respectively. The list is rounded out by the book of Judges, where the phrase appears eight times. I will look at these appearances starting with Deuteronomy and proceed in canonical order with the remaining books.

The six appearances of our phrase in Deuteronomy can just as easily be attributed to someone other than Moses in light of each of the given contexts. To begin, like many of the places where our phrase is used in conjunction with place names, the description of Edom's settlement in the land of the Horites (Deut. 2:22) could have been made at any time, although a later period seems most likely. Therefore, in most instances in the DtrH where our phrase appears in connection with place names, precise conclusions are impossible. Second, as I noted immediately above, two of the remaining five references are in quoted speech from YHWH (Deut. 11:4; 29:3 [Heb]). While it is indeed possible that Moses used this language as received directly from YHWH, it is just as valid to assign these notations to a later editor like Jeremiah, who used the phrase almost exclusively in quoted speech from YHWH.

Later editorial notations incorporating this phrase are perhaps the clearest in two of the three remaining occurrences: (1) Deut. 3:14

---

26. One could argue that the infrequent use of the phrase in Deuteronomy may point to the light editing of the predominantly Mosaic material.

(Jair's naming of Hawoth-jair; a parallel to Judg. 10:4); and (2) Deut. 34:6 (the location of Moses' burial place). Whereas one could argue that Joshua made the comment in the latter case, it would be more impressive coming from a much later period. As for Deut. 3:14, it is difficult to determine which came first, Deut. 3:14 or Judg. 10:4. Are we dealing with two separate Jairs from two different generations?[27] We do know that by the time of Ahab (c. 853 BCE) the towns of Bashan/Gilead where Jair lived were under the control of Aram (cf. 1 Kgs. 22:3; 2 Kgs. 10:32-33). Therefore, the recording of this historical notation in both Deuteronomy and Judges had to have occurred before the ninth century, thus ruling out a sixth-century date. Interestingly, under David and Solomon's rule this region in the Transjordan was still firmly in Israel's control (2 Sam. 24:6; 1 Kgs. 4:13, 19).

Next, Deut. 10:8 points to the role of the tribe of Levi as ministers before YHWH "unto this day." This editorial note could be assigned to the period of Moses; however, just as I concluded concerning the burial location of Moses, a later date would be more impressive. This conclusion makes sense in light of the context of verse 6. The calling of the tribe of Levi, perhaps for a second time, is placed in the context of Aaron's death, which occurred only a few months before the events of Deut. 10:8. Thus, a notation commending the long history of the service of the tribe of Levi would make the most sense at a much later date. At the same time, it is clear that this commendation of the tribe of Levi would not fit a sixth-century date, especially after the destruction of the temple when the Aaronic priests

---

27. Even though some question the redactional layers and the tensions between these two passages because Deuteronomy situates the site in Bashan whereas Judges places it in Gilead, the tensions are more apparent than real. According to Josh. 12:4-5; 13:30-31; and 17:1-5, Gilead and Bashan were both part of the inheritance of Manasseh and his son, Machir. Ownership of both regions overlapped, especially among the descendants of Manasseh. See the discussion by Geoghegan, *Time, Place, and Purpose*, 77–78; and Moshe Weinfeld, *Deuteronomy 1–11*, AB 5 (New York: Doubleday, 1991), 185.

had their cultic function significantly truncated. This is particularly poignant for an exilic priest like Ezekiel who served as a prophet rather than as a priest. Moreover, the fact that this phrase is used with a cultic nuance points perhaps to a priest like Abiathar.

To summarize, we may preliminarily note that the appearances of the phrase "unto this day" in Deuteronomy point just as much to later editorial work as they do to Moses. While we cannot be certain when this editorial work took place due to the infrequent use of the phrase in Deuteronomy, it still appears to fit best at a later period with someone like Abiathar, especially in light of Deut. 3:14, 10:8, and 34:6.[28] The scarcity of the phrase in Deuteronomy is offset by its prolific use in the book of Joshua, to which we now turn.

Joshua

Of the sixteen times the phrase is used in the book of Joshua, four of them appear in quoted speech, which may possibly be attributed to the latest editing strand of the DtrH (see the discussion above). Therefore, we are left with twelve occurrences of the phrase that fall within, or close to, the conquest period. However, upon closer examination it is evident that several of these twelve may have been later notations by someone living prior to the reign of Solomon, but not afterwards. For example, Josh. 15:63 is parallel to Judg. 1:21, which, as I have already pointed out, reflects a period prior to 1004 BCE. The repetition of the notation about the Jebusite presence in Jerusalem in both Joshua and Judges suggests that the compiler/ author of the books of Joshua and Judges was either the same person or at least was familiar with each of the books in question.[29] The

---

28. Geoghegan, *Time, Place, and Purpose*, 34, notes that a similar conclusion was reached by Abraham Kuenen in the German edition of his Dutch work. Cf. *Historisch-kritische Einleitung in die Bücher des Alten Testaments*, trans. T. Weber (Leipzig: Otto Schulze, 1887), 1:34. Kuenen attributed the inclusion of the phrase "unto this day" to the nameless authors of the JEDP sources.

notation recalling the presence of Canaanites at Gezer in Josh. 16:10 must have been prior to Solomon's era. Gezer was a wedding gift for Solomon's Egyptian wife from the pharaoh of Egypt c. 965 BCE (1 Kings 3; 9:15-16). It was at this time that the Canaanites were defeated and driven from Gezer. Thus, from these two events alone, it is obvious that the use of the phrase in the book of Joshua indicates that the events were recorded some time *after* they transpired in the conquest period but before c. 1004 and 965 BCE. Of course, the question still remains: "How long after?"

There is one other feature of Josh. 16:10 that may help us answer this question and narrow the time period to that of Abiathar. In 16:10, the author of the book of Joshua uses the term *Canaanites* to identify the inhabitants of Gezer. In the DtrH, the use of this ethnic designation appears most frequently in the book of Judges (sixteen times).[30] With Abiathar being a prime candidate for the authorship of Judges (see ch. 7 below), it goes without saying that our earlier connection becomes even more probable. Furthermore, the only other place the term *Canaanites* appears in the DtrH is in 2 Sam. 24:7 and 1 Kgs. 9:16, texts that both fall within the time period of Abiathar and his sons. Now, while it is true that this is by no means conclusive evidence, it does add weight to our ongoing hypothesis.

Seven of the remaining ten appearances of the phrase in the book of Joshua also point to a period of editing closer to the days of Joshua and David as opposed to the seventh or sixth centuries. The monuments put in place by the erecting of memorial stones (Josh. 4:9) or the heaping of stones over the bodies of slain adversaries, domestic and foreign (cf. Josh. 7:26 [2x]; 8:29; 10:27), doubtfully would have survived for seven to nine hundred years (approximate

29. While it may be possible that Abiathar just copied the phrase from the earlier book of Joshua, this conclusion does not appear to be as persuasive in light of the other notations that seem to suggest a later date for the editing of the book of Joshua (e.g. Josh. 16:10).
30. Cf. Judg. 1:1, 3, 4, 5, 9, 10, 17, 27, 28, 29 (2x), 30, 32, 33; 3:3, 5.

early date for the conquest: 1400 BCE—560 BCE = 840 years;[31] approximate late date for the conquest: 1240 BCE—560 BCE = 680 years).[32] The chance that these mounds of stones and monuments may have survived into the period of Abiathar (c. 260 to 400 years later) seems more plausible. In the case of Josh. 4:9, the memorial was to commemorate the crossing of the priests with the Ark of the Covenant, something of particular importance to a priest and his family.[33] What is more, Josh. 7:26a and 8:29b both exhibit the same grammatical structure which may betray one author/editor.[34] As for the remaining three occurrences in this category—the desolation of the city of Ai (Josh. 8:28); the relegating of the Gibeonites to slavery (Josh. 9:27); and the presence of Geshur and Maacath among the Israelites (Josh. 13:13)—all intimate a period prior to the death of David or early in Solomon's reign.[35]

In the case of Josh. 8:28, the chance that Ai was left uninhabited for close to nine hundred years is unlikely. We do know that Ai was resettled sometime prior to the exile of 586 BCE (cf. Ezra 2:28 and Neh. 7:32).[36] Furthermore, if Bryant Wood is correct in identifying

31. The year 560 is a rounded date for the final form of the DtrH as proposed by Noth, even though he notes specifically the date of 562 BCE as the *terminus a quo* based upon 2 Kgs. 25:27-30. Martin Noth, *The Deuteronomistic History*, JSOTSup 15 (Sheffield: JSOT, 1981), 12.

32. The repetition of the phrase "unto this day" for the continued presence of the stone memorial erected by Joshua and for the evidence of the heap of stones over Achan and the king of Ai could have lasted longer but such a conclusion seems to push the bounds of credulity. In the highlands of Israel, stones were the primary building material. It is very likely that piles of stones would have been robbed out to construct homes, terrace walls, etc.

33. Geoghegan, *Time, Place, and Purpose*, 88–89, has also noted the associations of the phrase "unto this day" and the author's priestly interests (e.g., 1 Sam. 5:5; 6:18; 2 Sam. 6:8).

34. So ibid., 76.

35. Ibid., 79–80. Geoghegan appears to be on the right track when he assigns Josh. 13:13-14 and Deut. 10:8-9 to the work of the Dtr because of the appearance of "unto this day" so close to the notation about the noninheritance of the tribe of Levi in both passages.

36. Of course, the migration of place names may also explain the settlement of a location close to the original Ai of Abraham's period, no doubt et-Tell. In this vein, I am fully aware of the debate surrounding the exact location of Abraham's and Joshua's Ai. While William Foxwell Albright identified et-Tell as the likely location of Ai—a position adopted by many scholars (see, for example, the recent comments by Christine Hayes, *Introduction to the Bible* [New Haven: Yale University Press, 2012], 192)—Albright's identification is not without its difficulties (see,

Khirbet el-Maqatir as the location of Joshua's Ai, then archaeological evidence shows that it was partially resettled in the Iron Age I (c. 1200–1000 BCE).[37] This, of course, would chronologically allow room for someone up to David's period to make a comment regarding the continued appearance of destruction at Ai. Second, the notation in Josh. 9:27 regarding the slavery of the Gibeonites at the time of the recording/editing of Joshua makes sense at any time after Joshua until the latter years of David. While one cannot be certain, it appears that by the time of 2 Sam. 21:1-14, the Gibeonites had gained a level of autonomy among the nation of Israel.[38] Moreover, by Solomon's reign, the city of Gibeon was a central shrine of sorts (cf. 1 Kgs. 3:4, 5; 9:2; 1 Chr. 16:39; 21:29; 2 Chr. 1:3, 13).

In this vein, one further note of interest in Josh. 9:27 needs to be addressed. In this verse the author notes that the Gibeonites were hewers of wood and water carriers for the children of Israel and for the *altar of the Lord* (italics mine). The fact that the cultic association is mentioned may betray a priest's interest in the role that the Gibeonites played in this regard. Even if the Gibeonites were still

for example, the refutation by Bryant Wood, "The Search for Joshua's Ai," in *Critical Issues in Early Israelite History*, ed. Richard S. Hess, Gerald A. Klingbeil, and Paul J. Ray Jr. [Winona Lake, IN: Eisenbrauns, 2008], 205–240, esp. 209–212). Since 2010, I have been excavating at the site of Khirbet el-Maqatir as a part of the archaeological team of the Associates for Biblical Research under the leadership of Dr. Bryant Wood. Topographical considerations and archaeological discoveries have helped build a case for Khirbet el-Maqatir as a potential site for Joshua's Ai (see further discussion in ibid., 230–40). Also, it is possible that the name "Ai" may not reflect the commonly held Hebrew meaning of "the ruin" but, rather, the general area of the Wadi-el Gayeh (see ibid., 240). In the 2013 dig season, we discovered a number of artifacts that will push forward Wood's dating and identification of the site as Joshua's Ai. One important find in particular was a scarab dating to the reign of Amenhotep II of the Eighteenth Dynasty of Egypt found in a locus with LBI pottery.

37. Ongoing archaeological work at Khirbet el-Maqatir has revealed Iron Age I dwellings along the inside portion of the northwestern wall of the old LBI fortress. The pottery from the squares in this area dates to this period in particular.

38. This may have something to do with Gibeonites being a part of David's military inner circle (cf. 1 Chr. 12:4). Also, it appears that they may have been allies of David in the civil war against the northern tribes after the death of Saul (cf. 2 Samuel 2; 3). That the Gibeonites detested Saul and his family goes without saying in light of 2 Sam. 21:1-14, esp. vv. 1-2.

subjugated at the time of David, this notation makes the most sense in the context of the tabernacle being at Gibeon. According to the Chronicler, this was during the reigns of David and Solomon (cf. 1 Chr. 16:39; 21:29).[39] Thus, the editor of this verse may have been a priest familiar with the cultic setting of Gibeon. Once again, this would fit someone like Abiathar or perhaps even the possible editorial work of his sons Jonathan or Ahimelech shortly after his death. In chapter 6 below, I will return to the importance of the role that the Gibeonites play in relation to Abiathar's possible interests especially from a geographical standpoint.

Next, in Josh. 13:13, the author notes the presence of the people of Geshur and Maacath among the Israelites. This point makes sense any time up until the events recorded in 1 Sam. 27:8-9. According to this passage, David annihilated the Geshurites prior to his accession to the throne in Hebron in 1010 BCE. If Abiathar had begun to record Israel's history prior to this event, then the *terminus ad quem* for Josh. 13:13 would have to be sometime before c. 1012 BCE.[40] At least by this time the Geshurites would have ceased to exist or their population would have been negligible.

We have now assessed thirteen of the sixteen appearances of the phrase "unto this day" in the book of Joshua. The remaining three could all have been recorded over an extensive time span: (1) the naming of Gilgal (Josh. 5:9); (2) Rahab's family's presence among the Israelites (Josh. 6:25); and (3) Caleb's inheritance of Hebron (Josh. 14:14). A couple of points should help to clarify my point in this regard. First, Gilgal is referenced in the Bible from the period of

---

39. The Chronicler makes it clear that the Ark of the Covenant was taken to Jerusalem by David, whereas the altar of sacrifice and the tabernacle of Moses remained at Gibeon under the control of Zadok and his family.

40. This date is derived from the calculation that David came to the throne in 1010 BCE. David was in Achish's land a year and four months prior to the death of Saul in 1010 BCE (1 Sam. 27:7). Thus the date would be c. 1012–1011 BCE.

Joshua until the eighth-century prophets Hosea, Amos, and Micah (cf. Hos. 4:15; 9:15; 12:11; Amos 4:4; 5:5; Mic. 6:5). As such, our catchphrase could be attributed to any number of people and periods. However, it is important to point out that Gilgal was a religious site of special interest to Samuel, Saul, David, and perhaps Abiathar (1 Sam. 7:16; 10:8; 11:14, 15; 13:4-15; 15:12-33; 2 Sam. 19:15, 40). Second, the reminder that Rahab still lived among the children of Israel also has a wide range of historical possibilities starting in the period of Joshua. This could be referring to a spiritual sense;[41] a literal sense reflecting comments by Joshua late in his life;[42] or possibly the presence of her offspring at a much later date.[43] Interestingly, the New Testament writers note Rahab's part in the genealogy of Jesus and her acts of faith (cf. Matt. 1:5; Heb. 11:31; Jas. 2:25). From the genealogy of Matthew it becomes clear that Rahab was the mother of Boaz—the great-grandfather of David (Ruth 4:21-22). Therefore, the author's recording of this tidbit of information in Josh. 6:25 may reflect his desire to make note of a heroic ancestress of King David.

Finally, in Josh. 14:14 the reader is reminded of Caleb's connection to the Canaanite city of Hebron. Because I will be handling this discussion in more detail in chapters 6 and 7 below, I will offer here

41. This was the conclusion of Augustine and early Christian interpreter Rabanus Maurus (776?–856), as noted by Geoghegan, *Time, Place, and Purpose*, 22.

42. Yehezkel Kaufmann, *The Biblical Account of the Conquest of Palestine* (Jerusalem: Magnes, 1953), 74.

43. So, too, the conclusion of early Reformation exegete Andreas Masius (1516–1573). For exact citation, see Geoghegan, *Time, Place, and Purpose*, 26. In the ancient Near East, it was a common understanding that an individual lived on in their offspring and could therefore be punished, postmortem, by striking out against their children. This is best reflected the Gibeonite request in 2 Sam. 21:1-14. See further comments by Herbert C. Brichto, "Kin, Cult, Land, Afterlife: A Biblical Complex," *HUCA* 44 (1973): 1–54, esp. 36–37. Here Brichto suggests that the Gibeonites' displaying of the bodies of Saul's kinfolk in 2 Samuel 21 was to cause Saul not to have rest in the afterlife. The Gibeonites, no doubt, followed the belief that one's continued earthly existence in the afterlife rested upon the continuation of one's family line. The killing of Saul's descendants would thus end Saul's "rest" in the afterlife. This idea is also developed by Henry Wheeler Robinson, *Corporate Personality in Ancient Israel* (Philadelphia: Fortress Press, 1967), 3–4.

only a few summary points. To begin, as the first capital of Judah (2 Sam. 2:1-3), Hebron would have held a special place in the life of both David and Abiathar. Second, Hebron was also a Levitical city of refuge (Josh. 20:7; 21:11, 13)—something of interest to a priest like Abiathar. Third, Caleb was a man of renown in Judah, David's tribe of origin. Finally, Hebron served as a home-away-from-home for Abiathar when he became a fugitive from Saul and Ishbosheth. Therefore, 14:14 could easily have been added as a means of bringing a level of recognition to Caleb and Hebron, a person and place that were important to both David and Abiathar.

We can conclude that even though these three final notations in Joshua could have come from the hand of Joshua later in his life,[44] it is also just as likely that they were added as later editing notations during the period of David's kingship over all Israel—the very period when Abiathar served as David's primary priest. Not surprisingly, all three of these final notations have direct connections to David and/or the priestly/cultic aspects of ancient Israel during the life and times of Abiathar. These types of parallels are also found in the book of Judges.

Judges

The phrase "unto this day" appears eight times in the book of Judges. Two of these (i.e., 1:21 and 10:4) have been addressed in our introductory discussion above and need not be repeated here. Of the remaining six, three deal with the naming of particular sites, which cannot be narrowed historically with any certainty (cf. Judg. 1:26; 15:19; 18:12). However, what is of interest is that 1:26 deals with an etiological account surrounding the cult site of Bethel and the two remaining passages deal with the naming of sites in the region to the southwest of Jerusalem—areas in the tribal region of Judah (see Joshua

---

44. That Joshua would offer a tribute to his old friend Caleb should not be surprising.

15) in which David and his men (Abiathar included) lived while on the run from Saul. In all three of these cases, Abiathar could easily have had access to this information and definitely would have been interested in the etiological details of Bethel—an area in his tribal region of Benjamin. Interestingly, Gary Rendsburg points out the antiquity of the notice regarding the land of the Hittites in Judg. 1:26 due to the collapse of the Hittite Empire in 1190 BCE.[45] Therefore, the source Abiathar employed may have been older as opposed to later.

Next, both Judg. 6:24 (Gideon's cult site at Ophrah) and 19:30 (the account about the Levite and his concubine) fit well on the pen of Abiathar the priest. What priest, especially one with such a high position in David's administration, would not want to point out the problems associated with improper worship? Moreover, the troubling account of the Levite and his concubine is set within the tribal region of Benjamin and in the hometown of Saul. Saul's hometown is disparaged by being likened unto Sodom and Gomorrah. That Abiathar detested Saul is an understatement, to say the least. I will deal more with this in chapter 7 below.

Finally, the phrase "unto *that* day" appears in Judg. 18:1, a variation of the phrase we have been studying. Here the author appears to be reflecting back on an earlier time when the tribe of Dan had not yet been allotted an inheritance. Of course, this is problematic if this portion of Judges postdates Joshua's day when each tribe had received an inheritance (Josh. 19:40-48). However, the Hebrew here is not as clear as one would like and the language may be interpreted in a way that is more reflective of Dan's lack of ability to subdue their allotted land. Furthermore, chapters 17–21 of Judges are known for being early and not in chronological order with the rest of the book of Judges. As such, it is possible that this notation in 18:1 happened

---

45. Gary A. Rendsburg, "A New Look at Pentateuchal *HW*," *Bib* 63, no. 3 (1982): 354–55.

before the actual tribal allotments of Joshua's day, especially if the priestly notations in 18:30 are any indication of an early period (i.e., Gershom, the son of *Moses*, served as priest for the tribe of Dan). Nonetheless, here again we see a use of the phrase in the context of cultic/priestly concerns. Thus, it is easy to see that, historically, Abiathar may have had rhetorical reasons for making the notations in every one of these final three appearances—a similar conclusion that may be drawn for most of the appearances of the phrase in Samuel.

1 and 2 Samuel

"Unto this day" appears thirteen times in the two books of Samuel. Of these occurrences, the majority point to someone other than the prophet Samuel as having actually written the phrase. Of the thirteen uses, only four actually appear before the recording of Samuel's death in 1 Sam. 25:1, and two of these appearances fall within quoted speech from YHWH and Samuel (1 Sam. 8:8 and 12:2 respectively)—see the discussion above. The two remaining uses of the phrase before 1 Samuel 25, not surprisingly, are in the context of cultic concerns. The first, 1 Sam. 5:5, falls within the Ark narratives and deals with the refusal of the priests of Dagon and the people of Ashdod to step on the threshold of the temple due to YHWH's judgment on their god. According to the text, the presence of the Ark of the Covenant had caused the image of Dagon to fall prostrate before the Ark. This fall had caused the hands and the head of the idol figure to break off on the threshold of the doorway. Etiologically, this account explained the cultic policy among the priestly class and the general populace in Ashdod that prohibited them from treading on the threshold of the house of Dagon in Ashdod.

Even though this event happened before Abiathar would have been born (c. 1104 BCE appears to be the best date for the capture of the Ark by the Philistines[46]), he easily could have added it to the oral or written history of someone like Samuel. Furthermore, some scholars already attribute much of the Ark and Succession Narratives (2 Samuel 9—1 Kings 2) to Abiathar.[47] Apart from these concerns, there are more obvious reasons for looking to this priest as the most likely author. Two immediate facts point to Abiathar as penning this notation. First, textually we know that only Abiathar lived for a period of time with David among the Philistines (cf. 1 Sam. 23:9; 30:7).[48] Second, Ziklag, the city given to David by the Philistine king, Achish (cf. 1 Sam. 27:6), was within thirty miles of Ashdod! Clearly, Abiathar would have had access to, and contact with, the priests of Dagon. And third, one would expect a priest to be particularly intrigued about a superstition such as that recorded in 1 Sam. 5:5. What better way to show the superiority of Abiathar's God than to record this pagan practice in the context of the acts of YHWH against Israel's archenemy?[49] Again, while it is possible that Samuel or someone else might have heard about this superstition through hearsay, as I noted in my argument above, a period of time would have had to transpire for the superstition to take hold as a common practice. Thus, it makes the most sense having been recorded around a hundred years later rather than within just a few months or years of the actual event, namely, in Samuel's day.

46. Merrill, *Kingdom of Priests*, 257.
47. The assertion that Abiathar may have written portions of the DtrH is not new. Hans Duhm suggested that Abiathar wrote sections of 1 and 2 Samuel and 1 Kings. Cf. Hans Duhm, "Zur Geschichte der Alttestamentlichen Geschichtsschreibung," in *Festschrift für Theodor Plüss* (Basel: Helbing & Lichtenhahn, 1905), 118–63; and Gerhard von Rad, *The Problem of the Hexateuch and Other Essays*, trans. E. W. Trueman Dicken (London: Oliver and Boyd, 1966), 195 n.37. Similarly, in 1926, Leonhard Rost suggested that Abiathar was a possible candidate as an author for much of 1 and 2 Samuel; see his *Die Überlieferung von der Thronnachfolge Davids*, BWANT 3/6 (Stuttgart: Kholhammer, 1926); in English, *The Succession to the Throne of David* (Sheffield: Almond, 1982), 105.
48. Of course, David's soldiers and their families lived with him in Ziklag as well, but it is Abiathar, a man from the literate class, who stands out in this regard.
49. So, too, Geoghegan, *Time, Place, and Purpose*, 62.

In keeping with our preceding discussion, the record about the monument commemorating the return of the Ark of the Covenant (a huge stone in a field near Beth-shemesh; cf. 1 Sam. 6:18) points to the work of a priest. The fact that the phrase is used in two places in relation to the capture of the Ark points to the work of one author/editor. Furthermore, in light of our conclusions concerning 1 Sam. 5:5, it seems quite likely that Abiathar is in fact that author (see more in ch. 8 below).

The remaining nine appearances of the phrase in 1 and 2 Samuel all fall after the death of Samuel. Again, four of the nine occur within quoted speech from three different speakers; twice from Achish (1 Sam. 29:3, 6), once by David (1 Sam. 29:8), and once from YHWH (2 Sam. 7:6). With so many uses of our phrase in quoted speech by different speakers throughout the DtrH, it becomes more and more likely that this is indeed a device used by the editor(s) or compilers of the material. The remaining five occurrences of the phrase (1 Sam. 27:6; 30:25; 2 Sam. 4:3; 6:8; 18:18) could easily be linked to the work of Abiathar and those who came after him. On this latter point, it is evident that 1 Sam. 27:6 may have been written some time after c. 930 BCE and the division of the kingdom of Israel. The text records that since Achish gave Ziklag to David, the city has belonged to the kings of Judah. Now, while one could posit that this notation was recorded during the civil war between Judah and the northern tribes (during Abiathar's era; cf. 2 Samuel 2–4), a straightforward reading of the text intimates that this is after 930 BCE. Indeed, the phrase "Ziklag has belonged to the *kings of Judah*" (italics mine) pushes one in the direction of the period after David when a series of "kings" had controlled the city. This, then, is one of the first clear examples of post-Abiathar editing. Of course, one cannot be sure when this happened, but sometime before the fall of the Northern Kingdom to Assyria in 722 BCE seems most likely.

The editorial note in 1 Sam. 30:25 dealing with the law concerning the spoils of war also may come from a later hand than Abiathar, or it may be from within his own lifetime. David's institution of this law after the defeat of the Amalekites in 1 Samuel 30 would have been sometime c. 1012 BCE, the very period when Abiathar was present and giving David advice from the Lord (1 Sam. 30:7). If Abiathar lived some time past David's death in 970 BCE, which seems to be the case, this would have allowed time for the legislation to have been in effect for over four decades of war, of which David had his fair share. It was mainly during the lifetime of David that Israel expanded its kingdom to its greatest limits. Such legislation regarding booty and spoils would have been the most appropriate at this time. Furthermore, the language used in the passage to categorize David's new legislation as a "statute" (ḥōq) and an "ordinance" (mišpāṭ) in Israel smacks of priestly influence.[50] Finally, in verse 25 we also see that the legislation was for "Israel." The author does not make a distinction for the divided kingdom. As such, one is even more inclined to date this text prior to 930 BCE. Interestingly, Solomon's reign is marked by peace for the most part, whereas most of the later kings of Judah suffered constant setbacks and loss of territory.[51] Thus, the timeframe of this verse best fits David's and Abiathar's lifetimes.

Next, 2 Sam. 4:3 makes a parenthetical notation about the alien status of the family of the assassins of Ishbosheth—Baanah and Rechab. While one cannot be certain when this editorial note was added, it does fall well within the era of Abiathar and the events between 1010 and 1004 BCE. What is more, the author goes out

---

50. These two words also appear in tandem in the covenant ceremony of Joshua in Josh. 24:25 and in Ps. 81:4.

51. That is not to say that the kings of Israel and Judah never had successful campaigns where booty would have been divided but, rather, that David seemed to be the most successful in this regard. In the former case, one could look to the successes of Jehoshaphat against Moab (1 Kgs. 22:45; 2 Kings 3) and Amaziah's defeat of Edom (2 Kings 14).

of his way to point out that Rimmon's family, of which Baanah and Rechab were a part, was from the tribe of Benjamin and, more specifically, from the city of Beeroth. Beeroth, one of the four cities of the Gibeonites (cf. Josh. 9:17), just happens to be in proximity to Anathoth. Again, while the evidence is circumstantial, it is tantalizing.

The last two appearances of the phrase in Samuel are again connected with the naming of a site (2 Sam. 6:8) and the erecting of a monument (2 Sam. 18:18). In the first passage, the site is none other than the place of Uzzah the priest's death (cf. 2 Samuel 6). There can be no question that Abiathar was the key player in bringing up the Ark to Jerusalem and, as a priest, he no doubt even knew Uzzah and his family. Kiriath-jearim (1 Chr. 13:5-6), again one of the four cities of the Gibeonites, was on the border of the tribal region of Benjamin and only a few miles from Jerusalem. Finally, in the case of 2 Sam. 18:18, the longevity of the monument of Absalom may fit a wide range of dates; however, the later period of Abiathar's life is again just as likely and fitting, especially if the same author recorded the account of Absalom's revolt.

To summarize, in the books of Samuel nothing prohibits the assigning of most of the appearances of the phrase to Abiathar. In fact, most of them actually make the most sense coming from his observations. Apart from the four quoted-speech occurrences, only one other usage (1 Sam. 27:6) seems to be later than the priest's lifetime.

1 and 2 Kings

The books of Kings record the transition period between Abiathar and his descendants. In these books, fifteen occurrences of our phrase span the days of Solomon until the days of Manasseh—over 325 years. With such a long span of time, it is clear that the phrase either was adopted by a series of authors/editors or was used by one editor at a later date and imposed upon the earlier accounts. The latter seems unlikely in light of some of the specific details that are only germane to earlier time periods as opposed to the days of Manasseh or shortly thereafter. Thus, only an assessment of the specific details connected to particular eras will suffice to ameliorate the tension between the two options.

In light of our ongoing discussion regarding the likelihood of Abiathar's recording or editing of the events from Deuteronomy to 2 Samuel, is it possible to posit that Abiathar continued to write into the period of Solomon's reign? The answer to this query must be in the negative. While the five appearances of the phrase in 1 Kings fall within the reign of Solomon, or close to it, all of the notations are best ascribed to someone writing, or at least editing, the material closer to the end of Solomon's life or immediately thereafter. Of course, this does not preclude editorial work done by someone like one of Abiathar's sons. Indeed, many of the five notations actually fit best coming from either Jonathan or Ahimelech.

The first occurrence of the phrase appears in 1 Kgs. 8:8. Here, the author notes that the poles used to carry the Ark of the Covenant protrude from the inner sanctuary into the priestly region known as the holy place. It goes without saying that for one to observe this ongoing phenomenon, he would have to be a priest. Geoghegan points out that the appearance of the phrase ויהיו־שׁם (*wayyihyû šām*; "and they are there") in conjunction with "until this day" appears elsewhere only in Josh. 4:3, where the Ark is also part of the narrative. Moreover, he goes on to suggest that the grammatical connection to Deut. 10:5, where the same phrase (ויהיו־שׁם) is used to speak of the continued presence of the law in the Ark of the Covenant, connotes Dtr editing. [52] Of course, it could be argued that a priest from a later period is recalling or even connecting his language to the older legal tradition. Thus, the presence of the phrase in 1 Kgs. 8:8 does not mandate that both had to have been written by the same author.

One could also argue that it is possible that the phenomenon mentioned here in 1 Kgs. 8:8 may be from a much later period of observation (e.g., Josiah's era); however, with so many godless kings who ruled Judah, the odds that the poles of the Ark were still situated as such two or three hundred years later seems unlikely.[53] Furthermore, as will be demonstrated in the following discussion, in the context of the narrative of Solomon's life, many of the occurrences of the phrase fit closer to the actual events being recorded.

For example, textually we know that Ahimelech, the son of Abiathar, served as priest alongside the older (?) priest, Zadok (cf. 2 Sam. 8:17; 1 Chr. 24:6, 31).[54] If Ahimelech was an active priest during Solomon's reign, then perhaps he is the best source for this particular notation. He certainly would have served in the temple over a long enough period of time to prompt a peculiar observance such as this. It is certainly unlikely that Abiathar would have had access to the temple after being exiled by Solomon (cf. 1 Kgs. 2:26, 27, 35). Moreover, Abiathar, as an old man, would not have been alive long enough to witness this ongoing practice of placing the Ark in the inner sanctuary, as recorded in 1 Kgs. 8:8. It is at this juncture that Ahimelech or Jonathan appears to have taken up the mantle of their father's history and borrowed the language and phraseology used by their aged or now-deceased father.[55]

---

52. Geoghegan, *Time, Place, and Purpose*, 125. Besides these three occurrences, this phrase appears rarely in the OT (cf. Ruth 1:2; 2 Sam. 2:18; 4:3; 1 Chr. 12:40).

53. According to Exod. 25:14-15, the carrying poles were not to be removed from the rings on the Ark. Even if this prohibition remained in force until a much later date, this observation pushes against the belief that the text was written after 560 BCE when the temple was destroyed and the Ark lost.

54. Based upon the continued service of Zadok during the reign of Solomon, it appears that Zadok was a much younger priest than Abiathar. It is possible that Zadok was closer in age to Abiathar's son, Ahimelech.

This becomes apparent in the next three occurrences of the phrase (i.e., 1 Kgs. 9:13, 21; 10:12), which reflect observances both during and toward the end of Solomon's forty-year reign. The first notation takes place in Solomon's twentieth year (1 Kgs. 9:10). The author records Hiram's reaction to the twenty cities in the Galilee that Solomon had given/sold to him (1 Kgs. 9:13).[56] Hiram's dissatisfaction is immediately evident and he names the region "Kabul unto this day." Much like the place names mentioned above, how long this region was so designated cannot be determined. The complete absence of the regional name *Kabul* again in the OT seems to push against a longstanding tradition, especially after the kingdom divided in 930 BCE.[57] However, Geoghegan and Baruch Halpern are no doubt correct in connecting the region of Kabul with the disinherited Gershonite priests. This piece of information would interest the priestly class and would fit our thesis.[58]

The second appearance of the phrase in the same chapter (9:21) addresses the presence of Canaanite slave labor in Solomon's kingdom. The editor's comment here in verse 21 is specific to the reign of Solomon before the division of the kingdom in 930 BCE and thus fits well within the lifetime of one of Abiathar's sons. The final text, which falls within Solomon's lifetime, is found in 1 Kgs. 10:12. Here the author notes the abundance of imported almug/sandalwood

---

55. According to the Chronicler, Azariah, the great-great grandson of Zadok, was the priest in Solomon's temple (1 Chr. 6:10). Some may see chronological problems with this statement because Zadok was alive when Solomon came to the throne. However, at this time men had children at very young ages. So, if all the males of Zadok's line started having children between the ages of twelve and fifteen, then this scenario could very well have happened. Azariah could have been twenty to thirty years old when Zadok was between seventy and eighty years of age.
56. Twenty years into Solomon's reign (c. 950 BCE) would almost certainly preclude Abiathar's involvement in the writing and editing process. The already aged priest would either be deceased or would be too advanced in age to be involved in recording Israel's history.
57. Kabul is used only one other place in the OT in Josh. 19:27. Here it is the name of a city in the tribal region of Asher.
58. Geoghegan, *Time, Place, and Purpose,* 85–86; and Baruch Halpern, "Sectionalism and the Schism," *JBL* 93, no. 4 (1974): 519–32, esp. 522–23.

trees in Jerusalem, specifically those used during the construction of Solomon's house and the temple. After the death of Solomon and the division of the kingdom, these types of imports appear to have ceased. Therefore, the one who is making this comment, along with those noted immediately above, had to have been alive during the days of Solomon or shortly thereafter.

This conclusion may also be applied to the final appearance of our phrase prior to its use in the days of Elisha (c. mid-ninth century), almost one hundred years later. In 1 Kgs. 12:19, the author points out that after the foolish actions of Rehoboam (c. 930 BCE): "Israel has rebelled against the house of David unto this day." Two things need to be noted about this comment. First, the *terminus ad quem* has to be before the exile of the Northern Kingdom in 722 BCE. Second, the fact that the phrase "house of David" is used instead of the national designation "Judah" seems to point to a period closer to the actual events recorded. In this vein, the phrase "house of David" is used almost exclusively in the DtrH prior to, or in temporal proximity with, 1 Kgs. 12:19 (cf. 1 Sam. 20:16; 2 Sam. 3:1, 6; 1 Kgs. 12:20, 26; 13:2). The only other appearance of the phrase in the DtrH is in 2 Kgs. 17:21, where the author there refers to events from the division of the kingdom c. 930 BCE! Thus, in the appearance of the phrase in 2 Kgs. 17:21, the later author may have been borrowing the phrase from the earlier account.[59] Whoever used the phrase in 1 Kgs. 12:19 may have been living during the immediate aftermath of the division of the kingdom.

Finally, while the appearance of our phrase in the Josianic prophecy of the unnamed prophet in 1 Kgs. 13:2 may be telling of a source that was used by one of Abiathar's descendants, it is also

---

59. The only other place the phrase appears (with and without the inseparable prepositions in Hebrew) is three times in Isaiah (i.e., Isa. 7:2, 13; 22:22) and once in Jeremiah (Jer. 21:12). Both prophets may have adopted the phrase from the earlier history of Israel.

possible that the unnamed prophet's words were paraphrased by a later author/editor of this same material. Furthermore, based upon 2 Kgs. 13:23, it is quite possible that an editing during the period of Hezekiah took place sometime well after the events in question. Neither position is conclusive, to be sure, but it does push against a sixth-century date for the compilation of the material.

This brings us to the final ten appearances of "unto this day" in the last portion of the DtrH, namely, 2 Kings. The phrase is absent in the DtrH from 1 Kings 13 through 2 Kings 2.[60] Also, the last two of these ten occurrences (i.e., 2 Kgs. 20:17; 21:15) again appear in quoted speech on the lips of Isaiah and YHWH respectively (see the above discussion). Three more of the usages of the phrase occur within 2 Kings 17, which records the fall of Israel to Assyria (722 BCE) and the sin of the "transplanted" peoples in and around Samaria after that transforming event (cf. 2 Kgs. 17:23, 34, 41). The use of the phrase in 2 Kings 17 certainly dates to a period after 722 BCE and may very well reflect the beginning of the last editing of the DtrH. In light of our ongoing assertion that Jeremiah played a key role in this phase, it is possible that he made these comments sometime during his ministry, perhaps in the reign of Josiah, prior to the fall of Jerusalem in 586 BCE. In this vein, 2 Kgs. 17:41 is useful in determining a possible *terminus ad quem* for these particular comments in chapter 17. Here the author notes that the grandchildren of these mixed people groups in and around Samaria sinned just like their forefathers had. Beginning in 722 BCE and allowing somewhere between thirty and forty years for each generation would easily place the third generation of these foreigners within the early life and ministry of Jeremiah.[61]

---

60. This may be connected to many scholarly assertions that much of the Elijah/Elisha cycle of 1 Kings 17—2 Kings 13 was an independent source. I will address this further in ch. 10 below.

61. David lived about seventy years (2 Sam. 5:4, c. 1040–970 BCE; cf. Merrill, *Kingdom of Priests*, 261, 298) and Solomon appears to have lived about sixty years. Solomon came to the throne when he was sixteen to twenty years old in 970 BCE and died around forty years later in 930 BCE

The last five occurrences of the phrase (i.e., 2 Kgs. 2:22; 8:22; 10:27; 14:7; 16:6) come from a wide array of events and eras. The first, 2 Kgs. 2:22, falls within the account of Elisha's healing of the bitter waters at Jericho (c. mid-to-late ninth century). While I will deal with the Elijah and Elisha narrative in more detail in chapter 10 below, it is important to note that the editing could have happened anytime from c. 841 to 586 BCE.[62] The perspective, however, may be from the school of the prophets in Jericho (in the region of Benjamin), thus pointing to a source of northern origins for the Elijah/Elisha narratives.

The second and fourth occurrences are connected to a battle between Judah and Edom and as such need to be handled together (i.e., 2 Kgs. 8:22; 14:7). Second Kings 8:22 falls within the kingship of Jehoram (c. 848–841 BCE), Jehoshaphat's son, and relates how Edom rebelled against Jehoram and the kings of Judah "unto this day." Second Kings 14:7 records the renaming of Sela to Joktheel, after King Amaziah (796–767 BCE) resubjugated Edom.[63] We can pinpoint when this resubjugation took place by further noting that not long after Amaziah's defeat of Edom, he challenged Jehoash, king of Israel, to a battle. Amaziah was soundly defeated at that time. This

---

(cf. 1 Kgs. 11:42; 2 Chr. 12:13 [Josephus *Ant* 8:211 suggests Solomon was only fourteen and reigned for eighty years]). Rehoboam lived about fifty-eight years (1 Kgs. 14:21; cf. Merrill, *Kingdom of Priests*, 336–37). Using the average lifespan of sixty years, if the first generation of exiles in Samaria were between twenty-five and thirty years of age when they were exiled to Samaria in 722 BCE, then the first generation would have died off sometime around 690–680 BCE. The second generation would have been born around 720 and would have died off around 660–650 BCE. The third generation would have been born about 700 BCE and would have started dying off about 640–630 BCE. Jeremiah started his ministry around 626 BCE and thus his early life and ministry would have overlapped with this third generation.

62. According to the context of this passage, the healing of the waters appears to have taken place early in the ministry of Elisha (c. 841 BCE). Therefore, the comment could have been anytime thereafter.

63. Despite the textual difficulties, B. Obed, "Neighbors on the East," in *The World History of the Jewish People*, vol. 4, part 1: *The Age of the Monarchies: Political History*, ed. Abraham Malamat (Jerusalem: Masada, 1979), 255, points to Edom's regaining its independence in 2 Kgs. 16:6 and the Tiglath-pileser III inscription mentioning an Edomite king named Qaushmalaku who paid tribute at that time.

battle between Judah and Israel was sometime during the reign of Jehoash (798–782 BCE), narrowing the window for the first reference in 8:22 to no later than 782 BCE—the last year of Jehoash's reign. Because we know that Amaziah reconquered Edom sometime during his reign (cf. 2 Kgs. 14:1-7; 2 Chr. 25:14), the first notation had to have been recorded between the last date of Jehoram (i.e., 841 BCE) and the death of Jehoash (c. 782 BCE).[64] Thus, the statement in 2 Kgs. 8:22 appears to have been recorded under the godly reigns of Joash or Amaziah (early). This resonates well with the role the priests, Jehoiada in particular, played during Joash's reign. Even though it is uncertain where Jehoiada fits among the families of the priests (no Zadokite reference is made to him), the priests of Anathoth would have been familiar with the inner political workings of Judah at that time. On the other hand, the latter occurrence in 2 Kgs. 14:7 noting the renaming of Sela to Joktheel may have been very close to the events themselves (i.e., during the reign of Amaziah), or it may have been added in the latest strand of editing. However, as I have noted above, the appearance of the phrase with place names is extremely difficult to pin point.[65]

The remaining pair of appearances of our phrase are in 2 Kgs. 10:27 and 16:6. The former records how Jehu (841–814 BCE) made the temple of Baal in Samaria a latrine "unto this day." While the date for such an event could range anywhere from 841 to 722 BCE, what is most intriguing is that the phrase is again used in the recording of a cultic tradition whereby a pagan shrine appears in a less-than-flattering light (see the discussion above about the shrine of Dagon in

---

64. The Chronicler notes that during the days of Ahaz, the Edomites were once again independent to the point of taking captives from Judah (cf. 2 Chr. 28:17).

65. It appears that Sela regained its name with Edom's independence by the period of Isaiah and Hezekiah. In Isa. 16:1 and 42:11, the prophet addresses the area of Edom as Sela, not Joktheel. After Hezekiah's defeat by Sennacherib, Judah lost much of its territory and its vassal countries like Edom. Of course, Edom may have gained independence even before this sometime between 782 and 701 BCE.

1 Sam. 5:5). Even though it is in a negative sense, the notation makes the most sense coming from someone of the priestly line who had an issue with Baal worship. It goes without saying that the priests of the northern region, Benjamin and Anathoth included, would have savored the opportunity to include this tidbit of history. Finally, 2 Kgs. 16:6 records the capture of Elath (modern-day Eilat) by the Aramean king, Rezin, and Aram's occupation of the site "unto this day." Now, while the verse has a number of textual issues (i.e., did Aram occupy it or did Edom?),[66] as it now appears the *terminus a quo* is c. 735 BCE (the beginning of the Syro-Ephramite war) and the *terminus ad quem* could be any time up until the fall of Aram, first to the Assyrians (c. 731 BCE), and later to the Babylonians in 586 BCE, or shortly thereafter. This last appearance of our phrase is impossible to narrow any further, but still does not preclude Anathothian origination.[67]

Initial Conclusions

Our extensive analysis of the phrase "unto this day" in the DtrH has yielded a number of interesting conclusions. First, it is evident that many of the occurrences of the phrase before 1 Kings could easily have come from the hand of Abiathar. As a matter of fact, a number of them fit most appropriately in his context and from his perspective. Second, those notations that appear in the life of Solomon (2 Kings 1–12) fit well on the pen of one of Abiathar's sons. Third, those

---

66. Merrill, *Kingdom of Priests*, 420, posits that Elath was handed over to Edom, and that Aram did not occupy the southern port city.

67. Interestingly, Duane L. Christensen, "A New Israel: The Righteous from among All Nations," in *Israel's Apostasy and Restoration: Essays in Honor of Roland K. Harrison*, ed. Avraham Gileadi (Grand Rapids: Baker, 1987), 256, points up that Edom actually allied with Nebuchadnezzar against Judah. If this is the case, and if "Edom" should be read for "Aram," then Edom controlled the area even after 586 BCE. Malachi 4:1-4 records that by Malachi's day, Edom was a desolation (c. 480–433 BCE) even though some people remained in the land. See further, J. R. Bartlett, "Edom," *ABD* 2:287–95, esp. 292–93.

appearances coming after the life of Solomon, and a few of the earlier occurrences, could have either been added during the last layer of editing by someone like Jeremiah or may have been added by a number of compilers and/or editors from Abiathar's lineage and/or the priests of Anathoth. Fourth, at several junctures it has been pointed out that the geographical context points to the tribal regions of Judah and Benjamin (i.e., the southern region of ancient Israel).[68] In this vein, Jeffrey Geoghegan's conclusion seems fitting:

> Most apparent among the various occurrences of "unto this day" is its use in connection with southern entities or in contexts that reflect southern concerns. In fact, its use reflects a *detailed* knowledge of the south that is virtually lacking from the north. . . . In contrast, three of the five northern locations said to exist "unto this day" are large geographical areas consisting of numerous cities (Deut 3:14; Josh 13:13; Judg 10:4), not individual objects or sites. The only *individual* objects in the north said to persist "unto this day" are the altar to YHWH at Ophrah (Judg 6:24) and the destroyed pillar and temple of Baal in Samaria (2 Kgs 10:27), both of which, . . . share the distinction of being former sites of Baal worship.[69]

It is clear that the southern focus of the author(s) is telling of the region of his origin and those places most familiar to him. It is also in keeping with our thesis because the priests of Anathoth actually lived and worked out of the very region where many of these sites are located. As members of the tribe of Benjamin, who also lived on the border region with Judah, this family is as good a prospect as any to be the authors of this material. Fifth, many places where our phrase is used falls within the context of cultic/priestly interests and/

---

68. So, too, the position of Hans Walter Wolff, "The Kerygma of the Deuteronomistic Historical Work," in *Reconsidering Israel and Judah: Recent Studies on the Deuteronomistic History*, ed. Gary N. Knoppers and J. Gordon McConville (Winona Lake, IN: Eisenbrauns, 2000), 63.

69. Geoghegan, *Time, Place, and Purpose*, 62, 64, see also 89–91 (italics his). For a detailed map with all of the geographical sites connected to the phrase "unto this day" plotted in their suggested locations in relation to Judah and Benjamin, see ibid., 63.

or the proper handling of the Ark of the Covenant (e.g., Josh. 4:9; 9:27; 1 Sam. 5:5; 6:18; 2 Sam. 6:8; 1 Kgs. 8:8; 2 Kgs. 10:27). Indeed, Geoghegan notes that "'until this day' is used more times with the Ark of the Covenant than with any other object or institution in ancient Israel."[70] Sixth, one of the other unique features, which appears in conjunction with our phrase, is the common geographical and political notations dealing with Edom and their rebellion and subjugation (Deut. 2:22; 2 Kgs. 8:22; 14:7; 16:6).[71] While on the surface some may question the presence of the Edomite connections, when they are viewed as originating on the pen of Abiathar and his family they make sense. Abiathar's entire family had been killed by none other than Doeg the Edomite (1 Samuel 22)! One could understand why Edom's rebellion would be included here. In a similar vein, the rebellion of Israel makes sense in light of Saul's (i.e., the Northern Kingdom) direct connection to this same event (2 Samuel 2–4; 1 Kgs. 12:19).[72] Finally, as has been pointed up throughout our discussion, very few of the appearances of the phrase fit historically after 586 BCE. This final conclusion alone pushes against the scholarly status quo of a late editing and compiling of most, if not all, of the material where our phrase appears.

A Brief Analysis of Jeffrey Geoghegan's Work

Jeffrey Geoghegan's 2006 work on the phrase "until this day" has filled a gap within DtrH studies and has paved the way for serious discussions on the who, when, why, and how of authorship issues in the DtrH. He has also done an exemplary job of summarizing

---

70. Ibid., 88.
71. Ibid., 67. Note that many of these appear after the time of Abiathar but could easily fall within the era of his sons and descendants.
72. Of course, both Abiathar and Saul were from the tribe of Benjamin. However, the northern tribes sided with Saul and later, under Ishbosheth, rebelled against the house of Judah. Judah (i.e., David) became the preservers of Abiathar and his family (see further, in ch. 7).

the history of scholarship on both the use of our phrase and the present state of DtrH scholarship.[73] As such, as I have been assessing the use of this phrase in the DtrH, at key points I have noted the conclusions and research of Geoghegan. His in-depth analysis has been illuminating and in many ways supportive of my ongoing thesis. Because many of my conclusions parallel Geoghegan's, with the exception of the dating of several of the occurrences of our phrase, I find it necessary to offer a brief critique of his work in light of my ongoing thesis. I begin this critique with the disclaimer that I had completed my initial exegetical analysis of the use of the phrase in the DtrH *before* I read or interacted with Geoghegan's work. I found it interesting that many of his conclusions in many ways mirrored those of mine! However, there were still some distinct differences between our theses that need to be addressed, especially in areas where I feel Geoghegan did not go far enough with his conclusions.

To begin, many of the areas where I deviate from Geoghegan's thesis have to do with his apparent presuppositional stance in relation to the dating of the book of Deuteronomy and in his assertion that every occurrence of our phrase falls in the late preexilic period. In the first case, I have pointed out above that there is just as much evidence to merit an early date (c. fifteenth century BCE) for the completed work of Deuteronomy as there is for a late date (c. 621 BCE). Thus, Dtr's interest in Deuteronomic ideas and laws simply may be reflective of any priest throughout the history of Israel, not just a priest or prophet from a late preexilic period.

Similarly, Geoghegan insists that the editorial work of Dtr can be identified by the obvious "Deuteronomistic language" used by this late preexilic author.[74] However, as I have already noted in chapter 1 above, scholarship is now beginning to question the validity of

73. Ibid., chs. 1 and 4.
74. Ibid., 127–28.

what exactly defines "Deuteronomic" language.[75] Is this phenomenon strictly from the Josianic period or is the language in the DtrH something that authors, especially priestly authors, employed over a period of time? Geoghegan fails to consider the possibility that perhaps the reason that the language is Deuteronomic is because it *is* from a priestly school from earlier periods—a school familiar with Deuteronomic law.[76] Geoghegan himself draws the conclusion that the editorial work was done by an individual or small group interested in the cult and Deuteronomic legislation. However, he does not allow for the possibility of earlier compilation and editorial work done by these priests.

Geoghegan also asserts that any of the appearances of the phrase in Deuteronomy must come from a later hand—as late as Jeremiah.[77] While this is indeed possible, the amount of material from the book of Deuteronomy that Geoghegan places on the pen of the later Dtr is problematic in light of the equally legitimate theory of an early Deuteronomy fashioned after a Hittite treaty. Nevertheless, even though I feel Geoghegan is correct in assigning many of the appearances of "unto this day" to an editor, had he allowed for the possibility that the occurrences of the phrase in Deuteronomy may have been the result of *minor* editing from an earlier period (as I posit), he may have been closer to answering more of the nagging questions of authorship.

---

75. See, for example, the conclusions of Robert R. Wilson, "Who Was the Deuteronomist? (Who Was Not the Deuteronomist?): Reflections on Pan-Deuteronomism," in *Those Elusive Deuteronomists: The Phenomenon of Pan-Deuteronomism*, ed. Linda S. Schearing and Steven L. McKenzie, JSOTSup 268 (Sheffield: Sheffield Academic Press, 1999), 78–79; and Gordon Wenham, "The Date of Deuteronomy: Linch-pin of Old Testament Criticism. Part One," *Them* 10, no. 3 (1985): 19.
76. Note also comments by James Robson, "The Literary Composition of Deuteronomy," in *Interpreting Deuteronomy: Issues and Approaches*, ed. David G. Firth and Philip S. Johnston (Downers Grove, IL: IVP Academic, 2012), 47.
77. Geoghegan, *Time, Place, and Purpose*, 142.

In this vein, because Geoghegan seeks to flatten out the use of the phrase and assign it to one hand at a later period, he often forces obvious earlier occurrences of the phrase to conform to his thesis (e.g., Josh. 4:9; 7:26; 13:13; 15:63; 16:10; 1 Kgs. 10:12; 12:19; 2 Kgs. 17:23, 34, 41). If Geoghegan had followed his own observations about an earlier form of the DtrH (in whatever form it took) and had allowed for the use and reuse of the phrase within a select group or community of authors/compilers, then the tensions would have been alleviated.[78] For example, when dealing with the appearances of the phrase in the Tetrateuch, Geoghegan posits, "At a minimum, this evidence suggests that Dtr was familiar with the use of the phrase in the Tetrateuch, allowing him to imitate it in his own writing."[79] This, of course, begs the question, If Dtr could "imitate" the appearance of the phrase in the Tetrateuch, why could he not also "imitate" the use of the phrase from an earlier DtrH "school" or circle in Anathoth, especially if it is Jeremiah, as Geoghegan conjectures at the end of his study? This also obtains for the use of the phrase by Isaiah, Ezekiel, Nehemiah, Ezra, and the Chronicler. Did they borrow the phrase from Dtr?

These concerns being noted, I still feel Geoghegan is more correct in his assessment than he is wrong. For example, I feel Geoghegan is on the right track in his critique of the work of scholars such as those in the Göttingen School (i.e., Smend, Veijola, and Dietrich). Their proposed DtrP (prophetic) and DtrN (nomistic) layers of the DtrH actually work best if merged into a preexilic DtrH written by one Dtr, who had both priestly and prophetic interests. They would have also been closer to the conclusions of scholars such as Cross, and to the reality of the text as we have it.[80]

---

78. E.g., ibid., 159.
79. Ibid., 156. See also his similar conclusion on pp. 152, 159.
80. Ibid., 152–53.

Also, Geoghegan's identification of the central location from which the DtrH was written (i.e., near Jerusalem and the border region with the northern tribes), along with Dtr's pro-Judahite and Davidic stance, is, in my evaluation, correct and to be taken seriously. What is more, Geoghegan correctly points up that Jeremiah is the most likely candidate for the final editing of the DtrH and may in fact be Dtr—a position in concert with my own.[81] Finally, Geoghegan's identification of Dtr as being a "representative of northern priestly/prophetic circles" is perhaps one of the most telling conclusions he makes.[82] Unfortunately, he only hints at the possible connections of Dtr to the priests of Anathoth in two brief footnotes.[83]

Nevertheless, Geoghegan still falls short of the mark by not attempting to answer the question of *why* certain accounts within the DtrH were written and *who* would have had the motives to do so. Had these concerns been teased out without holding to the presupposition that Dtr had to be a single person from a much later period, as opposed to a "school" with a somewhat long tradition of recording Israel's and Judah's history, then these very important questions may have been answered.[84] Surprisingly, Geoghegan teeters on the edge of "getting it right" when he makes two somewhat conflicting statements in the same paragraph. He notes, "This unity of use [of the phrase 'unto this day'] and perspective could not easily derive from 'many different redactors.' . . . Even so, the consistency of redactional procedure and religio-political perspective reflected in the use of 'until this day' across the DH strongly suggests

---

81. Ibid., 138, 153–58.
82. Ibid., 149–51. These "northern" priests could have been both those living in the region of Anathoth or refugees from the Assyrian invasion of 722 BCE. However, I do reject Geoghegan's assertion that the Deuteronomic law was the product of these northern priests that was later discovered in the temple in 621 BCE—de Wette's "pious fraud" scenario. On this latter point, see ibid., 250.
83. Ibid., 137 n.50 and 151 n.21.
84. Ibid., 143.

that the compilation of Israel's history fell to an individual or *small group* working in close association" (italics mine).[85] Sadly, Geoghegan stops short of fleshing out who this "small group" may have been. It is in answering the questions of who, when, and why that one may begin to focus the microscope on a particular group of individuals who have many of the qualities that Geoghegan and others have long noted—our priests from Anathoth. It is to this analysis that I now turn.

85. Ibid.

PART II

An Analysis of the Texts

5

The Editing of the Book of Deuteronomy

In the second half of this book, I will examine each book of the DtrH in order to determine how, if at all, the priestly authors from Anathoth may have influenced their content and shaping. While the bulk of my discussion in this second half is reserved for the books of Joshua to Kings, it is still important to assess what, if any, influence the priests from Anathoth may have had on the book of Deuteronomy. Nevertheless, I begin this analysis with the disclaimer that I accept the existence of earlier source material that may have comprised "proto" forms of at least Deuteronomy through 1 Samuel.[1] It is these "proto" works that Abiathar, and those that followed him, began to fashion into a sustained history, which culminated in the sixth century with the final editing of the DtrH by Jeremiah or Baruch.

---

1. As will be demonstrated in ch. 7, the book of Judges falls into a unique category. Pre-Abiathar material is obviously incorporated into the earliest presentation of Judges, which Abiathar uses for rhetorical purposes in his pro-Davidic/anti-Saulide polemic.

The existence of earlier strands of material, in some cases large blocks from the preexilic period, is in no way a novel idea.[2] Indeed, this has been pretty much assumed by scholars for the past century. Now, whether those strands were written by the Yahwist, Elohist, Nathan, Gad, Samuel, or some other figure of a given era is an entirely different, and at times heated, debate. Nevertheless, my ongoing theory concerning these earliest strands is rooted in the generally accepted scholarly perspective that these strands/sources actually did exist. Therefore, moving forward I will scrutinize the content of each book to determine exactly what portions may have been written by these earlier writers at Anathoth.[3]

Of course, in making such a supposition, scholars are sure to challenge this premise, especially in relation to issues of "late Deuteronomic influence" on the work. For certain, they will ask: "Exactly how much of it was written by these proposed earlier writers?" As will be demonstrated throughout the remainder of this work, it appears that more material, not less, came from these authors in Anathoth. To be more specific, it is my contention that large portions of the DtrH, especially prior to 2 Kings 11, were already shaped pretty much in their final forms prior to the final editing in the sixth century. The book of Deuteronomy, however, is one

2. Abraham Kuenen, *Het onstaan van de Historische Boeken des Ouden Verbonds*, vol. 1 of *Historisch-kritisch onderzoek naar het ontstaan en de verzameling van de boeken des Ouden Verbonds*, 3 vols. (Leiden: Engels, 1861), 249–82, as cited by Jeremy Hutton, *The Transjordanian Palimpsest: The Overwritten Texts of Personal Exile and Transformation in the Deuteronomistic History*, BZAW 396 (Berlin: de Gruyter, 2009), 89 n.36 (see there for further bibliography). See also F. García López, *Le Deutéronome: Une Loi prêchée*, CaE 63 (Paris: Cerf, 1988), 12–13.

3. Scholars of the earlier source-critical perspective suggested that the JEDP sources of the Torah extended into the DtrH. Cf., for example, D. Karl Budde, *Die Bücher Richter und Samuel, ihre Quellen und ihr Aufbau* (Giessen: Ricker, 1890); Carl Heinrich Cornill, *Einleitung in das Alte Testament*, GTW 2/1 (Freiburg: Mohr Siebeck, 1891); Immanuel Benzinger, *Jahvist und Elohist in den Königsbüchern*, BWANT 27 (Berlin: Kohlhammer, 1921); Ernst Sellin, *Introduction to the Old Testament*, trans. W. Montgomery (London: Hodder & Stoughton, 1923) [German: *Einleitung in das Alte Testament*, ETB 2 (Leipzig: Quelle & Meyer, 1910)]. This list as cited by Hutton; see further bibliography in Hutton, *Transjordanian Palimpsest*, 82 n.6.

book within this corpus that appears to have had the least amount of shaping by any author/editor prior to Dtr's adoption of its theological principles as he/they fashioned the history of Israel.[4] What follows is an assessment of the text of Deuteronomy, which is in no way as parsed as did Noth or those who followed him.[5] With this caveat, and because I have already handled aspects of the book of Deuteronomy above, we now turn to a brief discussion on the editorial work in the book of Deuteronomy.

The Book of Deuteronomy: An Assessment

... the idea of a deuteronomistic redaction of Deuteronomy rests on the unanimous consensus of exegetes.[6]

Even though such a conclusion as this by Thomas Römer may be true, when maximalists read Deuteronomy, they insist that Mosaic material is present in the book of Deuteronomy. The predominant use of first-person pronouns, both singular and plural,[7] is one of the

---

4. Some may suggest a level of naïveté in such a statement; yet there is absolutely no evidence beyond theory to suggest otherwise.

5. For Noth's work on the book of Deuteronomy, see Martin Noth, *The Deuteronomistic History*, JSOTSup 15 (Sheffield: JSOT, 1981), 26–35.

6. Thomas Römer, "Deuteronomy in Search of Origins," in *Reconsidering Israel and Judah: Recent Studies on the Deuteronomistic History*, ed. Gary N. Knoppers and J. Gordon McConville (Winona Lake, IN: Eisenbrauns, 2000), 115. Of course, there is the problem of who did this redaction and when this took place. Idem, "The Book of Deuteronomy," in *The History of Israel's Traditions: The Heritage of Martin Noth*, ed. Steven L. McKenzie and M. Patrick Graham, JSOTSup 182 (Sheffield: Sheffield Academic Press, 1994), 194–95, points out the earlier tradition of von Rad in assigning authorship of Deuteronomy to the Levitical priesthood (of which I agree in part), but goes on to note that many scholars today look for the authors of Deuteronomy among the wisdom tradition of the Jerusalem court scribes. On this, see Moshe Weinfeld, *Deuteronomy and the Deuteronomistic School* (Oxford: Clarendon, 1972), 244–319, esp. 274. Römer's conclusion in this regard merits quoting: "But there are also Levitical and prophetic interests in Deuteronomy, where much place is given to the elders. So it is too rigid to identify the authors of Deuteronomy definitely with any one professional class" ("Book of Deuteronomy," 195). While I may disagree with Römer's perspective of a "coalition" or "reforming party," he is nonetheless correct in alleviating the rejection of priestly involvement.

7. There are no fewer than 500 appearances of first-person pronouns, both personal and possessive, in the book of Deuteronomy (I, me, my, mine, we, our, us). This also reflects the use of these pronouns in the direct speech of YHWH. On the oscillation between singular and

reasons why more conservative interpreters assign the majority of the work to Moses even though minimalists would argue that the text is only written as such to give the appearance of this perspective (see the discussion in chs. 1 and 3 above).[8] Nevertheless, where scholars from both perspectives are beginning to find common ground is in the portions of Deuteronomy where Moses' name appears in the third person.[9] Not surprisingly, Moses' name appears most frequently in the chapters often assigned to editors or to Noth's Dtr. In this vein, in chapters 1–4 the name "Moses" is given in editorial comments no fewer than seven times. His name appears once in 5:1 and then not again until chapters 27 (vv. 1, 9, 11) and 29 (vv. 1, 2). In chapters 31–34, large portions of which are often assigned to later editors, Moses' name is used repeatedly (twenty-five times). These data, of course, align well with the general belief that chapters 5–26 form the heart of the "original" book of Deuteronomy.[10] It is for this reason that I will concentrate most of my analysis on chapters 1–4 and 31–34.[11]

plural forms of *you* in Deuteronomy, cf. Römer, "Deuteronomy in Search of Origins," 118–19, esp. nn.24–27 for bibliography.

8. See, for example, ibid., 117–18, 120.

9. While it is possible that Moses could have recorded his account in the third person as in the book of Exodus, it does not appear to be the case here in Deuteronomy. The book of Deuteronomy is recorded as direct addresses to the children of Israel thus accounting for the frequency of the first-person pronouns. It is when this pattern is broken that editorial work seems to make the most sense.

10. Of course, any number of variations of this statement could be argued by a given scholar. See, for example, the comments of Römer ("Deuteronomy in Search of Origins," 114) and the various scholarly positions he notes in nn.6–8. Here, Römer suggests that the original block was chs. 12–18, which in turn was given an introduction (i.e., 6:4ff.) and a conclusion (i.e., chs. 26–34). On the other hand, Richard E. Friedman, *The Exile and Biblical Narrative: The Formation of the Deuteronomistic and Priestly Works*, HSM 22 (Chico, CA: Scholars, 1981), 1 n.3, says that chs. 1–3 and 31–34 were the later additions. See also the conclusions of Alexander Rofé, *Deuteronomy: Issues and Interpretation* (London: T&T Clark, 2002), 6–9; and the summary of Noth's work by Antony F. Campbell, "Martin Noth and the Deuteronomistic History," in McKenzie and Graham, eds., *History of Israel's Traditions*, 29–62, at 33.

11. Noth did see the bulk of 4:44—30:20 as the older portions of Deuteronomy.

Deuteronomy 1–4

In our previous discussion concerning the importance of the phrases "beyond the Jordan" and "unto this day," we discovered many areas where it appears that later editors were at work throughout the DtrH. In this regard, in the book of Deuteronomy there appear to be places where editors/authors may have inserted non-Mosaic material for rhetorical purposes. Most of these editorial notations appear in the narrative portions of the book—both at the beginning and end. The most telling of these editorial comments appears within chapters 1–4—a position noted by many scholars. For example, Noth assigned good portions of these introductory chapters to Dtr.[12] While I am unwilling to go to the length that Noth went in assigning the entirety of the narrative material of these first four chapters to a later editor, there are, nonetheless, at least six obvious editorial notations that stand out, covering approximately twenty-six-and-a-half verses (cf. 1:1-5; 2:10-12, 20-23; 3:8-11, 13b-14; 4:41-49).

To begin, in Deuteronomy 1:1-5 the editor situates his reader not only within the Mosaic era, but also geographically in the Transjordan even though it is clear that the editor is already in Canaan/Israel. This is made clear by the use of the phrase "across the Jordan" not once, but twice in verses 1 and 5 (see the discussion in ch. 4 above). Serving as an inclusio, this phrase alerts the reader to the editorial activity here in the introduction to the book of Deuteronomy. What is more, the reader is also introduced to the two kings of the Transjordan: Sihon and Og (v. 4). At first glance, the introduction of these kings so early in the book appears out of place, seeing how Moses does not actually deal with the account of the defeat of these kings until chapter 3. While this early introduction

---

12. This assertion by Noth has become axiomatic among DtrH scholars. Most reject an early date for the book of Deuteronomy and instead accept the 621 BCE date postulated by de Wette.

may appear benign, it in fact may serve as a clue to the editor's literary purposes. I will return to this shortly.

Within the remaining five editorial notations in chapters 2–4 (i.e., 2:10-12, 20-23; 3:8-11, 13b-14; 4:41-49), every one of the pericopes makes some comment about the giants in the Transjordan who were directly related to Sihon and Og.[13] These kings, the editor notes, are related in some way to the Anakim (2:10, 11, 21; cf. also noneditorial notes about the Anakim in 1:28 and 9:2), Rephaim (2:11, 20; 3:11, 13), Zamzummim (2:20), and the Emim (2:10, 11).[14] Furthermore, Deuteronomy 3 records how these kings and their ilk were conquered by Moses and the Israelites. Interestingly, four of the five editorial notations fall within close proximity of one of the two phrases we mentioned in chapter 4, namely, "beyond the Jordan" and "unto this day" (cf. 3:8; 4:41, 46, 47, and 2:22; 3:14 respectively).[15] Thus, in chapter 3, editorial blocks appear in two places (vv. 8-11 and 13b-14) that are bookended by the use of the phrases "beyond the Jordan" and "unto this day" (vv. 8, 14 respectively). The editor also goes out of his way to include in the narrative the description of Og's bed, which shows the giant's immense size (3:11).[16] Similarly, "unto this day" (2:22) falls in the midst of the editorial notation of 2:20-23—again dealing with the large stature of the Transjordanian peoples conquered by Moses and the Israelites. The final appearance of an editorial note in the first four chapters falls within the last verses of chapter 4 (vv. 41-49). Here, the phrase "beyond the Jordan" is used

---

13. Sihon, king of the Amorites, appears twenty-four times in the DtrH, and Og, king of Bashan, appears seventeen times.

14. Robert Polzin, *Moses and the Deuteronomist: A Literary Study of the Deuteronomic History I. Deuteronomy, Joshua, Judges* (Bloomington: Indiana University Press, 1993), 31, points out the work of the editor in these texts.

15. The editorial note in 2:10-12 does not use either phrase "beyond the Jordan" or "unto this day," but does reference the giants.

16. See also the comments of Jeffrey C. Geoghegan, *The Time, Place, and Purpose of the Deuteronomistic History: The Evidence of "Until This Day,"* BJS 347 (Providence, RI: Brown University Press, 2006), 143–44.

three times (vv. 41, 46-47) in the context of the Levitical cities set aside as cities of refuge (i.e., Bezer, Ramoth, and Golan; cf. 4:43), while Sihon and Og are again referenced in 4:46-47.

What exactly does the editor's use of the phrases "unto this day" and "beyond the Jordan" in relation to the destruction of Sihon and Og tell us about his rhetorical purposes? Now, while it is understandable for Moses to recount the destruction of the kings in the Transjordan in his final speeches, it is the editor who repeatedly stresses this great feat and also emphasizes their immense size (Deut. 2:10, 21; 3:11). It seems obvious that he wanted to draw out something of importance about Israel and Moses' conquering of the giants in the Transjordan (I will deal with the Levitical cities in 4:41-49 momentarily).

At the outset of the book of Deuteronomy, it appears that the editor is seeking to draw a direct connection to the other great giant slayers in Israel's history—Caleb and David (cf. Josh. 14:12-15 and 1 Samuel 17; 2 Sam. 21:15-22). Even the giants of David's day appear to have been descended from the Anakim, not the Sea Peoples (Josh. 11:22). Their defeat was a momentous occasion for the nation of Israel, but, even more importantly, for the tribe of Judah. First, Caleb is remembered—the great conqueror of Hebron (David's first capital), the Judahite leader par excellence of the conquest period, who is often mentioned in tandem with Joshua (Num. 14:6, 30, 38; 26:65; Josh. 14:6, 13). Second, David is remembered—the greatest of the kings of Israel, the slayer of Goliath and the deliverer of Israel. In this regard, David's destruction of the giants was an event that occasioned the beginning of the end for the Philistine city-states.

Rhetorically, the editor desired to honor the two great men of Judah—one, a founding father of the tribe, and the other, its greatest king. He did this by connecting them to Israel's greatest leader and lawgiver, Moses. Moreover, Hebron, the haunt of the Anakim, was not only a Levitical city of refuge but also a home-away-from-home for Abiathar for over seven-and-a-half years as David ruled Judah (2 Sam. 2:1-3, 11)! In this context, Deuteronomy 4:41-49 becomes important and telling of the editor's bent. The editor, before he begins the extended legal sections and teaching of Moses in Deuteronomy 5–26, betrays his personal biases and background. In this regard, as a Levitical priest, he points out the three cities of refuge in the Transjordan. Dtr (and his circle), being from the priestly class, would find this type of information important.

Even though this conclusion does not fit with the presuppositions of those who argue for a Josianic editing, it does support our thesis. The compiler of this material remained faithful to the Mosaic content and tradition handed down to him but added key notations that had importance for his day and age. In this vein, a sixth-century editing does not serve a clear rhetorical function as it does coming from David's era; Josiah, while a great king, was not a giant slayer.[17]

Deuteronomy 5-30

Unlike these opening four chapters, the body of the book of Deuteronomy (i.e., chs. 5–26) shows little evidence of editorial interjections. On the contrary, we only see clear textual evidence of potential editorial work in 10:6-9 and possibly 11:30.[18] Deuteronomy 10:6-9 says,

> Now the sons of Israel journeyed from Beeroth of the sons of Jaaqan to Moserah. There Aaron died and there he was buried and Eleazar his son ministered as priest in his place. From there they journeyed to Gudgodah, to Jotbathah—a land of streams of water. At that time the

17. Gary N. Knoppers, "Prayer and Propaganda: Solomon's Dedication of the Temple and the Deuteronomist's Program," *CBQ* 57, no. 2 (1995): 243, notes that, as confirmed by the prayer of Solomon in the dedication of the temple (cf. 1 Kgs. 8:14-21, 55-61), David and Moses are the two most dominant figures in the DtrH.

18. So, too, Polzin, *Moses and the Deuteronomist*, 33.

Lord set apart the tribe of Levi to carry the Ark of the Covenant of YHWH; to stand before YHWH to minister and to bless in his name, unto this day. Therefore, Levi has neither portion nor inheritance with his brothers; YHWH, he is his inheritance just as YHWH your God spoke to him.

Interestingly, this editorial note in the midst of chapter 10 records the death of Aaron and the transition of the priesthood to Eleazar (v. 6); a short travelogue and record of the calling of the tribe of Levi (vv. 7-8); and finally a comment about Levi's noninheritance in the land (v. 9). Now, while it could easily be argued that Moses recorded this, the telling part is again the phrase "unto this day" in verse 8. As in our discussion in chapter 4, this phrase would make the most sense coming from a later time period. Furthermore, the information recorded in this parenthetical aside is all about the history of the Levites, something Abiathar and his family would have been familiar with. Of course, this editorial notation on its own does not prove a particular date for the editing of Deuteronomy, for anyone from Moses' day until Jeremiah's ministry could have made this interjection. Moreover, the simple phrase "unto this day" itself may have been the only later addition. However, in light of the editorial notations in chapters 1–4, one is pushed in favor of Abiathar's era when all these possible insertions are considered together.

On the other hand, the evidence in Deuteronomy 11:30 is not as conclusive. There are no fewer than three options as to where this information could have originated: (1) it may have come from a later hand because of the specific Cisjordan geographical information; (2) the spies could have easily given Moses this information; or (3) it may have been common knowledge from the region in general. Whatever the situation, the questionable editorial work of 11:30 is offset by the clear editorial hand(s) at work in chapters 31–34.

Deuteronomy 31–34

Unlike chapters 1–4, the editorial work that appears in the final narrative portions of Deuteronomy is a little harder to pinpoint to a particular author/editor. For example, it is pretty clear that chapters 31–34 had varying levels of editorial and/or authorial work; however, a number of possibilities have been offered to explain it. For example, from earliest times, chapter 34, which records Moses' death, has been scrutinized in this regard. Did Moses record his own death (a common assumption in the early church) or did Joshua add this chapter (cf. *Baba Bathra* 14b)?[19] How could a later author know what was seen by Moses on Mt. Nebo and what YHWH had said to him (34:1-4)? Of course, one could speculate that Joshua, as in the past, had gone with Moses up on Mt. Nebo and had seen and heard those things that were later recorded before leaving Moses to die alone—thus the reason "no man knows his burial place" (v. 6). However, if my argument above is accurate, the appearance of the phrase "unto this day" also in 34:6 denotes a much later time, perhaps even than that of Joshua. As such, Abiathar's involvement makes sense.

There is, however, a text in the closing chapters of Deuteronomy that may show evidence of a late editorial insertion perhaps from the time of Jeremiah. In 29:24-28 [Heb], Moses recounts what the response of the nations will be when Israel is taken into exile. Verse

---

19. For example, Jerome (342–420) in his *Adversus Helvidium* 1.7 writes, "Likewise at the end of Deuteronomy, 'And Moses the servant of the LORD died there in the land of Moab according to the word of the LORD, and he buried him in Geth, near the house of Phogor. And no one knows his burial place until this day.' We must certainly understand by 'this day' the time of the composition of the history, whether you prefer the view that Moses was the author of the Pentateuch or that Ezra restored it. In either case I make no objections." As cited by Geoghegan, *Time, Place, and Purpose*, 20. See also comments by Jeffrey Tigay, "The Significance of the End of Deuteronomy (Deuteronomy 34:10-12)," in *Texts, Temples, and Traditions: A Tribute to Menahem Haran*, ed. Michael V. Fox, et al. (Winona Lake, IN: Eisenbrauns, 1996), 137–43.

27 states, "And YHWH will uproot them from their land, in anger and in rage and in great wrath, and he will cast them into another land, *as it is this day*" (italics added). Here the Hebrew phrase כיום הזה (*kayyôm hazzeh*) is different than the phrase we examined in our previous chapter, which we have seen appears in a wide range of possible eras. However, the phrase used here in verse 27 is one Jeremiah often used (11:5; 25:18; 32:20; 44:6, 23). Thus, the final notation "as it is this day" may reflect the editor's note either about the exile of the Northern Kingdom in 722 BCE or, more likely, the exile of Judah in the early sixth century. In this case, Jeremiah would be the best candidate for being the editor.

Next, editorial insertions at 31:9-10a, 14-16a, 22-25, 30; 32:44-46a, 48-52 vary as to content and possible eras of insertion. There can be no doubt that these are recorded some time after Moses' death. Again, the question is whether they are the editorial notes of Joshua or of a later hand. The notations dealing directly with the priests (i.e., in 31:9-10a, 24-30) causes one to prefer a priestly editor, although one cannot be certain or dogmatic here. If our earlier assertion is correct concerning the editorial work and rhetorical purposes of the editor of chapters 1–4, then a priestly editor would be preferred.

Our final area of possible editorial activity in Deuteronomy is in the blessing of chapter 33 that Moses prayed over the nation before his death. Now, to be certain, there is nothing that would preclude most of what appears in chapter 33 as coming predominantly from the hand of Moses; however, Moses' blessings on the tribes are nonetheless interesting. The editorial notes found in 33:1, 4 are similar to those found throughout the book and are for the most part inconclusive when trying to determine an editor. Nevertheless, the extended blessings found in verses 8-11 and 13-17 may tell us something about who edited the material. Perhaps the editor added a few extra words for his own tribe? Unfortunately, verses 8-11 record the extended blessing of Levi, and verses 13-17, of Joseph (i.e., Ephraim and Manasseh)—both of whom are related to our proposed editors—priests such as Abiathar or Jeremiah, and Joshua, an Ephraimite (cf. 1 Chr. 7:20-27). Thus, we are no further ahead in our assessment of this particular chapter. Indeed, it is possible that Moses simply extended his blessings on these two tribes and nothing more.

Conclusion

We can conclude our assessment of the book of Deuteronomy by noting that it is indeed possible that Joshua, Abiathar, and Jeremiah may have all had a hand in the editorial history of the book, but nothing precludes us from asserting that Moses played a major role in contributing to the "proto" form of Deuteronomy. To be sure, though, when it comes to the editing of the bulk of the work, the best rhetorical evidence is for someone from David's era such as Abiathar. However, the temporal proximity that Joshua shared with Moses does not rule him out for several of the closing remarks found in chapter 34. While some of our assessment has proven fruitful, the book of Joshua may give up more of its secrets with a similar analysis. It is to this enterprise that I now turn.

6

The Editing of the Book of Joshua

The examination of Joshua as a literary work might begin with the form of the whole and the form of its parts and the relation between them. . . . it is a literary work that belongs to a series, a book attached by literal repetition to the books that precede and follow. It becomes obvious, then, that the books are about people and eras, real people or types, and epochs that follow each other but also clearly overlap. The parts of the book, similarly, are phases in a single career and periods in the era that follow each other and backtrack to earlier times.[1]

Brian Peckham's assertions indeed provide a summation of how the book of Joshua interconnects with the DtrH. Yet, the book of Joshua *begins* the block of material in the Hebrew Bible known as the *nebî'îm* (the "Prophets"). Jewish tradition assigns this book's authorship to Joshua—a position held by many within more conservative circles. Conversely, mainline scholarship has assigned it to Dtr. In keeping

---

1. Brian Peckham, "The Significance of the Book of Joshua in Noth's Theory of the Deuteronomistic History," in *The History of Israel's Traditions: The Heritage of Martin Noth*, ed. Steven L. McKenzie and M. Patrick Graham, JSOTSup 182 (Sheffield: Sheffield Academic Press, 1994), 229.

with the conclusions in my previous chapter, I believe that large portions of the material in the book that bears his name originated with Joshua or someone close to him.[2] The accounts of the conquest, especially those of Jericho and Ai, betray eyewitness-type material. Yet, this eyewitness content should not detract one from the similarities in authorial intent and concerns that point to a later editorial hand for the larger DtrH.

Another concern is the question of the book's prophetic nature. If the book of Joshua serves as the first book within the *nebî'îm*, does this force us to label both the book and the man "prophetic"? To be sure, Joshua does not have the prophetic flare of 1 and 2 Kings, but prophetic aspects are nonetheless present. In light of our earlier discussion on the prophetic tendencies of Dtr, it should not be surprising to find Joshua, to a degree, presented with a prophetic nuance. Of course, the prophetic aspect of Joshua the man rests upon one's presuppositional stance on this topic.[3] Nonetheless, at least textually, Joshua's actions and words do in fact betray his prophet-like stature. For example, in 3:13 Joshua predicts the parting of the Jordan River when the priests' feet touch the water's edge, which in turn is fulfilled in 3:15-16.[4] Or one could also marshal the prophetic-like nature of Joshua's controversial "longest day" in chapter 10; Joshua's prediction of the chaos of the judges' period (23:12-16); or his closing

---

2. For a discussion on the prehistory of the book of Joshua, see Martin Noth, *Das Buch Joshua*, 2d ed., HAT 7 (Tübingen: Mohr, 1953), 11–16.

3. For a discussion on how the book of Joshua meets the criteria of "prophecy," see Gordon Oeste, "The Shaping of a Prophet: Joshua in the Deuteronomistic History," in *Prophets, Prophecy, and Ancient Israelite Historiography*, ed. Mark J. Boda and Lissa M. Wray Beal (Winona Lake, IN: Eisenbrauns, 2013), 23–41.

4. Ibid., 31–38. Oeste goes on to give a number of examples where these types of prophetic events occur in the book of Joshua. For example, Joshua's intercession for Israel after the sin of Achan parallels that of Moses and Samuel—YHWH responds with specific instructions (Joshua 7; note also the similar role that Gad plays for David in 2 Samuel 24); the curse on Jericho and its fulfillment (cf. 1 Kgs. 16:34); Joshua predicts that Israel will be unable to keep the covenant (24:19-20), which is fulfilled in the book of Judges (Judg. 2:1-5, 10-11; 3:6-8; 10:13-14); and, of course, his prophet-like speech in chapter 24.

speech of chapter 24. We have no reason not to assign many of these and other acts to Joshua, acts that Dtr *later* incorporated into his history. Nevertheless, there can be no doubt that portions of Joshua were updated at a period subsequent to Joshua.

Evidence of Editorial Activity: Joshua 1–5

In our discussion on the phrase "unto this day" in chapter 4 above, I presented several instances where Abiathar fits the role of editor for the book of Joshua. What is more, even though the books of Joshua, Judges, and Samuel fall within the "Former Prophets," they do not reflect the clear prophetic underpinnings that 1 and 2 Kings display. This should not be surprising in light of the possibility of Jeremiah's dominant role in compiling the latter book—after all, he was both priest *and* prophet. Conversely, Abiathar, who served mainly as a high priest of sorts under David's rule, appears to have not been as focused on the prophetic aspects unless, of course, they were already present in his extant sources. Therefore, the book of Joshua is in keeping with the narrative style of the first three books of the *nebî'îm* and the way Abiathar apparently liked to record his history.

The book of Joshua begins with an editorial notation.[5] Joshua 1:1 shows signs of later editorial work, especially when viewed in light of Judg. 1:1 and 2 Sam. 1:1. Because I argue in chapter 7 that Judg. 1:1 is part of Abiathar's polemic against the Saulides and propaganda for David's rule, we need to assess all three verses together, working somewhat in reverse order. The texts read as follows (italics mine in all three verses):

---

5. Rudolf Smend, "The Law and the Nations: A Contribution to Deuteronomistic Tradition History," *Reconsidering Israel and Judah: Recent Studies on the Deuteronomistic History*, ed. Gary N. Knoppers and J. Gordon McConville (Winona Lake, IN: Eisenbrauns, 2000), 96, attributes Josh. 1:1-9 and the ending of the book of Deuteronomy to the work of Dtr.

Now it came to pass after the death of Moses the servant of YHWH that YHWH spoke to Joshua the son of Nun, Moses' servant *saying* . . . (Josh. 1:1)

Now it came to pass after the death of Joshua that the sons of Israel inquired of YHWH *saying*: "Who will go up for us against the Canaanites first to fight against them?" (Judg. 1:1)

Now it came to pass after the death of Saul when David had returned from the slaughter of the Amalekites that David stayed in Ziklag for two days. (2 Sam. 1:1)

The first phrase in all three of these texts in the Hebrew is exactly the same: [X] ויהי אחרי מות (*wayᵉhî ʾaḥărê môṯ* [X]). Furthermore, in the first two, the phrase is followed by the same word, *saying* (לאמר *lēʾmōr*). In the book of Joshua, YHWH speaks to Joshua, whereas in the book of Judges, the people speak to YHWH. It is very important to note that this phrase only appears in these three books of the DtrH.[6] Clearly, the author/editor of this portion of the DtrH wanted his readers to draw a connection between these three books—perhaps as *his* contribution to Israel's history? Not surprisingly, this phrase is used to mark the death of the three dominant leaders of Israel up until the time of David.[7] Moses was the giver of the law, Joshua was the conquest leader, and Saul was Israel's first king. In each case, the death of the leader marked a key transition in Israel's history.[8] This is no doubt the reason why Samuel's death is not recorded as such. Although Samuel was a great leader and marked the transition from

6. This phrase does appear in Gen. 25:11 when noting the death of Abraham. The editorial implication for this singular appearance outside of the DtrH is beyond the scope of this present work but may indicate that Abiathar was familiar with how the Pentateuch framed the death of Israel's founding father. Of course, some may argue that the borrowing is in the opposite direction.

7. The formula, "and [X] slept with his fathers," which is used for David's death and the kings that followed him, differs immensely. I will deal with this in ch. 10.

8. So, too, Barry Webb, *The Book of Judges: An Integrated Reading*, JSOTSup 46 (Sheffield: JSOT, 1987), 210.

the judges' period to the monarchy, his final years and his death were eclipsed by an overlapping with Saul's rule—the first king. The use of this phrase alone seems to point to an editor or compiler of this block of material who was contemporaneous with David; David's death notice being a key indicator of a different editor.

The connection between these three verses is also important in light of the rhetorical function of Judg. 1:1. This verse is an integral part of the inclusio of Judges, whereby the author focuses on the tribe of Judah. If my findings about Abiathar being the author of the book of Judges are correct (see ch. 7), then his use of the phrase in Judges leads one to the conclusion that he could easily have played a role in editing the books of Joshua and Samuel as well. This conclusion is further supported by what follows in the book of Joshua.

In Josh. 1:7 and 18, we also find a unifying theme and an inclusio of sorts that holds the first chapter together, namely the people's and YHWH's command to Joshua to be courageous. The actual phrase is "only be strong and courageous" (רק חזק ואמיץ *raq ḥāzaq wᵉˀĕmaṣ*).[9] A truncated form of this phrase also occurs in Josh. 1:6, 9, and 10:25 and parallels Moses' commands to Joshua in Deut. 31:6, 7, 23.[10] Moreover, in Josh. 1:9, just before the phrase "be strong and courageous," we find YHWH's command to Joshua: "Have I not commanded you" (הלוא צויתיך *hălōˀ ṣiwwîṯîḵā*). Interestingly, the only other time these two phrases appear together is in 2 Sam. 13:28 (slightly altered). Here, Absalom is commanding his men to execute Amnon for the rape of Absalom's sister, Tamar (2 Samuel 13). Based upon its use in Joshua, it appears that the author of 2 Samuel is trying to present Absalom as a "god-like" character in a

---

9. Jeffrey C. Geoghegan, *The Time, Place, and Purpose of the Deuteronomistic History: The Evidence of "Until This Day,"* BJS 347 (Providence, RI: Brown University Press, 2006), 153 n.25, 154–55, argues that the use of רק ("only") shows Dtr editorial activity.

10. The Chronicler places this phrase from Deuteronomy on the lips of David to Solomon (twice; cf. 1 Chr. 22:13; 28:20) and on the lips of Hezekiah to his people (2 Chr. 32:7).

negative sense. Absalom usurps the power to execute his brother from the God-appointed king and then goes on to usurp the God-given throne of David.[11] Again, Abiathar would have witnessed these events. Abiathar had a vested interest in protecting his friend David from a killer—much like David protected Abiathar from the killer, Saul. What is more, as will be demonstrated in chapter 9, the author of 2 Samuel 14–19 wants his reader to juxtapose David's struggle with Absalom with Joshua's entry and conquest of the land!

Next, the parallels between Josh. 1:4; Deut. 1:7; and 11:24 in identifying the boundaries of the promised land (i.e., from Lebanon to the great river Euphrates), along with the phrase "which I swore to your fathers" (*'ăšer nišba'tî la'ăḇōṯām*) in 1:6 (see also Deut. 10:11; 31:20; and in part in Deut. 1:8), shows that the editor was familiar with the introduction and content of Deuteronomy. Indeed, Gordon Wenham concludes, "So close is the affinity of outlook between Deuteronomy and Joshua that it is reasonable to suppose that both books were edited by the same man or school."[12] Also, it is worth noting that it was only under the rule of David that the promised land came close to reaching these boundaries (cf. 1 Kgs. 4:21).[13] Thus, it appears that this first chapter in Joshua, much like the first chapter of Deuteronomy, shows evidence of purposeful editorial work. This may not prove Abiathar's involvement, but if he was the editor of the

11. A number of scholars have written on the idea of Joshua as "an ideal royal figure." Cf. Gerald E. Gerbrandt, *Kingship According to the Deuteronomistic History*, SBLDS 87 (Atlanta: Scholars, 1986), 116–23; Moshe Weinfeld, *Deuteronomy and the Deuteronomistic School* (Oxford: Clarendon, 1972), 246, 359; Richard D. Nelson, "Josiah in the Book of Joshua," *JBL* 100, no. 4 (1981): 531–40; and J. Roy Porter, "The Succession of Joshua," in Knoppers and McConville, eds., *Reconsidering Israel and Judah*, 139–62.

12. Gordon J. Wenham, "The Deuteronomic Theology of the Book of Joshua," *JBL* 90, no. 2 (1971): 148.

13. For a discussion on the tensions between the boundaries of the promised land as promised to the Patriarchs and those actually gained by the nation of Israel, see Yehezkel Kaufmann, *The Biblical Account of the Conquest of Palestine* (Jerusalem: Magnes, 1953), 46–51.

introductory material of Deuteronomy, as I have argued above, then it is very possible that he did so here as well.

A number of other phrases appear within this opening chapter that betrays the compiler's familiarity with the book of Deuteronomy. In the context of cultic or legal concerns, the idea of "not turning to the right or the left" (cf. Deut. 5:32; 17:11, 20; 28:14; 2 Kgs. 22:2; 2 Chr. 34:2)[14] appears not only as part of YHWH's *command* to Joshua, but also as an inclusio to the book of Joshua (Josh. 1:7; 23:6).[15] It does not appear again in the DtrH until its use as part of the *assessment* of Josiah in 2 Kgs. 22:2 ("he did not turn to the right or the left")—a book whose editorial work is connected to Jeremiah (see ch. 10). Several possible conclusions can be drawn from this data: (1) Abiathar and Jeremiah separately borrowed the phrase from Deuteronomy for the books of Joshua and Kings respectively; (2) Jeremiah adopted the phrase from Abiathar's earlier use in the books of Deuteronomy and Joshua; or (3) Jeremiah may have been the one who used the phrase in both cases, not only to frame the book of Joshua but also to draw a parallel between Joshua and Josiah. In this vein, Richard Nelson and Jeffrey Geoghegan insist that the Josianic redactor of the books of Joshua and Kings wanted to connect these two great leaders through a series of acts and events.[16] However, if it is the later Dtr who is doing the editing of these books at this point, why did he use the phrase for Josiah in an *assessment* fashion and only as a *command* for Joshua? Moreover, why did Dtr not give this glowing assessment for some of the other great leaders of Israel's history, especially the prototypical king, David?[17] As we will demonstrate,

---

14. The Chronicler borrows the phrase from 2 Kings 22.
15. The inclusio-like phrase "to the Great Sea towards the setting of the sun" also appears in Josh. 1:4 and 23:4. For a detail analysis of the different phrases and connections between the beginning and the end of the book of Joshua, see Peckham, "Significance," 229–32.
16. Nelson, "Josiah in the Book of Joshua," 531–40, esp. 535–37; Geoghegan, *Time, Place, and Purpose*, 93–95.

more parallels can be drawn between Joshua and David, as opposed to Josiah. Furthermore, if our theory is correct and Abiathar did compile the books of Joshua, Judges, and Samuel, then perhaps the lacuna for David is due to the fact that Abiathar gave none of Israel's great leaders this type of assessment; neither to Joshua, nor to his friend David, and certainly not for Saul. Abiathar knew David and his faults, especially with Bathsheba and Uriah. Similarly, Joshua had also failed in the Gibeonite fiasco that had directly impacted the tribal allotment of Abiathar/Benjamin (see more below). However, if Jeremiah is doing the final editing and compiling of the DtrH, whose work is predominantly isolated to the book of Kings, then he easily could have picked up on the use of the phrase from his sources, most likely of which was Deuteronomy, and applied it to Josiah only.

We may conclude this portion of the discussion by saying that while any of these solutions are possible, none are overly satisfying, although Abiathar's non-use of the phrase is more convincing than Jeremiah's failure to assign it to either Joshua or David. At best, it is inconclusive; however, an earlier compilation of the material by Abiathar is not precluded by a late redaction by Jeremiah. It may even be best to conclude that the similarities between the early DtrH books (especially Deuteronomy) and Kings may have more to do with the authors' priestly interests in the law and the fact they are working from the same priestly tradition in Anathoth.[18]

---

17. "Superlative evaluations" appear for Moses, Solomon, Hezekiah, and Josiah (cf. Deut. 34:10; 1 Kgs. 3:12; 2 Kgs. 18:5; 23:25). One could argue that David is praised somewhat in this manner (see 1 Kgs. 14:9). In the case of Solomon, the elevation of his status has to do with his wisdom, not the greatness of his reign or his following of YHWH. Cf. also Weinfeld, *Deuteronomy and the Deuteronomic School*, 359.

18. Contra Gary N. Knoppers, "Rethinking the Relationship between Deuteronomy and the Deuteronomistic History: The Case of Kings," *CBQ* 63, no. 3 (2001): 393–415, who concludes that the DtrH "reflects the concerns and priorities of scribes and governmental officials at Jerusalem's royal court" (408). There is nothing within the DtrH that precludes a priestly and prophetic focus and interest.

While we could go on listing a number of words and phrases in the opening chapter of Joshua that find connections with the book of Deuteronomy, other factors may yield more fruit. For example, it is clear that *someone* wanted to present Joshua as another Moses, but the question is, Who?[19] The character parallels are obvious: (1) the author presents Joshua as hearing directly from YHWH (1:1-9);[20] (2) he makes sure that Joshua reminds the people of the words/law of Moses (1:12-18); (3) he records that Joshua, like Moses, sends spies into the land (cf. 2:1; Numbers 13); (4) he highlights the crossing of the Jordan River with YHWH performing a Red Sea-crossing type of miracle (3:13-17; 4:23; Exodus 15); (5) he records Joshua meeting an angel of the Lord (5:13-15) who quotes the exact phrase that was spoken to Moses at the burning bush: "remove your sandals from your feet for the place where you are standing is holy" (cf. 5:15; Exod. 3:5);[21] and (6) finally, Joshua is presented as a leader who is vital to the conquest of the promised land just as Moses had been in the conquest of the Transjordan.[22]

In this context, the opening verses of chapter 1 are important to the author's purposes. YHWH reminds Joshua of the Patriarchal promises and commissions him to conquer the land—the land that YHWH had sworn to give to their fathers (1:1-9; cf. Deut. 31:7). Interestingly, this connection of "swearing oaths" to the "fathers" has its last appearance in Josh. 21:43-45.[23] The author's use of the promise to the fathers

---

19. For a detailed list of these parallels, see Wenham, "Deuteronomic Theology of the Book of Joshua," 145–46.

20. There are a number of other parallels that could be listed. For example, notice that Joshua holds forth his spear during the battle at Ai in the same way that Moses oversees the defeat of the Amalekites by holding up his hands during the battle (Josh. 8:26; Exod. 17:12).

21. There are only slight spelling variations between the two phrases in Exodus 3 and Joshua 5. Some of these differences could have something to do with the time gap between the recording of Moses' material and that of the editor of this portion of the DtrH.

22. See further the work of Porter, "The Succession of Joshua," 139–62; and Robert Polzin, *Moses and the Deuteronomist: A Literary Study of the Deuteronomic History I. Deuteronomy, Joshua, Judges* (Bloomington: Indiana University Press, 1993), 74–80.

as an inclusio here serves as a reminder to trust in YHWH for the fulfillment of YHWH's word—the ultimate fulfillment of which came in the period of David!

Returning to the question that we asked previously: Can we figure out who wanted to present Joshua as this "Moses-like" figure? Did Joshua do it himself or was it the work of Abiathar? In attempting to answer these questions, perhaps one final phrase may be of assistance, one that appears exclusively in Joshua and only in these opening chapters (i.e., 1:5; 3:7), and which reads, "Just as I have been with Moses, I will be with you" (כאשר הייתי עם משה אהיה עמך *kā'ăšer hāyîtî 'im mōšeh 'ehyeh 'immāk*). This phrase reflects the author's intent to show that YHWH was going to be with Joshua in his conquest of the promised land as YHWH had been with Moses in the conquest of the Transjordan. While the author *may* be Joshua himself, it may be that Abiathar was attempting to draw connections beyond the book of Joshua for rhetorical purposes. In this vein, the other great conquest leader of Israel, whom YHWH was with, was none other than David from the tribe of Judah (see also Judg. 1:1; 20:18, 28). The author of Samuel, no doubt Abiathar (see ch. 8), makes it clear that YHWH was with David from his earliest days in fighting the enemies of Israel (2 Sam. 5:10; see also 1 Samuel 17; 18:7; 30:8). Moreover, it was David who not only sought the direction of YHWH through general inquiry (1 Sam. 23:9-11; 30:7-9; 2 Sam. 2:1), but also in his efforts of conquest by asking YHWH directly: "Shall I go up" to conquer my enemies? (cf. 1 Sam. 30:8; 2 Sam. 5:19).[24] Not surprisingly, Abiathar played a key role in receiving the

---

23. See further, Thomas Römer, "Deuteronomy in Search of Origins," in Knoppers and McConville, eds., *Reconsidering Israel and Judah*, 132–33.

24. This phrase is only used elsewhere in the DtrH for Jehoshaphat in 1 Kgs. 22:6. This may reflect an ongoing tradition of editorial work as opposed to pointing to Jeremiah. One would expect Jeremiah to use this phrase for Josiah's expansion as well if the phrase originated with the prophet.

word of YHWH for David because he was the bearer of the ephod at that time. As noted above, it was through the conquests of David that the nation of Israel reached its greatest limits, which in many respects allowed the promises of the Patriarchs to come to fruition (1 Kgs. 4:21)—the same promises that are reiterated in Josh. 1:6. Therefore, in recording the opening chapter of Joshua, Abiathar points forward to his own day and age when his friend, David, served in the office of Joshua as the one to complete the divine commands to conquer Canaan. For indeed, the judges' period had been a complete disaster in this regard (see the discussion in ch. 7).

Next, Joshua 2 records the account of Rahab the harlot and the two spies. The narrative here is in keeping with eyewitness material and very likely comes from a source from the period of Joshua. However, this does not eliminate the possibility of later editorial work. For example, similar to our discussion on Deuteronomy in the previous chapter, Josh. 2:10 once again brings up the motif of Sihon and Og, who were defeated by Moses in the Transjordan.[25] Some of the other language that may be telling of later redactional work is found in Rahab's declaration in 2:11. Here, Rahab states that the God of the Israelites was "God in heaven above and on earth beneath" (אלהים בשמים ממעל ועל־הארץ מתחת *ʾĕlōhîm baššāmayim mimmaʿal weʿal-hāʾreṣ mittāḥat*). This phrase, unique to the DtrH, only occurs in one other place, namely 1 Kgs. 8:23.[26] In this latter passage, Solomon is praying a prayer to YHWH at the dedication of the temple. Now, apart from the fact that David and Solomon were direct descendants of Rahab,[27] it appears that the author desired to connect the strong

---

25. Antony F. Campbell and Mark A. O'Brien, *Unfolding the Deuteronomistic History: Origins, Upgrades, Present Text* (Minneapolis: Fortress Press, 2000), 129, also note the possibility of this being a later insertion.

26. So, too, ibid., 111.

27. Solomon is actually the great-great-great-grandson of Rahab and Salmon (cf. Ruth 4:20-22; Matt. 1:5).

priestly language reminiscent of Genesis 1 to Rahab in an effort to elevate her spiritual status. The date of the second speech is possibly within Abiathar's latter days, but it certainly is within the days of his two sons. Either one could have included the words of Solomon, based upon language in their father's work.[28]

A further connection between Joshua's and David's lifetimes appears in the verse that follows. In Josh. 2:12, Rahab makes the spies swear to her by YHWH that they will preserve her family when Israel attacks Jericho. The only other place where this similar language appears is in 1 Sam. 24:21, when Saul makes David swear by YHWH that he will preserve Saul's family after David comes to the throne. The two accounts record someone taking an oath in the name of YHWH for the purpose of preserving life, but more specifically, family members. Again, the author draws a connection between the conquest period/Rahab and the life of David. In a similar vein, slight variations of the phrase involving oath taking occur canonically from the book of Joshua to the early reign of Solomon in 1 Kings (cf. 9:19; Judg. 21:7; 1 Sam. 28:10; 2 Sam. 19:7; 1 Kgs. 1:17, 30; 2:8, 23, 42).[29] Whereas these may vary in context from general oath taking to covenant making, the interesting aspect here is where this phrase appears—the very period I have proposed that Abiathar and his sons were doing their editorial work! This chronological connection for the editing of this portion of Joshua is further bolstered by the editor's use of covenantal-type language.

In this regard, the idea of "showing kindness" (חֶסֶד ḥesed) to Rahab and her family appears twice in Josh. 2:12. While the meaning of the term חֶסֶד is notoriously difficult to interpret, throughout the DtrH

---

28. One of the main problems in identifying exact language within a biblical speech is whether or not the biblical account is a verbatim quotation or whether the authors took liberties to get the gist of the speech by adding their own wording. Even though I feel it is the latter, I still believe that the biblical speakers did say something very close to what is recorded.

29. The phrase "swear by YHWH" appears only in Zeph. 1:5 and Gen. 24:3 outside of the DtrH.

it seems to connote some type of covenant loyalty or favor. Again, the dominant use of the phrase appears in the early portions of the DtrH (Josh. 2:12; Judg. 8:35; 2 Sam. 3:8; 9:1, 3, 7; 10:2; 1 Kgs. 2:7 with variations).[30] As a matter of fact, all forms of חסד in the DtrH appear predominantly in Deuteronomy to 1 Kings 8 (Deut. 5:10; 7:9, 12; Josh. 2:12, 14; Judg. 1:24; 8:35; 1 Sam. 15:6; 20:8, 14, 15; 2 Sam. 2:5, 6; 3:8; 7:15; 9:1, 3, 7; 10:2; 15:20; 16:17; 22:26, 51; 1 Kgs. 2:7; 3:6; 4:10; 8:23; 20:31; note also its use in Ruth 1:8; 2:20; 3:10).[31] Note, however, that the appearance of the term in 1 Kgs. 20:31 is only recollecting an earlier period when חסד is said to have been the custom of Israel's kings. Whoever is using this concept, at least in the DtrH, appears to have been responsible for most of the editing or compiling up until the early reign of Solomon.

The final phrase of Joshua 2—"all the inhabitants of the land" (כל־ישבי הארץ *kol-yōšbê hā'āreṣ*)—not only serves as an inclusio for the dialogic section of chapter 2 (i.e., vv. 9-24) but may also point to the final period of editing under Jeremiah. Moreover, we also see the same phrase appearing on the lips of the Gibeonites in Josh. 9:24. This phrase appears only here in the DtrH and four times in Jeremiah. The verses from the book of Joshua read as follows:

> And she [Rahab] said to the men, "I know that YHWH has given to you the land and that the dread of you has fallen upon us and that *all the inhabitants of the land* have melted away before you." (2:9)

> And they [the spies] said to Joshua, "Surely YHWH has given all the land into our hands, and also *all the inhabitants of the land* have melted away before us." (2:24)

30. The phrase, with variations, also appears in Gen. 20:13; 21:23; 24:12; and 1 Chr. 19:2, with the Chronicles' passage paralleling 2 Sam. 10:2.
31. In the Tetrateuch, חסד appears in Genesis (11x); Exodus (4x); Leviticus (1x); Numbers (2x). Outside of the Tetrateuch חסד has the following frequency: 1 and 2 Chronicles (14x); Ezra (3x); Nehemiah (5x); Esther (2x); Job (3x); Psalms (128x); Proverbs (11x); Isaiah (8x); Jeremiah (6x); Lamentations (2x); Daniel (2x); Hosea (6x); Joel (1x); Jonah (2x); Micah (3x); Zechariah (1x).

> And they [the Gibeonites] answered Joshua and said, "Because it was certainly declared to your servants that YHWH your God had commanded Moses his servant to give to you all the land and to exterminate *all the inhabitants of the land* before you, therefore we feared exceedingly for our lives because of you and we have done this thing." (9:24)

The fact that the editor used this phrase as an inclusio for the dialogue between Rahab and the spies shows a level of intent in the organization of the material. Furthermore, the fact that three different people/groups use the same phrase is more apt to indicate editorial work than actual verbatim dialogue. Jeremiah comes to the fore in this regard because of the relative frequency in which the prophet uses this same phrase in his own work (cf. Jer. 1:14; 13:13; 25:29, 30).[32] In every occurrence in the book of Jeremiah, it is in direct speech/dialogue from YHWH and in the context of judgment! We have already noted the possibility of Jeremiah's use of distinct phraseology in quoted speech in chapter 4 above. Of course, it is possible that this phrase was used by the original author or an earlier editor. Indeed, one could argue that Joshua or Abiathar actually used it first, based upon its singular usage in Num. 33:52.[33] Then again, there is nothing barring Jeremiah from borrowing it from the books of Numbers or Joshua. Nevertheless, such instances do cause one to seriously consider what input Jeremiah had in the final editing of the earlier material.

While the connections to David in the opening two chapters of Joshua appear subtle, as the narrative develops this subtlety begins to change. We also begin to see more evidence of who the author may be. Indeed, the conquest of Jericho, Ai, Bethel, and the Gibeonite

---

32. The phrase also appears in Joel 1:14; 2:1; Zeph. 1:18; and Ps. 33:14.
33. I realize that the issue of dating the material in the Pentateuch is a much-debated area within biblical studies. However, it is possible that if a "proto-Pentateuch" existed before the putative "J" or "E" sources, then this phrase may have been part of that source.

fiasco reflect more about Abiathar and David than one might think. Chapters 3–5 turn to the process of preparing to take the land of Canaan. Here the priests take a decisive leadership role, with the Ark of the Covenant playing a key visual part of the Jordan crossing. In chapters 3 and 4 alone the priests (כהנים *kōhănîm*) and the Ark/Ark of the Covenant (ארון־הברית *'ărôn-habbᵉrît*) are referenced directly no fewer than twelve and sixteen times respectively and another nine and ten times respectively in chapter 6.[34] Chapter 5 focuses on the keeping of Passover and the circumcision of the nation before entering the land. While it is very likely that Joshua contributed to the source material of this portion of the account, especially the basic content of the dialogue between him and YHWH, it was still up to either Joshua or an editor to choose what to include in the final form. It goes without saying that editors and compilers were selective in what they included from their source material (cf. 2 Sam. 1:18; 1 Kgs. 11:41; 14:19, 29; 15:7, 23, 31, etc.). The fact that this section brings the cultic sphere to the forefront of the narrative may be telling of the biases of the editor. Moreover, in chapter 4 above, we have already discussed the presence of the phrase "unto this day" in relation to Abiathar's possible editing of portions of Joshua 4–6 (cf. Josh. 4:9; 5:9; 6:25).

The Conquest: Joshua 6–11

As noted in the above discussion, the opening six chapters in ways reflect the work of a priest, both in content and motive. At the

34. See also Brian Peckham, "The Composition of Joshua 3–4," *CBQ* 46, no. 3 (1984): 413–31; Jay A. Wilcoxen, "Narrative Structure and Cult Legend: A Study of Joshua 1–6," in *Transitions in Biblical Scholarship*, ed. J. C. Rylaarsdam (Chicago: University of Chicago Press, 1968), 43–70, esp. 47–70; Nicolai Winther-Nielson, "The Miraculous Grammar of Joshua 3–4," in *Biblical Hebrew and Discourse Linguistics*, ed. Robert D. Berger (Winona Lake, IN: Eisenbrauns, 1994), 300–319; and Hans-Joachim Kraus, "Gilgal: A Contribution to the History of Worship in Israel," in Knoppers and McConville, eds., *Reconsidering Israel and Judah*, 163–78 (German: "Gilgal: Ein Beitrag zur Kultusgeschichte Israels," *VT* 1, no. 3 [1951]: 181–99).

same time, it appears that aspects of the narrative reflect eyewitness testimony from the period of Joshua, especially portions related to the battle scenes. Here Walter Dietrich's concerns are pertinent. He notes, "the historical horizon of a redaction is as broad as the combined horizons of its sources."[35] Indeed, in each account we wrestle with the events of the distant period of the conquest and at the same time try to assess a history recorded at a later date. It appears that this history is told in a selective manner not only for history's sake, but also with a rhetorical purpose in mind. Yet, despite this dichotomy, what we have before us is the canonical text. Therefore, we need to discuss why the compiler included certain accounts while eliminating others. A further examination of the actual content of the rest of Joshua will perhaps help alleviate some of the ambiguity.

Joshua 6–11 comprises the three-pronged conquest of Canaan with the destruction of Jericho, Ai, and the Gibeonite fiasco occupying the majority of the narrative from 6:1—10:27. Indeed, only sixteen verses, which are very formulaic, are devoted to the rest of the southern conquest (cf. Josh. 10:28, 30, 32, 35, 39 for the formula).[36] It is clear that the conquest of these central cities was of interest to the author. Furthermore, Josh. 10:1 and 11:1 also follow a pattern whereby the kings of the south and north form their respective coalitions. Where the first three accounts of Jericho, Ai, and Gibeon are drawn out, it appears that the author wanted to get through the last two military campaigns very quickly.[37] To be sure, there must have been a number of noteworthy events as Israel encountered the Canaanites that did not make it into the book. But why is so much space devoted to the conquest of Jericho, Ai, and the defense of the Gibeonites at the

---

35. Walter Dietrich, "Martin Noth and the Future of the Deuteronomistic History," in McKenzie and Graham, eds., *History of Israel's Traditions*, 163.

36. The entire conquest covered more than seven years. Note further the formulaic expression of Josh. 10:28-41 and ch. 11 (esp. v. 18).

37. The northern campaign is covered in fifteen verses (Josh. 11:1-15).

beginning of the southern campaign? The answer to this question may lie in the compiler's desire to highlight his home region.

In chapter 4 above, we looked at the geographical perspective of the author of the DtrH. We concluded that he was most likely from the tribal region of Benjamin or Judah, perhaps even on the border of these two tribal allotments. Of course, Abiathar, a Benjaminite, not only lived in this region but also became familiar with Judah while traveling as a fugitive with David. Here in the book of Joshua, this factor takes on even more poignancy as we assess the nature of the content of the heart of the conquest narratives. Based upon Josh. 18:21, three of the cities within the tribal allotment of Benjamin included Jericho, Bethel (Ai would be included here; cf. Josh. 8:17), and the cities of Gibeon. What is more, the four Levitical cities for the priestly family of the sons of Kohath in the region of Benjamin were Gibeon, Geba, Almon, and Anathoth (Josh. 21:17-18)![38]

When one takes into account the geographical focus of the conquest narratives, some surprising conclusions can be drawn beyond the facile understanding that what we have here is merely a retelling of the historical events. First, it appears that the compiler of the material wanted his readers to understand how this region was conquered and how YHWH was central in bringing about that conquest (note especially Joshua's longest day in 10:12-14).[39] Second, he wanted his readers to understand why soldiers had died in the process of the conquest of one of those cities, namely Ai. It was not due to the weakness of YHWH; rather, it was the result of sin regarding the accursed thing—by a man from Judah, no less. Third,

---

38. See geographical comments concerning the tribe of Benjamin by Peckham, "Significance," 213–34, esp. 220.

39. For a discussion on the interpretive options for Joshua's longest day, see John Walton, *Ancient Near Eastern Thought and the Old Testament* (Grand Rapids: Baker Academic, 2006), 262–63; Baruch Margalit, "The Day the Sun Did Not Stand Still: A New Look at Joshua x 8–15," *VT* 42, no. 4 (1992): 466–91; John S. Holladay Jr., "The Day(s) the *Moon* Stood Still," *JBL* 87, no. 2 (1968): 166–78.

he wanted his readers to recognize the dangers of not consulting YHWH in important decisions. Much like the issue with the Gibeonites, Joshua had not consulted YHWH as to how to proceed in the conquest of Ai.[40] It was only after YHWH revealed the guilty man by casting lots (?)—no doubt with the aid of a priest—that order and blessing were restored (Josh. 7:14). Fourth, he wanted to explain why the Gibeonites had not been exterminated. Here he makes it clear that Joshua (an Ephraimite) and the elders of Israel had not consulted YHWH (Josh. 9:14). Thus, the author and his offspring were stuck dealing with the Gibeonites in their midst (1 Chr. 21:29; 2 Sam. 21:1-14; etc.).

The above conclusions are bolstered by the language used in Josh. 9:14 to assess the Gibeonite fiasco. The text says that the leaders of Israel—Joshua included—did not "ask from the mouth of YHWH" (ואת־פי יהוה לא שאלו *wᵉet-pî yhwh lōʾ šāʾālû*). Of course, this inquiry should have been mediated by the high priest through the Urim and Thummim (Num. 27:18-21; Deut. 33:8; see also 1 Sam. 28:6; Ezra 2:63; Neh. 7:65). Moses himself had commanded Joshua to inquire of YHWH through Eleazar in this manner (Num. 27:18-21). Fifth, the author wanted to show what happened to Canaanites who joined the covenant people through deception. They became hewers of wood and drawers of water in the service of the house of YHWH (Josh. 9:21, 23, 27). Notice that the author says three times that they are cursed (ארר *ʾārar* v. 23) in this manner. Furthermore, this account must be read in light of the Rahab pericope, whereby she and her family join the covenant people more as equals, exemplified by the fact that Rahab is in the direct lineage of David! She had negotiated her position because of her willingness to accept the sovereignty of

---

40. Here we see another parallel with the book of Deuteronomy (7:2; 20:10-18). Israel was to make no covenants with the Canaanites; Joshua failed in this regard.

YHWH and as a willing participant in the destruction of her own city and people.

One last verse, Josh. 9:26, is germane to our discussion: "And he did to them [the Gibeonites] accordingly, and *he* [Joshua] *delivered them from the hand of the sons of Israel* and they [Israel] did not kill them [the Gibeonites]" (italics mine). The idea of delivering someone into/ from the hand of another (cf. also Josh. 22:31; 24:10) finds parallels elsewhere in the DtrH (as early as Deut. 32:39). For example, in several places the author of Judges uses a similar phrase in recollecting Israel's history of deliverance (e.g., Judg. 2:16; 6:19; 8:24, 34; 9:17). And a variation of the phrase is also used heavily in 1 and 2 Samuel (i.e., 4:8; 7:3, 14; 10:18; 12:10, 11; 14:48; 17:37 [2x]; 2 Sam. 12:7).[41] Throughout, the author prefers to use the verb "to deliver" (נצל *nāṣal*) with the prepositional phrase "from the hand" (מיד *miyyad*). The irony in the text is that YHWH was supposed to deliver the Canaanites into the hands of the Israelites and now, because of their failure to include YHWH in their decision making, Joshua has to deliver the Canaanites from the hand of the Israelites—a picture that will be reversed in the judges' period. Of course, the dominant use of this concept in the books of Joshua, Judges, and Samuel points to someone from Abiathar's era.

Several other important indicators point to a compiler from the priestly class. As we have noted, the central role of the priests both explicitly and implicitly points in this direction. Also, the language at certain junctures seems to intimate this as well. For example, when Achan admits to his deception, he uses very formulaic language used only three times in the Bible. In Josh. 7:20, Achan says, "I have sinned

---

41. The use of the phrase in 1 and 2 Kings may have been borrowed by a later editor like Jeremiah (2 Kgs. 17:39; 18:29, 33, 34, 35 [2x]; 20:6). The phrase also appears in the Tetrateuch (Gen. 32:12; 37:21, 22; Exod. 2:19; 3:8; 18:9, 10; Num. 35:25), which may betray the author's knowledge of these texts. A similar phrase using כף (*kap̄*) appears infrequently (e.g., 2 Sam. 14:16; 19:10; 22:1).

against YHWH" (חטאתי ליהוה‎ ḥāṭāʾtî layhwh). The two other places where this language appears is on the lips of Pharaoh and David (Exod. 10:16; 2 Sam. 12:13). The similar language used in Samuel and Joshua appears purposeful. What we end up with are similar declarations of sin in three of the key periods of Israel's history: the exodus (Pharaoh), conquest (Achan), and the monarchical periods (David).[42] Abiathar could have easily been responsible for the latter two by adopting the language of Exod. 10:16.

We also need to consider the character parallels as they relate to the compiler's greater purposes. As I will demonstrate in chapter 7, character parallels, prevalent in Joshua, Judges, and Samuel, seem to be the author's literary technique of choice. This again points to an author with an overarching intent and purpose and who may have recorded good portions of these three books. Here in Joshua, Rahab and Achan form polar opposites. Victor Hamilton notes that Rahab is a female "outsider," who is both fearful and faithful. When she trusts in YHWH, she and her family become "insiders" and are allowed to live. Conversely, Achan is a male "insider," who is both fearless and faithless. When he disobeys YHWH, he and his family become "outsiders" and are killed.[43] And one must not forget the parallels with how Achan and his family end up. After they are executed, their bodies are burned and a great heap of stones are piled over them. The heaping of stones over one's body, of course, is also the end that awaits the king of Ai, the five kings of the south, and Absalom (Josh. 7:26; 8:29; 10:27; 2 Sam. 18:17). Notice that the last event falls within the lifetime of Abiathar.

In Josh. 8:1, another phrase from Deuteronomy appears, "Do not be afraid or dismayed" (אל־תירא ואל־תחת‎ ʾal-tîrāʾ wᵉal-tēḥāṯ). This

---

42. The truncated phrase "I have sinned" (חטאתי‎ ḥāṭāʾtî) appears in the record of Saul's fall in 1 Sam. 15:24, 30. However, Saul does not admit that his sin is against YHWH but merely YHWH's command.

43. Victor Hamilton, *Handbook on the Historical Books* (Grand Rapids: Baker Academic, 2008), 45.

word of encouragement is spoken by YHWH to Joshua and Israel after their initial loss at Ai and their execution of Achan. The phrase, which first appears in Deut. 1:21 and 31:8 on the lips of Moses, is also used by Joshua in Josh. 10:25. In the latter incident, Joshua encouraged his army with these words after they defeated the five kings of the southern coalition. These are the only places in the DtrH where the phrase is used and may point to Joshua as a source or to a priest who was familiar with the book of Deuteronomy.

In this vein, the first phrase in 8:2 "and you will do to [X]" also occurs in Deut. 3:2; 31:5; and 1 Sam. 24:4.[44] It is the latter appearance that is important. In this case, the phrase appears on the lips of David's men when Saul comes into the same cave where they and David are hiding. The verse reads, "And David's men said to him, 'Behold, the day which YHWH said to you, "Behold I am giving your enemy into your hand *and you shall do to him* as seems good in your eyes.'" So David arose and cut the edge of Saul's robe secretly" (italics mine). This again shows signs that the author was familiar not only with Deuteronomy but may have used it in Samuel as well. The one person who just happened to be on the run with David and who would have been aware of this encounter between David and Saul is, of course, Abiathar. This is also in keeping with our authorial assessment of the use of the phrase "unto this day" that appears twice in the same chapter (i.e., Josh. 8:28–29). It is at this juncture in chapter 8 that the geographical context switches from the destruction of Ai to the blessing and cursing ceremony on Ebal and Gerizim at Shechem. While this rapid shift is odd, it appears that the authorial intent in this shift at the heart of the conquest narrative may have to do with his desire to draw parallels between Joshua and David.

---

44. This phrase appears in Num. 21:34 as well, but it is in the context of the defeat of Og.

In Josh. 8:30-35, we not only again see language reminiscent of the book of Deuteronomy, but also character parallels with the book of Samuel.[45] Some even posit that what is being depicted by Joshua's actions on Mount Ebal are king-like acts. In this regard, J. Roy Porter points out that Joshua is doing what many kings do: they build altars (1 Sam. 14:35 [Saul]; 2 Sam. 24:25 [David]; 1 Kgs. 6:20; 9:25 [Solomon]; 1 Kgs. 12:33 [Jeroboam]; 1 Kgs. 16:32 [Ahab]; 2 Kgs. 16:10 [Ahaz]); they read the law (2 Kgs. 23:1-3); and they offer sacrifices (e.g., 1 Sam. 13:9; 2 Sam. 6:17).[46] Porter goes on to draw a connection between the successions of Joshua from Moses (Josh. 1:1-9) and Solomon from David (1 Kgs. 2:1-5).[47] Similarly, R. Nelson parallels Joshua and Josiah in this regard.[48] However, the ideal king to whom the author seeks to draw attention is not Josiah, but David. This is evinced through the narrative parallels woven into the larger fabric of Joshua 6–8.

In this vein, the narratives of Joshua 6–8 and 2 Samuel 5–7 not only need to be considered, but are of rhetorical importance. The parallels between these two blocks of material are numerous.

1. Both narratives begin with the conquering of an impregnable city (Joshua 6—Jericho//2 Sam. 5:6-9—Jerusalem).
2. Both cities are devoted to YHWH, one for destruction and the other as the place YHWH will dwell and be worshiped.
3. After the conquering of the impregnable cities, both ensuing

---

45. Note also the parallels between the curse associated with hanging someone on a tree in Josh. 8:29 (so, too, Josh. 10:27) and the legal pronouncements of Deut. 21:23.
46. Porter, "Succession of Joshua," 148–57, at 148–49. Even those who adopt a late date for much of the DtrH recognize the early nature of these connections. E.g., ibid., 154–55.
47. Ibid., 151. See also the similar work of Klaus Baltzer on 1 Chronicles 22 in *Das Bundesformular* (Neukirchen: Neukirchener, 1960), 79–84 (English: *The Covenant Formulary*, trans. David E. Green [Philadelphia: Fortress Press, 1971]). Porter, "Succession of Joshua," 153, also sees parallels with the installation of Saul as a "successor of Samuel."
48. Nelson, "Josiah in the Book of Joshua," 531–40, esp. 534. When faced with the key role David plays as the ideal king in the DtrH, Nelson erroneously suggests that David's status as the ideal king is not reality but, rather, is projected back into history based upon Josiah's traits (540).

battle narratives record the defeat of an enemy not once, but twice (cf. Joshua 7; 8:1-21—the people of Ai//2 Sam. 5:18-25—the Philistines).

4. Both battles take place at the direction of YHWH (Josh. 8:1//2 Sam. 5:19, 23, 24).

5. Both battles involve an ambush of sorts at the direction of YHWH (Josh. 8:2//2 Sam. 5:23)

6. Both leaders follow the exact commands of YHWH (Josh. 8:27//2 Sam. 5:25).

7. In both narratives, a man is killed for touching the holy things of YHWH: Achan, for taking that which was under the ban (Josh. 7:20-21)//Uzzah, for touching the Ark (2 Sam. 6:7).[49]

8. After the battles, Joshua and David gather the hosts of Israel (Josh. 8:33//2 Sam. 6:1-2).

9. Both leaders bring the Ark to a mountain for blessings (Josh. 8:33—Mount Ebal//2 Samuel 6—to Jerusalem).

10. Both build an altar and offer sacrifices (Josh. 8:30-31//2 Sam. 6:13, 17, 18 [where the altar building is implicit]).

11. In the accounts, priests are present (Josh. 8:33//2 Sam. 6:3, 4, 13 [implicit]).[50]

12. Both leaders offer whole burnt offerings (עלות 'ōlôṯ) and peace offerings (שלים šelîm).

13. Both offer blessings for the people and cursings (Josh. 8:33-34//2 Sam. 6:12, 18, 20, 23). In Joshua's case, it is a general blessing

---

49. Another parallel is the response of Joshua after the first defeat, he falls on his face before YHWH in fear of the people of Canaan and in anger/frustration (Josh. 7:5-9), whereas David was angry and afraid of YHWH for what he did to Uzzah (2 Sam. 6:8-9).

50. It is uncertain why the priests are not explicitly mentioned in 2 Samuel 6. It could have something to do with the fact that Abiathar is writing for an audience who knows that Abinadab and his family at Kiriath-jearim are in fact priests (cf. 2 Sam. 6:1-3). Or he may be trying to distance himself from the fiasco of the first attempt when the people were carrying the Ark on a cart and not properly by its poles. One should not make too much of this infraction in light of the distance the Ark had to travel to get to Jerusalem. Abiathar and David may have been being practical—obviously, this practicality was a mistake.

and curse, whereas, in David's case, it is blessing for the house of Obed-edom, the people and his house, with a curse falling upon Uzzah and Michal (2 Sam. 6:7, 23).

14. Both narratives appear in proximity to the phrase "unto this day" (Josh. 7:26 [2x]; 8:28, 29//2 Sam. 6:8; see my ch. 4), which, as we have noted, in many cases points to someone like Abiathar.

The one glaring absence in the parallels is the reading of the law by Joshua, and David's failure to do so in 2 Samuel 6. That is not to say it did not happen during the festivities in 2 Samuel 6 but, rather, the thing that David "gives" the people is literal food (i.e., cakes of dates, raisins, and figs) instead of the law of the Lord—spiritual "food." Then again, it appears that the reading of the law by the king was not a regular occurrence in David's day. Josiah is the only one we know who did so (2 Kgs. 23:1-3).

Finally, one must not overlook the presence of covenant making in the following chapters in each account. Joshua 9 tells of the Gibeonite fiasco and the covenant that ensued. This affected the nation negatively, but more specifically, the Levitical region of Benjamin. On the other hand, 2 Samuel 7 records the Davidic covenant, which would become a blessing for the entire nation, the tribe of Judah (and Benjamin) specifically. All of these connections, of course, mesh well with our assumption that Joshua is being depicted as a parallel to Israel's ideal king, David (or vice versa). Who else but Abiathar would have been familiar with so many aspects of David's life and the history and service of the Levites in both accounts? This familiarity with the life of David and his struggles comes through again at the end of the conquest narrative.

The "addendum-like" nature of Josh. 11:18-23 deviates from the typical narration up to this point. Indeed, the notation in 11:21-22 about the Anakim being defeated in Hebron and the hill country harks back to the opening chapter of Deuteronomy (see my ch. 5). Whereas, the defeat of the Anakim resounds a note of sweet justice for Joshua and Caleb in light of the Numbers 13 debacle (see especially Num. 13:33),[51] we are also told of, or should I say prepared for, the return of the Anakim in Gaza, Ashdod, and Gath at a later date (v. 22).[52] These cities of the Philistines in David's day would be the bane of David's existence. It is very possible that the link between the Anakim and David's day may point to the reality that Goliath and his fellow giants were not Philistine at all; they were descendants of the Anakim—Canaanites![53] Thus David, in many ways, did complete the conquest started under Joshua and Caleb. Of course, including the account of the Anakim would be something befitting Abiathar's rhetoric because of David's battles with Goliath and his descendants.

The Division of the Land: Joshua 12–22

Much of the material in chapters 12–22 has long been noted as possibly coming from a later hand.[54] To be sure, the annalistic nature of this block does perhaps point to a priestly author. In this vein, John Van Seters postulates that chapters 13–19 derive from the so-called "P" ("Priestly") source.[55] He also suggests that the integration of this material into the DtrH was achieved "partly by way of commentary"

---

51. Eugene Merrill, *Kingdom of Priests: A History of Old Testament Israel*, 2d ed. (Grand Rapids: Baker Academic, 2008), 138.

52. I agree with Kaufmann, *Biblical Account*, 79, that the absence of the Philistines here in Joshua points to an early date for the material.

53. So Merrill, *Kingdom of Priests*, 138.

54. K. L. Noll, "Deuteronomistic History or Deuteronomic Debate? (A Thought Experiment)," *JSOT* 31, no. 3 (2007): 313 n.6, suggests this.

55. John Van Seters, *In Search of History: Historiography in the Ancient World and the Origins of Biblical History* (New Haven: Yale University Press, 1983; repr. Winona Lake, IN: Eisenbrauns, 1997), 332–37; Gerhard von Rad, *The Problem of the Hexateuch and Other Essays*, trans. E. W. Trueman Dicken (Edinburgh/London: Oliver & Boyd, 1966), 79–93. Van Seters (336) suggests that "P" added chapters 13–19; 20:6, 9bβ; 21:1–42; 22:7–34; 24:28–33. Georg Fohrer, *Introduction to the Old Testament*, trans. David Green (London: SPCK, 1970), 203, suggests ch. 12; 13:15–33; chs. 14–19 (most of these); 21:1–42; and 22:9–34 derive from "P."

at key junctures, thus allowing for the insertion of the "P" material[56]—a suggestion I feel is legitimate, to a degree. Of course, where I would differ is in the dating of the original material of the DtrH and when the final form (with the lists integrated) was developed. The lists here could easily be attributed to the hand of a priest such as Abiathar.[57] It is also highly unlikely that the author fabricated lists for the sake of assigning them to the conquest period. It seems more appropriate that sources were used to this end (e.g., 12:7-24; 13:1-6, 7-33, etc.)—sources that no doubt come from the period of Joshua or shortly thereafter.[58] Interestingly, Porter again suggests that Joshua was appropriating king-like qualities when he apportioned the land (cf. 1 Sam. 8:14).[59] However, the connections may not be as strong as he supposes. In Josh. 14:1, Joshua is joined by Eleazar the *priest* and by the heads of the households of the tribes in the decision-making process. Later in 18:6, the allotments of land are determined by Joshua casting lots in the presence of YHWH—with the aid of the high priest (?). Simply put, someone had to be responsible for the division of the land. Furthermore, someone from his period must have recorded what portion each tribe received.

The speculative nature of who included these lists is unfruitful to our discussion, other than to note that a priest such as Abiathar is as good a candidate as any. But even this proposal does not preclude the input of earlier material from Joshua. What may be more useful is to determine when those lists may have been compiled or updated. If our assumptions have been correct thus far, Abiathar selectively compiled the conquest narratives from existing sources (with a focus on the Levites/Levi, Benjamin, and Judah) from Joshua's day and

---

56. Van Seters, *In Search of History*, 333.
57. For a bibliography of the varying opinions on the proposed priestly redactions of this portion of Joshua, see Peckham, "Significance," 226–27 nn.1–9.
58. Kaufmann, *Biblical Account*, 19–33.
59. Porter, "Succession of Joshua," 156–57.

added commentary along the way. In this regard, in chapter 13 it is interesting that the lack of an inheritance for the tribe of Levi seems to be a preoccupation of the author. Verses 14 and 33 serve as bookends to this block of material with a variation of whom and what was the Levites' inheritance. The two verses read,

> Only to the tribe of Levi he did not give an inheritance, *the offerings by fire to YHWH the God of Israel it shall be his inheritance* even as he said to him. (v. 14; italics mine)

> But to the tribe of Levi Moses did not give an inheritance, *YHWH the God of Israel, he was their inheritance* even as he said to them. (v. 33; italics mine)

Here the author notes that both YHWH and Moses commanded not to give Levi an inheritance. The first verse records that the *sacrifices* would be their inheritance and the second points to *YHWH* as their inheritance. Clearly, this was something that was on the mind of this priestly(?) author. Moreover, in 14:3, 4, and 18:7 the inheritance issues of the Levites appear again, with Eleazar the high priest playing a key role in the apportioning of the land, even being listed ahead of Joshua (Josh. 14:1)! What is more, Josh. 14:6-15 deals with Caleb's conquering of Hebron (a priestly city in Judah), which was David's first capital and Abiathar's second home. The chapter ends with the motif of the Anakim once again appearing in verses 12 and 15.

In chapter 15, Judah's territorial list is the first to appear, with obvious updating taking place that would match the period of David (15:8—Jerusalem; 15:9—Kiriath-jearim; 15:10—Chesalon) and later.[60] Verses 13-19 once again take up the conquest of Hebron by Caleb, a topic that reappears in Judg. 1:10-15. The last verse of chapter 15 (v. 63) is one of the more difficult passages in the book of Joshua,

---

60. In 15:38, it appears that the list had to have been updated after the time of 2 Kgs. 14:7, when Sela was renamed to Joktheel.

especially in light of Judg. 1:23 (see ch. 4 above). The text states, "Now the Jebusites, the ones living in Jerusalem, the sons of Judah were not able to dispossess them; therefore the Jebusites dwell with the sons of Judah in Jerusalem unto this day." At first glance, this text appears to be a direct contradiction to Judg. 1:23, where it is the Benjaminites who are unable to dispossess the Jebusites. However, as I will discuss in the next chapter, several factors could be in play: (1) both Benjamin and Judah may have attempted to conquer Jerusalem at different times; (2) the author may be speaking of the western city as opposed to the stronghold to the east, which later became the "city of David"; (3) the close association between the two tribes at a date after the division of the kingdom in 930 BCE (1 Kgs. 12:21, 23) may have caused the last editor—someone like Jeremiah—to see the two tribes as somewhat interchangeable and as a unified people within Judah.[61]

Chapters 16–19 record the allotment of the land. Chapters 16 and 17, although more laconic than chapter 15, deal exclusively with the inheritance of Ephraim and Manasseh. Interestingly, the high priest Eleazar plays a central role within this larger block (cf. 17:4; 19:51; see also 14:1; 21:1). Chapters 18 and 19 cover the last seven tribes' inheritance, with Benjamin's tribal allotment receiving priority of place and matching only the extensive listing afforded the tribe of Judah earlier (18:11-28). Not surprisingly, Simeon, from the region of Judah, comes next (19:1-9). From 19:10-48, the remaining five tribes are quickly covered. Joshua's inheritance completes the chapter (19:49-50). Once again, the tribe of Benjamin (and Judah's territory) takes priority. Not surprisingly, chapters 20 and 21 return to priestly concerns, with the assigning of the priestly cities of refuge (Kedesh, Shechem, Hebron, Bezer, Ramoth, and Golan) and the forty-eight

---

61. So, too, the conclusion of Geoghegan, *Time, Place, and Purpose*, 137.

Levitical cities respectively.[62] Yohanan Aharoni is no doubt correct when he places the completed list in the days of David.[63]

Chapter 22 brings to a close the conquest narrative with the words of Joshua to the Transjordan tribes in 22:4 harking back to those in 1:15: "YHWH has given rest (נוח *nûaḥ*) to your brothers." From 22:9-34, the author records the civil war that almost erupts over a misunderstanding between the Transjordan and Cisjordan tribes over the building of a commemorative altar. Priestly interests are pervasive, along with cultic language:[64] the word *altar* (מזבח *mizbēaḥ*) appears twelve times; the tabernacle is referenced twice (22:19, 29); the notion that the actions of the Transjordan tribes would make the land unclean (טמא *ṭāmēʾ*) is highlighted (22:19);[65] YHWH's name appears twenty-four times along with divine superlatives (22:22); Phinehas, the son of Eleazar the priest, oversees the confrontation (22:13, 30-32); and two key events related to cultic malfeasance from Israel's past are referenced (Peor and Achan; 22:17, 20). All of these are related as a warning against rebellion, cultic taboos, and disunity within Israel. These motifs would fit almost anytime during the nation's history; several times during the reign of David alone (2 Samuel 1–5; esp. 2:5, 9; and chs. 14–20).

Finally, within this chapter we find the phrase "far be it" from me/us (חלילה *ḥālîlāh*) (Josh. 22:29; 24:16). This phrase, which appears predominantly in Samuel (1 Sam. 2:30; 12:23; 14:45; 20:2, 9; 22:15; 24:7; 26:11; 2 Sam. 20:20 [2x]; 23:17; 1 Kgs. 21:3), is in keeping with our theory that the author of both books is the same.[66]

---

62. Scholars posit that Joshua 21 is from the time period of "either Josiah or the United Monarchy." Cf. Nelson, "Role of the Priesthood," 181. However, see the scathing, but accurate, critique of the Josianic perspective by Kaufmann, *Biblical Account*, 19–22.

63. Yohanan Aharoni, *The Land of the Bible: A Historical Geography*, trans. A. F. Rainey (Philadelphia: Westminster, 1967), 269–73, at 271.

64. Fohrer, *Introduction to the Old Testament*, 203, suggests that Josh. 22:9-34 derives from "P."

65. טמא *ṭāmēʾ* is used predominantly in Leviticus (128x); and in Numbers and Ezekiel (35x each).

To summarize, what is glaringly obvious in chapters 12–22 is the central role played by priestly concerns and the tribal allotments of Judah and Benjamin—all in keeping with our theory that Abiathar is compiling this history. Also, it is important to note the repetition of the phrase "unto this day" in chapters 13–22 (i.e., Josh. 13:13; 14:14; 15:63; 16:10; 22:3, 17), which may again point to Abiathar's era.

Joshua's Final Words: Joshua 23–24

Chapters 23–24 mark the final words of Joshua and the covenant ceremony at Shechem, respectively. As I noted in chapter 1, scholars have long highlighted the importance of the speeches within the work of the DtrH and how they appear to show the hand of Dtr. There is no lack of debate on which portions are original or later additions.[67] Indeed, one could argue that the study of Josh. 24:1-28 alone is a field all of its own with radically differing opinions.[68] I will not attempt to discuss those opinions here, but I do feel that S. David Sperling's conclusion that most of chapter 24 is unified and not necessarily the work of Dtr has merit, although I would disagree on the dating of the text.[69] These issues aside, what is clear is that the final author of these two chapters wanted them to be read together based upon the same lists of leaders in 23:2 and 24:1 (see also 8:33),

---

66. In 1 Kgs. 21:3, Naboth's quoted speech may be from Jeremiah's editorial work (see ch. 10 below).

67. See, for example, Thomas Römer, "Book-Endings in Joshua and the Question of the So-Called Deuteronomistic History," in *Raising up a Faithful Exegete*, ed. Kurt L. Noll and Brooks Schramm (Winona Lake, IN: Eisenbrauns, 2010), 85–99, esp. 92–99.

68. See, for example, the comments by S. David Sperling, "Joshua 24 Re-examined," *HUCA* 58 (1987): 119–36, esp. 119, and his interaction with the work of John Van Seters, "Joshua 24 and the Problem of Tradition in the Old Testament," in *In the Shelter of Elyon: Essays on Ancient Palestinian Life and Literature in Honor of G. W. Ahlström*, JSOTSup 31 (Sheffield: JSOT, 1984), 139–58; and Lothar Perlitt, *Bundestheologie im Alten Testament* (Neukirchen-Vluyn: Neukirchener, 1969), 239–84.

69. Sperling, "Joshua 24 Re-examined," 120, 136, dates it to Jeroboam II's reign (c. 786–746 BCE). See also Sperling's detailed linguistic analysis on pp. 122–33. George Mendenhall, "Covenant Forms in Israelite Tradition," *BA* 17, no. 3 (1954): 67, suggested that the covenantal form and basic content appear to be from Joshua's period or shortly thereafter.

the appearance of the "book of the law" (23:6; 24:26 cf. also 1:8; 8:31, 34), and the use of "covenant" (23:16; 24:25; note also the use of the covenant language "cling" [דבק *dābaq*] 23:8, 9, 16; cf. Deut. 10:20). Much like Moses, Joshua warns the people about breaking the covenant by practicing idolatry (23:7, 16; 24:14, 15, 20, 23) and intermarriage (23:12), actions that would result in the loss of the land (23:13, 15, 16). Not surprisingly, these will be the very issues that cause the chaos recorded in the book of Judges.

This linking of books is evinced by the intentional textual connections between the books of Joshua and Judges that appear in the closing verses of chapter 24. While the ordering varies slightly, several verses are almost verbatim (cf. 24:28-31; Judg. 2:6-9).[70] Moreover, if Porter's assertion that Joshua's actions in chapter 24 portray true kingship,[71] then this chapter serves as an excellent transition to the book of Judges and the failure of the judges' period when kingship was desired (Judg. 17:6; 21:25; 1 Samuel 8). This presentation, along with the motif of covenant (cf. 2 Samuel 7), makes for an excellent link to the importance of ideal kingship and the role performed by David—the first God-focused king after the judges' period, and the king against whom every other king would be measured. Before the author completed this book, however, he saw the need to insert one last priestly notation about the "changing of the guard" (24:33)—a final glimpse of sorts into the mind of the author.

---

70. It is also interesting that Josh. 24:32; Judg. 2:10; and Exod. 1:8 all share a common motif; language reflective of Joseph's day. Joshua 24:32 mentions the burying of Joseph's bones and the Judges and Exodus passages use the same phraseology connected to the period after Joseph's death; "now a new [X] arose who did not know [X]." The connections are clearly meaningful.
71. Porter, "Succession of Joshua," 155; Geo Widengren, "King and Covenant," *JSS* 2, no. 1 (1957): 1–32, esp. 13–17. Widengren suggests that Moses, Joshua, Solomon, Joash, Josiah, Ezra, and the postexilic kings of Judah all are presented performing the role of the king by reading the law and renewing the covenant during the New Year's festival (usually on an elevated platform).

Conclusion

The book of Joshua betrays numerous examples of editing that shed light on who compiled this portion of the DtrH. Connections to the period of David and the geographical regions of Benjamin and Judah point to an author familiar with, and sympathetic to, these areas and concerns. Furthermore, the parallels between David and Joshua as the two great conquest leaders should not be overlooked or downplayed. The predominant priestly and cultic concerns betray a priestly hand as well. In each case, Abiathar could very well have been the compiler of older traditions while shaping them with an eye to his region and interests. These same concerns continue to rise to the surface in the book of Judges; however, the genre of apologia becomes blended with the chaotic history of the judges' period. It is to this we now turn.

7

The Book of Judges: An Apology for Kingship

The dominance of Martin Noth's analysis of Deuteronomy–2 Kings in terms of an original Deuteronomic work in which the judges period began with Judg. 2.6sqq. and ended with Samuel's speech in 1 Samuel 12 has strongly disposed subsequent scholarship against giving serious consideration to Judges as a literary unit in its own right.[1]

These comments by Barry Webb highlight the problem within DtrH studies when one attempts to isolate authors of the DtrH. The all-too-often rejection of a prehistory for individual books within the DtrH has hampered more holistic studies of a given book. Fortunately, some are beginning to consider the possibility of an earlier existence of books or blocks of the DtrH that may have served different rhetorical functions.[2] In this vein, scholars such as J. Gordon

---

1. Barry Webb, *The Book of Judges: An Integrated Reading*, JSOTSup 46 (Sheffield: JSOT, 1987), 207.
2. See, for example, Mark Leuchter, *Samuel and the Shaping of Tradition* (New York: Oxford University Press, 2013), 20.

McConville and Claus Westermann are pushing the discussion in the right direction. Westermann's conclusion that the books of the DtrH may have had a separate redactional history may be close to reality in light of their possible use in a given era.[3] For example, Westermann notes that the accounts of the Judges looks more like family stories.[4] Indeed, as I will argue in this chapter, the author may have incorporated such stories for a rhetorical reason. The book of Judges may have been a piece of pro-Davidic and anti-Saulide propaganda that circulated separately for a period of time before being incorporated into the DtrH.[5]

Steven L. McKenzie has rightly noted that Deuteronomy, Joshua, and Judges do not fit the traditional genre of "history" as do Samuel and Kings.[6] Some of this diversity may have to do with the fact that scholars have downplayed the propagandistic aspects of the history. In the same way that Deuteronomy may have first served as a legal

---

3. Cf. J. Gordon McConville, "The Old Testament Historical Books in Modern Scholarship," *Them* 22, no. 3 (1997): 3–13, esp. 8–11; and Claus Westermann, *Die Geschichtsbücher des Alten Testaments: gab es ein deuteronomistisches Geschichtewerk?* (Kaiser: Gütersloher, 1994). Similarly, Gordon J. Wenham, "The Deuteronomic Theology of the Book of Joshua," *JBL* 90, no. 2 (1971): 148, notes the problem with apparent conflicting theological outlooks of different books of the DtrH, whereas Hartmut N. Rösel, "Does a Comprehensive 'Leitmotiv' Exist in the Deuteronomistic History?," in *The Future of the Deuteronomistic History*, ed. Thomas Römer (Leuven: Leuven University Press, 2000), 211, concludes that the theory of the DtrH should be abandoned because of the lack of a central guiding "Leitmotiv." For an opposite position, see Thomas Römer, "The Book of Deuteronomy," in *The History of Israel's Traditions: The Heritage of Martin Noth*, ed. Steven L. McKenzie and M. Patrick Graham, JSOTSup 182 (Sheffield: Sheffield Academic Press, 1994), 210 n.2. See also the assessment of the trend exemplified by Westermann in Gary N. Knoppers, "Is There a Future for the Deuteronomistic History?," in Römer, ed., *Future of the Deuteronomistic History*, 119–34.

4. Westermann, *Die Geschichtsbücher des Alten Testaments*, 33–36, as noted by McConville, "Old Testament Historical Books in Modern Scholarship," 8.

5. I cannot agree with Iain Provan, *Hezekiah and the Books of Kings: A Contribution to the Debate about the Composition of the Deuteronomistic History*, BZAW 172 (Berlin: de Gruyter, 1988), 169, 173, that Joshua and Judges were added at a much later date to the DtrH. It appears that these books may have been the key components around which the rest of the DtrH was built. Note also the role of "propaganda" in the ancient world: Keith W. Whitelam, "The Defence of David," *JSOT* 29 (1984): 61–87, esp. 65–68.

6. Steven L. McKenzie, "The Books of Kings in the Deuteronomistic History," in McKenzie and Graham, eds., *History of Israel's Traditions*, 300.

tractate from Moses, as opposed to merely an "introduction" to the DtrH, Judges appears to have had a greater rhetorical purpose than a mere recitation of the chaotic period of the judges. Of course, this does not preclude Abiathar from being the person who later incorporated the work into his ongoing history, nor does it exclude the possibility that Jeremiah may have edited portions of the book in order to match his particular agenda.

Structurally, we also have to deal with the numerous parallels between the opening chapters of Judges and the book of Joshua. Scholars have long struggled with the redactional history of Judg. 1:1—2:5, and we certainly will not settle it here.[7] For example, Georg Fohrer posits that this block was originally the closing to the book of Joshua.[8] Similarly, Noth posited that Joshua 24—Judges 2:5 was later than Dtr and that the book originally continued to 1 Samuel 12.[9] Conversely, Yehezkel Kaufmann defends the antiquity of the opening material in Judges, suggesting that it should be dated to a period shortly after Joshua when the tribes continued the wars with the Canaanites.[10]

With such diversity of opinions, one is left wondering what role this opening material played and why it was added. However, if our conclusion that Abiathar compiled the book of Joshua is correct, then the parallels between these two books make sense, especially if Abiathar borrowed from his earlier work (i.e., Joshua) to fashion a polemic for Davidic kingship that circulated as a separate document (i.e., Judges). Thus, chapter 1 of Judges is not only important for introducing this new literary treatise, but it also served as an inclusio

---

7. For a discussion on the redactional history of this material, see John Van Seters, *In Search of History: Historiography in the Ancient World and the Origins of Biblical History* (New Haven: Yale University Press, 1983; repr., Winona Lake, IN: Eisenbrauns, 1997), 337–42.

8. Georg Fohrer, *Introduction to the Old Testament*, trans. David Green (London: SPCK, 1970), 197.

9. Martin Noth, *The Deuteronomistic History*, JSOTSup 15 (Sheffield: JSOT, 1981), 9, 42.

10. Yehezkel Kaufmann, *The Biblical Account of the Conquest of Palestine* (Jerusalem: Magnes, 1953), 82–86.

introducing the positive leadership role of the tribe of Judah in conquering the land and in leading the nation as a whole (cf. Judg. 1:1; 20:18). In this vein, Robert Polzin's assessment that Judg. 1:1—3:6 forms a unified literary construct appears correct. Polzin avers that Judg. 1:1—2:5 gives the linear history after Joshua's death, whereas 2:6-23 is circular in that it shows the reason why Israel fell into sin (esp. vv. 10-15).[11] This latter portion sets up the cycle that will unfold in the body of the book.[12] In this regard, Mark O'Brien outlines the cycle as follows: (1) accusation of infidelity (3:7, 12; 4:1; 6:1; 10:6; 13:1); (2) oppression by an enemy (3:8, 12; 4:2; 6:1; 10:7; 13:1); (3) cry to God (3:9, 15; 4:3; 6:6; 10:10a); (4) God raises a deliverer (3:9, 15); (5) subjugation of the enemy (3:10, 30; 4:23; 8:28; 11:33); and (6) a period of rest (3:11, 30; 5:31; 8:28).[13] Interestingly, this same cycle could be applied to the reign of Saul, perhaps with the exception of section 6 of the cycle. Even though Saul had initial successes (cf. 1 Samuel 11; 14), when he failed to follow YHWH the cycle had to be completed by a new leader. For this reason, section 6 and, to a large degree, section 5 of the cycle, were not truly fulfilled until David came to the throne.

On the macro-structural level, Alexander Rofé argues that Joshua 24—1 Samuel 12 minus Judg. 1:1—3:11 and chapters 17–21

---

11. Robert Polzin, *Moses and the Deuteronomist: A Literary Study of the Deuteronomic History I. Deuteronomy, Joshua, Judges* (Bloomington: Indiana University Press, 1993), 151.

12. Contra O'Brien's negative assessment of Polzin's hypothesis (Mark A. O'Brien, "Judges and the Deuteronomistic History," in McKenzie and Graham, eds., *History of Israel's Traditions*, 235–59, at 256), the indictment of the angel at Bochim (2:2b) does not necessarily contradict the statement in 2:7 that the children of Israel worshiped YHWH all the days of Joshua and the elders that followed him. The fact that the people entered covenants with the Canaanites was not a new phenomenon, especially during the period of the conquest and later under the kings (e.g., Joshua with the Gibeonites; David and Solomon with Hiram and Egypt respectively); yet, in each case the nation, for all intents and purposes, followed YHWH. This appears to be noted in 2:2b in order to show the proverbial "chink in the armor," which will be the undoing of Israel. And indeed, this is the case for the judges' generation as well as the period of the kings! For an excellent summary of the history of scholarship on Judges, see ibid., 239–53.

13. Ibid., 236–37 n.3.

comprised the original history of the judges' period from a "North-Israelite account."[14] Of course he has to excise the Othniel account in 3:7-11 in order to gain an entire "northern" perspective—a move that is unnecessary in light of my discussion below. Thus, Rofé lists the judges as follows: Joshua [Ephraimite], Ehud [Benjaminite], Deborah [Mt. Ephraim], Barak [Naphtali], Gideon [Manasseh], Jephthah [Transjordanian Gileadite], Samson [Dan], Eli [priest at Shiloh], and Samuel [Ephraimite].[15] Rofé goes on to note correctly the role northern cult sites play in this block: Shechem (Josh. 21:1, 25), Ophrah (Judg. 6:24—Galilee region), Mizpah of Gilead (Judg. 11:11), Shiloh (1 Sam. 1:7, 9, etc.), Mizpah of Benjamin (1 Sam. 7:5-9), Ramah (1 Sam. 7:17; 9:5-25), and Gilgal (1 Sam. 11:15).[16]

In some ways, Rofé's pointing up of the northern perspective is in keeping with my argument below and in chapter 8. Abiathar, a priest from the northern tribe of Benjamin, was reaching out to his fellow northerners during the civil war between David and Ishbosheth in an attempt to convince them of the failure of the judges *and* of Saul, who in many ways was "judge-like." Abiathar could have easily modified an existing history, or fashioned it himself based upon northern accounts such as Rofé has noted. The major problem with Rofé's theory is that he dates the work to the eighth century—long after any polemic would make sense.[17] It is to this issue that we now turn.

---

14. Alexander Rofé, "Ephraimite Versus Deuteronomistic History," in *Reconsidering Israel and Judah: Recent Studies on the Deuteronomistic History*, ed. Gary N. Knoppers and J. Gordon McConville (Winona Lake, IN: Eisenbrauns, 2000), 465.

15. Ibid., 465. See also A. D. H. Mayes, *The Story of Israel Between Settlement and Exile: A Redactional Study of the Deuteronomistic History* (London: SCM, 1983), 81, who does the same thing with Judg. 3:7-11.

16. Rofé, "Ephraimite Versus Deuteronomistic History," 466.

17. Ibid., 474. With the exception of slight revisions, the remainder of ch. 7 was originally published under the title, "Could Abiathar, the Priest, Be the Author of Judges?" *BibSac* 170, no. 680 (2013): 432–52. Used by permission.

Judges as a Pro-Davidic Polemic

In 1967, J. P. U. Lilley mused, ". . . a fresh appraisal of Judges as a literary work, starting from the assumptions of authorship rather than of redaction, could lead to a more satisfying interpretation of the book than is to be found in the standard commentaries, and could help to resolve some of the major problems which have been raised."[18] Sadly, in his article Lilley never went on to posit a potential author of the material, even though he makes an excellent argument for the book's unity and the methodology of the anonymous author.[19] Thus, nearly fifty years later, readers are left still pondering the question, Who could have penned the earliest form of this book? Without fail, scholarship has taken the circuitous route, bantering around the possibilities of multiple layers of redaction and editing throughout the centuries but always ending up with the nebulous, but safe, choice of Dtr as the main editor/compiler/author or some combination of these.[20]

Apart from these typical redactional proposals of the past hundred or so years,[21] the traditional Jewish perspective on the authorship of

18. J. P. U. Lilley, "A Literary Appreciation of the Book of Judges," *TynBul* 18 (1967): 95.
19. See also the work of D. W. Gooding, "The Composition of the Book of Judges," in *Eretz-Israel, Archaeological Historical and Geographic Studies, Vol. 16: Harry M. Orlinsky Volume*, ed. B. A. Levine and A. Malamat (Jerusalem: Israel Exploration Society, 1982), 70–79; and Alexander Globe, "Enemies Round About: Disintegrative Structure in the Book of Judges," in *Mappings of the Biblical Terrain*, ed. Vincent L. Tollers and John R. Maier (Lewisburg, PA: Bucknell University Press, 1990), 233–51 (as cited by Gale Yee, "Introduction: Why Judges?" in *Judges and Method: New Approaches in Biblical Studies*, ed. Gale Yee [Minneapolis: Fortress Press, 1995], 10 nn.2, 3).
20. For example, see the paradigmatic approach by Wolfgang Richter, *Traditionsgeschichtliche Untersuchungen zum Richterbuch*, Bonner Biblische Beiträge 18 (Bonn: P. Hanstein, 1963); Globe, "Enemies Round About," 235–39; and comments by James D. Martin, *The Book of Judges* (Cambridge: Cambridge University Press, 1975), 5–9. Martin speaks of "blocks of material," "collections of stories," "a collection of hero sagas," and how Dtr "inserted" material at will and added "appendices" to suit—of course, none of which ever finds a consensus among scholars.
21. Even as of 1967, Lilley ("A Literary Appreciation," 94) opined about the futility of source-critical and redactional exercises forced upon the biblical books with no consensus ever being reached. For some examples of the redaction-critical theories applied to Judges, see D. Karl

Judges has for centuries leaned toward Samuel as the most logical choice for the bulk of the source material (*Baba Bathra* 14b).[22] Open any Old Testament introduction and this is one of the first facts mentioned when dealing with the authorship of Judges.[23] While it is possible that some of the source material found in Judges could have been penned by Samuel, or someone close to him,[24] the textual, structural, and rhetorical aspects of the final form push against it.[25] Because of more recent, focused studies on the polemical nature of the book, one is forced to consider other possibilities. In this chapter, we will examine the authorial implications of the oft-noted anti-Saulide polemic and how this polemic betrays a particularly raucous period in Israel's history when kingship was needed. However, not just any king would do, Judahite kingship was vital. One person stands out as a possible candidate for promoting this type of kingship, namely Abiathar, the friend and priest to David.

Budde, *Das Buch der Richter*, KHC 7 (Leipzig: J. C. B. Mohr, 1897), 110–11 (here notations on chs. 17–21); David M. Gunn, "Narrative Patterns and Oral Tradition in Judges and Samuel," *VT* 24, no. 3 (1974): 286–317; Robert G. Boling, *Judges: Introduction, Translation, and Commentary*, AB 6A (New York: Doubleday, 1975), 30; William J. Dumbrell, "'In Those Days There Was No King in Israel; Every Man Did What Was Right in His Own Eyes': The Purpose of the Book of Judges Reconsidered," *JSOT* 25 (1983): 23–33. For a bibliographic list of studies related to the topic of the redaction of Judges, see Victor H. Matthews, *Judges & Ruth* (Cambridge: Cambridge University Press, 2004), 23–24. Cyril J. Barber, *A Narrative of God's Power: Judges* (Neptune, NJ: Loizeaux Bros., 1990), 240 n.13, comments, "Because the majority of scholars have allowed for numerous redactors, the authorship of the book has been unnecessarily obscured." See further Barber's list of scholars who posit long redactional histories of Judges (ibid.).

22. Rabbi Chaim Dov Rabinowitz, *Commentary on the Books of Yehoshua Shoftim; Da'ath Sofrim Torah, Prophets, Sacred Writings*, trans. Rabbi S. Carmel (New York/Jerusalem: H. Vagshal, 2004), 177.

23. See Otto Kaiser, *Introduction to the Old Testament* (Oxford: Western Printing Services, 1975), 142; Peter Craigie, *The Old Testament: Its Background, Growth, and Content* (Nashville: Abingdon, 1986), 131; Andrew Hill and John Walton, *A Survey of the Old Testament* (Grand Rapids: Zondervan, 1991), 173; William Lasor, et al., *Old Testament Survey*, 2d ed. (Grand Rapids: Eerdmans, 1996), 161.

24. Barber, *Judges*, 19–20, suggests that Samuel or someone from his prophetic school authored Judges.

25. Lilley's presentation is paradigmatic of those who argue for the unity of the book (cf. "A Literary Appreciation," 94–102).

An Anti-Saulide Polemic in Its Historical Context

Many scholars have now come to realize that the book of Judges may have served as more than a mere Deuteronomistic recitation of the history of Israel prior to the monarchy. Along with the clear religio-political message and the apparent push for kingship, a growing number of scholars now view Judges, in whole or in part, as an anti-Saulide polemic.[26] From this conclusion, some scholars attempt to determine the period of Israel's history when such a rendition of the nation's past would best serve any practical function. Indeed, the anti-Saulide perspective requires a certain historical setting, as well as an author with motive and opportunity to fashion it.

26. See Arthur E. Cundall, "Judges—An Apology for the Monarchy?" *ExpTim* 81, no. 6 (1970): 178–81; Hans-Winfried Jüngling, *Richter 19–Ein Plädoyer für das Königtum*, AnBib 84 (Rome: Biblical Institute Press, 1981), 43–44; Raymond Dillard and Tremper Longman III, *An Introduction to the Old Testament* (Grand Rapids: Zondervan, 1994), 121; Robert H. O'Connell, *The Rhetoric of the Book of Judges*, VTSup 63 (Leiden: Brill, 1996); Matthews, *Judges & Ruth*, 8; Terry L. Brensinger, *Judges* (Scottdale, PA: Herald, 1999), 21; Yairah Amit, *Hidden Polemics in Biblical Narrative*, BIS 25 (Leiden: Brill, 2000), 178–88; Tammi J. Schneider, *Judges*, Berit Olam: Studies in Hebrew Narrative & Poetry (Collegeville, MN: Liturgical, 2000); A. D. H. Mayes, "Deuteronomistic Royal Ideology in Judges 17–21," *BibInt* 9, no. 3 (2001): 241–58; Marc Zvi Brettler, *The Book of Judges* (New York: Routledge, 2002); and idem, "The Book of Judges: Literature as Politics," *JBL* 108, no. 3 (1989): 395–418; Yee, "Introduction: Why Judges?" 3; Marvin Sweeney, "Davidic Polemic in the Book of Judges," *VT* 47, no. 4 (1997): 517–29. See also comments on the need for leadership in Judges promoted by Brian Irwin, "Not Just Any King: Abimelech, the Northern Monarchy, and the Final Form of Judges," *JBL* 131, no. 3 (2012): 445.On the other hand, contra Dumbrell, "In Those Days There Was No King in Israel," 30; and Boling, *Judges*, 293 (cf. also idem, Boling, "Judges, Book of," *ABD* 3:1113), who argue against the pro-monarchic thrust of Judges by misconstruing the phrase "in those days there was no king in Israel and every man did what was right in his own eyes" to mean "that the time had arrived once again for every man to do what was right before YHWH without any sacral political apparatus to get in the way" (here Boling, 293). Thus, both assert that this reference refers to YHWH's kingship as opposed to an earthly king. Of course, this is in keeping with their presupposition that the text it to be dated to the Babylonian exile. A straightforward reading of the text in no way leads one to this interpretation apart from such a presupposition. Also, the appearance of the truncated phrase "in those days there was no king in Israel" in 18:1 and 19:1 hardly supports such a reading in light of what follows.

Nine Proposed Dates for Judges

Robert O'Connell lists nine of the most commonly proffered time periods when the "religious-political situation" could have fostered the "compilation/redaction" of Judges.[27] These include:

1. that described in 1 Samuel 1–11/12, a situation in which Saul had established a monarchy that had not yet fallen into disfavour (c. 1053 BCE); [Keil and Delitzsch][28]

2. that described in 2 Samuel 1–4, a situation that had not yet seen the rule of the Davidic monarchy extended to include the Ephraimite league of tribes (c. 1011–1004 BCE); [O'Connell; Keil and Delitzsch, Bush, Young][29]

3. a situation subsequent to the beginning of David's rule over all Israel from Jerusalem (post–1004 BCE); [A. E. Cundall][30]

4. the aftermath of the division of the monarchy in which Jeroboam I established a calf cult at Dan and Bethel and a non-Levitical priesthood at various cult centres (post–931 BCE, cf. 1 Kgs. 12); [M. Brettler][31]

5. the aftermath of Tiglath-pileser III's subjugation in 734 BCE of all the northern kingdom of Israel except Samaria; [Soggin][32]

---

27. O'Connell, *Rhetoric*, 305–6. Square brackets (i.e., [ ]) have been added to show the scholars who hold each position as presented by O'Connell—this list has been added to for the purpose of updating and bolstering O'Connell's list.

28. Carl Friedrich Keil and Franz Delitzsch, *Joshua, Judges, Ruth, 1 and 2 Samuel*, COT 2 (Edinburgh: T&T Clark, 1866–1891; repr., Peabody, MA: Hendrickson, 2001),182. Keil offers two options for the dating of Judges: (1) the period of Saul; or (2) the period of David before his capture of Jerusalem.

29. O'Connell, *Rhetoric*, 308; Keil, *Judges*, 182; George Bush, *Notes on Judges* (New York: Newman & Ivison, 1852; repr., Minneapolis: James & Klock, 1976), v. Edward J. Young, *An Introduction to the Old Testament*, 3d ed. (Grand Rapids: Eerdmans, 1965), 169, 170, concludes that it had to be before the "early days of David."

30. Arthur E. Cundall and Leon Morris, *Judges and Ruth: An Introduction and Commentary* (London: Tyndale, 1968), 26–27. Interestingly, Susan Niditch, *Judges: A Commentary*, OTL (Louisville: Westminster John Knox, 2008), 8, suggests there is material spanning the periods from "pre-tenth century" up until 586 BCE.

31. Brettler, "Literature as Politics," 417.

6. the aftermath of the fall of Samaria in 722 BCE; [D. Block][33]

7. a pre-exilic situation subsequent to Josiah's reform of 621 BCE (i.e. a 'deuteronomic' compilation/redaction); [R. G. Boling; F. M. Cross][34]

8. the exilic aftermath of the 587 BCE deportation of Babylon (i.e. a 'deuteronomistic' compilation/redaction; or a 'postdeuteronomistic' compilation/redaction); [A. D. H. Mayes; W. J. Dumbrell][35] and

9. a postexilic situation of the 5th or 4th C. BCE (i.e. a redaction of JE [by Rje] and D [the 'deuteronomic redactor']; or of Rp [the 'priestly redactor']).[36] [G. F. Moore; C. F. Burney; J. Gray][37]

While space does not allow for a detailed refutation of every one of these various positions, a few summary comments are in order. First, from the anti-Saulide polemic perspective, any attempt to place the *Sitz im Leben* of Judges during or after the exile (i.e., positions 8 and 9 above) is not historically probable. The clear bias toward the Davidic dynasty at this time as presented in the rest of the DtrH, not to mention Chronicles, betrays this pro-Davidic stance. What is more, the supremacy of the line of David extends even after the exile. This is evinced in the choice of Zerubbabel, a descendant of David, to lead the first return of the exiles back to Judah (Ezra 3:2, 8; 5:2; Neh.

---

32. Alberto Soggin, *Judges*, trans. John Bowden, OTL (Philadelphia: Westminster, 1981), 278, intimates that this is the setting, at least for chs. 17–18.

33. Daniel Block, *Judges, Ruth*, NAC 6 (Nashville: Broadman and Holman, 1999), 64–67, suggests sometime after the evil reign of Manasseh.

34. Boling, *Judges*, 30, 35, 36; and Frank Moore Cross, *Canaanite Myth and Hebrew Epic: Essays in the History of the Religion of Israel* (Cambridge: Harvard University Press, 1973), 250–54, 287–89.

35. A. D. H. Mayes, *Judges* (Sheffield: JSOT, 1985), 15, 33; and Dumbrell, "'In Those Days,'" 29.

36. O'Connell, *Rhetoric*, 305–306.

37. George F. Moore, *A Critical and Exegetical Commentary on Judges* (Edinburgh: Clark, 1895), xxxiv, xxxv; C. F. Burney, *The Book of Judges with Introduction and Notes*, 2d ed. (London: Rivingtons, 1920), 1; John Gray, ed., *Joshua, Judges, Ruth*, 2d ed. (Basingstoke/Grand Rapids: Morgan & Scott/Eerdmans, 1986), 232.

12:1, etc.). Finally, arguments for a resurgence of the line of Saul in the exilic and postexilic periods do not comport textually.[38]

Second, the period of the divided monarchy (post-931 BCE—positions 4–7) would not fit the anti-Benjamin rhetoric prevalent throughout Judges, especially in chapters 19–21. It is clear that Benjamin had sided with Judah during the war between Rehoboam and Jeroboam I (1 Kgs. 12:21). Any polemic that would have presented Benjamin in such an unfavorable light surely would have driven a wedge between this relationship (see the discussion below for issues surrounding the 722 BCE date).

Third, the biblical support for position 3 is anemic at best. Textually, there is no credible Saulide challenge to David's throne at this time, with the possible exception of two events during Absalom's coup: Ziba's false (?) indictment against Mephibosheth (2 Sam. 16:3), and Shimei's curse (2 Sam. 16:5).[39] To begin with, the events of the coup take place during a very narrow historical window (2 Samuel 15–18).[40] It is unlikely that someone would have written an entire polemic in such a brief period to garner support for David. Note also that at the end of this short coup, the house of Saul actually joins the throngs to welcome David back to the throne of Israel (2 Sam. 19:16-18)—hardly a picture of wanton rebellion. As for the Shimei

---

38. The only Saulide to play a key role in a postexilic text is Mordecai in the book of Esther, but here he is in a foreign setting, not Judah (Est. 2:5).

39. Although James C. Vanderkam, "Davidic Complicity in the Deaths of Abner and Eshbaal: A Historical and Redactional Study," *JBL* 99, no. 4 (1980): 535, asserts that much of 2 Samuel is devoted to Saulide events challenging David's right to the throne (e.g., 6:14-23—Michal despises David; 16:1-4—Ziba tricks David concerning Mephibosheth; 20:1-22—the rebellion of Sheba the Benjaminite after the failed coup of Absalom; 21:1-14—the Gibeonite incident involving the death of seven sons of Saul), most of these incidents are in no way tangible threats to the throne of David—perhaps with the exception of Sheba's rebellion, of which there is no evidence that he was a Saulide.

40. The text is silent as to the length of Absalom's coup. Nevertheless, the fact that Saul's grandson does not wash his clothes or trim his mustache during the coup seems to suggest weeks or months as opposed to years (2 Sam. 19:24). On the other hand, the civil war between the house of Saul and David in 2 Samuel 2–4 may have lasted up to seven-and-a-half years—ample time to devise and write a polemic!

and Ziba episodes, in the former case, even if Shimei's threat was credible, this event occurred much later in David's rule as opposed to the "beginning" of it, not to mention the period of Shimei's obstinacy was relatively short-lived. Furthermore, this threat to the throne was from David's own family, thus begging the question as to why there would be any need for anti-Saulide rhetoric. In the latter case, Ziba's actions seem suspect at best in light of David's declaration in 1 Samuel 9. Ziba appears to have been waiting for the opportunity to remove the yoke of his servanthood to Mephibosheth that David placed upon him. By bringing a false accusation against Mephibosheth, at David's most vulnerable time, Ziba's calculated accusation paid dividends. Mephibosheth's contrition and explanation to David after the coup seems to militate against Ziba's indictment (2 Sam. 19:24-30).

Also, David's unfettered rule becomes even more evident when one considers the events of 2 Sam. 21:1-14. Here David acts with impunity by handing over seven descendants of Saul to the Gibeonites to be sacrificed in order to end the famine in Israel. Surely, if there was any amount of Saulide support in Israel, this act would not have gone unchecked.[41]

Finally, position 1 is untenable due to the textual witness; the basis upon which one must adjudicate evidence. At this time, almost all Israel supported Saul's rule, at least up until his fall into sin (1 Samuel 13; 15). Those who rejected Saul's leadership (1 Sam. 10:27)

---

41. It is clear that 2 Sam. 21:1-14 is not in chronological order canonically. Most scholars note that this pericope fits best between 2 Samuel 8 and 9. It was perhaps David's surrendering of the seven sons of Saul to the Gibeonites that Shimei was alluding to in 2 Sam. 16:5-8. However, one man's rant hardly seems a fitting reason around which to develop an entire polemic. For comments about the chronological placement of 2 Sam. 21:1-14, see Leonhard Rost, *Die Überlieferung von der Thronnachfolge Davids*, BWANT 3/6 (Stuttgart: Kohlhammer, 1926) (English: *The Succession to the Throne of David*, trans. Michael D. Rutter and David M. Gunn [Sheffield: Almond, 1982], 66); Leo G. Perdue, "Is There Anyone Left of the House of Saul . . . ? Ambiguity and the Characterization of David in the Succession Narrative," *JSOT* 30 (1984): 75; Simeon Chavel, "Compositry and Creativity in 2 Samuel 21:1-14," *JBL* 122, no. 1 (2003): 45–50. See also the suggested redaction process of 2 Sam. 21:1-14 as outlined by D. Karl Budde, *Die Bücher Samuel erklärt*, KHC 8 (Tübingen and Leipzig: J. C. B. Mohr, 1902), 304.

were silenced after his defeat of the Ammonites (1 Sam. 11:12). Furthermore, until the Philistines killed Saul (1 Samuel 31), even David supported Saul's right to the throne as YHWH's anointed king (1 Samuel 24; 26:9-10; 2 Sam. 1:14). Therefore, the *terminus a quo* is after the death of Saul (1 Samuel 31) and the *terminus ad quem* must be before the rise of David to rule over all Israel (2 Samuel 5). In this vein, K. W. Whitelam notes that Davidic propaganda would have been most effective when David was initially coming to power.[42] That leaves only one logical historical period for the writing/compiling of Judges, at least as an anti-Saulide polemic: position 2, as per O'Connell.[43]

Textual Support for Position 2

Nine texts in Judges allude to potential chronological settings in which Judges may have been written. These include: 1:21b, 29; 18:30, 31; 21:19; 17:6; 18:1; 19:1; 21:25. These will be handled *seriatim*.

First, 1:21b states, "so the Jebusites have lived with the sons of Benjamin in Jerusalem to this day."[44] As noted in chapter 4 above, this parenthetical aside tells of a time prior to the capture of Jebus/Jerusalem by David (2 Sam. 5:6-9)—a situation anterior to the civil war between Ishbosheth and David.[45] Furthermore, contextually,

---

42. Whitelam, "Defence of David," 67, 69.

43. O'Connell, *Rhetoric*, 306–307. D. R. Davis, "A Proposed Life-Setting for the Book of Judges" (PhD diss., Southern Baptist Theological Seminary, 1978), has also suggested an early date for Judges (the latter entry as cited by Dillard and Longman, *Introduction*, 122). For a more detailed handling of these issues, see further O'Connell, *Rhetoric*, 332–38.

44. Based upon this passage, Herbert Wolf, *Judges*, EBC 3 (Grand Rapids: Zondervan, 1992), 378, also asserts that the period of the early monarchy is a probable date for the authorship of Judges.

45. The designation "Jerusalem" as opposed to "Jebus" may be a later scribal updating or the recognized name of the extended city (i.e., both Urusalim and Jebus). Also, the contradiction of 1:8 and 1:21b is more apparent than real. Not only could there be a time span between these two verses when the city may have been originally destroyed and then re-inhabited by the Jebusites, but more likely, it may reflect two events when the city on the southwest hill (i.e., Urusalim) was destroyed (1:8) but not the eastern "stronghold" of the city where the Jebusites

chapter 1 mentions a number of other facts pointing to a central focus on Judah which betrays an authorial bias: (1) Judah is given a divine mandate to lead (1:2); (2) they have supremacy over their enemies (1:3–11); and (3) Othniel and Caleb, Judahite leaders from Hebron,[46] play a dominant role in leading their tribe and Israel.

Second, in 1:29 the text notes that "the Canaanites dwelled in Gezer" among the Israelites at that time. This notation intimates that the compilation of the book had to occur sometime before Egypt's capture of Gezer and the subsequent gifting of said city to Solomon (1 Kgs. 9:16; c. 960s BCE).[47]

The third passage, 18:30, creates difficulties for an early date. Here, the note that a cult shrine was in Dan "until the day of the captivity of the land" causes many to posit a date after 722 BCE.[48] Four possible explanations have been given. First, chapters 17–18 may be a later addition denouncing Jeroboam's cult shrine in Dan. Second, the text may be original, thus proving that Judges was written after the exile of 722 BCE (2 Kgs. 15:29).[49] Third, the text may be corrupted due to a scribal error. Fourth, when coupled with 18:31, the text may be interpreted to reflect the actual period of the Judges.

While the arguments for and against these positions are detailed, suffice it to say that option 1 (i.e., the complete removal of chapters

---

dwelled (see R. Pearce S. Hubbard, "The Topography of Ancient Jerusalem," *PEQ* 98 [1966]: 130–54, esp. 135–37 and the diagram on 136). David indeed conquered every portion of the city, with the text specifically noting that he dwelled in this מצודה (*mᵉṣûḏāh*, "stronghold"; 2 Sam. 5:9). On this twofold conquering of the city, see Boling, *Judges*, 55.

46. Hebron, a city of refuge (Josh. 21:13), was David's capital city and Abiathar's home.

47. Young, *Introduction*, 169, goes on to suggest that the primacy of Sidon (Judg. 3:3) over Tyre as the chief city of Phoenicia points to a time before the twelfth century BCE. However, the pinpointing of the twelfth century by a simple reference to the Sidonians as opposed to Tyre is not persuasive, especially in light of the appearance of the term "Sidonians" by itself at a much later period (cf. 1 Kgs. 11:5, 33; 16:31; 2 Kgs. 23:13). In 1 Kgs. 16:31, Jezebel is actually called the daughter of Ethbaal the "king" of the Sidonians (c. ninth century).

48. Bush, *Notes on Judges*, v, argues—no doubt correctly—against a 722 BCE date by suggesting that the Philistines captured the region of Dan at the same time they captured the Ark of the Covenant and destroyed Shiloh (1 Samuel 4).

49. Block, *Judges, Ruth*, 66.

17–18) is not appealing because it would destroy the overall structure of the book. However, even though one could argue that verses 30-32 are a later gloss,[50] a position that is purely speculative, there seems to be a better explanation. Second, those who opt from a straightforward reading of the text fail to account for the problem of how an anti-Saulide polemic fits at this time. Furthermore, one would also have to believe that there was an ongoing questionable cult site in Dan from the period of the judges until 722 BCE (over three hundred years!). This site, officiated over by descendants of Moses no less,[51] would have had to survive the judgeship of Samuel and the reigns of Saul, David, and Solomon, who were all cultic reformers to some degree (cf. 1 Sam. 7:4; 1 Sam. 28:3; 1 Kings 5–7).[52] Moreover, if a cult site had been present in Dan from the judges' period onward, then Jeroboam I would not have needed to establish one there when he came to power (1 Kgs. 12:29). Thus, this understanding has too many historical, practical, and theological problems to merit its acceptance. Third, some posit that the word הָאָרֶץ (*hāʾāreṣ*, "the land") at the end of 18:30 should be emended to read הָאָרֹן (*hāʾārōn*, "the Ark") due to a scribal error.[53] Thus, the text would reflect the captivity of the Ark by the Philistines at Aphek in 1104 BCE (1 Samuel 4). While emending the text would solve the late-date problem, there may be another option that preserves the text.

It seems more likely that the situation being presented in 18:30 must be understood in light of 18:31, namely that the cult shrine in Dan lasted "all the days the house of God was in Shiloh."[54] During

---

50. Typical of this perspective is that of Budde, *Das Buch der Richter*, 123–24.

51. Jewish scribes emended the text to remove any connection of Moses to the cult site in Dan. They added a raised *nun* after the *mem*, thus changing מֹשֶׁה (*mōšeh*, "Moses") to מנשׁה (*menaššeh*, "Manasseh").

52. So Wolf, *Judges*, 378.

53. See, for example, ibid., 378; and Young, *Introduction*, 170.

Saul's later reign, the tabernacle was at Nob (1 Samuel 21), whereas during David's early reign it was at Gibeon (1 Chr. 16:39; 21:29); yet no mention is made of these sites in this text—suggesting an earlier date. What is more, 18:31 makes it clear that the Danite shrine rivaled the Shiloh site, the official cult site during the late judges' period (1 Samuel 1–4; c. 1050 BCE). Interestingly, Jerusalem, the religious site par excellence, is not mentioned, something one would expect from Dtr if this portion of Judges had been written post-722 BCE.[55] In light of these inconsistencies, it is perhaps safer to concur with Carl Friedrich Keil and Franz Delitzsch that the phrase "until the captivity of the land" (18:30) must refer to an unknown time when the region of Dan fell into enemy hands, well before 722 BCE.[56]

The fifth verse, 21:19, makes a parenthetical notation about the location of Shiloh as if the people no longer knew where the site was. This only makes sense if the specific location of Shiloh was unknown to the generation of the author.[57] As noted above, Nob and Gibeon had supplanted Shiloh after its destruction by the Philistines (cf. Ps. 78:59-64; Jer. 7:12-14). Someone writing at a later date (i.e., in David's day) may have needed this notation. Now, to be fair, any time after Shiloh's destruction may have fostered this side note, but when all the passages in question are considered, the former perspective obtains.

Finally, texts six through nine record the phrase "in those days there was no king in Israel" (בימים ההם אין מלך בישראל) *bayyāmîm hāhēm 'ēyn melek bᵉyiśrā'ēl*, cf. 17:6; 18:1; 19:1; 21:25).[58] From this

---

54. Contra Matthews, *Judges & Ruth*, 4, who states that Shiloh is not mentioned in Judges as a central shrine.

55. O'Connell, *Rhetoric*, 334.

56. Keil, *Judges*, 316–18. For a brief discussion against this position, see Soggin, *Judges*, 276–77.

57. Niditch, *Judges*, 185, also notes the problem of including this aside on Shiloh but does not offer a convincing reason as to why it is there.

58. Similar to the discussion above, some scholars posit that בימים ההם אין מלך בישראל ("In those days there was no king in Israel") does not point to an earthly king but, rather, to the rejection

phrase alone, the writing of Judges fits most logically after the establishment of the monarchy. While this phrase allows for any period during the monarchy, again, the anti-Saulide polemic helps narrow the focus.

In light of these chronological cues, one is able to hone in on a particular timeframe for the fashioning of Judges. Moreover, the canonical considerations noted above help narrow this search even more. It is for this reason that O'Connell's conclusion that 2 Samuel 1–4 is the "*Sitz im Text*" that best fits the message of Judges takes on a particular poignancy when searching for an author. However, O'Connell stops short of venturing a guess but, rather, states that 2 Samuel 1–4 is the "ostensible situation in which Judges was composed."[59]

From this vantage point, it appears that the "ostensible situation" seems to be a logical place to begin a search for a possible author of Judges. The prolonged struggle between David and Ishbosheth after Saul's death (i.e., 2 Samuel 1–4) seems to be a historically fitting period. The political upheaval that the civil war would have engendered would have required some form of diplomatic appeal between the two sides—a reality alluded to in 2 Sam. 3:14-17.[60]

---

of YHWH as king. Two of the more recent scholars to hold this view are Block, *Judges, Ruth*, 59, 476; and Gregory T. K. Wong, *Compositional Strategy of the Book of Judges: An Inductive, Rhetorical Study*, VTSup 111 (Leiden: Brill, 2006), 212–23. Both authors posit that the phrase does not support a call for an earthly monarch due to the negative connotations leveled against kingship in the book (e.g., Gideon's refusal in ch. 8 to be king, and Abimelech's usurpation of kingship in ch. 9). However, contra Wong, if the author of Judges wanted to stress that it was YHWH's kingship which was rejected by Israel, he could have made this fact much clearer than the cryptic expression found here. We also see that the nation did not reject YHWH in the closing chapters because they call on YHWH (i.e., 20:18, 27; 21:2, 3; cf. also 20:1) and they call themselves the "people of God" (20:2).

59. O'Connell, *Rhetoric*, 308.

60. In v. 17, Abner accuses the elders of Israel of "seeking David in times past to be king over them." There obviously was some event or thing that caused the elders of the northern tribes to desire David's leadership. It may have in fact been some form of propagandistic tractate like Judges that had influenced them in this direction. This is not unprecedented, especially in light of David's olive branch to Jabesh-gilead after Saul's death (2 Sam. 2:5-7) and his sending of messengers to the new king of Ammon (2 Sam. 10:1-2).

Judges thus became a propagandistic tractate promoting a unified nation under Davidic rule. Only this outcome would end the internal turmoil that was weakening both factions before their common enemies (e.g., the Philistines).

Possible Authors of Judges

The next task is to find an author who lived within this narrow historical window, and who would have had distinct qualifications for the task of preparing a polemical tractate against the Saulides. Even though scholars rarely venture a guess about the author of Judges, they do often point out his unique perspectives and biases.[61] Having taken several of these postulations into consideration, one is tasked with identifying an individual who, at the bare minimum, would have needed the following qualifications:

1. He would need to be privy to many of the intimate life details of both Saul and David.[62]
2. He would have to have an intense dislike for Saul—a motive for removing the Saulides from the throne.[63]
3. He would need to be pro-Davidic, with an unshakeable belief that David was YHWH's choice to be king.[64]

---

61. Of course, these qualifications are often blurred with those of the putative Dtr.
62. Gerhard von Rad, *The Problem of the Hexateuch and Other Essays*, trans. E. W. Trueman Dicken (London: Oliver and Boyd, 1966), 195, notes the author of many of the accounts in the DtrH had to have "an intimate knowledge of what went on in the court. His portrayal of personalities and events breathes an atmosphere which must silence any doubts as to the reliability of his account. He displays a penetrating understanding of human nature, and his characterization of David is particularly impressive. The King is shown consistently in a warm sympathetic light, and is treated with great respect, although the writer always preserved an unfettered liberty of judgment with regard to him. He never reveals his faults of omission and commission . . ."
63. So Peter Miscall, *The Workings of Old Testament Narrative*, SBLSS (Philadelphia: Fortress Press, 1983), 134, who concludes his comments on the events of 1 Sam. 22:20-23 by stating ". . . the episode ends with Abiathar bound to David for his protection."
64. So Wolf, *Judges*, 379; and Globe, "Enemies Round About," 234, 250, who note the central focus on proper kingship from Judah. Young, *Introduction*, 170, points up the call of Judges for a "righteous" king. It did not take long before Saul's lack of righteousness appeared (cf. 1

4. He would need access, direct or otherwise, to oral or written materials (e.g., "proto-Samuel") that told the history/legends of the leaders of various tribes of this era.[65]

5. He would have to have a strong interest in proper YHWH worship.[66]

6. He would have to be literate.

Based upon these criteria, one of the prophets of the period—namely Samuel, Gad, or Nathan—immediately comes to mind. Therefore, a closer evaluation of these candidates is in order.

As noted in the introduction to this chapter, some modern commentators, following Jewish tradition (cf. *Baba-Bathra* 14b and 15a), propose that Samuel is in fact the author.[67] However, the likelihood of Samuel writing an anti-Saulide polemic in order to further the monarchy under David does not seem logical. Even though one may argue that Samuel anointed and supported David (1 Sam. 19:18), Samuel was not known for his wholehearted support of the institution (1 Samuel 8; 12:11). In light of this, one can assume that he would not have taken the time to fashion an elaborate polemic

---

Samuel 13; 15). David is thus the most righteous of the kings at this time, one whose life was the benchmark against which all ensuing kings were measured (cf. 1 Kgs. 9:4; 11:6; 14:8; 15:3; 2 Kgs. 14:3, etc.).

65. So Block, *Judges, Ruth*, 54. Block goes on to note that "the sources used undoubtedly go back to eyewitnesses" (54 n.154). See below for the discussion on Abiathar's "eyewitness" sources.

66. Even though Wolf, *Judges*, 377, notes the priestly nature of Judges 17–21 and points up the oft-held position that the author lived in the exilic period, this need not be the case. Keil, *Judges*, 181, draws attention to the author's focus on the "Mosaic law and legal worship." Niditch, *Judges*, 11, suggests that "conservative northern Levitical circles" were responsible for adding the "theologian's voice" post-722 BCE. Interestingly, when dealing with the author of the "Ark Narratives" of 1 Samuel (hailing from the same time period of Judges; see 1 Sam. 12:11), Rost, *Succession*, 63, comments that ". . . we looked for him among the community of priests of the ark in Jerusalem. The whole content of his narrative points this way, especially the attention paid to cultic issues."

67. See, for example, Bush, *Notes on Judges*, v. Keil, *Judges*, 182, also acknowledges the possibility of Samuel as author but goes on also to suggest one of his successors in the prophetic school. It is possible that the author was Samuel's successor; however, not necessarily from the prophetic school but, rather, the priestly office.

to foster its continuation. Now, that is not to say that he did not contribute any of the material found in Judges but, rather, that the goal of the polemic does not lend itself to Samuel's stated position. Moreover, recent character-trait studies comparing particular judges to Saul betray the period in which the book of Judges was compiled (see the appendix, below).[68] One particular parallel is the death scenes of Abimelech and Saul (cf. Judg. 9:54 and 1 Sam. 31:4).[69] If this parallel is intentional, then Samuel could not have fashioned this section of Judges.[70] Samuel's death occurs several years *before* Saul's death and David's ascension to the throne (1 Sam. 25:1). Moreover, contra Moshe Garsiel, the author of Judges and Samuel is not setting up parallels because of his distrust of the monarchy.[71] On the contrary, he is setting up parallels with the judges and the early monarchy, particularly Saul, to show what *type* of monarchy is wrong.

68. Beyond the many links between the life of Saul and the judges, the character parallels made evident by several scholars show the apparent purposeful connections between Saul and Gideon and Abimelech. See O'Connell, *Rhetoric of the Book of Judges*, 292, 296, 309–10; Schneider, *Judges*, 148; Peter R. Ackroyd, *The First Book of Samuel* (Cambridge: Cambridge University Press, 1971), 227; Bruce Birch, "The Development of the Tradition on the Anointing of Saul in 1 Sam. 9:1—10:16," *JBL* 90, no. 1 (1971): 61–64; Moshe Garsiel, *The First Book of Samuel: A Literary Study of Comparative Structure, Analogies, and Parallels* (Jerusalem: Revivim, 1985), 78–81, 94–99; and Sam Dragga, "In the Shadow of the Judges: The Failure of Saul," *JSOT* 38 (1987): 39–46. Also see comments by Mayes, "Deuteronomistic Royal Ideology," 245.

69. One could also note similarities between Samson's burial by his family and Saul's burial by the men of Jabesh-gilead (cf. Judg. 16:31//1 Sam. 31:11-13).

70. While one could argue that the book of Samuel later influenced the writing of Judges, this still does not account for the "ostensible" setting of the book of Judges in the period of 2 Samuel 1–4. It is possible that Samuel may have recorded portions of 1 Samuel before he died, thus allowing the author of Judges to glean from his records (see more on this below). However, it is just as legitimate to suggest that the author's firsthand knowledge about the life of Saul and his shortcomings, something Abiathar would have surely known, may have informed his writing—certainly Samuel was not the only one to know about the downward spiral of Saul. Either way, the historical setting is within a very confined period of Saul's later reign and David's rise to the throne. See further comments on textual dependency by O'Connell, *Rhetoric of the Book of Judges*, 309–10.

71. Garsiel, *First Book of Samuel*, 140.

Another problem with Samuel's authorship is the apparent lack of prophetic pronouncements in Judges that are typical of the book of Samuel.[72] While the book of Samuel is not as blatantly "prophetic" as 1 and 2 Kings,[73] it does betray a clear prophetic voice.[74] Judges, however, has a more priestly tone by its use of priestly themes and terminology.[75] Furthermore, YHWH addresses the nation directly in Judges—the norm during the Mosaic/priesthood era (Judg. 10:11-14). In light of these concerns, Samuel does not appear to be the most likely choice.

Next, while both Gad and Nathan definitely meet the qualifications of numbers 6 (cf. 1 Chr. 29:29; 2 Chr. 9:29—Nathan only), 3, 4, and possibly 5, the likelihood of them meeting qualifications 1 and 2 finds no clear textual support. What is more, Gad is only mentioned once in David's period as a fugitive (1 Sam. 13:7),[76] and textually Nathan does not appear until 2 Samuel 7, long

72. That is, if we concur with Jewish tradition concerning Samuel's authorship of his self-titled book; see *Baba Bathra* 14b, 15a.

73. For example, in every chapter of 1 Kings 12–17 there is a word from a prophet followed by its fulfillment.

74. Even though Samuel served as both priest and prophet, the book bearing his name reflects more of a prophetic voice. Cf. 1 Sam. 3:11-21—prophecy given; ch. 4—prophecy fulfilled; 7:3—prophecy given; 7:4-14—prophecy fulfilled. See further, 8:10-18; 9:15-16, 20; 10:1-8, 9-11; 12:16-18, 20-25; 13:13-14; 15:1-3, 16-23, 28, 29; 16:1-3, etc. With the exception of one case (i.e., Judg. 6:8) the prophetic pronouncements in Judges come from angels, not a prophet (cf. 2:1, 4; 5:23; 6:11, 12, 20-22; 13:3, 6, 9, 13, 15-18, 20, 21). Interestingly, this one appearance of an unnamed prophet is followed up by the appearance of an angel.

75. See, for example, the use of מצות (*miṣṓṯ*, "commandments") in 2:17 and 3:4; אפוד (*'ēpôd*, "ephod") in 8:27; 17:5; 18:14, 17, 18, 20 (note that the term *ephod* is used in relation to Samuel only twice in 1 Samuel cf. 2:18, 28); לוי (*lēwî*, "Levite") in 17:7, 9-13; 18:3, 15; 19:1; 20:4 ("Levites" is used once in 1 Sam. 6:15); פסילים (*pᵉsîlîm*, "idols") in 3:19, 26 תרפים (*terāpîm*, "household idols") in 17:5; 18:14, 17, 18, 20; סיני (*sînay*, "Sinai") in 5:5; the mention of the cult site at Shiloh (cf. 18:31; 21:12, 19, 21); and the quotation from the Mosaic legislation איש הישר בעיניו יעשה (*'îš hayāšār bᵉ'êynāyw ya'áśeh*, "each man did what was right in his own eyes"; cf. Judg. 17:6; 21:25//Deut. 12:8). Thus, contra Dumbrell, "In Those Days," 29, who argues for a late redaction focusing on the prophetic perspective of Judges, a priestly focus is evident. See more on the priestly perspective below. The Ark of the Covenant does appear predominantly in 1 Samuel, but not so much within the context of proper worship (cf. Judg. 20:27).

76. Benjamin Mazar, "The Military Élite of King David," *VT* 13, no. 3 (1963): 311, suggests that Gad was a fugitive with David. However, there is no textual support for this assertion. The

after David's throne was firmly established (2 Sam. 7:1). Even though these two prophets are excellent prospects, with Gad being most acceptable of the two, they both lack solid motive for writing an anti-Saulide polemic. Nonetheless, there is still one person whose life's experiences mesh best with the above-stated qualifications. It is, of course, Abiathar from Anathoth.[77]

The Qualifications of Abiathar Examined

1. *He would need to be privy to many of the intimate life details of both Saul and David.*[78] The account of Saul's massacre of the priests at Nob (1 Sam. 22:11-23) introduces Abiathar, the son of Ahimelech, the only survivor of the pogrom (see more in ch. 8). David's remorse for having indirectly caused the deaths of the eighty-five priests and their families allied Abiathar with the would-be king. The ensuing interaction between David and Abiathar points up several important factors regarding their relationship. First, Abiathar became a fugitive with David as he tried to stay one step ahead of Saul and his men. Second, it is obvious that David trusted Abiathar and relied on his cultic services.[79] For example, on at least two occasions Abiathar consulted the ephod for David while on the lam (1 Sam. 23:6-9; 30:7). Third, Abiathar served and remained loyal to David from their first interaction in 1 Samuel 22 until Abiathar's exile by Solomon in 1

Chronicler does note that Gad influenced David when he centralized worship in Jerusalem (2 Chr. 29:25).

77. As early as 1926, Rost, in his work *Die Überlieferung von der Thronnachfolge Davids*, suggested that Abiathar was a possible candidate as an author of good portions of 1 and 2 Samuel.

78. The assessment in this section does not negate the proposition that the author, whether Abiathar or someone else, may have had more than one agenda in writing the book. As Lilley, "A Literary Appreciation," 95, notes, "Purpose may be discovered by noting certain remarks, by observing the writer's selectivity, by discerning patterns in his work. However, an author may conceivably have more than one purpose, not all equally in view in any one paragraph or section."

79. Vanderkam, "Davidic Complicity," 526–27, also notes the sacerdotal benefits of David's interaction with Abiathar. He asserts that because of Abiathar's standing in the priestly families, he would have been a valuable asset to David when he gained the throne.

Kings 2. David also appointed Abiathar as one of his chief priests after his kingdom was established (2 Sam. 8:17). It is clear that David and Abiathar's time together as fugitives cemented their relationship that lasted for decades to come. Interestingly, it is Abiathar's close relationship as David's priest and fellow fugitive that saved his life after Adonijah's ill-conceived coup (1 Kgs. 2:26). It goes without saying that during this long friendship, Abiathar would have been able to learn about David the man, and his history. Further, he would have been able to gain valuable character information about Saul, with whom David had spent the majority of his teen years and early adulthood. Therefore, Abiathar meets this first qualification easily.

2. *He would have to have an intense dislike for Saul—a motive for removing the Saulides from the throne.* That Abiathar disliked Saul would be an understatement to say the least. He clearly would have had a motive to write an anti-Saulide polemic. As noted above, Saul had killed his entire family, and then had forced the young priest to become a fugitive in his own country. Abiathar's resentment of Saul would have been compounded in light of the fact that his family had been supportive of Saul during his reign up until their massacre—Ahimelech's defense of his innocence reinforces this conclusion (1 Sam. 22:14-15). Saul's paranoia and tunnel vision added to the injustice of the act.

Saul also forced Abiathar, now bereft of family, to flee from his tribal region of Benjamin to the southern reaches of Judah. His disgust for Saul's injustice and cruelty, coupled with his knowledge that David was YHWH's choice to rule in Saul's place, would have driven Abiathar to reach out to his fellow Israelites in the north to support the better choice for king. Abiathar had not only a motive, but a vested interest in trying to influence the northern tribes in this regard. Thus, Abiathar is a fitting author of an anti-Saulide polemic when placed within this context.

3. *He would need to be pro-Davidic, with an unshakeable belief that David was YHWH's choice to be king.*[80] It is very likely that Abiathar interacted with Samuel, thus becoming aware of David's anointing. Samuel's support of David would have cemented Abiathar's belief that David was YHWH's chosen leader.[81] On at least one occasion, David, no doubt with Abiathar in tow, actually fled from Saul to be with Samuel in Ramah (1 Sam. 19:18-22)—a few miles from Abiathar's original home town of Nob.[82] David's interaction with Samuel at this time would have given Abiathar opportunity to converse with Samuel. Beyond this, however, even if Abiathar had never heard about the anointing of David directly from Samuel, he would have

---

80. Contra Block, *Judges, Ruth*, 57–59, esp. 57 n.156, who intimates an anti-Judah polemic in Judges based upon three passages: 1:5-7; 5:2-31; 15:9-13. Concerning the first text, Block's assertion that "Judah's Canaanite-style brutality towards Adoni-bezek" reflects poorly on Judah is hardly a problem in light of ANE brutality and that practiced by David against the Moabites (2 Sam. 8:2). Second, Judah's absence in Judges 5 may have had more to do with the way the tribes were divided and geographically separated by the Philistines at the time. After all, Judah was in the extreme south. What is more, in 5:17 Dan and Asher are mentioned as not coming to the battle but their distance is also noted (i.e., by the sea, to the south and north of the tribes listed). Thus, they may have been unable to get to the battle even though it was expected. Furthermore, besides Asher and Dan, only seven tribes are actually mentioned as fighting. Levi was perhaps exempted, but Gad and Simeon, besides Judah, are also absent. Interestingly, Simeon and Judah both occupied the extreme southlands. One cannot be certain why Gad is not mentioned. This can hardly be a reason to propose some slight against Judah. Finally, the only remaining account is that of Judah giving up Samson to the Philistines in 15:9-13. This text, above all else, shows the need for kingship. The men of Judah, the tribe geographically the closest to the Philistines, are worried about their very existence—this is the reason they gave up Samson. Of no surprise is a similar action by the men of Judah against David when Saul was on a murderous rampage (1 Samuel 23). This, however, did not diminish Judah's central role in bringing David to the throne, twice (cf. 2 Sam. 2:4; 19:14-43). Basing an argument on these three pericopes as evidence against Judah is very tenuous when Judg. 1:2 and 20:18 make the central role of Judah very clear, especially when it comes to leading the nation. Amazingly, concerning this last point, Block later (67) goes against his own assertions by noting the pro-Judahite perspective of the author, even going so far as to saying that the author was from Judah!
81. First Samuel 22:20 records that Abiathar "fled after David" after he escaped from Saul. This causes one to conclude that Abiathar may have already known about David's call to the throne. Abiathar must have recognized this fact and decided to cast his lot in with David the would-be king.
82. After Saul's sin in the Amalakite/Agag fiasco, Samuel never saw Saul again (1 Sam. 15:35) and later even feared for his own life (1 Sam. 16:2; 19:18).

known about it from David himself, or one of David's trustworthy followers.

A natural outgrowth of Abiathar's acceptance of David as the better/rightful king of Israel would be his pro-Davidic/Judah stance. Abiathar owed David his life for allowing him to come under his protection.[83] As long as David lived and reigned, even from Hebron, Abiathar would be safe. If, however, David were to fail to win the civil war with Ishbosheth, Abiathar's life would have been in jeopardy under renewed Saulide rule. A propaganda tractate such as Judges would have aided his own cause as much as that of David's. Abiathar therefore had a vested interest in David's successful rise to the throne. Beyond these obvious pro-Davidic sentiments rooted in his fear of Saul, Abiathar's relationship with David obviously became more than a mere union of convenience. Indeed, Abiathar and David formed a close relationship and deep trust that lasted for over forty years. The depth of this relationship is seen later in David's life when the king relied on Abiathar and his son Jonathan to relay information to him concerning Absalom's coup (2 Sam. 15:35-36)—actions clearly betraying his pro-Davidic stance. This association was obviously more than a priest–king relationship. David's trust in Abiathar in the midst of the coup reflected a level of confidence beyond one of the normal cultic association.

It is quite clear that somewhere along their path of friendship Abiathar came to believe that David was YHWH's choice for the throne. The adversity they shared had solidified this bond that would

---

83. According to Schneider, *Judges*, xiv, "The book of Judges is concerned with seeking an answer to a straightforward question, 'Who is going to lead Israel?'" (1:1; 20:18).

last a lifetime.[84] For this reason, he qualifies as a man capable of writing a pro-Davidic, anti-Saulide polemic.

4. *He would need access, direct or otherwise, to oral or written materials (e.g., "proto-Samuel") that told the history/legends of the leaders of various tribes of this era.*[85] The diversity of the material found in Judges leads one to conclude that the author used a multiplicity of oral and written sources.[86] Abiathar's relationship with David, his men, and Samuel, goes a long way in explaining this diversity. Beyond his interaction with David, Abiathar would have had ample opportunity to gain important "history" from those who traveled in David's circle.[87] To begin, during David's years as a fugitive he accrued individuals from various backgrounds and tribes (1 Chr. 12:1-8), most of whom later joined his army (1 Sam. 22:2; 1 Chronicles 12).[88] It is reasonable to conceive that soldiers sitting around a campfire would have recounted the various legends of their tribal heroes/judges.[89] Abiathar

84. Abiathar remained a close ally and priest of David until the early reign of Solomon. It was only his poor choice to support Adonijah's bid for the throne during his later years that evoked Solomon's disfavor (1 Kgs. 1:19—2:27). At no point does the text record David's rejection of Abiathar all the days of his life. Ultimately, it was Solomon's respect for Abiathar's service to his father David through David's early struggle for the throne that had prevented Solomon from having Abiathar executed for treason (2 Kgs. 2:26).

85. So Block, *Judges, Ruth*, 54. Block goes on to note that "the sources used undoubtedly go back to eyewitnesses" (54 n.154).

86. Cf. ibid., 54–57. Block concludes that, based on archaeological records, "it is conceivable that written versions of all these sources [i.e., those in Judges] were produced shortly after the events, in some instances perhaps even by eyewitnesses. . . . Information from these documents was utilized selectively and arranged and shaped in accordance with his [i.e., the author's] rhetorical and theological purposes" (57). Bush, *Notes on Judges*, v, points up the need for the author to have at his disposal a number of public registers and records but suggests that these sources were used by Samuel.

87. Boling, *Judges*, 32, notes the historical nature of the material in Judges but goes on to posit that the "nuclear narratives" are "folkloric" coming from a "guild of professional storytellers in premonarchical Israel." While Boling appears to be correct about the historical, folkloric, and premonarchical nature of the narratives, there is no evidence for or reason why this material had to be from a "guild of professional storytellers." Is one to believe that people could not relate a story about their heroes without being from a "professional guild"?

88. See comments by Yee, "Introduction: Why Judges," 6. Yee notes the tribal character of these stories and how they may have circulated as such.

89. Lilley, *A Literary Appreciation*, 102, notes well that the aim of the author was to selectively record the principle feats of the great men of that time. And contra Block, *Judges, Ruth*, 55–56,

would have had access to these accounts if they had indeed started as oral tradition.[90]

As for the written sources, even if Abiathar did not have direct contact with Samuel, he certainly would have met Gad and Nathan.[91] For example, in 1 Sam. 22:5, the same chapter that records the slaughter of Abiathar's family and his flight to David's side, Gad met David to warn him about Saul's intentions.[92] Moreover, few would debate the role that both Gad and Nathan played in David's court. Thus, Abiathar would have had access to written sources passed down from Samuel to Gad and Nathan (1 Chr. 29:29; 2 Chr. 9:29).[93]

On a side note, the inclusion of the acts of Caleb and Othniel in Judges 1, both of whom were credited with conquering Hebron (cf. Josh. 14:13; 15:13-19; Judg. 1:19-20), highlights the importance of this city and its founders in the book of Judges. Abiathar lived with David in Hebron for over seven years (2 Samuel 2; 11). While Abiathar was there, he certainly would have had access to written or oral materials concerning the history and great feats of Othniel

who speculates that these "hero-stories" were placed in an anthology "long before our text was written"—the truth is no one knows how they were passed on. Gray may be closer to reality when he notes how oral tradition played a key role in the preservation of these accounts. He goes on to suggest that most of the accounts of the judges ". . . were sober historical traditions conserved locally, possibly in saga form, among those who had been involved in the events narrated." Cf. John Gray, ed., *Joshua, Judges and Ruth* (London: Thomas Nelson, 1967), 207.

90. Matthews, *Judges & Ruth*, 3, comments, "It is quite likely that much of the received text of the Book of Judges was drawn from oral tradition—especially 'hero' stories—based on the cultural memories of each of the tribes or regions of ancient Israel." It is also possible that the original form of the book of Judges may have been more irenic to the northern tribes based upon the inclusion of hero stories from diverse tribes. Indeed, Dtr may have reformatted these stories with a more negative twist (so Block, *Judges, Ruth*, 56). On the other hand, it is just as likely that Abiathar may have included the "good, the bad, and the ugly" in order to show how all past "heroes" failed to be the ideal leader—unlike David.

91. As noted earlier, Nathan first appears in 2 Samuel 7 to address the issue of building the temple in Jerusalem and then again in 2 Samuel 12 in his confrontation of David concerning the king's sin with Bathsheba. Nathan no doubt is much younger than David and Gad (cf. 1 Kings 1).

92. Although Gad reappears in 2 Samuel 24, most agree that these closing chapters of 2 Samuel are not in chronological order.

93. Block, *Judges, Ruth*, 56, notes the strong likelihood that the author had access to prophetic sources, "perhaps even Samuel himself."

and Caleb.[94] Interestingly, many scholars note the "model" nature of Othniel as a Judahite judge.[95] Perhaps this explains why these stories find priority in Judges—Abiathar's host city and home-away-from-home. Thus, Abiathar fits the profile of having access to both written and oral sources and motive for developing certain aspects of them.

5. *He would have to have a strong interest in proper YHWH worship.*[96] While some aver that proper cultic observance has a very small part to play in the book of Judges,[97] the truth is that this appears to be one of the reasons the book is written—to show the need for a return to proper YHWH worship as opposed to random Levites hiring out their services and suffering humiliation at the hands of entire cities and tribes (Judges 17–21).[98] The fact that Abiathar was associated with the main priestly family of the time (i.e., Eli; cf. 1 Sam. 14:3; 1 Kgs. 2:27) and was a priest by occupation qualifies him as a likely candidate for desiring proper YHWH worship. This also

---

94. It is likely that while Abiathar lived in the priestly city of Hebron, he would have had access to conquest records if they existed (e.g., Judg. 1:10-15 = Josh. 15:13-14; Judg. 1:27-28 = Josh. 17:12-13; Judg. 1:34 = Josh. 19:47; Judg. 1:21 = Josh. 15:63; Judg. 1:29 = Josh. 16:10; list used from Block, *Judges, Ruth*, 56).

95. See Brettler, "Literature as Politics," 404–405; and idem, *Book of Judges*, 111; Boling, *Judges*, 82; Schneider, *Judges*, 38; Webb, *Book of Judges*, 127; J. Clinton McCann, *Judges*, Interpretation (Louisville: John Knox, 2002), 43; and Sweeney, "Davidic Polemic," 524.

96. See also n. 66 above. Boling, *Judges*, 29 (see also idem, "Judges, Book of," 1115–16), propounds that the "theological updating across the centuries was confined almost exclusively to the connectives between the units." See further his neatly proposed redaction process on p. 30 and comments on p. 37. However, there is no way to prove that this was in fact the case. Scholarly theories suggesting that "intrusions" into the text can be ascertained have faltered over the past 150 years due to their sheer speculative nature and lack of consensus. Indeed, Boling (33–34) goes on to criticize such approaches employed by earlier scholars! For a paradigmatic critique of the weaknesses of these types of theories, see the work of Eugene Merrill, "Deuteronomy and de Wette: A Fresh Look at a Fallacious Premise," *JESOT* 1, no. 1 (2012): 25–42.

97. Matthews, *Judges & Ruth*, 4. To be fair, Matthews goes on to point out that the purpose of the "editors" may have been to offer an "intentional caricature of events and thus an argument for law and order" (4). This is in fact the purpose!

98. Uwe Becker, *Richterzeit und Königtum: Redaktionsgeschichtliche Studien zum Richterbuch*, BZAW192 (Berlin: de Gruyter, 1990), 257–99, who sees chs. 20–21 coming from a priestly hand, although in the postexilic period (as cited by Mayes, 254 n.41). See also comments by Gale Yee, "Ideological Criticism: Judges 17–21 and the Dismembered Body," in idem, ed., *Judges and Method*, 146–70, esp. 158–61.

helps explain the mention of the cult site at Ophrah (6:24), the Ark (20:27), and the author's knowledge of Shiloh (18:31; 21:12, 19, 21).[99] In this vein, the specific information about cult shrines and their duration of existence (Judges 17–20, esp. 18:30-31—see above) is fitting coming from the pen of Abiathar, who was from the region of the cult sites in question.[100] It is only logical that a priest would want some level of uniformity in YHWH worship while moving away from random shrines that led to the profaning of YHWH's name. Interestingly, Robert Boling even hints at the thematic and literary parallels between the Levitical material (e.g., Deuteronomy and the Holiness Code) and the book of Judges.[101]

Canonically, David's first act after conquering Jerusalem was to bring the Ark of the Covenant into his new capital and begin some form of centralized worship of YHWH (cf. 2 Sam. 6:1; 1 Chr. 15:11-12). Abiathar's previous cultic service to the would-be king (see 1 Sam. 23:6-9; 30:7; 2 Sam. 2:1—implicit) must have influenced David in this and many other matters concerning YHWH worship. As already noted, it is very likely that Abiathar had direct contact with the pro-YHWH prophets, Samuel, Gad, and Nathan. In light of the cultic bent of Judges, Abiathar once again fits the profile of author.

6. *He would have to be literate.* Because I have already covered this topic in chapter 1 above, only a few summary notes will be given here. The priestly community has long been recognized as a literate class of society in Israel as well as in the ANE.[102] To assume that

---

99. So Block, *Judges, Ruth*, 57. Block avers that the author "must have been a Judahite" (67) who was "schooled in the Torah of Moses."

100. The cult centers of Bethel, Shiloh, Gilgal, and Mizpah are all within twenty miles of Jerusalem while Nob was approximately two-and-a-half miles north of Jerusalem. The central location of this priestly city would have served well as a central lodging area for priests who served at these key sites. Beyond this, proper worship would have been an important part of Abiathar's teaching, especially if he had contact with Samuel, which the text seems to imply.

101. Boling, *Judges*, 32–33. Even though Boling's perspective on the authorship of this material does not mesh with the theory being presented here, he is correct in noting the Levitical/priestly nature of Judges.

Abiathar was among that select group is a given. Even if Abiathar was illiterate, which is unlikely, David employed scribes during his rule, of which Abiathar could have availed himself (e.g., 2 Sam. 8:16-17; 20:25). Therefore, Abiathar would have had the means, or at least the connections, to write an anti-Saulide polemic.

Some Final Notes

Before ending this discussion, one final facet needs to be addressed which is pertinent to our authorship discussion. Scholars have often queried about the uniqueness/randomness of Jotham's fable in the book of Judges.[103] According to Noth, Judges 9 was part of Dtr's

102. See S. S. Laurie, "The History of Early Education: The Semitic Races," *The School Review* 1, no. 8 (1893): 482–90; J. Philip Hyatt, "The Writing of an Old Testament Book," *BA* 6, no. 4 (1943): 72; S. Yeivin, "Social, Religious and Cultural Trends In Jerusalem under the Davidic Dynasty," *VT* 3, no. 2 (1953): 149–66; Erica Reiner, "Fortune-Telling in Mesopotamia," *JNES* 19, no. 1 (1960): 23; John J. Collins, *Daniel*, Hermeneia (Minneapolis: Fortress Press, 1993), 138; Ian Young, "Israelite Literacy: Interpreting the Evidence: Part II," *VT* 48, no. 3 (1998): 408–22; and Duane Garrett, *Rethinking Genesis* (Tain, UK: Christian Focus Publications, 2000), 208–10. See also p. 24 n.55.

103. For example, Soggin, *Judges*, 173, 175; Albert Vincent, *Le Livre des Juges, Le Livre de Ruth* (Paris: Les Editions du Cerf, 1952), 76; Eugene H. Maly, "The Jotham Fable—Anti-Monarchical?" *CBQ* 22, no. 3 (1960): 300, 301; and Baruch Halpern, "The Rise of Abimelek Ben-Jerubbaal," *HAR* 2 (1978): 79. For further analysis on ch. 9, see Halpern, "The Rise of Abimelek Ben-Jerubbaal," 79–100, esp. 80–81, 92–96; and Irwin, "Not Just Any King," 446. Others have suggested that this chapter is an "anti-monarchical tractate;" cf. Hugo Gressmann, *Die Anfänge Israels (von 2. Mosis bis Richter und Ruth) übers., erklärt und mit Einleitungen versehen* (Göttingen: Vandenhoeck & Ruprecht, 1914), 219–20; Richter, *Richterbuch*, 285–86; Martin Buber, *Kingship of God* (New York: Harper & Row, 1967), 75, posits, albeit incorrectly, that not just ch. 9, but the entire book is anti-monarchical; Frank Crüsemann, *Der Widerstand gegen das Königtum: Die antikoniglichen Texte des alten Testamentes und der Kampf um den fruhen israelitischen Staat*, WMANT 49 (Neukirchen-Vluyn: Neukirchener, 1978), 32–42 (on the redaction of Jotham's fable, see esp. 39); John Bright, *A History of Israel*, 4th ed. (Philadelphia: Westminster, 2000), 182, 273 n.7; Soggin, *Judges*, 173–94, esp. 176–77; Niditch, *Judges*, 114–18.For a perspective showing how Jotham's Fable promotes proper or a particular type of monarchy/leadership, cf. Maly, "Jotham Fable," 299–305; Gordon Oeste, *Legitimacy, Illegitimacy, and the Right to Rule: Windows on Abimelech's Rise and Demise in Judges 9* (New York: T&T Clark, 2011), 84–87, 221–27; idem, "Butchered Brothers and Betrayed Families: Degenerating Kinship Structures in the Book of Judges," *JSOT* 35, no. 3 (2011): 295–316; and Irwin, "Not Just Any King," 447–53. See competing perspectives as presented by Naomi Steinberg, "Social Scientific Criticism: Judges 9 and Issues of Kinship," in Yee, ed., *Judges and Method*, 45–64, esp. 53–63.

work.[104] It is possible that Abiathar, as the "Dtr," included Jotham's polemic against Abimelech in Judges 9 as a miniature autobiographical reflection on the senseless, murderous acts that Saul propagated against his family.[105] In essence, both Abiathar and Jotham call out to any and all who will listen, saying, "I am from the north like you, brothers and sisters, listen to my warning, do not allow a usurper to sit on the throne lest you all be consumed!"[106] Thus, Jotham's fable, as does Abiathar's anti-Saulide polemic, stresses the negative impact of throne usurpation. In both cases, Abimelech and Ishbosheth came to the throne without divine sanction by allowing family members to crown them as king (cf. Judg. 9:6//2 Sam. 2:8-9).[107] Judges 9 thus becomes a subtle plea from Abiathar to his audience to accept his message and embrace YHWH's choice for king—David—not the usurper, Ishbosheth. If they refuse to listen, evil will befall them as it had Abimelech and those of Shechem.

Next, the anti-Benjamin rhetoric that appears in Judges 19–21 must be read in the light of Saulide connections. Even though Abiathar was from Benjamin, he zeroes in on particular regions of Benjamin that are directly connected to Saul. Because a number of scholars have written on these chapters at length, only a few summary marks will be given.[108] First, the Levite and Saul have several points of contact, the main one being the hewing of the concubine into twelve pieces (cf. Judg. 19:29; 1 Sam. 11:7).[109] Second, geographical

---

104. Noth, *Deuteronomistic History*, 20.

105. Maly, "Jotham Fable," 300, in fact does suggest that the fable has been "introduced as a literary figure by the author of the account."

106. It is not a coincidence that the author of Judges has Jotham standing upon Gerizim to deliver his fable. This is the same mountain that the tribe of Levi (i.e., Abiathar's tribe) was to stand upon and pronounce blessings upon Israel (Deut. 27:12).

107. Abner was a first cousin once removed to Ishbosheth (1 Sam. 14:50-51).

108. Brettler, "Literature as Politics," 395–418; idem, *Book of Judges*, 84–91; and Amit, *Hidden Polemics*, 178–88.

109. Amit, *Hidden Polemics*, 181–82, suggests several parallels, including the common theme of donkeys (19:3, 10, 19, 21, 28, compared to 1 Sam. 9:3, 5, 20, etc.) and the consulting of a servant (cf. Judg. 19:11; 1 Sam. 9:6-8).

place names in these chapters point to Saul as well.[110] Saul's home was located in Gibeah (cf. Judges 19–20; 1 Sam. 15:34; see also 1 Sam. 11:4; 2 Sam. 21:6; Isa. 10:29). And the men of Jabesh-gilead, who are disparaged in the Judges' account, played a key role in establishing Saul on the throne (1 Samuel 11).[111] It is particularly noteworthy that Judg. 20:13 and 1 Sam. 11:12 have the same phraseology in the context of accounts about the region of Gibeah—"Give up the men that we may put them to death."[112] Similarly, the cities of Ramah, Rimmon, and Mizpah may be connected to events in Saul's life.[113] Thus, we may conclude with Marc Zvi Brettler that this account serves to ". . . make Saul look bad. He comes from a tribe, indeed from a city of rapists and murderers, who are unwilling to own up to their own wrongdoings."[114]

Finally, a couple of other key issues stand out in the author's polemic for kingship. First, the depravity of the men of Benjamin and their failure to adhere to the dictates of the majority of Israel brought about mass destruction and death. This finds a fitting parallel in the civil war between David and Ishbosheth (e.g., 2 Sam. 2:24-28). The message is clear: civil war only hurts the nation's unity and can threaten the annihilation of entire tribes. Second, the inclusio

---

110. Ibid., 181–83. Amit has correctly noted the connection between the Levite and David's hometown, Bethlehem-Judah. However, I cannot agree with Amit's connection of Jebus to David in this account, at least as it relates in a positive sense. In 19:12, Jebus is disparaged and would not have reflected positively on David. It would, however, have fit in the period prior to David's capture of it as I suggest (see 2 Sam. 5:1-9).

111. Brettler, "Literature as Politics," 413. Also, in 2 Sam. 2:4-7 the people of Jabesh-gilead appear to reject David's olive branch for peace after the death of Saul.

112. Robert Polzin, *Samuel and the Deuteronomist: A Literary Study of the Deuteronomistic History, Part 2: 1 Samuel* (San Francisco: Harper & Row, 1989), 113.

113. According to Amit, *Hidden Polemics*, 180, Ramah, the hometown of Samuel, appears to have little literary value in ch. 19 other than to bring out another aspect of the polemic against Saul. Also, Amit (181) points up that Rimmon is the place where Saul had rested with 600 men (1 Sam. 14:2). Finally, Mizpah was the location of Saul's official anointing by Samuel (1 Sam. 10:17-27) and is used in ch. 20 as the staging ground for the attack on Benjamin.

114. Brettler, *Book of Judges*, 89.

focusing on YHWH's choice of Judah for leadership cannot be overstated (Judg. 1:1//20:18).

Conclusion

We may conclude this chapter by noting that most scholars now recognize that Judges contains some level of an anti-Saulide polemic. What they fail to do is offer a viable option for when and who could have fashioned such an intricate character and content polemic. What has been suggested here answers these two key questions and opens the door for future rhetorical analyses, such as presented in the "Some Final Notes" section immediately above. It is safe to conclude that Judges as an anti-Saulide polemic was commissioned by David at Hebron. This conclusion takes seriously the canonical text and scholarly hypotheses such as that advocated by O'Connell. At the same time, this conjecture does not preclude the possibility that Judges was later reworked before being added to the DtrH by either Abiathar himself or someone as distant as Jeremiah.[115] Abiathar had the necessary qualifications, the motive, and opportunity to write Judges as a means to draw a war-torn nation together under the banner of one king. Legends, histories, and character parallels gave Abiathar a ready pool of material to be organized into a fitting tribute to his friend and ruler at Hebron while rallying support from the northern tribes to reject Saulide rule and bring peace and stability to a nation in turmoil. Yet, even then, his priestly duty to instruct the

---

115. Lilley's proposition appears valid when he avers that "The assumption of 'authorship' does not rule out the possibility of additions and later editing, still less does it deny the possibility of identifying sources; it simply takes as a principle that one should begin by looking for the maximum rather than the minimum unity of plan" ("A Literary Appreciation," 95). On the other hand, Matthews's (*Judges & Ruth*, 5–6) supposition that Judges started in an oral form in the monarchic period and was later recorded to support Josiah's administration (c. 640–609 BCE) lacks not only textual support, but also fails to take seriously the work of scholars who have shown the polemical nature of Judges. Moreover, such positions do not answer the canonical and historical issues of when such a polemic would have had optimum clout.

nation concerning the proper worship of YHWH broke through as he trumpeted his explicit call for a return to YHWH and an implicit polemic for David, Israel's God-appointed king.

8

1 Samuel: History vs. Polemic

For the story of Saul and David Dtr. had access to an extensive collection of Saul–David traditions compiled long before Dtr. from different elements—the old tradition on Saul and, in particular, the story of the rise of David and the story of the Davidic succession. As in the occupation story, the existence of this traditional material absolved Dtr. from the need to organize and construct the narrative himself. Once he has stated his fundamental position on the institution of the monarchy in no uncertain terms (1 Sam. 8–12), he has little need to interpose in the traditional account his own judgments and interpretations, particularly as the tradition itself gives a detailed account of the rapid downfall of Saul, the first king . . .[1]

While Noth identifies the extensive collections of the Saul and David traditions incorporated by Dtr into his DtrH, he does not offer a good answer to the basic question: If Dtr is so anti-monarchical, why is he so pro-Davidic—after all, David is a king! This only makes sense if Dtr, that is, the author of the books of Samuel, is a friend of David, or if he supports the Davidic kingship in general. In this case, it is just

---

1. Martin Noth, *The Deuteronomistic History*, JSOTSup 15 (Sheffield: JSOT, 1981), 54.

as valid to say that Dtr is not "anti-monarchic" per se but, rather, is attempting to promote a certain *type* of kingship. Nevertheless, even though I cannot agree totally with Noth's postulations on the Dtr's perspective of the monarchy, the rest of his assessment is actually more astute than most scholars today give him credit for.[2] Noth's assertion of the existence of "traditional material" points to historical work well before the generally accepted date of Dtr,[3] to a time, I would argue, most fittingly in Abiathar's day.[4]

Well-intentioned scholars have also "identified" a number of redactional layers in this portion of the DtrH. For example, P. Kyle McCarter argues for two redactions of the book of Samuel (i.e., Dtr1 and Dtr2), with the majority of the redactional work appearing in the first redaction during Josiah's era.[5] While such redactional activity is possible, this still does not negate the fact that the proposed antiquity of the material at the heart of the DtrH (1 Samuel 1—1 Kings 2), as pointed up by Noth, may be best explained by the fact that Abiathar lived and breathed much of what was written. And as we have seen for the books of Joshua and Judges, for those portions where he was not around to have an eyewitness vantage point, sources, both

---

2. See, for example, the assessment of various scholars' opinions since Noth in Walter Dietrich and Thomas Naumann, "The David–Saul Narrative," in *Reconsidering Israel and Judah: Recent Studies on the Deuteronomistic History*, ed. Gary N. Knoppers and J. Gordon McConville (Winona Lake, IN: Eisenbrauns, 2000), 308–13.

3. So, too, ibid., 310.

4. I am aware of the trend within scholarship to date an increasing amount of the material in 1 and 2 Samuel to a much later date. However, this trend takes into account neither the rhetorical reasons for why these texts were preserved nor what function they served at that time. For example, see Thomas Römer, *The So-called Deuteronomistic History: A Sociological, Historical, and Literary Introduction* (London: T&T Clark, 2005), 93–94.

5. Cf. P. Kyle McCarter, "The Books of Samuel," in *The History of Israel's Traditions: The Heritage of Martin Noth*, ed. Steven L. McKenzie and M. Patrick Graham, JSOTSup 182 (Sheffield: Sheffield Academic Press, 1994), 265. These divisions can be tabulated as follows: Dtr1—1 Sam. 2:27-36; 3:11-14; 4:18b; 7:2aβ-4, 6b, 13-17; 8:8; 12:6-15, 19b (?), 20b-22, 24-25; 13:1-2; 14:47-51; 17 (passim); 20:11-17, 23, 40-42; 23:14-24:23; 25:28-31; 2 Sam. 2:10a(?), 11 (?); 3:9-10, 17-18a (?), 18b, 28-29; 5:1-2, 4-5 (?), 12; 6:21; 7:1b, 9b-11a, 13a, 16, 22b-24 (?), 25-26, 29bα; 8:14b-15 (?); 14:9; 15:24aβ (?); 21:7; Dtr2—1 Sam. 12:25; 2 Sam. 7:22b-24 (?); 15:24aβ (?).

written and oral, helped flesh out the earlier picture. Thus, Noth is correct in his observation that the final Dtr (be it Jeremiah or Baruch) did only minor editing to the received tradition of Samuel.

The Authorship of Samuel

Over the past two thousand years, scholars have proposed a number of authorship options for the book of Samuel. Medieval rabbi and exegete Don Isaac Abravanel (1437–1508), following Jewish tradition to a degree (see *Baba-Bathra* 14b), suggested that the book of Samuel was written by Samuel, Nathan, and Gad—each attributing the material from his own day (see 1 Chr. 29:29). He concluded that the one who combined this material was none other than Jeremiah.[6] On the other hand, Christian exegete Rabanus Maurus (776?–865) posited that David finished Samuel's book where the aged prophet had left off.[7] Twentieth-century scholars had similarly diverse opinions. For example, Leonhard Rost, building upon the conclusions of A. Klostermann, proposed that Ahimaaz, Zadok's son, wrote portions of Samuel.[8] And Hans Wilhelm Hertzberg suggested that Hushai, David's friend, may have played a role.[9] Georg Fohrer asserts that while only slight Dtr influence is observable in Samuel (as per Noth's theory), the "[p]rocedure and perspective are so different that the books cannot be derived from a single author or redactor."[10]

---

6. Jeffrey C. Geoghegan, *The Time, Place, and Purpose of the Deuteronomistic History: The Evidence of "Until This Day,"* BJS 347 (Providence, RI: Brown University Press, 2006), 17.

7. Ibid., 22.

8. Leonhard Rost, *The Succession to the Throne of David*, trans. Michael D. Rutter and David M. Gunn (Sheffield: Almond, 1982), 105 (German: *Die Überlieferung von der Thronnachfolge Davids*, BWANT 3/6 [Stuttgart: Kohlhammer, 1926]). Cf. also A. Klostermann, *Die Bücher Samuelis und der Könige*, KKHSANT 3 (Nördlingen: Beck, 1887).

9. Hans Wilhelm Hertzberg, *I & II Samuel* (Philadelphia: Westminster, 1964), 379. Gillian Keys, *The Wages of Sin: A Reappraisal of the 'Succession Narrative,'* JSOTSup 221 (Sheffield: Sheffield Academic Press, 1996), 212, plays it safe with the "prophetic school" of the exilic period.

10. Georg Fohrer, *Introduction to the Old Testament*, trans. David Green (London: SPCK, 1970), 194.

Another issue when dealing with the authorship of the book of Samuel is the obvious continuation of the judges' period into 1 Samuel. On this problem, David Jobling quips,

> Has the narrator ever released this reader from the instructions of Judges 2 . . . ? When the *Philistines* appear [in 1 Samuel], she will recall that they were not dealt with in Judges according to established convention—the formulae for foreigners' subjugation to Israel (see Judg. 3:30, 4:23 etc.) were missing at the end of the Samson account . . . but the reader will surely let out a cry of recognition when she comes to 1 Samuel 7, which returns fully to the logic of the judge-cycles, including a subjugation formula: 'So the Philistines were subdued' (7:13).[11]

To be sure, Jobling is in fact correct when it comes to the connectivity of the historical periods handled in these two books. However, it appears that the history was bifurcated for a reason. Apart from the rhetorical arguments presented in the previous chapter, one could also postulate that Abiathar, of the line of Eli, did not want to connect himself and the revered Samuel directly with the chaos of the judges' era. Moreover, Abravanel and Maurus's assumption that Samuel played a part in authoring portions of Samuel may be correct. Samuel may very well have originally connected the source material found in Judges and 1 Samuel and only at a later period did Abiathar split it apart for the purpose of the polemic presented in the book of Judges.[12] Thus, Judges 17–21 (and, to a degree, ch. 9) served as a divider to drive home the type of kingship/leadership that was *not* needed—the very thing that is picked up in 1 Samuel 8.

Furthermore, contra Römer, the book of Samuel clearly exhibits a unified rhetorical outlook that in some cases flashes back to earlier books of the DtrH.[13] First Samuel presents the birth of Samuel and his

---

11. David Jobling, "What, If Anything, Is 1 Samuel," *SJOT* 7, no. 1 (1993): 23 (italics original).
12. Alexander Rofé, "Ephraimite Versus Deuteronomistic History," in Knoppers and McConville, eds., *Reconsidering Israel and Judah*, 465, argues for an early source, which included Joshua 24–1 Samuel 12.

death, the first appearance of Saul and his death, and introduces us to David—the boy, the giant killer, and the outlaw turned mercenary. By the end of the book Israel's experiment with the monarchy hangs in the balance with the death of Saul.[14] Second Samuel fills this lacuna bringing to the fore, once again, David—the right *type* of king. Finally, whereas 1 Samuel is inextricably linked to the judges' period, within the second half of Samuel we also find reflections on Joshua, the great conquest leader, mirrored in the narrative accounts of David—we will return to this shortly. Therefore, the cohesiveness of motifs within both books of Samuel highlights not only the unity of the work, but also the rhetorical links with the two books that precede it.[15]

Regardless of how one may approach the book of Samuel, the reader still finds a series of accounts that betray the author's respect for Samuel and the Ark (1 Samuel 1–7), his disdain for the Saulide monarchy (1 Samuel 8–31), an apology for David's right to the throne (1 Samuel 13—2 Samuel 4), a picture of David as the new Joshua (2 Samuel 5–10; 13–20), and the sad plight of David's family when the sin of adultery and murder precipitate God's fourfold judgment (2 Samuel 11—1 Kings 2). Due to these sins, the final years of David's life are marred by his sons' internecine struggles for

---

13. Römer, *So-called Deuteronomistic History*, 92, suggests that "the books of Samuel are among the least unified and the least homogeneous within the Former Prophets."

14. See also the work of Walter Dietrich, *David, Saul und die Propheten: Das Verhältnis von Religion und Politik nach den prophetischen Überlieferungen vom frühesten Königtum in Israel*, BWANT 122 (Stuttgart: Kohlhammer, 1987); and J. P. Fokkelman, *Narrative Art and Poetry in the Books of Samuel. A Full Interpretation Based on Stylistic and Structural Analysis II: The Crossing Fates (1 Sam. 13–31 & 2 Sam. 1)* (Assen: Van Gorcum, 1986).

15. See, for example, the list of intertwined motifs in Dietrich and Naumann, "The David–Saul Narrative," 305–307. See also the commentary by Keys, *The Wages of Sin: A Reappraisal of the 'Succession Narrative'* (1996).

succession—a conflict that will see three sons die by the sword.[16] In each facet of this outline, Abiathar's input may be seen.

The End of the Judges: 1 Samuel 1–12

Samuel's Ministry: 1 Samuel 1–3

The prophet Samuel is the dominant figure in 1 Samuel 1–12. Much of the content in these first twelve chapters appears to be a literary unity and perhaps derives from Samuel himself or someone close to him.[17] The eyewitness-type accounts of these chapters push one to this conclusion.[18] In this vein, chapters 1–3 could easily have come from the hand of Samuel, especially those words which were close to the heart of his mother (1 Samuel 1–2).[19] In these chapters, we also see the prophetic element begin to rise to the surface. Much of the prophetic material points forward to events that will unfold from 1 Samuel 4 to the early period of Solomon. Now, while many scholars may presuppositionally relegate these "prophecies" to hypothesized redactional layers,[20] as they stand, these early prophecies serve not

16. So too T. C. G. Thornton, "Solomonic Apologetic in Samuel and Kings," *CQR* 169, no. 371 (1968): 162.

17. Lyle M. Eslinger, *Kingship of God in Crisis: A Close Reading of Samuel 1–12*, BLS 10 (Decatur, GA: Almond, 1985), 425, also sees unity in these chapters. For an overview of the tradition layers of 1 Samuel 7–15, see Bruce Birch, *The Rise of the Israelite Monarchy: The Growth and Development of I Samuel 7–15*, SBLDS 27 (Missoula: Scholars, 1976), 1–7.

18. John Van Seters, *In Search of History: Historiography in the Ancient World and the Origins of Biblical History* (New Haven: Yale University Press, 1983; repr. Winona Lake, IN: Eisenbrauns, 1997), 353, concludes that Dtr is responsible for combining the sources in the first seven chapters.

19. Marsha White, "'The History of Saul's Rise': Saulide State Propaganda in 1 Samuel 1–14," in *'A Wise and Discerning Mind': Essays in Honor of Burke O. Long*, ed. Saul M. Olyan and Robert C. Culley, BJS 325 (Providence, RI: Brown University Press, 2000), 287–91, suggests that the constant nuanced use of שׁאל (*šāʾal*, "to ask") in Samuel's birth narrative served as a means of introducing Samuel into the Saul narrative while subtly looking forward to Saul. Note also the linguistic parallels between chs. 1 and 9. Such connections do point to unified authorship of this portion. Cf. P. Kyle McCarter, *I Samuel: A New Translation with Introduction: Notes and Commentary*, AB 8 (Garden City, NY: Doubleday, 1980), 172; and Eslinger, *Kingship of God in Crisis*, 285–86.

only as a means of vindicating the ministries of the prophets but also as an integral part of the following narrative. For example, the prophetic announcement that Eli's sons would be judged, and that Eli's line would be cut off from the priesthood (1 Sam. 2:27-36), finds fulfillment in Hophni and Phinehas's deaths (1 Samuel 4) and Abiathar's removal from the priestly office at the hands of Solomon (1 Kgs. 2:26; see the discussion below). The new "faithful priest" to come no doubt is Samuel, who is revealed as both prophet and priest in the ensuing account.[21] Moreover, the use of the phrase "an enduring house" (בית־נאמן *bayit-ne'ĕmān*) in 1 Sam. 2:35 looks forward to the Davidic covenant of 2 Samuel 7 (1 Sam. 25:28; 2 Sam. 7:16) and on to YHWH's promise to Jeroboam I, which the new king failed to live up to (1 Kgs. 11:38).[22]

Of course, some may argue that Abiathar would never include material detrimental to him and his family. However, Noth's assumption that Dtr honored his sources obtains here.[23] Abiathar allowed the prophetic announcement of 1 Samuel 2 to stand. As a priest, Abiathar, like any faithful priest, would want sin judged, even if it was in his own family. To a degree, the legitimate judgment on Hophni and Phinehas is counterbalanced by the sympathy evoked by the massacre of Abiathar's innocent family at Nob (1 Samuel 22),

---

20. E.g., Helga Weippert, "'Histories' and 'History': Promise and Fulfillment in the Deuteronomistic Historical Work," in Knoppers and McConville, eds., *Reconsidering Israel and Judah*, 60.

21. So, too, Mark Leuchter, *Samuel and the Shaping of Tradition* (New York: Oxford University Press, 2013), 34. On the other hand, some posit that this could also be Zadok. There are almost Messianic overtones to 1 Sam. 2:35-36. Note especially the appearance of משיח (*mašiaḥ* "anointed one") in v. 35 and the connections with 2 Sam. 7:12. Richard D. Nelson, "The Role of the Priesthood in the Deuteronomistic History," in Knoppers and McConville, eds., *Reconsidering Israel and Judah*, 186, downplays any future role of the prophecy beyond Abiathar being deposed in 1 Kings 2. See also Robert Polzin, *Samuel and the Deuteronomist: A Literary Study of the Deuteronomistic History, Part 2: 1 Samuel* (San Francisco: Harper & Row, 1989), 41, who points to Samuel but does not exclude future fulfillment.

22. See also Nelson, "Role of the Priesthood," 184.

23. Noth, *Deuteronomistic History*, 96.

even though some may see this latter event as part of the fulfillment of the prophecy of chapter 2 as well.[24] Finally, chapter 3 reflects the personal experiences of Samuel as a boy and helps serve as the back story for these opening chapters. He is the voice of YHWH, something rare in those days (3:1, 20, 21). The use of prophetic doublets, here against Eli's house (once from an unnamed prophet and once from the boy Samuel; cf. 1 Sam. 2:27-36; 3:11-14), will be a dominant motif as we move forward.[25]

Before advancing to the putative Ark Narratives of 4:1—7:1 (hereafter AN), a couple of points need to be addressed concerning Abiathar's use of Samuel's written or oral sources—sources that may comprise the majority of 1 Sam. 1:1—16:4. First, one must keep in mind that Samuel was like an adopted son to Eli (1 Samuel 2–3) and, as such, his connection to the Elides would have been profound, something Abiathar as a great-great-grandson of Eli would have known. Second, because of this connection and Samuel's connections to David, Abiathar would have had a deep respect for Samuel and his opinions, especially on the monarchy. This respect may be the reason that Samuel is not presented in a negative light, with the exception of his sons' indiscretions (1 Sam. 8:2-3). And here it is possible that Abiathar is pointing out that even someone as great as Samuel could have sons who were scoundrels, much like Eli's two sons. This may have been his way of lessening the sting of God's judgment on his ancestors. Of course, this judgment is inextricably linked to the so-called AN.[26]

---

24. E.g. White, "'History of Saul's Rise,'" 291–92.
25. Contra, Robert Karl Gnuse, *The Dream Theophany of Samuel: Its Structure in Relation to Ancient Near Eastern Dreams and Its Theological Significance* (Lanham, MD: University Press of America, 1984), 2, who sees Samuel's dream in ch. 3 as "a late literary creation cast in the form of an ancient Near Eastern message dream theophany" and chs. 1–3 as a "literary creation." There is no reason not to find a level of historicity in these chapters based upon their importance to the overall narrative complex.

The Ark Narratives: 1 Samuel 4–7

Leonhard Rost suggested that 4:1b—7:1 (and 2 Sam. 6:1-23)[27] represent a separate tradition.[28] Upon closer scrutiny, however, it becomes clear that these chapters are such a fundamental part of the book of Samuel that it is hard to divorce them from what follows.[29] As just noted, the prophecy against Eli's sons in chapter 2 finds fulfillment in this block (4:4-22). Moreover, the central role of the Philistines as the enemy of Israel harks back to the days of Samson (Judges 13–16), while looking forward to Saul and David's encounters with them. Even though Samuel may have been responsible for the heart of the narratives, Abiathar's input appears at key junctures especially with the common refrain "unto this day" (5:5; 6:18; see ch. 4).

It is also possible that much of 1 Samuel 4 may have come from family tradition within Abiathar's immediate household. Abiathar was in fact the grandson of Phinehas's older son Ahitub (cf. 14:3; 22:9, 11, 12, 20), and such tragedy in conjunction with a defeat would have been common family knowledge, to be sure. Moreover, the author's note that a "man from *Benjamin*" came to give the news of the defeat of Israel (4:12) is a telling parenthetical notation. Apart from the fact that any priest from Eli's family would have known about the horror of the loss of the Ark, especially under the watch of the Elides, the Dagon—YHWH confrontation and tradition in chapter 5 easily could have been added by Abiathar in light of his time with David in

---

26. See also the work of Antony F. Campbell, *The Ark Narrative (1 Sam 4–6; 2 Sam 6): A Form-critical and Traditio-Historical Study*, SBLDS 16 (Missoula: Scholars, 1975). Campbell (6) starts his analysis with the basic acceptance of Rost's theory.

27. For a further delineation of what Rost proposed was not part of the original AN, see ibid., 8.

28. Leonhard Rost, *Die Überlieferung von der Thronnachfolge Davids* (BWANT 3/6; Stuttgart: Kohlhammer, 1926) in English, *The Succession to the Throne of David*, trans. Michael D. Rutter and David M. Gunn (Great Britain: Almond, 1982).

29. So, too, Nadav Na'aman, "The Pre-Deuteronomistic Story of Saul and Its Historical Significance," *CBQ* 54, no. 4 (1992): 654.

Philistia (see the discussion in ch. 4 above). Finally, in several places of chapter 6 we also find references to priestly interests. For example: "guilt" (אשם 'āšām) and "whole burnt" (עלה 'ōlāh) offerings (6:4, 8, 15) are mentioned; a reference to the exodus tradition appears (6:6); the role of Levites is pointed out (6:15); and the Levitical city of Beth-shemesh appears seven times (6:9-20). Now, to be sure, much of this is conjecture, but the weight of evidence does point toward Abiathar or someone of his household.[30]

Nevertheless, this "conjecture" becomes more realistic when understood in the light of the rhetorical purpose for the inclusion of the AN in the account of 1 Samuel. Yes, the connections both before and after the narrative show that this block is important to the whole. However, it also shows why the Ark is not in Shiloh under the control of the Elides, and it answers the questions as to why David has to go to Kiriath-jearim to bring it up to Jerusalem. More importantly, the AN of 1 Samuel 4–7 and 2 Samuel 6 reflects the period of early centralization at a national level during the Davidic monarchy. The individuals who would push such an agenda are few, to be sure.

Finally, while I am not in complete agreement with Rost and Antony Campbell that 2 Samuel 6 was an integral part of a separate AN, Campbell's assessment of who wrote these narratives, and why, has bearing on our thesis. He notes,

> . . . they should be viewed as men of the stamp of Abiathar, who were not afraid to leave their sanctuary and engage in the national arena. . . . [the Narrative] is not merely to justify and legitimate the new sanctuary of the ark in Jerusalem, nor merely to justify and legitimate the new royal regime of David in Jerusalem. Encompassing these and going beyond them, it draws a caesura which marks the old epoch with rejection and Yahweh's departure, and the new epoch with election and Yahweh's return.[31]

---

30. Rost, *Die Überlieferung*, 151–52, argues that the author is likely from the circle of priests in Jerusalem from the time of David or the early rule of Solomon.

Not surprisingly, YHWH's humbling/defeat of the Philistines and his return "home" by way of Beth-shemesh and Kiriath-jearim serves as a precursor to David's final defeat of the Philistines (2 Sam. 5:18-25; 8:1) and his bringing of the Ark into Jerusalem (2 Samuel 6). The narratives of 1 Samuel 4–7 and 2 Samuel 6 also serve as a stern warning to all Israel, even for YHWH's chosen king David, that YHWH is not to be taken lightly. The Philistines, the people of Beth-shemesh, and Uzzah learned this the hard way. A similar lack of respect for YHWH will be the undoing of the kingship of Saul.

The Institution of the Monarchy: 1 Samuel 8–12

First Samuel 7:2—8:3 serves as a literary transition from the judges to the monarchy.[32] Here we find the last hurrah of the judges' period (7:15),[33] and a flashback to the good old days much like in the days of Joshua (cf. 7:3-6; Joshua 24). The people remove their idols and repent before YHWH (7:3-6); Samuel, much like Moses, offers intercession to YHWH for the people with burnt offerings (7:9); and YHWH goes out and fights for Israel (7:10). So complete is the defeat of the Philistines that the text says that they did not enter the borders of Israel again (7:13). Of course, we know that this is germane only to the period of Samuel, thus betraying the source's origins.[34] Abiathar presents the reason why Israel seeks a king; like the judges before Samuel, Samuel's sons are corrupt (8:1-3). Therefore, the monarchy is needed to correct injustice in the land (cf. Judges 17–21), even

---

31. Campbell, *Ark Narrative*, 251, 252.
32. For an overview of the proposed redactional issues in chs. 7–12, see A. D. H. Mayes, *The Story of Israel Between Settlement and Exile: A Redactional Study of the Deuteronomistic History* (London: SCM, 1983), 85–102.
33. See also ibid., 93.
34. Contra Mayes (ibid., 98), who sees this text as a fabrication. There is no reason not to accept that Samuel oversaw a decisive victory at that time. The concluding statement of the Philistines not returning to the region of Israel is no more felicitous than the similar declaration in Elisha's day (2 Kgs. 6:23).

though the institution itself may lead to similar injustices.[35] These potential injustices are highlighted in the so-called anti-monarchic traditions of 1 Samuel 8 and 12.

Based upon ANE context and precedent, most of Samuel's denunciation of the monarchy in 1 Samuel 8 and 12 appears to be original to the prophet.[36] Nevertheless, scholars still conjecture that two literary strands comprise this material, one pro-monarchic (9:1—10:16; 11:1-11, 15; 13:2-7a; 13:15b—14:48), and the other an anti-monarchic perspective added at a later date (7:2—8:22; 10:17-27a; 12:1-25).[37] However, it is possible that in these "anti-monarchical" sections what we are seeing is the raw emotion and rhetoric of an aged and rejected prophet and priest offering a real warning to the people about the dangers of kingship.[38] As Baruch Halpern puts it, "The sacral league, the so-called theocracy, Samuel himself, did not 'go gentle' into the night of kings."[39] To be sure, Abiathar would have had every reason to include these "anti-monarchic" accounts in *his* history, especially in light of Saul's atrocities against Abiathar's family (1 Samuel 22), and David's

---

35. Ibid., 99.
36. Isaac Mendelsohn, "Samuel's Denunciation of Kingship in the Light of the Akkadian Documents from Ugarit," *BASOR* 143 (1956): 17–22. Here, Mendelsohn argues that parallel texts from the eighteenth to thirteenth centuries BCE at Alalakh and Ugarit point to the original nature of Samuel's speech. See also comments by F. Langlamet, "Les récits de l'institution de la royauté (I Samuel, VII–XII): De Wellhausen aux travaux récents," *RB* 77, no. 2 (1970): 186–87. For the literary connections between chs. 1–7 and 8–12, see Eslinger, *Kingship of God in Crisis*, 425–27.
37. White, "'History of Saul's Rise,'" 273. See also Langlamet, "Les récits de l'institution," 186–99; and Mayes, *Story of Israel*, 86.
38. Baruch Halpern, *The Constitution of the Monarchy in Israel*, HSM 25 (Chico, CA: Scholars, 1981), 150–51, offers an appropriate word of caution about such labels as *anti-monarchic* or *pro-monarchic* given the sophistication of the ancient authors, the context, and the language used. Note also the concerns of Steven L. McKenzie, "The Trouble with Kingship," in *Israel Constructs Its History: Deuteronomistic Historiography in Recent Research*, ed. Albert de Pury, Thomas Römer, and Jean-Daniel Macchi, JSOTSup 306 (Sheffield: JSOT, 1994), 307–308; and the narrative-critical insights by Lyle Eslinger, "Viewpoints and Points of View in Samuel 8–12," *JSOT* 26 (1983): 61–76, esp. 65–70.
39. Halpern, *Constitution of the Monarchy*, 256.

transgressions against Uriah and Bathsheba (2 Samuel 11).[40] Indeed, absolute power corrupts absolutely![41] Interestingly, even if the narrative derived from the hand of one of Abiathar's sons during the reign of Solomon,[42] these words would prove applicable even then in light of Solomon's heavy taxation on the land (1 Kgs. 4:1-24; 12:4), and Solomon's unilateral "gift" of twenty northern cities in the Galilee to Hiram—some Levitical (1 Kgs. 9:10-13)! One certainly does not need to look into the distant future of Israel's history for the seedbed of such hostility toward the monarchy.

These issues aside, there are also parallels that the author wanted to draw about the *type* of kingship that was best suited for Israel. Whereas the words of Samuel in ways reflect a wounded ego, and rightly so, Abiathar uses the warnings of Samuel rhetorically.[43] More than one of Samuel's warnings finds fulfillment, not so much in the actions of David but, rather, in the life of Saul. For example, Samuel warns the people that the king would "take" (לקח *lāqaḥ*) their young men into the army (8:12)—a fact that is realized when Saul "took" (לקח *lāqaḥ*) David (18:2) for this purpose. And it is not coincidental that the author draws a very different picture of the way David built his army—men coming and joining David on their own accord (22:1-2). Even Abiathar willingly ran to David's side for protection (23:6). Samuel also warns that the king will take the best

---

40. Brian Peckham, "The Deuteronomistic History of Saul and David," *ZAW* 97, no. 2 (1985): 190–209, argues for two separate sources in the narrative of Saul and David coming from a later date. However, the apparent "competing" outlooks may be reflected in Samuel and Abiathar's different historical agendas.

41. Mayes, *Story of Israel*, 95, dates these "anti-monarchic" texts between David's consolidation of the kingdom and its division after the death of Solomon.

42. So, too, ibid., 94. Gary N. Knoppers, *Two Nations under God: The Reign of Solomon and the Rise of Jeroboam*, HSM 52 (Atlanta: Scholars, 1993), 5, suggests a writer from a much later period is recalling Solomon's oppressive taxation.

43. Steven L. McKenzie, "The Trouble with Kingship," in de Pury, Römer, and Macchi, eds., *Israel Constructs Its History*, 286, argues for the unity of chs. 8–12 compiled from sources by Dtr. In this case, I would agree with McKenzie perhaps with the exception of the dating of the editing.

of the land—the fulfillment of which is found on the very lips of Saul (cf. 8:14-15; 22:7). Even the pomp and circumstance of the kings is noted by Samuel. He points out that the king will take Israel's young men and have them run before his chariots—a clear picture of the usurper, Absalom (2 Sam. 15:1; see also 1 Kgs. 1:5). Finally, the desire of the people to be "like all the nations" (ככל־הגוים *k^{e}ḵol-hagôyim*; 1 Sam. 8:5, 20) parallels Deut. 17:14 and Moses' prophetic word about kingship (Deut. 17:14-20). A priest like Abiathar would have noted this, to be sure.

In chapters 9–11, the author again draws on disparate sources from Samuel and his era. In this vein, Gary N. Knoppers states,

> . . . the tradent culled various traditions, recast them, and supplemented them to defend the cause of David, enhancing his claims to be God's rightful choice as king over the entire nation. Older sources depicting Saul's stature and beauty (1 Sam. 9:2; 10:23), his heroic deeds (1 Samuel 11), his anointing (1 Sam. 9:17; 10:1; cf. 12:3, 5) and finally his elevation to kingship (1 Sam. 10:17-27) are not suppressed. Instead, these materials lend to a sense of tension and drama to the overall structure of the narrative.[44]

Knoppers is indeed correct. Moreover, how the author chooses to relate these accounts to his readers speaks volumes.[45] Even when Samuel and Saul meet for the first time, the happy occasion has a tone of foreboding.[46] The author draws parallels between Saul and Gideon (9:21; cf. Judg. 6:15; see the appendix for character parallels),

---

44. Knoppers, *Two Nations under God*, 34. Antony F. Campbell, *Of Prophets and Kings: A Late Ninth-Century Document (1 Samuel 1–2 Kings 10)*, CBQMS 17 (Washington, DC: Catholic Biblical Association of America, 1986), 203, posits that the history of David's rise may have begun with 1 Samuel 9, thus removing any need for a history of Saul.
45. Moshe Garsiel, *The First Book of Samuel: A Literary Study of Comparative Structures, Analogies and Parallels* (Jerusalem: Revivim, 1985), 81–84, gives a forceful refutation of the supposed positive portrayal of Saul in these chapters.
46. Murray L. Newman Jr., *The People of the Covenant: A Study of Israel from Moses to the Monarchy* (New York: Abingdon, 1962), 129–30, posits three different Saul traditions that were joined (1 Sam. 10:17-27; 9:1-10:16; ch. 11).

and Absalom (9:1-2; 2 Sam. 14:25-26). Both Saul and Absalom were handsome (טוב and יפה *ṭôḇ* and *yāp̄eh* respectively), better than all who were in Israel, and uniquely featured—one tall, the other with long hair.[47] Moreover, in chapter 10 one cannot miss the parallels between the scene of Saul's anointing and the Achan debacle of Joshua 7 (cf. 10:17-22; Josh. 7:16-23). Lots are cast, one tribe is taken, then a family, and then a man. Achan had hidden his loot in his tent and Saul hid himself in the baggage! At least Achan had the nerve to stand before his accuser; Saul was too scared to stand before Samuel in a moment of celebration.

Furthermore, distinct differences are highlighted between Saul and David's anointing.[48] Saul has to have his heart changed by God (10:9), whereas David's heart is already like God's (13:14). Saul is chosen by casting lots (10:20-21), whereas David is chosen by the direct voice of YHWH (16:3, 12). Saul receives three signs of his acceptance (10:3-6); David requires none. Saul is praised by the people at his anointing (10:24); David is greeted with no fanfare and is disdained by Eliab, Saul, and Goliath (17:28, 33, 43). Also in chapter 11, the only positive event in the presentation of Saul is overshadowed by the numerous parallels with the events of Judges 19–21. One can almost sense the distaste that Abiathar has for Saul as he records the

---

47. The irony is that the uniqueness about each man is associated with their deaths. Saul loses his head in battle (he is no longer "head and shoulders" above everyone else; 1 Sam. 31:9), and it appears as though Absalom's hair is his undoing in battle (2 Sam. 18:9-15).

48. See also the work of Campbell, *Of Prophets and Kings*, 2 nn.3–4, and the list of studies he presents as being relevant to 1 and 2 Samuel. Campbell suggests that 1 Samuel—2 Kings 10 comes from prophetic circles originating in the Northern Kingdom in the late ninth century BCE. His theory is based upon similarities in the anointing scenes of Saul (1 Sam. 9:1—10:16), David (1 Sam. 16:1-13), and Jehu (2 Kgs. 9:1-13). However, one is left wondering if the later author of the ninth century could not just have easily borrowed the parallels from the earlier author, or that this was just the way anointing was done when prophets were involved! Further, Campbell notes the "private" nature of the anointing scenes as pointing to key parallels. However, in the case of David and Jehu, kings were already on the throne, thus causing the need for secrecy (Saul and Joram). In Saul's case, Samuel kept the anointing secret because he wanted to make the anointing of Saul official at Mizpah.

history of the transition to *his* monarchy—so much so that he cannot stop himself from noting the key connections to a bygone era when Gibeah and Jabesh-gilead were key players in Israel's horrific past. Also, the paring up of a body into pieces (the concubine and the oxen cf. Judg. 19:29//1 Sam. 11:7) is used to get the nation's attention and go to war.[49] On the one hand, when Israel is challenged in 1 Samuel 11, Saul's anger is aroused and threats are made to anyone who does not come to the battle. On the other hand, when Israel is challenged in 1 Samuel 17, David makes no threats but takes care of the situation singlehandedly with the aid of YHWH.

One of Noth's proposed key transitional speeches written by Dtr, 1 Samuel 12 (actually starting in 11:14),[50] serves to make the break, at least in a formal sense, between the judges' era (12:9-11) and the monarchy.[51] Even here, one last time in the classic prophetic style, Samuel warns the people of their sin in asking for a king. Literarily, the author gives the revered prophet his "space" and allows Samuel to present the conditional nature of the kingship (12:14, 15, 24, 25). Samuel does not go "gently into the night" but continues to serve beside Saul until the day of his death (cf. chs. 13; 15; 16; 19), quite literally (cf. ch. 28—posthumously). However, in the interim, the cracks in Saul's "armor" begin to appear as Abiathar recounts a unified history rife with the need for a change of kingship.[52] Abiathar will use the power of the pen to tell the nation that David was the man for the throne and it was God who placed him there.

---

49. So too Polzin, *Samuel and the Deuteronomist*, 108–14.

50. So too Fokkelman, *Narrative Art and Poetry*, 1:481.

51. Note that the MT and LXX[BA] have "Samuel" at 1 Sam. 12:11, whereas the LXX[L] and Syriac have "Samson." Cf. Mark A. O'Brien, "Judges and the Deuteronomistic History," in McKenzie and Graham, eds., *History of Israel's Traditions*, 238 n.2.

52. I tend to agree with Eslinger, *Kingship of God in Crisis*, 425–28, that chs. 1–12 are in fact a unity and need to be read as such.

An Apology for David's "Usurpation" of the Throne: 1 Samuel 13—2 Samuel 10

P. Kyle McCarter has forcefully, and no doubt correctly, argued that much of the account of David's "rise to the throne" in 1 Sam. 16:14—2 Sam. 5:10 comes from someone living in the period of David and serves as an apologia for David's replacement of Saul as king in Israel.[53] David, at least to the outside observer, appeared to have usurped the throne from his master Saul, thus shifting the balance of power from the northern tribes (Benjamin in particular) to the region of Judah.[54] The audience of the apologia would have been the elite and nobility of the region.[55] Interestingly, it is during this very time within Hittite circles that an apologetic genre appeared

---

53. P. Kyle McCarter, "The Apology of David," *JBL* 99, no. 4 (1980): 489–504, esp. 495. For a list of those passages that McCarter labels "later additions," see 492–93. A similar date is accepted by Baruch Halpern, "Erasing History: The Minimalist Assault on Ancient Israel," *BRev* 11, no. 6 (1995): 47 n.22; and White, "'History of Saul's Rise,'" 281. Artur Weiser, "Die Legitimation des Königs David: Zur Eigenart und Entstehung der sogen. Geschichte von Davids Aufstieg," *VT* 16, no. 3 (1966): 351, places it in the period of Solomon. McCarter notes that as of 1980 the majority position was to see the unity of much of the Succession Narratives (490). So, too, Keith Whitelam, "The Defence of David," *JSOT* 29 (1984): 61–87, esp. 75–76. See also comments by Walter Brueggemann, *David's Truth in Israel's Imagination and Memory* (Philadelphia, Fortress Press, 1985), 19–23. Brueggemann argues against the idea of the David–Saul narratives being labeled "propaganda." He prefers the label "tribal" literature where the "marginal" can rise to power.

54. E.g., Niels Peter Lemche, "David's Rise," *JSOT* 10 (1978): 2–25, propounds that once the propagandistic layers are removed, what is left is a dark picture of David, who is nothing more than a calculating and manipulative turncoat who works his way to the top. See similar conclusions by Baruch Halpern, *David's Secret Demons: Messiah, Murderer, Traitor, King* (Grand Rapids: Eerdmans, 2001). Halpern goes so far as to call David a "serial killer" (73); Steven L. McKenzie, *King David: A Biography* (New York: Oxford University Press, 2000), 111–27, calls David an "assassin"; and James C. VanderKam, "Davidic Complicity in the Deaths of Abner and Eshbaal: A Historical and Redactional Study," *JBL* 99, no. 4 (1980): 521–39. Walter Brueggemann, *First and Second Samuel*, Interpretation (Louisville: John Knox, 1990), 373, suggests the closing chapters of 2 Samuel (esp. 2 Sam. 21:1-14) are meant to offer an ironic counter perspective of a perfect David. However, for a more balanced approach, see my article "The Gibeonite Revenge of 2 Sam. 21:1-14: Another Example of David's Darker Side or a Picture of a Shrewd Monarch?" *JESOT* 1, no. 2 (2012): 201–222; and Dietrich's and Naumann's ("The David–Saul Narrative," 305) short, but astute and cogent, critique of Lemche's and other minimalists' approaches to the David–Saul account.

55. So Whitelam, "Defence of David," 76.

which was used to legitimate a usurper's right to the throne.[56] We have already noted in chapter 1 above the likelihood of scribal activity in Iron Age Israel, and the possibility that scribes were at work forming this type of literature for burgeoning kingdoms.

Of course, several important concepts converge with these literary and historical revelations. First, it goes without saying that whoever wrote this material is pro-Davidic.[57] Second, he most likely was from the region of the southern tribes. Third, he had to be alive during the period of David's reign in Jerusalem, especially toward the latter period. Fourth, he had to have a motive for seeing David on the throne (see ch. 7). And fifth, if he did use the Hittite "usurper" genre, the author needed to have access to it, either written or oral. When these concerns are taken into consideration, again one person comes to mind—Abiathar. He had all of the qualifications and he would have had access to Hittite military and administrative culture from at least one of the named Hittite mercenaries of David—Uriah or Ahimelech (1 Sam. 26:6).[58] Nevertheless, even if Abiathar did

---

56. McCarter, "Apology of David," 495–96. McCarter notes the work of Harry A. Hoffner Jr., "Propaganda and Political Justification in Hittite Historiography," in *Unity and Diversity: Essays in the History, Literature, and religion of the Ancient Near East*, ed. Hans Goedicke and J. J. M. Roberts (Baltimore: Johns Hopkins University Press, 1975), 49–62. For the actual Hittite text, see Edgar H. Sturtevant and George Bechtel, *A Hittite Chrestomathy*, Special Publications of the Linguistic Society of America, William Dwight Whitney Linguistics Series (Philadelphia: University of Pennsylvania, 1935), 42–99. For an overview of the genre form, see Jeremy Hutton, *The Transjordanian Palimpsest: The Overwritten Texts of Personal Exile and Transformation in the Deuteronomistic History*, BZAW 396 (Berlin: de Gruyter, 2009), 161–64. See also the bibliography by Whitelam, "Defence of David," 84 n.36.

57. Contra *Polzin, Samuel and the Deuteronomist*, 217, who argues that the narrative of "David's rise to power is contrived as much against him as for him." Even though the narrative shows David with his blemishes, it also presents him in the best light possible under difficult circumstances.

58. Interestingly, Ahimelech's name means "brother of the king". Hittite soldiers had to swear allegiance to the Hittite king; therefore, any type of usurpation would have directly affected a soldier. There can be little doubt that Uriah and Ahimelech, if they were in fact mercenaries from Hatti, would have known these inner workings of the Hittite monarchy. For an example of the oaths that were sworn, see Elisabeth Meier Tetlow, *Women, Crime, and Punishment in Ancient Law and Society*, 2 vols. (New York: Continuum, 2005), 1:193–94; Richard H. Beal, "Hittite Military Organization," in *Civilizations of the Ancient Near East*, ed. Jack M. Sasson, 4 vols. (New York: Scribner, 1995), 1:547–548; and "The Soldiers' Oath," trans. Albrecht

not know about the Hittite genre, the concept had to have been somewhat commonplace in the ancient world of this time.[59]

McCarter's thematic appraisal of 1 Sam. 16:14—2 Sam. 5:10 captures the heart of the apologetic nature of this block of material and bears repeating here. He suggests that this material serves to answer seven charges against David's right to rule: (1) David sought to advance himself at court at Saul's expense (16:19-22; 18:20-23; 19:4-5); (2) David was a deserter (19:9-17; 20:1-21:1; 26:19); (3) David was an outlaw (26:18-21); (4) David was a Philistine mercenary (27:1; 27:8-12; 30); and (5-7) David was implicated in Saul's, Abner's, and Ishbaal's deaths (1 Samuel 24; 26; 29:1-2, 11; 2 Sam. 1:14-16—Saul; 2 Samuel 2-3—Abner; 2 Sam. 4:2-12—Ishbaal).[60]

For McCarter, the *Sitz im Text* where such an apology fits may be during the revolt of Sheba or the historical situation that fostered the complaints of Shimei (cf. 2 Sam. 20:1-22; 16:8-9 respectively)—the general period seems best. Thus, an apology such as this would have been appropriate during the latter period of David's life (ca. 980s BCE?). It was then that his administration was marked with corruption and injustice (e.g., 2 Samuel 11–13); the king was showing signs of political weakness during the coup of Absalom (2 Samuel 14–18); and the northern tribes were rethinking their loyalty to the crown (2 Samuel 19–20). Of course, this is in keeping with my theory that the book of Judges served a similar purpose at the *beginning* of David's reign, especially during the civil war between the north and the south c. 1004 BCE (see the discussion in the previous chapter).

At this point, it is only fitting that we work through the seven "charges" posited by McCarter, adding any further commentary from

---

Goetze, in *Ancient Near Eastern Texts Relating to the Old Testament,* 3rd ed., ed. James Pritchard (Princeton: Princeton University Press, 1969), 353–54.

59. So, too, McCarter, "Apology of David," 498.

60. Ibid., 499–502. So, too, Robert P. Gordon, "David's Rise and Saul's Demise: Narrative Analogy in 1 Samuel 24–26," *TynBul* 31 (1980): 37–64, esp. 39–40.

the text that is needed while looking for clues about who may have authored them. Following redaction critics' "acceptable" divisions of 1 Samuel, McCarter suggests that the apology should begin with the Spirit's departure from Saul in 1 Sam. 16:14a.[61] While this is indeed a transitional moment in the life of Saul, one may better be served to go back to chapter 15 or even 13 to find the best starting point for the apologia. It seems clear that the author is actually using these earlier accounts to flesh out the reason *why* the Spirit departed from Saul in 16:14a. To start one's apology as abruptly as suggested by McCarter would naturally beg such a question.

As I noted earlier, the books of 1 and 2 Samuel reflect the work of one author, perhaps with minimal editing at a later date. As such, much of what precedes McCarter's apologia may have served as its back story or prequel.[62] Thus, 1 Samuel 1–15 may have played just as big a role in setting up the story as the apology itself. Indeed, it is within these earlier chapters of Samuel that we first see character parallels with the earlier judges that betray Saul's weaknesses (see the appendix).[63] Therefore, we need not begin with 1 Sam. 16:14a, as McCarter suggests. Indeed, if Noth's theory about important speeches marking key junctures in the DtrH is correct, then immediately following Samuel's speech in 1 Samuel 12 seems an appropriate place to begin this apology.[64] Not surprisingly, in 13:1 we do in fact find a formulaic "reintroduction" to the life and reign of Saul.[65]

---

61. McCarter, "Apology of David," 502. For a brief discussion on the redactional delimiting of the block, see ibid., 491–92.

62. For a range of opinions on where in 1 Samuel David's rise to power actually should begin, see Dietrich and Naumann, "The David–Saul Narrative," 294. It is clear that there is no consensus.

63. White, "'History of Saul's Rise,'" 281–82, argues that a pro-Saul account existed, which was altered to present a back story for David's rise to the throne. She dates this source to Saul's reign (283–84).

64. David Jobling, "What, If Anything, Is 1 Samuel," *SJOT* 7, no. 1 (1993): 17–31, at 19. Jobling points out the clear break between 1 Samuel 12 and 13.

The Apologia's Introduction: 1 Samuel 13–15

David Jobling correctly labels 1 Sam. 13:1 as "the first rejection account" of Saul, suggesting that Saul's "reign had not really begun in chs. 9–12."[66] Therefore, the events that ensue relegate the earlier victory of Saul against the Ammonites (1 Samuel 11) to another sphere and begin by showing Saul's complete and utter failure as a leader.[67] Not surprisingly, the formulaic expressions for Israel's first kings begins in 1 Sam. 13:1 (Saul), and continues in 2 Sam. 2:10 (Saul's son Ishbosheth), and 2 Sam. 5:4-5 (David). It is noteworthy that in these instances the formula is not the same or as complete as the later formula in Kings, and clearly reflects the work of someone from David's era! Thus, in Saul and Ishbosheth's introductions not only is the mother's name of the king not mentioned, as it is for the Judean kings, but also their capital city is lacking (e.g., 1 Kgs. 14:21; 15:10; 22:42). Moreover, Saul's formulaic introduction is notoriously problematic with Saul's age and the full extent of his reign missing. In this regard, Jobling's conspiracy-like theory about 13:1 is intriguing. He queries, "Did someone decide that these data should not be part of Israel's memory, that they should be consigned to oblivion?"[68] He finds it hard to fathom that any scribe would not have corrected such an error for Israel's first king! In keeping with our theory, perhaps

---

65. Interestingly, this division is clearly presented in the title of Fokkelman's book, *Narrative Art and Poetry in the Books of Samuel. A Full Interpretation Based on Stylistic and Structural Analysis II: The Crossing Fates (I Sam. 13–31 & II Sam. 1)* (Assen: Van Gorcum, 1986). For the text-critical problems surrounding 1 Sam. 13:1, see S. R. Driver, *Notes on the Hebrew Text and the Topography of the Books of Samuel*, 2d ed. (Oxford: Clarendon, 1960), 96–97; or Hertzberg, *I & II Samuel*, 103.

66. David Jobling, *1 Samuel*, Berit Olam (Collegeville, MN: Liturgical, 1998), 79.

67. White, "'History of Saul's Rise,'" 271–92, argues for a separate pro-Saulide apology in 1 Samuel 1–14. However, even after she removes the anti-Saulide, pro-Davidic, and anti-monarchy portions (i.e., 1 Sam. 7:2—8:22; 10:8, 11-12, 17-27a; 12:1-25; 13:7b-15a, 21), what remains of chs. 13 and 14 are still far from being "pro"-Saul in the strictest sense of the term. Saul is pictured as a bumbling idiot for the most part, while his son Jonathan is the true hero!

68. Jobling, *1 Samuel*, 80.

this lacuna was purposeful. Was Abiathar trying to leave traces of his disdain for Saul?

After the problematic formulaic introduction of Saul in 13:1, we are introduced for the first time to Saul's son, Jonathan, who just happens also to be David's best friend (we will return to the importance of this below).[69] Unlike the earlier history of Saul's defeat of the Ammonites, it is not Saul but his son Jonathan, with a smaller military force than his father (one thousand men as opposed to two thousand men), who has the first military victory in this block of the narrative (13:2).[70] Moreover, it is Saul's men who are in fear for their lives under the king's leadership (13:6).[71] It is here that we find Saul's disobedience to the command of God, which becomes the impetus for the departure of the Spirit noted in 1 Sam. 16:14a, and for Saul's removal from the throne. Note also that Jonathan is not implicated in this event, and, as is clear from his comments in 14:6, he is willing to allow YHWH to save by the few (that is, soldiers) in contradistinction to Saul's fearful attitude (cf. 13:11–14:6).[72] Furthermore, it is at this point that the reader is introduced, albeit indirectly, to David by YHWH's desire to replace Saul with a "man after his own heart" (13:14). Verses 13 and 14 not only introduce what the ideal king will look like spiritually, but they also function as the first apologetic reason for Saul's removal—his disobedience—a clear refutation against the charge that David initiated throne usurpation.[73]

---

69. Hutton, *Tranjordanian Palimpsest*, 145, propounds two separate histories of David's rise to the throne: one included Saul as the precursor to David and the other Jonathan.
70. Cf. also Garsiel, *First Book of Samuel*, 84–87.
71. The character parallels between the lives of Gideon and Saul should not be lost here. Gideon begins his military career with the men of Israel hiding in strongholds, caves, and dens (Judg. 6:2). Saul's military career in ch. 13 starts with his men hiding in caves, pits, thickets, cliffs, and cellars (1 Sam. 13:6).
72. Garsiel, *First Book of Samuel*, 86.

This account also appears to have been adopted from a source, perhaps even from an eyewitness such as Samuel himself (e.g., 14:8-15a). Obviously, Abiathar was not there; he probably was too young. Moreover, unlike what follows in chapter 14, the description of Jonathan's battle in chapter 13 is terse (13:3) and the account shows signs of potential secondary notations (13:19-22) that could have been added by anyone from the general period—Abiathar included. Interestingly, the events of chapters 13 and 14 just happen to fall, once again, within the geographic region of Benjamin, close to Abiathar's home.

Chapter 14 records a second battle, which is again initiated at the hand of Jonathan, not Saul (14:1-14). Once again, in this account Jonathan will turn out to be the true hero of the battle, at least in the eyes of the people (14:44-45).[74] It is verse 3 that stands out as important for answering our ongoing question of authorship. The author sees fit to identify—up front, mind you—the priest who was "on duty" that day. And it just happens to be Ahijah, the uncle of Abiathar (cf. 14:3; 22:9, 11, 12, 20)![75] The detailed genealogy of verse 3 is no doubt for this very purpose. Whereas some may see the connection of the Elides to Saul here in a negative light, there is nothing in the text that presents Ahijah as being anything

---

73. Na'aman, "The Pre-Deuteronomistic Story of Saul," 646–47, argues that the anti-Saulide aspects of the account are from Dtr—a fitting connection to my ongoing theory—apart from the issues of dating the work of Dtr.

74. So, too, Jobling, *1 Samuel*, 95; Whitelam, "Defence of David," 72; and Polzin, *Samuel and the Deuteronomist*, 174.

75. The family lineage of Eli is as follows: Eli had two sons, Hophni and Phinehas (1 Sam. 1:3), who both died in battle against the Philistines (1 Sam. 4:21). Phinehas had two sons, Ahitub, his older boy (1 Sam. 14:3), and Ichabod, his youngest (the child born on the day Phinehas died in battle cf. 1 Sam. 4:21). Ahitub had two sons, Ahimelech (1 Sam. 22:9, who was killed at Nob by Saul; cf. 1 Sam. 22:19), and Ahijah (mentioned here in 1 Sam. 14:3). Abiathar was the son of Ahimelech (1 Sam. 22:20), and it appears that Abiathar had two sons, Jonathan (2 Sam. 15:27; 1 Kgs. 1:42) and Ahimelech (named after his grandfather [?]; 2 Sam. 8:17; 1 Chr. 24:6). Note Zadok was the son of an Ahitub (2 Sam. 8:17), of the lineage of Eleazar, Aaron's son (1 Chr. 6:3, 8), but this is a different person than Abiathar's grandfather, Ahitub (cf. 1 Sam. 22:9, 11, 12, 20).

but an upright and loyal priest available to the king. Abiathar may be using this account as support for his father's claims of loyalty and innocence in 1 Sam. 22:15. The author goes on to make it clear that Ahijah was there throughout the battle, thus explaining the detail and the eyewitness nature of this chapter (14:3, 18, 19) compared to the previous one. Therefore, Abiathar's source probably was his own uncle. What is more, the account is not at all flattering to Saul. On the contrary, the author stresses how Saul got in the way of the battle's success (14:24, 30; cf. David's success in 1 Sam. 19:8),[76] and how YHWH delivered Israel in spite of Saul's ineptitude (14:23). Saul even thwarts Ahijah's inquiry to YHWH (14:19) and allows his troops to break the Mosaic Law by eating food with blood in it (14:32-34; cf. Deut. 12:16). Saul is always playing catch up—always one step behind, spiritually and militarily, where he, as king, should be. Moreover, he is presented in less-than-flattering terms, as exemplified by his own son's declaration that he has "troubled" (14:29; עכר 'ākar) Israel.[77] This is the same term that is used later in the DtrH to describe Ahab (1 Kgs. 18:18). This assessment by Jonathan is due to Saul's rash vow (see character parallels in the appendix), which causes the army to gain only a partial victory (14:46).

One can also see evidence of a priestly hand in chapter 14 with an anti-Saulide bent. To begin, the battle is overseen by a priest with the ephod and the Ark (14:3, 18). Second, the priest inquires of YHWH but is thwarted the first time by Saul, and is left unanswered the second time (14:19, 36-37). Third, an altar is built (14:35), Saul's first—no doubt a negative assessment of the king—and lots are cast (14:41-42).[78] Finally, the chapter ends with an assessment of Saul's

---

76. Whitelam, "Defence of David," 72.
77. Tony W. Cartledge, *1 & 2 Samuel* (Macon, GA: Smyth & Helwys, 2001), 181, rightly notes that the two battles in chs. 13 and 14 serve to highlight the emerging conflict between Jonathan and Saul.

ensuing actions after the battle. Saul is a rash man who "seizes" (לכד *lākad*) the kingdom of Israel (14:47). In fulfillment of Samuel's warnings in 1 Sam. 8:11-12, Saul forcibly enlists into his army any mighty man he sees (14:52). Once David shows his valor (1 Samuel 17), he will have no way of getting out of being in Saul's army—a reality that happened when Saul "took" (לקח *lāqaḥ*) David and would not allow him to return to his father's house (1 Sam. 18:2).

Before we leave this important chapter, there are a couple of points that reinforce the introductory nature of this block of material. First, by the end of the narrative we are told that, much like stirring up a hornet's nest, Saul had "caused vexation" (ירשיע *yaršia'*) for his enemies. David will be the one ultimately to subdue those that Saul only harassed.[79] Second, in 14:47-51 the reader is introduced to several of the key players who will appear later in David's life: his enemies to be defeated (Moab, Ammon, Edom, Zobah, and the Philistines), and the family of Saul, especially Jonathan, Merab, Michal, and Abner. Finally, the only remotely positive assessment of Saul to be found in this pericope is in his defeat of the Amalekites (14:48); however, as we will soon see, this will be the second great failure of Saul, which will pave the way for David.

Chapter 15 serves the author's rhetorical purposes by recording the second rejection of Saul. As already noted above in 1 Samuel 2–3, common to the DtrH *and* OT narratives, when someone receives a double promise, prophecy, or dream, it means it is sure to come

---

78. The fact that the author notes that this is Saul's *first* altar to YHWH could be a note of sarcasm or it may have something to do with the previous account in ch. 13. Did Saul not build a proper altar to YHWH on which to offer his burnt offerings in 13:9-10? Or is the author trying to point out that unlike the Patriarchs, who built altars regularly (Gen. 12:7, 8; 13:18; 22:9; 26:25; 33:20, etc.), Saul did not?

79. Contra White, "'History of Saul's Rise,'" 278–79, who suggests that Saul has fulfilled his mandate to deliver Israel from her enemies, as seen in the conclusion of 14:47-48. It is strange that the author would use this term as opposed to something like "subdued" (כנע *kāna'* ; Judg. 8:28).

to pass (cf. Gen. 28:12-15; 31:10-13; 37:5-10; 41:1-7; Judg. 6:36-40; 13:1-20; 1 Sam. 2:27-36; 3:11-14; 1 Kgs. 3:5-14; 9:2-9; Daniel 2; 7, etc.).[80] The presentation here is in no way favorable to Saul, as he is pictured in direct disobedience to the word of YHWH (15:26)—again—and will not even acknowledge YHWH as his own God (15:21). The destruction of Amalek was to be carried out according to Deut. 25:17-19. Now, while Samuel could have recorded this event, any priest of the period could have included it to show the fulfillment of the Deuteronomic law. Thus, in chapter 15, for the second time in three chapters, Samuel declares the removal of the kingdom from Saul (15:28). In chapter 13, Samuel had said that YHWH was giving the kingdom to a "man after his own heart," but now he is even more precise; it will be given to his "neighbor" (רֵעַ *rēya*'). The double entendre is evident and the irony that Benjamin borders Judah would not have been lost on the original audience. The account fittingly ends by noting that Samuel did not see Saul again until the day of his death.[81] Furthermore, YHWH "repented" (נחם *nāḥam*) that he had made Saul king over Israel (15:35). Masterfully, chapters 13–15, and especially this last verse, sets up the scene for the anointing of David in chapter 16.

Before we leave this chapter a few final things need to be pointed out concerning authorship and the rhetorical purpose of Abiathar. First, in 15:6 the author again leaves us a clue that seems to point to Abiathar, even though he must have used a source such as Samuel. Here the author makes a parenthetical notation about the deliverance of the Kenites from the midst of the Amalekites. At first glance, textually, this seems a little awkward with the flow of the narrative

---

80. Note also the doublets for anointing a king (1 Sam. 9:17; 10:1—Saul; 1 Sam. 16:1-13; 2 Sam. 5:1-3—David).

81. The question of the "day of whose death" arises here. The Hebrew seems to intimate that it is Saul's death, and thus this notation may be pointing forward to Samuel's postmortem encounter with Saul at the home of the witch of Endor (1 Sam. 28:15-19).

and even out of place until one takes into account that the Kenites were partial to David later during his time on the lam (30:29)—Abiathar in tow. David even patronized them with gifts from the spoils of none other than the Amalekites! Second, the issues of Saul's desire to sacrifice that which was already devoted (חרם ḥērem) to YHWH would not have been lost on a priest (cf. 15:21; Lev. 27:29). Third, with but a few exceptions, from this point on in the narrative until David's death, David and Abiathar could easily become the primary sources for the narrative. Samuel moves to a secondary role.[82] Fourth, the twofold rejection of Saul for disobedience gives us the reason *why* that the Spirit departed from Saul—the place that McCarter begins his apologia.

David's Rise and Fall from Prominence: 1 Samuel 16–31

Chapters 16–31 deal with Saul's interaction with David—mostly negative. Of course, it is in chapter 16 that we see the Spirit departing from Saul and resting upon David—a confirmation of both of Samuel's earlier prophecies to Saul (13:14; 15:23). Chapters 16 and 17 are, again, by no means pro-Saul. Not surprisingly, one cannot miss the subtle jab at Saul, when Samuel is attracted to Eliab's physical stature, but is nonetheless rejected by YHWH (16:6-7). Also, the Spirit rests on David at the very moment of his anointing, whereas Saul's anointing is delayed (cf. 10:6, 10; 11:6; 16:13).[83] As for the apologia perspective of McCarter, from the outset of Saul's encounters with David it is Saul who seeks to keep David close (16:18, 19, 22) and in his service. David is merely following Saul's commands.

In chapter 17, the author pits Saul's ineptitude and fear against David's innocent trust in YHWH.[84] Again, the slighting of Saul

---

82. David or Samuel could have been the source for 1 Sam. 16:1-13.
83. White, "'History of Saul's Rise,'" 283.

comes through as the author parallels David's and Saul's first encounter with the people of Israel after their initial anointing (cf. 1 Sam. 10:1; 16:13). David comes to the battle carrying provisions for his brothers and Saul; leaves it with the "baggage" (כלי $k^e l\hat{i}$) and the "baggage" keeper; runs to the battle lines; and ultimately challenges a giant (17:22). Earlier, we had seen that Saul had hid himself in the "baggage" (כלי) before he was declared king (1 Sam. 10:22). Furthermore, while the man who is head and shoulders above his compatriots cowers in fear (ירא $y\bar{a}r\bar{e}$';17:11), David, the young man, goes out and fights Israel's battles—he behaves as the king![85] Indeed, Goliath's challenge was intended for Israel's "champion"—in this case, it is David not Saul. Much like we saw in chapters 13 and 14 where Jonathan is the hero, here Saul fails once again to be the leader.

One other note of importance to our apologetic theme that is sometimes overlooked is the threefold question and response that David asks and receives regarding the plight of the man who kills Goliath (17:25, 27, 30). Saul is supposed to give that man his daughter, and he and his family will be "free" (חפשי $hop\check{s}\hat{i}$) in Israel.[86] Of course, Saul is not a man of his word and thus the author seeks to point out this very fact by the threefold question.[87] Instead of David and his family being free, Saul "takes" (לקח $l\bar{a}qah$) David by force into his army, and later, David and his family will have to run from a crazed Saul to Moab and Philistia (22:3-4; 27:1; chs. 29–30).

---

84. See similar comments by Weiser, "Die Legitimation des Königs David," 331.
85. For an erudite discussion on the problems of when David was "known" by Saul (1 Sam. 16; 17:55-58), see Polzin, *Samuel and the Deuteronomist*, 171–76. For a series of essays on the textual variants of 1 Samuel 17, see Dominique Barthélem, David Wooding, Johan Lust, and Emanuel Tov, *The Story of David and Goliath: Textual and Literary Criticism: Papers of a Joint Research Venture*, OBO 73 (Göttingen: Vandenhoeck & Ruprecht, 1986).
86. This no doubt refers to an exemption from taxation. Cf. McCarter, *I Samuel*, 304.
87. For a full discussion on Saul's failure to honor his word, see Brian Peterson, "The Gibeonite Revenge of 2 Sam 21:1–14: Another Example of David's Darker Side or a Picture of a Shrewd Monarch?" *JESOT* 1, no. 2 (2012): 201–22.

In this vein, Robert Polzin rightly connects chapters 14 and 17 and goes on to note that when David refused to be called the "son" of Saul (cf. 17:58), Jonathan saw in David a man after his own heart who would stand up to his father, Saul. It is for this reason that they became close friends (18:1). In the same way that Jonathan had stood up to his father (14:29, 43), here David declares his fidelity to his biological father, Jesse, thus rejecting Saul's overture for him to become his son. Therefore, 1 Sam. 18:2 declares that Saul "took" (לקח *lāqaḥ*) David—by force (?) (cf. 8:11-12; 18:13)—and made him one of his soldiers.[88] One can see clearly the battle lines being drawn, with Saul on one side and David and Jonathan on the other. This is further heightened by Jonathan's removal of his robe, armor, belt, and sword and giving them to David (18:4). Where David had rejected Saul's armor, he accepts Jonathan's. Moreover, Jonathan enters a covenant (ברית *bᵉrît*) with David (18:3). Thus, the author establishes from the outset that Jonathan, by these acts, has relinquished his rights to the kingdom and has abdicated the throne to David—a fact that will be vocalized in 1 Sam. 23:17. David has not grasped for the throne at all; it has been given to him freely.

Beyond the Jonathan–David associations in chapter 18, the author draws out a number of clear apologetic-like aspects within the narrative that present David in the best light and Saul as the oppressor. The author could not make David's innocence any clearer than in his comments of chapter 18. Even though Saul forced David into the army, David prospered (18:5, 14, 15, 27); the people and the army loved him (18:5-7, 16, 30); Saul feared him (18:12, 29); David did not seek position through marriage with the king's daughters (18:18, 23); and YHWH was with David (18:12, 14, 28) and

---

88. Polzin, *Samuel and the Deuteronomist*, 175–76. See also comments by Francesca Aran Murphy, *1 Samuel* (Grand Rapids: Brazos, 2010), 183.

protected him (18:11) even when Saul devised evil against him (18:11, 17, 21, 25).

The author continues to evoke sympathy for David in chapter 19. Here the author presents four scenes wherein Saul attempts to kill an innocent David four times. Whereas before Saul had tried to mask his attempts on David's life (via the Philistines and a dowry), in 1 Sam. 19:1 Saul plainly commands Jonathan and his men to put David to death. Even though there is a period of respite for David at the end of the first scene (19:6-7), once David again has military success (19:8), Saul goes back to his old ways and tries to kill David himself (19:10). In the narrative of chapter 19, Jonathan (19:2-6),[89] David himself (19:10), Michal (19:11-17), and YHWH/Samuel save David (19:18-24) from Saul. As an apology, the author wants his audience to know that none of Saul's machinations will prosper against YHWH's anointed—even Saul's own family are a party with David.

Chapter 20 narrows the reader's focus to Jonathan's obvious desire to see David's success and for him to survive to sit on the throne of Israel. Jonathan and David enter a covenant of peace, which extends to their offspring (20:1-23, 42). Just to make sure that the reader is aware of Jonathan's allegiance to David, seven times Jonathan affirms that he only wants what is best for David (20:4, 9, 13, 17, 30, 32, 34). For showing kindness to David, Jonathan is met with a barrage of curses as the crazed Saul even tries to kill his own son in the same manner he had used on David three other times (20:30, 33). Saul's bouts of insane anger and paranoia force an innocent David to run for his life.

Coming almost at the midpoint of chapters 13–31, chapters 21 and 22 serve as the apex of Saul's paranoid rage. It should be no surprise that these chapters just happen to focus on an introduction

---

89. Whitelam, "Defence of David," 73, draws out how Jonathan intercedes for David in the same way that the people had interceded for Jonathan in 1 Sam. 14:45.

to the family of Abiathar at Nob and their senseless murder by Saul. Who better to know and record the details of this encounter than the only survivor? In the account, Abiathar's father, Ahimelech, is presented as truly innocent of any wrongdoing, as David takes full blame for their deaths (22:22).[90] Ahimelech declares his innocence of any malice toward Saul. He had only shown due respect and honor to Saul's best soldier, and son-in-law, David (22:14). Nevertheless, his cries of innocence fall on deaf ears as the maniacal insanity of Saul's action is juxtaposed with the godly reverence and fear of his soldiers for the priests of YHWH (22:17). It was a hated Edomite who carries out the butchering of eighty-five innocent priests, not counting their wives and children (22:18). Saul performed a *ḥerem*-like act against his own people—and priests at that![91] Furthermore, at this key juncture Abiathar is introduced to the reader as the sole survivor. The young and no doubt influential priest runs to none other than David (22:20-23).[92]

In this regard, if Abiathar's livelihood as part of the priestly family had been copying scrolls (e.g., the law) and performing priestly duties for King Saul, how would he survive now that that occupation was gone? Abiathar needed to find someone who could use his crafts and, in exchange, offer him a means of providing for himself. Ryan Byrne's assessment of scribal activity in the Iron I period becomes relevant in this situation. When commenting on how Iron Age I scribes survived, he notes that working for warlords "ranks far below the ideal form of intellectual patronage, but it does afford survival."[93] In essence, David had become a "warlord" due to Saul's

---

90. Contrary to some (e.g., White, "'History of Saul's Rise,'" 291–92) who see this massacre as justifiable, based upon the anti-Elide prophecy of 1 Samuel 2, this presentation is nothing but positive toward the priests at Nob and their innocence.

91. So, too, Whitelam, "Defence of David," 73.

92. VanderKam, "Davidic Complicity," 526–27, correctly points up the importance of Abiathar to David's cause.

93. Ryan Byrne, "The Refuge of Scribalism in Iron I Palestine," *BASOR* 345 (2007): 22.

insane jealousy (cf. 22:1-2). Abiathar knew David would be able to offer him an existence when the rest of the nation under Saul's rule sought his life as a survivor of the massacre. It is in this historical context that the words of David in 22:23 find poignancy and relevance to our discussion. David says to Abiathar, "Remain with me, do not be afraid, for he who is seeking my life is seeking your life, for you will be safe with me." This statement not only sets the stage for Abiathar's long friendship with David, but also presents the motive for Abiathar's waxing eloquent through an apologia on behalf of a wronged man and the rightful king—David. As noted in chapter 7 above, David's words to Abiathar in verse 23 give the reason for why Abiathar would desire David to be on the throne. As long as a Saulide was on the throne, Abiathar's life would be in danger! What better motive for writing an apology, or should I say, apologies, for David the son of Jesse?[94]

The focus of chapters 23–31 switches predominantly to David as he acts like the true king of Israel, exemplified by his concern for the city of Keilah, which he delivers from the hand of the Philistines (23:1-6). Moreover, in chapters 23 and 24 both Jonathan and Saul acknowledge that David will be the next king (23:17; 24:20), as the author records the reaffirmation of the covenant between Jonathan and David (23:18). Authorial clues again come to the surface when David inquires of YHWH about his battle at Keilah, and whether he should remain in the city (23:1, 4, 10-12). Tucked in between these notations about his inquiries is a note that Abiathar had come to David with an ephod when he escaped from Saul's massacre (23:6, 9). Abiathar is the one who is giving David his spiritual direction! This certainly would account for the eyewitness perspective concerning

---

94. When David finally came to the throne, his administrators includes scribes (cf. 2 Sam. 8:16-18; 20:23-26). Even if Abiathar was not literate, which is unlikely, David did have scribes that Abiathar could utilize.

David's cat-and-mouse game with Saul (see esp. 24:11). We also see evidence of David's complete innocence as he refuses to kill Saul when he had the chance (24:10-11). In this encounter, David finally acquiesces and identifies Saul as his "father" (אב 'āḇ; cf. 17:58), and Saul calls David his "son" (בן bēn; 24:16). David insists that it will not be him who will settle the dispute between them but, rather, YHWH will be their judge and will avenge David (24:12, 15).

One should also not overlook the rhetorical importance of the Nabal and Abigail account sandwiched between the two accounts of David's chances to kill Saul (1 Samuel 24; 26).[95] Not only does this chapter read like an eyewitness account, but it also serves the rhetorical purpose of showing both David's willingness and ability to avenge himself on those who mistreated him, and his restraint. The Saul–Nabal parallels would not have been lost on the reader, especially when the latter is presented with king-like status (25:36). Nabal, like Saul, misused the "services" of David and his men (25:15-16).[96] Furthermore, the repetition of "contend/plead a cause" (ריב rîḇ; cf. 24:16 [Heb]; 25:39), "evil" (רע ra'; 24:10, 12, 18; 25:7, 16, 17, 21, 26, 28, 39 [2x]), and "good" (טוב ṭôḇ; 24:18, 19, 20 [2x]; 25:3, 8, 15, 21, 30, 36), show direct literary parallels between chapters 24 and 25 in particular.[97] The idea of Saul "playing the fool" (הסכלתי hiskaltî) in 26:21 (see also 13:13) harks back to the very meaning of Nabal's name (25:25; cf. also 25:37).[98] There are good reasons why Abiathar placed these three accounts together. First, even though David had two opportunities to kill Saul, Abiathar makes it clear that the reason David did not do so was not because he was scared to

---

95. For a detailed narrative analysis of these three chapters, see Paul Borgman, *David, Saul, & God: Discovering and Ancient Story* (New York: Oxford University Press, 2008), 79–95. Borgman sees unity here as well.

96. Gordon, "David's Rise and Saul's Demise," 44–48.

97. Ibid., 47–50.

98. Ibid., 50–51. Gordon (51) rightly points out the play on words in 1 Sam. 25:37 where the wine leaves Nabal just as a wineskin (נֵבֶל nēḇel; 25:18) is emptied.

"take out" someone who had offended him but, rather, because of his respect for Saul as YHWH's anointed. Second, the author shows that David did not suffer from "blood-guilt" (25:31),[99] which Saul was guilty of (1 Samuel 22; 2 Sam. 21:1). Thus, the picture that the author presents is of a man of restraint when it comes to his master Saul.[100] YHWH, not David, had to remove Saul from the throne. Any charges against David in this vein must be dropped.

Another point of interest is the author's use of "anointed" (מָשִׁיחַ *mᵉšîaḥ*) in the nominal form in these chapters. It is true that David refused to kill Saul because of his anointing, but is there more going on here than what at first meets the eye? One must keep in mind that Saul was not scared to kill God's anointed servant, David (16:13). Nor was he afraid to wipe out an entire town of God's anointed priests at Nob (1 Samuel 22). Here it appears that Abiathar is drawing upon this motif as a not-too-subtle reminder of the differences between Saul and David. Not surprisingly, the nominal use of מָשִׁיחַ appears only in Samuel in the DtrH and is used predominantly in Leviticus (cf. Lev. 4:3, 5, 16; 6:15; 1 Sam. 2:10, 35; 12:3, 5; 16:6; 24:7 [2x], 11; 26:9, 11, 16, 23; 2 Sam. 1:14, 16; 19:22; 22:51; 23:1)![101] Also, one needs to take into account David's cutting of the "hem of the robe" of Saul (כְּנַף־הַמְּעִיל *kᵉnap-hammᵉ'îl*) in 1 Sam. 24:5 [Heb] and how it harks back to the only other appearance of this phrase in the OT in 1 Sam. 15:27. In the latter incident, after Saul tore Samuel's hem, Samuel declared the kingdom was going to be taken from Saul.[102] In

---

99. So, too, Borgman, *David, Saul, & God*, 85–86.

100. Jon D. Levenson, "1 Samuel 25 as Literature and as History," *CBQ* 40, no. 1 (1978): 23–24, suggests that David's restraint in killing Nabal is a foreshadowing of his lack of restrain in killing Uriah.

101. The verbal form appears numerous times throughout the DtrH; yet even in these places they appear predominantly within the timeframe or the possible corpus of Abiathar. Judg. 9:8, 15, 16; 1 Sam. 10:1; 15:1, 17; 16:3, 12, 13; 2 Sam. 1:21; 2:4, 7; 3:39; 5:3, 17; 12:7; 19:11; 1 Kgs. 1:34, 39, 45; 5:15; 19:15, 16 [2x]; 2 Kgs. 9:3, 6, 12; 11:12; 23:30.

102. Gordon, "David's Rise and Saul's Demise," 55–56.

1 Sam. 24:5, David had symbolically taken possession of the throne by cutting Saul's hem. This symbolic action—not his to take—is what troubled David after the fact (24:5).[103]

Finally, David's double warning to Saul in chapters 24 and 26 (24:12; 26:24; cf. also 25:38–39—note David's words about Nabal) harks back to our earlier discussion in 1 Samuel 13 and 15 on the rhetorical role of doublets in bring to pass the plan of God.[104] There, the two chapters divided by a chapter depicting the *poor* character of Saul (ch. 14) pointed to the loss of Saul's kingdom at the word of Samuel. Here we see the double word from David that YHWH will judge between him and Saul about who is the truly righteous one. The intervening chapter (i.e., ch. 25) thus shows the *good* character of David in the area of self-restraint. Moreover, one cannot overlook the olive branch extended to David by Saul when he says, "return to me my son David" (26:21). David's response to Saul's overture— "behold *the* spear of the king, let one of the young men come over and retrieve it" (26:22; italics added for emphasis)—makes it clear that David would not allow himself to be in harm's way of Saul's spear ever again.[105] Of course, this sets up for the final five chapters of 1 Samuel as David's call for YHWH's vengeance plays out for all Israel to see.

The rapid downward spiral of Saul's demise unfolds in these final chapters. In chapter 27, David is forced to flee to Philistia, thus

103. See comments by Martin Noth, "Remarks on the Sixth Volume of the Mari Texts," *JSS* 1, no. 4 (1956): 322–33, esp. 329–31.
104. I tend to agree with Gordon, "David's Rise and Saul's Demise," 58, in his denunciation of David Jobling (*The Sense of Biblical Narrative: Three Structural Analyses in the Old Testament [1 Samuel 13–31, Numbers 11–12, 1 Kings 17–18]* JSOTSup 7 [Sheffield: JSOT, 1978], 22), when Jobling suggests that the doubled account in chapters 24 and 26 does not "make sufficient sense." On the contrary, as we have seen at the beginning of the book of Samuel, the use of doublets serves as proof that YHWH will indeed vindicate David and bring judgment on Saul.
105. Gordon, "David's Rise and Saul's Demise," 60. While the Hebrew *qere* does not have the definite article on the word for "spear," the author may have wanted to stress the importance of David's act in denying a return to Saul especially in light of Saul's use of a spear in his earlier attempts to kill David (1 Sam. 18:10–11).

removing him from Saul's reach—David is willing to be deprived of his homeland to preserve his life, and to keep peace between him and Saul. As such, chapters 28–31 must be read as a unit.[106] In 1 Sam. 28:1-2, David becomes the bodyguard for Achish, the king of Gath (28:2). These verses are then separated by the account of Saul's encounter with the hag of Endor (28:3-25). Moreover, 28:3-25, along with chapters 30 and 31, serves as parallel battle scenes; one in Judah, the other at Gilboa (I will deal with ch. 29 in a moment). In these closing chapters, the author wanted to set up a side-by-side comparison between the two candidates for the throne, a "meanwhile-back-at-the-ranch" scenario for Saul, while David and Abiathar experienced life in real time with Achish, and in Ziklag.[107] The seven key comparisons are as follows:

1. Both leaders face impossible odds: David returns to Ziklag and finds it destroyed by the Amalekites (whom Saul was supposed to have killed in 1 Samuel 15),[108] while Saul faces the uncertainty of battle with the Philistines (28:3-5).

2. Saul tries to hear from YHWH but YHWH is silent (28:5, 6), whereas David gets a direct word from YHWH (30:7-8; note with Abiathar's help).

3. When Saul is distressed and facing death, he consults a medium (28:7–25); when David is distressed and facing death, he consults YHWH through the priest, Abiathar (30:6).[109]

4. Saul loses his battle to the Philistines (ch. 31), whereas David wins his battle because YHWH is with him (30:17-24).

5. Saul takes his own life, and his three sons die (31:2), whereas David recovers all (30:18-19).[110]

---

106. So, too, the conclusion of Garsiel, *First Book of* Samuel, 133–37.
107. So, too, ibid., 137.
108. Cf. ibid., 134–35.
109. So, too, Cartledge, *1 & 2 Samuel*, 332.

6. Saul's armor is sent to all the people of the Philistines as trophies of war with Israel (31:9), while David sends the spoils of war to the leaders of the surrounding cities (30:26-31).

7. Saul's time as king is over, whereas David prepares for his time on the throne by sending these gifts to his friends.

One could easily go on, but the point the author makes is clear: David is the right man for the throne. As for chapter 29, this chapter serves as an integral part of the apology to prove that David in fact did *not* take part in the battle against Saul and Israel in chapter 31. Abiathar makes it clear that David was not present because he was fighting his own battle back in Judah. What is even more telling in this regard is the double entendre in David's words to Achish in 28:2a, when Achish insisted that David accompany him in battle against Saul. David replies: "Surely you will find out what your servant can do." Here it is very possible that David had every intention of joining Jonathan and Saul against the Philistines.[111] This is bolstered by the concerns of the Philistine commanders in 29:4. Next, whether one wants to accept the account of the medium at Endor as factual or not, what is evident is that the author records that Samuel returned from the dead long enough to connect all the proverbial dots for Saul. Samuel declares that YHWH is against Saul, that the kingdom will in fact be David's, and that YHWH's word regarding Saul's sin in 1 Samuel 15 is going to be fulfilled as prophesied (28:16-18). David has nothing to do with what is about to happen. Finally, the authorial perspective also points to Abiathar. His use of "unto this day" four times in these chapters (29:3, 6, 8; 30:25; see discussion in ch. 4 above)

---

110. The circumstances and method of Saul's death must be read in the light of Abiathar's other apology, namely, Judges and the Abimelech account (Judg. 9:54). So, too, Garsiel, *First Book of Samuel*, 139.

111. Contra VanderKam, "Davidic Complicity," 526. The entire narrative is depicting David's deception of the Philistines (e.g., 1 Sam. 21:13-15; 27:8-12).

and the eyewitness detail of what happened during David's battle as opposed to the laconic nature of Saul's battle (cf. 1 Sam. 28:1-2 and chs. 29–30 versus 28:5-25; 31) pushes one in this direction. As for Saul's encounter with the witch, Abiathar could have easily found out about this from one of Saul's men (e.g., see 2 Sam. 2:4b). Certainly an account as dramatic as this would have been told long after Saul's death.

Conclusion

The first book of Samuel ends with the tragic deaths of Saul and his three oldest sons. The author, which in many cases points to Abiathar, has recorded the transition from the judges' period to the monarchy while juxtaposing the two options for kingship—Saul or David. From McCarter's apologia perspective, up to this point the author has shown David's complete innocence in his actions toward Saul and his refusal to take the throne. We have seen that David did not seek to advance himself in the court at Saul's expense—YHWH promoted and protected David at every turn. In fact, even after Saul "took" David into his army, David took every opportunity to give Saul his due respect (18:30; 24:8-12; 26:17-20). Second, David had not deserted Saul; Saul had forced him away by threatening to kill him at least four times. Third, David was not an outlaw per se but, rather, was forced to survive by despoiling Israel's enemies (27:8; 30:9-18). Fourth, David was never a Philistines mercenary, but he did deceive them into thinking such (ch. 27; 28:1-2). Fifth, David was in no way implicated in Saul's death—David was busy fighting his own battles in the region of Judah (ch. 30). Finally, Jonathan, the heir apparent, on several occasions not only showed his love for David but accepted David's right to the throne (cf. 18:1, 3, 4; 19:2-6; 23:16), as did Saul (1 Sam. 24:20). However, David's path to the throne of all Israel was still far from smooth. Even though Saul and Jonathan are dead, David still had one major hurdle to overcome: to convince the northern tribes that he is the best man for the job above Saul's son Ishbosheth.

9

—

2 Samuel: The Apology Continues—David's Fall from Grace

The history of David's rise, then, is a narrative that promulgates a political point of view supported by theological interpretation of the events it recounts. Its purpose is to show that David's accession to the throne was lawful and that the events leading up to his proclamation as king over all Israel were guided by the will of the god of Israel.[1]

P. Kyle McCarter's summation of David's rise to the throne is indeed what we have seen thus far in the narrative of 1 Samuel. All along his narrative journey, the author presents YHWH as directing the path of David toward the throne of a united Israel (1 Sam. 18:12, 14, 28; 2 Sam. 5:3). However, David remains to be cleared of two lingering charges: Is he responsible for the deaths of Abner and Ishbosheth? The opening chapters of 2 Samuel answer this very question.

---

1. P. Kyle McCarter, "The Apology of David," *JBL* 99, no. 4 (1980): 494–95. See also Artur Weiser, "Die Legitimation des Königs David: Zur Eigenart und Entstehung der sogen Geschichte von Davids Aufstieg," *VT* 16, no. 3 (1966): 325–54, esp. 326.

McCarter opts to end his apologia at 2 Sam. 5:10; however, the notice of David's accession to the throne in 2 Sam. 5:3 serves as a natural conclusion to David's long trek to the throne. This is reinforced by both literary markers and structural clues. To begin, the author's use of the regnal formulas at 1 Sam. 13:1 and 2 Sam. 5:4 delimits the apologia quite naturally—thus what lies between them forms a unit. Even though Ishbosheth has a regnal formula appearing in 2 Sam. 2:10, it is overshadowed by the appended notice of Judah's rejection of his kingship. Moreover, structurally, the two accounts of messengers coming to David with "good news" form an inclusio (cf. 1:1-16 and 4:1-12) that reinforces the notion that David was innocent of the final two charges involving the deaths of Abner and Ishbosheth.[2] On the heels of this inclusio, the content of 2 Sam. 5:1-3 quickly brings the apologia to a close as David is pictured being anointed king over all Israel at Hebron.

On the macro-structural level, the struggle with the Amalekites has been a thread that has recurred throughout this apologia. Saul's failure to exterminate the Amalekites had cost him the throne (1 Samuel 15). And the Amalekites were responsible for burning David's city of Ziklag and kidnapping his family (1 Samuel 30). Ironically, an Amalekite, of all people, is the one who brings David the "good tidings" of Saul's death (2 Sam. 1:2-8). Little did the unnamed Amalekite know that he was the last person who David would want to see, especially bearing this type of news. Also, if the author had not made it clear enough earlier that David loved Saul and Jonathan, he certainly makes it clarion through David's harsh response to the

---

2. Contra, J. P. Fokkelman, *Narrative Art and Poetry in the Books of Samuel. A Full Interpretation Based on Stylistic and Structural Analysis III: Throne and City (II Sam. 2–8 & 21–24)* (Assen: Van Gorcum, 1990), 25, who appears to bifurcate these two accounts. And contra James C. VanderKam, "Davidic Complicity in the Deaths of Abner and Eshbaal: A Historical and Redactional Study," *JBL* 99, no. 4 (1980): 522, who feels 2:8—4:12 belongs to the Court History.

Amalekite's confession (1:14-16) and through David's eulogy—a ballad that immortalized Saul and Jonathan (1:17-27).

Some Final Notes on "David's Rise to the Throne"

Before moving to our next section, a few minor points concerning authorial perspective and McCarter's apologia remain to be addressed from 2 Samuel 2–5. First, 2 Sam. 2:1-4 shows David again inquiring of YHWH regarding the choice of his first capital. David's choice of Hebron, a Levitical city, again may betray the influence of Abiathar. Second, David is shown extending an olive branch to the men of Jabesh-gilead, who were not only some of Saul's staunchest allies (1 Sam. 31:11-13), but also lived within twenty-five miles of Mahanaim, the new capital of Israel (2:8). Their rejection of David's overture for peace (2:4b-7) makes it clear that David was not responsible for the ensuing civil war.[3] On a side note, in 2:4b the author includes the notation that the men of Judah had told David about the actions of the men of Jabesh Gilead in recovering Saul and his sons' bodies from Beth-shean. This could be where Abiathar got the truncated battle report used in 1 Samuel 31. Third, the author points out the weakness of Ishbosheth as a king, as exemplified in his inability to thwart Abner's indiscretions with Rizpah (3:6-13)—David's decisiveness and strength as king is thus juxtaposed with Ishbosheth's weakness. Fourth, the sixth charge against David—his complicity in Abner's death—is also debunked and blamed on the duplicitous and vindictive actions of Joab (3:19-39) with all the people acknowledging David's innocence (3:35-39). Fifth, in 4:2-3 the phrase "unto this day" appears in conjunction with Ishbosheth's assassination plot, which just happens to be linked with a family from the tribal region of Benjamin; details Abiathar would have known (see ch. 4 above).

---

3. Later annalistic insertions may account for notations such as those found in 2 Sam. 2:10-11.

Finally, David's harsh treatment of Ishbosheth's assassins is meant to convince the reader that David was not complicit in the death of Ishbosheth (4:9-12). With this final vindicating notation, the apologia begun in 1 Samuel 13 is brought to a fitting close in 5:1-3.

In 2 Samuel 2–5, the author also introduces, somewhat awkwardly at times, several people and concerns that will be integral to the following narratives (cf. 1 Sam. 14:49-51). For example, even though the civil war between David and Ishbosheth is long (seven years and six months; see 5:5), surprisingly, only one battle is mentioned. The battle scene at Gibeon (2:12-32), again in the tribal region of Benjamin, not only tells the reader that David's forces are stronger than Ishbosheth's (2:31; 3:1), but also records the reason why Joab wants to kill Abner (cf. 2:22; 3:27). Moreover, the sons born to David at Hebron are named, three of whom will be vital to the following narrative: Amnon, Absalom, and Adonijah (3:2-5; cf. chs. 13; 14–18; 1 Kings 1–2 respectively). Finally, characters who will be a part of the ensuing narrative are noted: David's wife, Michal, is returned (cf. 3:14-16; ch. 6), and Mephibosheth is introduced just before Ishbosheth's assassination (cf. 4:4; 9; 16:3).

Now, while it is certainly possible that these insertions may be later additions, there is nothing that precludes Abiathar himself from going back at a later date and adding these comments in order to thread the earlier independent apologia into the next two blocks of Israel's history: David as the next Joshua (2 Sam. 5:6—10:19); and the putative Succession Narrative (2 Samuel 9–20; 1 Kings 1–2).[4] As we move forward, I will demonstrate that authorial perspective once again points to Abiathar (or one of his sons) as the best candidate for writing much of these last two blocks of David's history.

---

4. Leonard Rost, *The Succession to the Throne of David* (Sheffield: Almond, 1982), argues that the Succession Narrative includes 2 Samuel 9–20 and 1 Kings 1–2.

The Pro-Jonathan Content of the David Apologia

Before moving on to the next block in 2 Samuel, one last emendation needs to be made to McCarter's apologia theory. While I believe he is correct in his dating of the text and in his presentation of the basic "charges" from which David needed vindication, McCarter has missed a key motif of the apologia, namely, the pro-Jonathan stance. In this vein, the narrative of 1 Samuel 13:1—2 Sam. 5:3, while defending David, also offers sustained praise for Jonathan through his military exploits (1 Samuel 13–14); his friendship and love for David (1 Samuel 18–23); his relinquishing of the throne (1 Sam. 23:17); his valiant death at the side of a Spirit-rejected father (1 Samuel 31); and through David's eulogy (2 Sam. 1:22-27). Scholars are hard-pressed to explain how this motif aligns with a seventh- or sixth-century date.[5] However, once these texts are placed within a tenth-century context, as McCarter and a few others have posited, this subtheme makes perfect sense. David, as king, would have needed to "sign off" on the apology written on his behalf. He makes sure that his best friend is presented in glowing terms and that Jonathan's death, while honorable, was no fault of his own. There is no reason to doubt that Abiathar, another one of David's friends, respected Jonathan any less.

David as a Second Joshua: 2 Samuel 5:6—8:14

As already handled in some detail in chapter 6 above, the author of 2 Sam. 5:6—8:14 presents David, not Saul, as the true successor of Joshua.[6] Here I will only highlight a few of the key connections. The judges' era had been a long pause in the leadership history of

---

5. Marsha White, "'The History of Saul's Rise': Saulide State Propaganda in 1 Samuel 1–14," in *'A Wise and Discerning Mind': Essays in Honor of Burke O. Long*, ed. Saul M. Olyan and Robert C. Culley, BJS 325 (Providence, RI: Brown University Press, 2000), 283–84, sees the pro-Saul narrative as also promoting Jonathan as Saul's successor. While this is possible, it seems more likely that the text was originally recorded to elevate and praise Jonathan's prowess in battle and record David's love for his friend (cf. 1 Sam. 20:17; 2 Sam. 1:17-27).

Israel, with varying degrees of success. Now, however, David would complete what the judges and Saul had been unable to accomplish: the total subjugation of the land of Canaan. Not surprisingly, the author begins the record of David's success as the next Joshua by focusing on the one city—on the border of Benjamin and Judah, please note—that had eluded the total control of Israel since the conquest and judges' period: Jerusalem (Josh. 15:63; Judg. 1:21). Jerusalem becomes the first step in David's "conquest" of his new kingdom, just as Jericho had served a similar function for Joshua (Joshua 6; 2 Sam. 5:6-9). While the parallels are only general, they are nonetheless present.

To begin, the twofold conquest of Ai finds affinity with David's double encounter with the Philistines (Joshua 7–8; 2 Sam. 5:17-25). And, as with Joshua, before David can complete his "conquest" of Israel's enemies he has to ameliorate YHWH's wrath against him and Israel for improperly handling that which was devoted to YHWH (cf. Joshua 7; 2 Samuel 6)—in each case someone from Judah touches that which was devoted to YHWH, and in turn dies (Achan and Uzzah). Once this is achieved, and YHWH's presence (i.e., the Ark) is with David, he can move forward to conquer the enemy—a similar scenario found in the conquest narrative. Finally, mirrored in Joshua's actions at Jericho (Josh. 6:19, 24), 2 Sam. 8:10-11 tells us that David dedicated the precious metals from the spoils of war to YHWH (i.e., silver, gold, and bronze).[7] Nowhere else in the DtrH do we find such a connection, not even with Josiah!

---

6. Another subtle jab against Saul's right to the throne appears in 2 Sam. 6:21-23. Michal's ability to have children would have helped David claim the throne, but he does not take this opportunity (2 Sam. 6:23). Cf. Walter Dietrich and Thomas Naumann, "The David–Saul Narrative," in *Reconsidering Israel and Judah: Recent Studies on the Deuteronomistic History*, ed. Gary N. Knoppers and J. Gordon McConville (Winona Lake, IN: Eisenbrauns, 2000), 307.

7. Note that iron is included in Joshua's day as a precious metal but not in David's day. This points to the early date of the Joshua source when iron was considered rare (cf. Deut. 3:11). Iron in David's day was a relatively common commodity.

Next, Nathan's prophecy in 2 Samuel 7 has garnered many scholarly opinions as to who wrote it and when.[8] Also, the text appears chronologically out of place. The content of this chapter is in a period when David had rest from all his enemies (7:1)—something obviously not the case in light of 2 Sam. 8:1.[9] If our Joshua/David parallels are valid, the odd chronological ordering makes sense in light of the order of the covenant motif in Josh. 8:30—9:27. Interestingly, further connections to the conquest and the period of the judges are alluded to in 2 Samuel 7 (2 Sam. 7:10, 11). Following on the heels of chapter 7, David goes on to subdue the land and complete the "conquest" (see esp. 2 Sam. 8:15)—a similar feature that follows the covenant motif of Josh. 8:30—9:27 (see Joshua 10–11). Not surprisingly, with the exception of the short-lived revolt of Sheba in 2 Samuel 20, no further battles take place in the Cisjordan in 2 Samuel. The rest of the battles recorded in 2 Samuel take place in the Transjordan (2 Samuel 10–11).

Also central to 2 Samuel 7 is the introduction to the future temple construction project. Surprisingly, no reference to Solomon as the one who will build the future temple is ever made. One would expect such a clarification, especially if the later Dtr is not above "naming names" when needed (cf. 1 Kgs. 13:2)—as is often propounded by DtrH scholars. There may, however, be good reason why Solomon's name is not included at this juncture in the temple-construction narrative of 2 Samuel 7, especially if Abiathar, or his son Jonathan (see more on this in ch. 10 below), is the one recording this portion

8. See Martin Noth, *The Deuteronomistic History*, JSOTSup 15 (Sheffield: JSOT, 1981), 59, 87; Walter Dietrich, "Martin Noth and the Future of the Deuteronomistic History," in *The History of Israel's Traditions: The Heritage of Martin Noth*, ed. Steven L. McKenzie and M. Patrick Graham, JSOTSup 182 (Sheffield: Sheffield Academic Press, 1994), 169; Helga Weippert, "'Histories' and 'History': Promise and Fulfillment in the Deuteronomistic Historical Work," in Knoppers and McConville, eds., *Reconsidering Israel and Judah*, 59.
9. Richard D. Nelson, "Josiah in the Book of Joshua," *JBL* 100, no. 4 (1981): 533, notes the clear links between Josh. 1:3, 5 and 2 Sam. 7:9-10.

of David's history. Abiathar may have wanted to fashion his source in such a way that allowed him enough wiggle room for plausible deniability about who exactly was to be the next king after David. After all, Abiathar, as we will see in 1 Kings 1–2, chose poorly in Adonijah. Notice that the text of 2 Sam. 7:12-13 says, "When your days are fulfilled and you lay down with your fathers, I will raise up your *seed* after you who will come forth from you and I will establish his kingdom. He certainly will build a house for my name and I will establish the throne of his kingdom forever" (italics mine). Now, to be sure, the wording here certainly points to Solomon, but then, hindsight is always 20/20. DtrH scholars have been so focused on reading their presuppositions back into the narrative that they fail to consider the remote possibility that this material may have been composed as early as Abiathar's exile to Anathoth—a fitting period when David had "rest from all his enemies" (7:1). Furthermore, for most people, rhetorical concerns are secondary. Yet, one must answer the question: What was the rhetorical function of these texts for the earliest audience? If we stop and consider the possibility of the text coming from Abiathar, then the ambiguity in the text, which is regularly filled in by DtrH scholars (i.e., with Solomon's name), makes sense.[10] Moreover, is Abiathar taking the opportunity to take a jab at Nathan the prophet for "getting it wrong" concerning the will of YHWH in relation to David's construction of the temple (7:3-4)? Is this Abiathar's way of alluding to the possibility that Nathan's siding with Solomon as "YHWH's choice" was incorrect? First Kings 1–2 makes it clear that there were two competing factions trying to put their man on the throne—Abiathar and Nathan being on opposing sides.

---

10. Contra Noth, *Deuteronomistic History*, 59, 87; and Dietrich, "Martin Noth," 158, who insert Solomon's name into the discussion without giving it a second thought.

Finally, if our earlier assessment of the authorship of the book of Joshua is correct, and if the scholarly consensus on the early dating of much of the Samuel material is legitimate,[11] then these parallels would date to the Davidic era and perhaps to Abiathar. Abiathar chose to include accounts about the conquering of Jerusalem, the future home of the Ark (5:6-9; ch. 6); the births of David's children in Jerusalem (5:13-16)—perhaps a negative assessment for Solomon in light of his possible connection to the native inhabitants of Jerusalem (5:13—see the discussion below); the bringing up of the Ark to Jerusalem and the priestly interests presented there (ch. 6); the issuing of YHWH's covenantal blessing to David and his prayers before YHWH (ch. 7); and finally, much like the period of Joshua, with YHWH's help (8:14), the land had rest with David administering justice (מֹשְׁפֹּט mišpāṭ) and righteousness (צדקה ṣᵉdāqāh) for his people (cf. 8:15; Josh. 11:23; 23:1). Finally, chapter 8 ends with a list, Abiathar included, of those who were a part of David's administrative team, thus bringing to a close this portion of the David/Joshua parallels (8:15-18).[12] The rest of 2 Samuel will answer the question: Who will succeed David?

The Succession Narrative: 2 Samuel 9—1 Kings 2

The axiomatic acceptance of the presumptive Succession Narrative (hereafter SN)[13] of 2 Samuel 9–2 Kings 2 (minus 2 Samuel 21–24) as proposed by Leonhard Rost has long held sway over scholarly assessment of this portion of the Samuel narrative even though some scholars question delimiting the narrative as such.[14] Based upon our

11. For example, R. Norman Whybray, *The Succession Narrative: A Study of II Samuel 9–20; I Kings 1 and 2*, SBT 9 (London: SCM, 1968), 48.

12. This may be a later insertion.

13. J. P. Fokkelman, *Narrative Art and Poetry in the Books of Samuel. A Full Interpretation Based on Stylistic and Structural Analysis I: King David (II Sam 9–20 & I Kings 1–2)* (Assen: Van Gorcum, 1981).

14. See, for example, Gillian Keys, *The Wages of Sin: A Reappraisal of the 'Succession Narrative,'* JSOTSup 221 (Sheffield: Sheffield Academic Press, 1996), 71–82. Keys (86) argues, what I feel

discussion immediately above, I propose that the narrative of 2 Samuel 9–20 (I will deal with chs. 21–24 separately) presents a unified, but sad picture of YHWH's judgment on the house of David for his sin with Bathsheba, and for his leniency with his sons' sins.[15] Whereas some may seek to present David's leniency with his sons in a positive sense—showing his excessive love—in essence, the author makes it clear that this was his undoing, which led to Absalom's revolt.[16] In fact, Abiathar (or one of his sons) may be showing how leniency when handling one's sons, a common motif in Samuel (e.g., Eli, Samuel, and now David), can lead to chaos often affecting the innocent around them.[17] Even Abiathar was led astray when he sided with the spoiled, Adonijah (see 1 Kgs. 1:6), thus losing his long-held office of high priest.[18]

incorrectly, that another author penned chs. 1–9 and 21–24; yet she still suggests a unity to the book. Joseph Blenkinsopp, "Another Contribution to the Succession Narrative Debate (2 Samuel 11–20; 1 Kings 1–2)," *JSOT* 38, no. 1 (2013): 35–58, argues for the coherency of the SN although he starts at 2 Samuel 11. See also the designation "Court History" as proposed by John Van Seters, *The Biblical Saga of King David* (Winona Lake, IN: Eisenbrauns, 2009).

15. Ibid., 210–12. Keys also sees these chapters as a block. Tomoo Ishida, *History and Historical Writing in Ancient Israel: Studies in Biblical Historiography* (Leiden: Brill, 1999), 134, suggests that the SN is a criticism against David's regime. However, this hardly seems likely in light of the pro-David sympathies throughout.

16. P. Kyle McCarter, "Plots, True or False:" The Succession Narrative as Court Apologetic," *Int* 35, no. 4 (1981): 366.

17. Contra Walter Brueggemann, *David's Truth in Israel's Imagination and Memory* (Philadelphia: Fortress Press, 1985), 20, who calls the author of the David material, "naïvely enthusiastic for David." What we actually see is an author who dares to show David's true colors and point out "David's affronts."

18. One would think that Abiathar would have been alerted to the actions of Adonijah, especially due to the similarities between Adonijah's actions and Absalom's coup (cf. 2 Sam. 15:1; 1 Kgs. 1:5; there is, however, a difference in the language of 2 Sam. 15:1—"a chariot and horses"—as opposed to "a chariot and horsemen" in 1 Kgs. 1:5). It is also possible that old age or Joab's influence may have caused Abiathar's poor choice. Indeed, Ishida, *History and Historical Writing*, 133, also suggests Abiathar's role was minimal. Note also the parallel of Adonijah's attempt to take one of David's concubines as Absalom had done earlier (cf. 2 Sam. 16:20–22; 1 Kgs. 2:13–25). Tomoo Ishida, "Adonijah the Son of Haggith and His Supporters: An Inquiry into Problems about History and Historiography," in *The Future of Biblical Studies—The Hebrew Scriptures*, ed. Richard E. Friedman and H. G. M. Williamson (Atlanta: Scholars, 1987), 173, sees this latter pericope as a later Solomonic addition to the Adonijah account. See further, Ishida's numerous parallels between Adonijah and Absalom's coup on p. 176.

It has also been posited that the SN is an apologia for Solomon's rise to the throne,[19] composed by a "near contemporary of David and a member of the court."[20] As such, several authors for this material have been suggested.[21] For example, Rost, following the work of A. Klostermann, suggests Ahimaaz, Zadok's son, wrote the work, whereas Hans Wilhelm Hertzberg proposes Hushai, David's friend.[22] However, as we shall demonstrate, when this block is closely examined, especially in conjunction with 1 Kings 3–11, it is difficult to vindicate its usage as a pro-Solomonic apologia. To begin, the pro-David-and-Solomon Chronicler omits the SN, no doubt because it was not the most flattering for either David or Solomon.[23] Also, nowhere in the text do we see Solomon's name mentioned as a candidate for the throne until Nathan and Bathsheba collude (?) to approach the aged King David and propose that Solomon be the next king (1 Kgs. 1:11-31).[24] Yes, Solomon appears at the end of

---

19. E.g., T. C. G. Thornton, "Solomonic Apologetic in Samuel and Kings," *CQR* 169, no. 371 (1968): 159–66; Whybray, *Succession Narrative*, 54–55; James W. Flanagan, "Court History or Succession Document? A Study of 2 Samuel 9–20 and 1 Kings 1–2," *JBL* 91, no. 2 (1972): 172–81; Ishida, "Adonijah the Son of Haggith," 165–87, argues for a pro-Solomonic apology in 1 Kings 1–2. See Ishida's revised essay in *History and Historical Writing*, 102–36. In his updated essay (135–36), he suggests that one of Nathan's followers was the author of the SN (2 Samuel 2—1 Kgs. 2:46b), sometime in the first half of Solomon's reign

20. Whybray, *Succession Narrative*, 11. Whybray concludes that as of his day there is "almost universal agreement" on this point. David M. Gunn, *The Story of King David*, JSOTSup 6 (Sheffield: JSOT, 1982), 65, notes the general consensus that 1 Kgs. 2:2b-4, 10-11, 27 are the work of Dtr. For a further listing of those holding an early date, see Keys, *Wages of Sin*, 184–88.

21. Contra Weiser, "Die Legitimation des Königs David," 329, who sees a different author beginning in 2 Samuel 9.

22. Leonhard Rost, *The Succession to the Throne of David*, trans. Michael D. Rutter and David M. Gunn (Sheffield: Almond, 1982), 105. Cf. also A. Klostermann, *Die Bücher Samuelis und der Könige*, Kurzgefasster Kommentar zu den heiligen Schriften Alten und Neuen Testamentes (Nördlingen: Beck, 1887); Hans Wilhelm Hertzberg, *I & II Samuel* (Philadelphia: Westminster, 1964), 379. Like many more recent scholars, Keys, *Wages of Sin*, 212, plays it safe by suggesting that the authorship of this material was undertaken by the "prophetic school" of the exilic period.

23. So, too, Keith Whitelam, "The Defence of David," *JSOT* 29 (1984): 70–71; and Whybray, *Succession Narrative*, 13. Interestingly Whybray (54) goes on to conclude that the narrative was written early in the reign of Solomon. This hardly seems likely, especially if Solomon is not presented in the most positive light.

chapter 12 as the next son of David by Bathsheba.[25] And yes, the text says that YHWH "loved" Solomon. But this in no way equates to a declaration that Solomon was to be the next king.[26] Furthermore, in Abiathar's eyes, primogeniture would dictate that Adonijah, the next son in line to the throne after the death of Absalom, would serve as king.[27] Now to be clear, I am not saying that David had *not* told Bathsheba that Solomon would be the next king but, rather, that the way it is presented textually, Abiathar remains somewhat "innocent" of the charge leveled against him by Solomon in 1 Kgs. 2:26. What is more, in the very next verse (1 Kgs. 2:27), the author clarifies that the dismissal of Abiathar was not solely due to his poor choice but, rather, in order to "fulfill the word of YHWH which he spoke concerning the house of Eli in Shiloh."[28] And even though some scholars argue over the legitimacy of the prophecy in 1 Sam. 2:27-36, the fact that it was actually included in the DtrH shows that it served its very

24. So the conclusion of Timo Veijola, "Solomon: Bathsheba's Firstborn," in Knoppers and McConville, eds., *Reconsidering Israel and Judah*, 357; Ishida, "Adonijah the Son of Haggith," 175–76; and intimated by Gerhard von Rad, *The Problem of the Hexateuch and Other Essays*, trans. E. W. Trueman Dicken (London: Oliver and Boyd, 1966), 188.

25. While Veijola, "Solomon," 340–57, argues that Solomon was in fact the son of the adulterous relationship between David and Bathsheba—that is, there never was a "first" child—his conclusions are based upon suppositions that run counter to a straightforward reading of 2 Sam. 12:14-23. Several narrative changes would be required throughout ch. 12 in order to foster such a conclusion. Furthermore, if Abiathar is the author of the material, he would have been more than willing to include such "truth" in an effort to vindicate his choice of Adonijah.

26. So, too, Thornton, "Solomonic Apologetic," 160; and Gunn, *Story of King David*, 105–106. McCarter, "Plots, True or False," 361–62, recognizes the problem with this lacuna as he argues for a pro-Solomon apology and conveniently ascribes the earlier portion along with 1 Kings 1–2 to another hand(s)—a position adopted by Flanagan, "Court History or Succession Document?," 175, as well. Ishida, *History and Historical Writing*, 156, also struggles with this lacuna even though he, too, sees the SN as pro-Solomonic.

27. See also comments by Thornton, "Solomonic Apologetic," 161. Lucien Legrand, *The Bible on Culture* (Maryknoll, NY: Orbis, 2000), 21, postulates that because Solomon was born to a "Canaanite" mother (i.e., Bathsheba), he was supported by the large Canaanite population in Jerusalem (Jebus). Abiathar supported Adonijah the "Judahite," who was the son of Haggith, and lost (2 Sam. 3:4). However, there is just as much textual evidence to suggest that Bathsheba was from the tribe of Judah (cf. 2 Sam. 11:3; 23:34).

28. Gunn, *Story of King David*, 65, suggests that 1 Kgs. 2:27 was a later addition. While this is possible, perhaps even coming from one of Abiathar's sons, it is also possible that it was original, especially in light of the rhetorical context.

purpose.[29] Did Abiathar or his son Jonathan decide to include this prophecy to help explain later why the priest was a political casualty in Solomon's day?

Interestingly, the author did not show how Abiathar's removal fulfilled the earlier prophecy in toto, especially the extremely negative aspects (1 Sam. 2:36).[30] Thus, the "faithful priest" who will replace the Elides (1 Sam. 2:35), whether Samuel or Zadok, is not addressed here.[31] If it is supposed to be Zadok, the author makes sure it is not stressed.[32] Thus, Abiathar walks off the scene of Israel's history as a casualty of the sins of his forefathers. Indeed, his cultic service to David is actually highlighted in 1 Kgs. 2:26 by none other than Solomon himself—for the other key "conspirators," execution is their end (e.g., Joab, Adonijah, and, by extension, Shimei), but Abiathar lives on. Perhaps even to write another day!

Pushing against a pro-Solomonic apologia also is the issue of how the main characters are presented in the narrative. Nathan, Solomon, and Bathsheba are not presented in the most favorable light. For example, Norman Whybray concludes that the author paints a picture of Bathsheba "as a good-natured, rather stupid woman who was a natural prey both to more passionate and to cleverer men."[33] She allowed David to take her; Nathan to use her; and Adonijah,

---

29. See, for example, the comments by Richard D. Nelson, "The Role of the Priesthood in the Deuteronomistic History," in Knoppers and McConville, eds., *Reconsidering Israel and Judah*, 183-184. Nelson sees most of the prophecy as original except for verse 35. I am a firm believer that the prophecy was not a fabrication by a later hand but, rather, a true word from YHWH—a word that Abiathar included, in some ways, to vindicate his actions but also to show the truthfulness of the prophets' words.

30. Ibid., 185–86. Nelson correctly notes that Abiathar's removal did not fulfill the entire prophecy of 1 Sam. 2:36, namely, the bowing down and the begging of his sons.

31. Contra Tony W. Cartledge, *1 & 2 Samuel* (Macon, GA: Smyth & Helwys, 2001), 59. There is no direct evidence that the prophecy of 1 Samuel 2 is meant for Zadok per se. Indeed, if the text was recorded in Josiah's day, as propounded by Cartledge, one would expect a clearer connection.

32. So too Nelson, "Role of the Priesthood," 186–87.

33. Whybray, *Succession Narrative*, 40.

in a back-door manner, to ask for the throne. Solomon does not even appear in the narrative until 1 Kings 1 and then is silent until his mother and Nathan see that he is placed on the throne.[34] And Solomon is not anointed at the command of YHWH but, rather, of David.[35] Nathan, on the other hand, who only appears in 2 Samuel 7; 12; and 1 Kings 1, appears to take advantage of David's aged state to push for Solomon's candidacy for the throne.[36] Moreover, as noted above, 2 Sam. 7:3 records a subtle jab at Nathan for "getting it wrong" regarding who would build the temple. YHWH had to step in and correct the prophet. It is possible that Abiathar is suggesting that because Nathan has been wrong in the past, perhaps he was wrong in his choice of Solomon (1 Kgs. 1:11-14). The fact that Abiathar and Nathan end up on opposite sides of the succession debate in 1 Kings 1–2 may be evidence that there was a rift between them. The SN thus becomes Abiathar's way of telling the facts of history from *his* perspective.

Rhetorically, the SN also shows stylistic similarities with earlier material. For example, the author's way of introducing characters who appear later in the narrative obtains here as well (cf. 1 Sam. 2:12-17; 14:49-52; 2 Sam. 3:2-6, etc.). For example, 2 Samuel 9 has inclusio-like traits with 2 Samuel 19, whereby the reader is introduced to Mephibosheth and Ziba and the region of Lo-debar (9:4, 5; 17:27). At the same time, the narrative links back to David's promises to Jonathan in 1 Sam. 20:15. Chapter 9 also needs to be read in light of chapter 10. In the former chapter, David shows kindness

---

34. Gunn, *Story of King David*, 106, notes this silence as well. On the other hand, Lienhard Delekat, "Tendenz und Theologie der David-Salomo-Erzählung," in *Das ferne und nahe Wort Festschrift Leonhard Rost*, BZAW 105 (Berlin: Topelmann, 1967), 26–36, argues that the text is anti-Solomon *and* anti-David. As cited by McCarter, "Plots, True or False," 259 n.9.

35. So, too, Flanagan, "Court History or Succession Document?," 175.

36. I am not meaning to question the prophetic calling or status of Nathan, especially in light of 2 Sam. 12:1-12, but, rather, that it is possible that Abiathar, or one of his sons, is including certain facts to lessen the sting of his banishment.

(חסד ḥesed; cf. 9:1, 7; 10:2 [2x]) to an "enemy" (Mephibosheth) of the throne. In turn, that "enemy" accepts David's overture and is treated favorably. Conversely, in chapter 10, the Ammonites, supposed "friends" of the throne, balk at David's overture of condolences and suffer the consequences. Of course, the ensuing Ammonite war also serves as the backdrop for the events of chapters 11–12. Thus we can conclude that chapters 9 and 10 are integral to what follows and what comes before.

Next, whereas in chapters 9 and 10 David is presented in a more favorable light, chapters 11–12 paint a picture of David that is less than flattering. Nevertheless, even after David sins with Bathsheba he is presented in a positive light despite the gravity of the event. Indeed, scholars look to events such as these as evidence of Dtr's positive evaluation of both David and his reign.[37] Priestly perspectives also appear in these chapters. For example, in 11:4 Bathsheba is said to have purified herself of her "uncleanness" (טמאה ṭum'āh) after her adultery with David—a term that abounds in priestly literature (e.g., Lev. 5:3; 7:20, 21; 14:19, 15:3, esp. Lev. 15:25, 26, etc.). Interestingly, other than two references in Judg. 13:7, 14 (another proposed book by Abiathar), this term only appears here in the DtrH. Moreover, the Ark is mentioned (11:11); explicit connections are made with the book of Judges (cf. 11:21; Judg. 9:52-53); and David is said to have done "evil in the sight of YHWH" (11:27; 12:9)—a common refrain in the Mosaic Law and the DtrH, which is also used for Saul (cf. 1 Sam. 15:19; Deut. 4:25; 9:18; 17:2; 31:29). We also see a subtle, but important, link back to the evil actions of Saul. Nathan tells David that YHWH knew that he used the "sword" of the Ammonites to kill Uriah (12:9). Saul had also tried to use the "sword" of the Philistines to kill David (1 Sam. 18:25). In both cases, a woman who

37. E.g., Dietrich, "Martin Noth," 169.

was to be a wife (Michal), or was the wife of another (Bathsheba), is the central focus. Finally, chapter 12 also serves as the backdrop for the fulfillment of the fourfold prophecy against David and his house (12:6), the fulfillment of which occupies the narrative from chapters 13 through 20. It is likely that Abiathar's use of Nathan's prophecy reflects a period prior to the succession disagreement, which plays itself out in 1 Kings 1–2 (see more on the chronological problems above).

From an authorial perspective, in this block we do not see blind favor granted to David, as is often leveled against Dtr. As a priest, Abiathar would have detested what David had done with Bathsheba, especially the Saul-like manner in which he acted. Abiathar may have also loathed David's actions if the priest was a close friend of Uriah, after spending years on the run together from Saul. Moreover, Abiathar would have been an eyewitness to many of the goings-on in the court. Thus, he obviously framed the remainder of the SN in such a way as to show how David's sin affected the lives of his family, and how that sin had ramifications for the entire nation. Indeed, this was perhaps the main reason Abiathar sided against Solomon in the first place. Solomon was a product of David and Bathsheba. Even though he was loved by God, Solomon was still not the ideal king in Abiathar's mind.

Chapters 13–20 trace the downward spiral of David's history, as many of God's blessings to David are removed. Amnon rapes his half-sister Tamar (13:1-20); Absalom kills Amnon (13:22-39); intrigue ensues between Absalom, David, and Abner (ch. 14); and Absalom mounts a coup against his father that ends with Absalom losing his life (chs. 15–19). Thus, in the aftermath of David's sin, David is expelled from the "promised land" and forced back to the region where the children of Israel had first started the conquest in Joshua 1. That the author desires to show parallels between these blocks of material should not be surprising, especially if Abiathar is the author of both. This material would have been in the forefront of his thinking, to be sure.

Therefore, as I noted in chapter 6, the account of David's battle for the "promised land" during Absalom's coup in many ways reflects motifs found in Joshua's conquest of the promised land—although in many ways reversed. The narrative parallels that occur betray the same hand in the editing and compiling process. These motifs include:

1. The rebellion against David is triggered by the blowing of a ram's horn, whereas Joshua's conquest of Jericho is triggered by the blowing of a ram's horn (2 Sam. 15:10//Josh. 6:20).

2. In both accounts, a man from Judah is responsible for troubling Israel, Absalom and Achan respectively (2 Sam. 15:14//Josh. 7:1).

3. David sends two spies to know the weaknesses of his enemy, Absalom (2 Sam. 15:27-28), and Joshua sends two spies to find the weakness of Jericho (Josh. 2:1).

4. The Ark goes with the people, but David sends it back to Jerusalem where it belongs; Joshua takes the Ark with him so it will end up "where it belongs" (2 Sam. 15:24-29//Josh. 3:8-17).

5. The two spies are almost discovered by the enemy in both accounts, but are protected by a woman (cf. 2 Sam. 17:17-21//Josh. 2:2-7).

6. The battle for the promised land takes place in the Transjordan in David's day, whereas the battle for the promised land takes place in Canaan in Joshua's day (2 Sam. 17:24//Josh. 3:13–4:1).

7. David's provisions cease as he *leaves* the promised land but he is given food and supplies from his *friends* in the Transjordan (2 Sam. 17:27-29; 19:32), whereas in Joshua's day, the people's provisions cease on the day they *leave* the Transjordan and are

provided for by their *enemy's* crops in the promised land (Josh. 5:12).

8. Oath taking is in both accounts (2 Sam. 18:5; 19:23//Josh. 2:12; 9:15).

9. The side that had the blessing of YHWH wins (2 Sam. 18:7//Joshua 6; 8–12).

10. In both accounts, people who have gone against YHWH and his leaders (Absalom and Achan, the king of Ai, the five kings of the south) end up dead with a heap of stones over them (2 Sam. 18:17//Josh. 7:26; 8:29; 10:27).[38]

11. The tribes meet at Gilgal (Joshua's base camp during the conquest) to welcome David back (2 Sam. 19:15//Josh. 4:19).

12. When David returns to the promised land, he is met by a host of people who swear allegiance to him, whereas Joshua is met with hostility (2 Sam. 19:11-43//Joshua 6–12).

13. David is presented as the "angel of God" when he crosses the Jordan, whereas Joshua meets a "man of God" when he crosses the Jordan (2 Sam. 19:27//Josh. 5:13-15).

14. Both leaders are met by people dressed in tattered clothing and unkempt: Mephibosheth and the Gibeonites (2 Sam. 19:24//Josh. 9:5).

15. David and Joshua are challenged to display wisdom in making a decision about the affairs of these people that meet them (2 Sam. 19:24-32//Joshua 9).

16. In both cases, neither leader seeks God's guidance in that decision (2 Sam. 19:27//Josh. 9:14).

17. In both accounts, the people who are adjudicated by David and Joshua end up being lowered in their social status or position: Mephibosheth loses half of his wealth and is now equal with

---

38. The account of the five kings of the southern coalition ends with their being executed and their bodies sealed in a cave with large stones over the mouth of the cave.

his servant Ziba, whereas the Gibeonites are forced to become hewers of wood and drawers of water (2 Sam. 19:29//Josh. 9:27).

18. After an initial victory, more hostilities ensue: civil war for David; the northern and southern campaigns for Joshua (2 Samuel 20//Joshua 10–12).

19. Both leaders are faced with the possibilities of civil war after the cessation of hostilities (2 Samuel 20//Josh. 22:9-34).

20. Both potential civil wars are averted by a parley: an old woman with Joab, whereas in Joshua's day the leaders of the Transjordan tribes meet with Phinehas and the Cisjordan leaders (2 Sam. 20:16-22//Josh. 22:30-34).

21. David is confronted with internal dissent from one man named Sheba, who causes trouble for the renewed nation, and Joshua has to deal with the sin of Achan, which causes trouble for the nation (2 Samuel 20//Joshua 7).

22. A woman plays a key role in the fall of a city and in saving a city (2 Sam. 20:16-22//Josh. 6:23-25).

It goes without saying that these parallel motifs point to unity of authorship. Moreover, the eyewitness perspective lends itself to both Abiathar (15:24, 29, 35; 19:11) and his son Jonathan (17:15-21). Also, terms that appear in this block show unity with earlier material (e.g., Deut. 25:10//2 Sam. 15:30). For example, three different times David is likened to an "angel of God," which harks back to 1 Samuel (cf. 1 Sam. 29:9; 2 Sam. 14:17, 20; 19:28 [Heb]). And 2 Sam. 20:23-26 ends with a similar list of David's administrators, as seen in 8:16-18.[39] This seems to point to the completion of a block of material for a given time period. The chapters that follow in 2 Samuel 21–24 may serve

---

39. Similar entries include: Joab, Beniah, Jehoshaphat, Zadok. Different entries include: Adoram was over the forced labor; Sheva was scribe vs. Seraiah in 20:17; Ira was also a priest (20:26); David's sons were chief ministers (8:18); and Abiathar's son, Ahimelech, is priest in 8:17. The latter entry seems to point to a later list than that of ch. 20.

as an appendix to Samuel, added late in David's life. Nevertheless, the material in these closing chapters still may reflect Abiathar's day, as opposed to an exilic or postexilic addendum.

The Putative Appendix to Samuel: 2 Samuel 21–24

Scholars have also long struggled with the purpose of the presumed appendix of 2 Samuel 21–24.[40] Was it original to the work of 2 Samuel, or was it a later addition? If we argue that 1 Kings 1–2 is in fact not directly tied to the book of 2 Samuel, then perhaps a new picture emerges. Chapters 21–24 are not so much an appendix as they are a highly structured conclusion to the life of David in preparation for his successor.[41] I have presented the merits of this perspective elsewhere, so I will only summarize them here.[42] These chapters present eight key motifs that show that the throne is ready for the next king.

1. The threat from past curses on the land (i.e., famine) is eliminated (21:1-14).
2. David's age has restricted him in battle, thus a new king is needed (21:15-17).

---

40. See, for example, the comments of Keys, *Wages of Sin*, 69–70.
41. Many have noted the chiastic structure of this block. See, for example, Julius Wellhausen, *Die Composition des Hexateuchs und der historischen Bücher des Alten Testaments*, 3d ed. (Berlin: Georg Reimer, 1899), 260–63, esp. 260–61; Joyce Baldwin, *1 and 2 Samuel*, TOTC (Downers Grove, IL: InterVarsity, 1988), 282–83; P. Kyle McCarter, *II Samuel: A New Translation with Introduction: Notes and Commentary*, AB 9 (Garden City, NY: Doubleday, 1984), 18; A. A. Anderson, *2 Samuel*, WBC 11 (Dallas: Word, 1989), 248. An example of the oft-cited chiastic structure is that offered by Anderson:
A. Offense of Saul and its expiation (21:1-14)
  B. Lists of heroes and their exploits (21:15-22)
   C. David's praise of Yahweh (22:1-51)
   C' Yahweh's oracle to David (23:1-7)
  B' Lists of heroes and their exploits (23:8-39)
A' Offense of David and its expiation (24:1-25)
42. Brian Peterson, "The Gibeonite Revenge of 2 Sam. 21:1-14: Another Example of David's Darker Side or a Picture of a Shrewd Monarch?" *JESOT* 1, no. 2 (2012): 201–222, esp. 216–20.

3. The threat of Philistine giants is removed from the land (21:18-22).

4. David is at peace with his God and is ready to die (22:1-51).

5. In typical "Dtr" style, David's final words have been spoken (23:1-7).

6. David's loyal bodyguard is in place, ready to aid the new king (23:8-39).

7. YHWH is at peace with the nation for its past sins (24:1-25).

8. The future site for the temple has been identified (24:18).

These chapters also vary chronologically, reinforcing the perspective that the author arranged them for thematic/rhetorical purposes.[43] For example, even though 2 Sam. 21:1-14 probably should be placed before 2 Samuel 9,[44] it also serves as another reminder of Saul's transgressions, which is the reason David gave up seven sons of Saul. Saul broke the oath that was sworn before YHWH in Joshua's day (Joshua 9).[45] There can be little doubt that many from the northern tribes saw in David's actions another chance to rid himself of the Saulides (see Shimei's words in 2 Sam. 16:7-8).[46] However, from the author's perspective, David was merely trying to avoid disaster from the famine that came upon the nation as judgment for Saul's misplaced "zeal." Chronologically, chapter 24 also appears to be from an earlier period when David was able-bodied and ready for war. Furthermore, much of the language of David's song in chapter 22 reflects priestly concerns,[47] and chapter 24 includes the site of the

---

43. For the proposed dating of the different units in these chapters, see Keys, *Wages of Sin*, 84–85.

44. So, too, VanderKam, "Davidic Complicity," 537.

45. Even though the actions taken in 21:1-14 are against the laws of Deut. 21:23, the Gibeonites are not Israelite and therefore are not bound by this law.

46. So, too, Robert P. Gordon, "David's Rise and Saul's Demise: Narrative Analogy in 1 Samuel 24–26," *TynBul* 31 (1980): 40.

47. See, for example, the theophanic imagery in 24:7-16 and the use of terms such as "ordinances" (משפט *mišpōṭ*; 22:23) "statutes" (חקת *ḥuqōṯ*; 22:23), "blameless" (תמים *tāmîm*), and "iniquity" (עון *'āwōn*; 22:24, 26, 31, 33).

future temple location—a concept that would be of interest to a priest. However, once again, nowhere do we see Solomon mentioned in these chapters. Thus, they must represent a perspective either before Solomon's rise to the throne when Adonijah was the logical choice, or later when someone was trying to suppress Solomon's importance in the turbulent time of transition; the former seems appropriate.

Conclusion

The author of 2 Samuel has provided the reader with four key blocks of material reflecting periods of David's kingship: (1) the transition to the throne of all Israel after the civil war (1:1—5:3); (2) David as the next Joshua figure (5:6—8:14); (3) David's strength as a king, his fall from grace, and the repercussions of his sin (chs. 9–20); and (4) the preparations for a new king (chs. 21–24). However, ever since David's fourfold self-judgment in 2 Sam. 12:6, the narrative has shown how this word has come to pass (cf. also 2 Sam. 12:11-12//16:21-22). From chapters 12–19, three of David's sons had died: (1) the unnamed son of Bathsheba (12:18), (2) Amnon (13:28-29), and (3) Absalom (18:15). It is not until 1 Kings 1–2 that we see the final death recorded, thus again pointing to a unity of rhetorical intent and perhaps in authorship.

10

---

1 and 2 Kings: The Anathothian Tradition

The privileged position given to Kings generally in the discussion also has the effect of de-emphasizing important themes and characteristics in the other books . . .[1]

J. Gordon McConville's assessment speaks volumes in light of the current state of DtrH studies, especially for the book of Kings. While McConville is speaking about the influence of Deuteronomic theology on Kings, his conclusion obtains for a number of other issues related to the DtrH. Invariably, scholars seek to flatten out the other books of the DtrH by forcing them into the proposed rhetorical mold of the book of Kings—a problematic stance in light of our discussion in chapters 7–9 above.[2] Scholars also tend to zero in on the diverse formulae in Kings as a means of identifying the different

---

1. J. Gordon McConville, "The Old Testament Historical Books in Modern Scholarship," in *Them* 22, no. 3 (1997): 11.
2. E.g., centralization of the cult in Jerusalem—one is hard pressed to see centralization as a dominant theme in the Elijah-Elisha cycle, yet it makes up almost half of Kings. Furthermore, I am not implying that a final editor could not have included theological biases throughout the final form but, rather, that it appears to have been more limited than most assert.

eras when certain religio-political concerns may have prevailed, thus affecting the whole of the DtrH—a methodology, as we will see, which has limited benefits at best. Because a number of recent studies have concentrated on these different formulae (e.g., regnal, death, prophetic), I will only highlight a few of the most important aspects germane to our study. Indeed, the scope of this work will not allow a replowing of ground that has already been thoroughly worked over.

Therefore, in this chapter I will continue to focus on macro thematic and rhetorical indicators that point to authorial perspective. Also, I do not seek to answer the nagging questions associated with the tedious redactional-layer debate, whether Hezekian, pre-Hezekian, Josianic, or later. Despite prevailing opinions, when it comes to the book of Kings, it is virtually impossible to have any level of certainty of when certain annalistic blocks were added.[3] However, when it comes to the *final* form of the book of Kings at least, I tend to agree with Steven L. McKenzie's perspective that the book appears to have predominantly one editor from the period of Josiah.[4] Of course, I would argue that this is Jeremiah or Baruch. However, this final editorial work does not preclude the possibility of several authors bringing together material over roughly a three-hundred-year period, which this later compiler edited into the book of Kings during the period of Josiah and then finalized in the exilic period. With this caveat, I do feel that the early portions of 1 Kings, as with the book of Samuel, reflect a perspective earlier as opposed to later in Israel's history.[5] Of course, this is not a novel perspective. For

3. Gary N. Knoppers, "Rethinking the Relationship between Deuteronomy and the Deuteronomistic History: The Case of Kings," *CBQ* 63, no. 3 (2001): 393, suggests that there was heavy editing done by Dtr(s).

4. Steven L. McKenzie, *The Trouble with Kings: The Composition of the Book of Kings in the Deuteronomistic History*, VTSup 42 (Leiden: Brill, 1991), 149.

5. See, for example, the comments by R. Ficker, "Komposition und Erzählung: Untersuchungen zur Ludeerzählung (1 S 4–6; 2 S 6) und zur Geschichte vom Aufstieg Davids (1 S 15–2 S 5)" (ThD diss., University of Heidelberg, 1977), who posits that much of 1 Samuel 16—1 Kings

example, Baruch Halpern and David S. Vanderhooft conclude that a Hezekian edition of the DtrH must have reached back to the United Monarchy, the judges' period and perhaps beyond—a reality, which I have attempted to highlight by this thesis.[6]

The Succession Narrative Concluded: 1 Kings 1–2

As initiated in the previous chapter, 1 Kings 1–2 completes the putative SN. Furthermore, in 1 Kings 1–11, Solomon is presented in a variety of lights: neutral (1 Kings 1–2), somewhat positive (1 Kings 3–10), and negative (1 Kings 11). With such a variety of perspectives, it is hardly likely that this block, or even chapters 1–2, served as an apologia for Solomon (see the discussion in ch. 9). In this vein, the narrative flow and rhetoric of 1 Kings changes from the earlier apologetic tones of Judges and Samuel. As suggested in the previous chapter, it is possible that Abiathar's son, Jonathan, picked up where his father's history left off and recorded these two chapters (maybe more) as a means of offering some vindication for his father's actions in the Adonijah fiasco. He also brings the fourfold curse motif to a close.[7] This proposal finds support in the eyewitness nature of the events of 1 Kings 1–2.

In 1 Kings 1, Jonathan resurfaces, only this time as the bearer of bad news to Adonijah. This naturally begs the question: Why wasn't Jonathan with his father, Joab, Adonijah, and the other celebrants at En-rogel? Jonathan apparently did not approve of his father's alliance with Adonijah and came to En-rogel to warn Abiathar of

---

2 was concluded by the early reign of Solomon. As noted by Walter Dietrich and Thomas Naumann, "The David–Saul Narrative," in *Reconsidering Israel and Judah: Recent Studies on the Deuteronomistic History*, ed. Gary N. Knoppers and J. Gordon McConville (Winona Lake, IN: Eisenbrauns, 2000), 313.

6. Baruch Halpern and David S. Vanderhooft, "The Editions of Kings in the 7th–6th Centuries b.c.e.," *HUCA* 62 (1991): 242.

7. It is possible that Jonathan may be responsible for the SN in totality.

the events transpiring in Jerusalem. Jonathan also was an eyewitness to Solomon's coronation in Jerusalem, and no doubt was in the palace of David when the speeches of Nathan and Bathsheba took place. This would explain the detail of the events leading up to Jonathan's trip to En-rogel, and the laconic description of Adonijah's celebrations—only one verse in length (1 Kgs. 1:9). That Jonathan may have been the author of this material is further bolstered by the fact that the longest sustained speech in 1 Kings 1 comes from Jonathan himself (1:43-48)![8]

It is clear that the author knew a lot about the inner workings of the court. He knew about David's inability to keep warm, and the Abishag "solution"; who was on whose side of the succession debate; Nathan and Bathsheba's plan; the coronation particulars; how and why Joab, Adonijah, and Shimei were dispatched. In the latter case, Shimei's execution was three years later than that of Adonijah and Joab (1 Kgs. 2:39), so whoever wrote the account was no doubt attached to the court. Surprisingly, no mention is made of whether Jonathan (or his brother Ahimelech) was banished with his father. If Jonathan had been a co-conspirator, he certainly would have been singled out for retribution with the others. Also of interest are the author's recorded reasons for why Abiathar escaped the death penalty. First, Solomon himself waived the punishment because Abiathar had faithfully carried the ephod for David, and had shared in David's afflictions while he was a fugitive from Saul—certainly not a negative assessment of the aged priest (2:26). Second, the author tempers Abiathar's responsibility in the failed-coronation fiasco by seeing the event as fulfilling the earlier anti-Elide prophecy (1 Sam. 2:31-36). He thus lays a good portion of the blame at the feet of this familial curse enacted by YHWH himself. Surprisingly, the author stops short

---

8. Nathan's speech is longer but it is interrupted by Bathsheba's speech to David. David's speech is third in length, with Bathsheba's being the shortest of the four main speakers in the chapter.

of applying the full prophecy, namely the negative aspects directed at Eli/Abiathar's sons (1 Sam. 2:33, 36)—Jonathan being one! Thus, Jonathan was not only protecting his father, but himself as well!

One may conclude, then, that although the authorial perspective of 1 Kings 1–2 points to one of Abiathar's two sons, Jonathan seems the most obvious choice. Therefore, Jonathan, Ahimaaz, and Zadok comprised the "younger generation," who stayed on after David's tenure as part of Solomon's court. However, even though Jonathan may have been supportive of Solomon early on, he, like many others, became disillusioned with Solomon's rule in his later years. It is to this portion of Solomon's story that we now turn.

Solomon's Rise and Fall: 1 Kings 3–11

Canonically, the book of Kings takes a marked shift in its literary style during the reign of Solomon.[9] Martin Noth posits that Dtr did not have narrative sources for the reign of Solomon like he did for David and Saul.[10] Similarly, McKenzie, in assessing Noth's work, notes, "For the rest of Solomon's reign, Dtr lacked the kind of running narrative that he had used for Saul and David and so was forced to construct his own account of disparate traditional materials. His primary source was the 'Book of the Acts of Solomon' that he cites in 11:41."[11] McKenzie goes on to suggest that the reign of Solomon was arranged into two distinct literary phases, each beginning with a theophany at Gibeon (3:4-15; 9:1-9). According to some, these two blocks also represent two distinct phases in Solomon's life: the pious and apostasy periods.[12] This assessment is correct, as is Noth's

---

9. For a detailed treatment of 1 Kings 1–14, see Gary Knoppers, *Two Nations under God: The Reign of Solomon and the Rise of Jeroboam*, HSM 52 (Atlanta: Scholars, 1993).

10. Martin Noth, *The Deuteronomistic History*, JSOTSup 15 (Sheffield: JSOT, 1981), 57.

11. Steven L. McKenzie, "The Books of Kings in the Deuteronomistic History," in *The History of Israel's Traditions: The Heritage of Martin Noth*, ed. Steven L. McKenzie and M. Patrick Graham, JSOTSup 182 (Sheffield: Sheffield Academic Press, 1994), 281–82.

identification of a distinct change in the format of the material. As touched on above, the differences at this juncture may be attributed to changes in writing styles; Jonathan took over writing the history started by his father. It is also possible that after the death of David, Jonathan's relationship with Solomon may not have been as close as his and his father's was with David. This would have limited the precise detail about the young king, as is common in the earlier books of the DtrH. This is particularly relevant for the period after the monarchy had become institutionalized—something Solomon excelled at enacting.

At the same time, scholars seek to attribute any negative assessment of Solomon's reign to a later editor who, during the reign of Josiah, inserted the material reflecting Solomon's apostasy as a means of legitimizing Josiah's purge of the former Northern Kingdom. Thus the argument is posited that because Solomon's malfeasance had in essence effected the secession of Israel, cultic reform could legitimate its return.[13] Now, while this is possible, it hardly seems likely that someone would go to such lengths to legitimate Josiah's reforms; after all, Hezekiah needed no such justification (2 Chr. 31:1). Rather, it seems that the author of 1 Kings 3–11, living in Solomon's day, is more interested in telling what the nature of Solomon's reign was like from beginning to end. It also is telling that after 1 Kings 12–14 (the period of Rehoboam and Jeroboam), the DtrH becomes very annalistic in nature.[14] Of course, this change would correspond closely to the death of Jonathan and the change in authors—perhaps to one of his sons or other priests at Anathoth.

Thus, Jonathan took up the mantle of Abiathar and recorded the history of the man who had deposed his father. Later, Jonathan, in

---

12. A. D. H. Mayes, *The Story of Israel Between Settlement and Exile: A Redactional Study of the Deuteronomistic History* (London: SCM, 1983), 109.

13. Halpern and Vanderhooft, "Editions of Kings," 242.

14. The Elijah and Elisha cycle excepted.

his old age, or even one of his sons, assessed Solomon's reign through the lens of the Deuteronomic law, namely, Deut. 17:14-20, especially vv. 14-17. Yes, Solomon had been blessed by wealth and fame, but instead of using his God-given wisdom and wealth for the good of the entire nation, he had lavishly spent the lion's share of it on himself (e.g., 1 Kgs. 10:14-22),[15] and the very things that YHWH had condemned in his law (i.e., multiplying horses and wives; cf. 1 Kgs. 4:26, 28; 10:25, 28; 11:1-4, 8 respectively; cf. also Deut. 7:1-6). Therefore, one does not need to adhere slavishly to the theory that the anti-Solomonic portion of the DtrH was added in Josiah's day; it fits just as well on the pen of Jonathan or someone close to him.

In this regard, even in the purported "positive" portion of the history of Solomon, one can already see the chinks in Solomon's armor. In 1 Kgs. 3:1, the reader is told that Solomon enters into a covenant with the pharaoh of Egypt by marrying his daughter—a clear violation of the law (Deut. 17:16; see also 1 Kgs. 5:12).[16] A subtle rebuke may also be present when one compares the time spent on Solomon's own house to that of the house of YHWH—thirteen years versus seven years respectively (cf. 1 Kgs. 6:38; 7:1). At the same time, the author tries to give an honest assessment of the positive elements of Solomon's early reign. Whether verses such as 3:2-3, 4:20, 25, or 6:11-14 are later additions or justification of Solomon's actions by Jonathan is difficult to adduce.[17] What is certain is that Solomon's judgment between the two harlots shows that YHWH's word concerning Solomon's wisdom had come to pass (3:16-28; see also 4:29-34).

15. In this vein, see also the comments by Baruch Halpern, "Sectionalism and the Schism," *JBL* 93, no. 4 (1974): 519–32, esp. 522–26. For a contrasting view, see Knoppers, "Rethinking the Relationship," 409–12.

16. So, too, J. Gordon McConville, "Narrative and Meaning in the Books of Kings," *Bib* 70, no. 1 (1989): 35.

17. 1 Kgs. 6:11-14 may be a later insertion due to its absence in the Old Greek and Lucianic witnesses. Cf. McKenzie, *Trouble with Kings*, 138.

What is more, the period of building the temple must have been an exciting time for all Israel, especially a priest. In this regard, the priestly interests and perspective are clearly evident when twelve verses out of four chapters (1 Kings 5–8) are devoted to the thirteen-year building project of Solomon's house (7:1-12) as compared to the temple and its dedication. Again, this priestly interest may lie with Jonathan or his brother, Ahimelech. Other possible authorial clues appear in the midst of the list of Solomon's district administrators. Ahimaaz (Zadok's son?) is mentioned, along with a notation that he married a daughter of Solomon (4:15). No doubt, Ahimaaz and Jonathan were friends; and this information would have been of interest to Jonathan (2 Sam. 15:27, 36; 17:17, 20). Of course, the eyewitness nature of many of the events of 1 Kings 3–10 points to someone like Jonathan as well.

Next, the temple dedication of 1 Kings 8 falls within the category of Dtr "speeches" proposed by Noth. While the scholarly opinions concerning the redactions and importance of this prayer are legion,[18] here I will only note that the content is that in which a priest surely would be interested. On the one hand, it is possible that this speech/prayer was incorporated into the DtrH by one of Abiathar's sons.[19] On the other hand, Gary Knopper's suggestion that Solomon's prayer which focuses on the temple as a place of prayer as opposed to sacrifice, fits well in the period of Jeremiah (i.e., Josiah and later) is also noteworthy.[20] Jeremiah's temple speech in chapter 7 addresses the issues of a repentant and right heart before YHWH as opposed to

18. See, for example, the work done by Gary N. Knoppers, "Prayer and Propaganda: Solomon's Dedication of the Temple and the Deuteronomist's Program," *CBQ* 57, no. 2 (1995): 229–54.

19. Antony F. Campbell, *Of Prophets and Kings: A Late Ninth-Century Document (1 Samuel 1–2 Kings 10)*, CBQMS 17 (Washington, DC: Catholic Biblical Association of America, 1986), 205, places 1 Kings 8 as the conclusion to the block of the DtrH that begins with 1 Samuel 13. However, see my discussion on the unity of Samuel in chapter 9.

20. Knoppers, "Prayer and Propaganda," 231–32, esp. 245–53. Knoppers (252) does point out the numerous sacrifices at the dedication as the work of the original Dtr and not from a later hand.

ritual sacrifice. Sacrifice would not save the people, but earnest prayer and proper conduct would.[21] Then again, what true priest of God would not want to see proper attitudes in this manner? Therefore, we are left to look at the broader narrative for more convincing authorial clues.

Before we leave the topic of the temple dedication, it is important to note one final point of interest. It is intriguing that once the Ark of the Covenant is placed within the temple that it is never mentioned again in the DtrH.[22] Two factors could account for this lacuna: (1) due to Abiathar's exile, his family may have had limited access to the temple and Ark; (2) it could be that the temple itself took on the central cultic role that the Ark once held.[23] In this regard, the fact that Jeremiah only mentions the Ark once, and only then in the context of the distant future when it will never be mentioned or come again to the people's mind (Jer. 3:16), may be telling of why the Ark is basically absent in the final form of Kings. Jeremiah certainly witnessed the destruction of the temple and the loss of the Ark to the Babylonians (of course, the latter is a debateable statement). When he was doing the final editing of the book of Kings, he could easily have had this prophecy in mind when he formulated these books.

The last portion of Solomon's reign in chapters 9–11 may be divided into two portions. Chapters 9–10 are relatively positive, whereas chapter 11 is a negative assessment of Solomon's final days.[24]

21. So, too, Thomas Römer, "How Did Jeremiah Become a Convert to Deuteronomistic Ideology?," in *Those Elusive Deuteronomists: The Phenomenon of Pan-Deuteronomism*, ed. Linda S. Schearing and Steven L. McKenzie, JSOTSup 268 (Sheffield: Sheffield Academic Press, 1999), 194. See also parallels between Jeremiah and Deuteronomy and the DtrH at Jer. 25:1-13//2 Kings 17; Jer. 11:3-4//Deut. 29:24//1 Kgs. 8:21; Jer. 11:4-5//Deut. 7:8; 8:18; Jer. 24:9-10//Deut. 28:25, 63. As noted by ibid., 194–95.

22. Knoppers, "Prayer and Propaganda," 231–32, esp. 242.

23. On the latter concept, see Martin Noth, "The Jerusalem Catastrophe of 587 b.c. and Its Significance for Israel," in *The Laws in the Pentateuch and Other Studies*, trans. D. R. Ap-Thomas (London: Oliver & Boyd, 1966), 262.

24. McConville, "Narrative and Meaning," 36–37, rightly points up the subtle jab at Solomon for needing the pharaoh to capture Gezer from the Canaanites (1 Kgs. 9:16).

Jonathan may have recorded this material, but he certainly would have been quite old or even dead by the time Solomon died. Therefore, a descendant of Jonathan may have taken over the history. This finds support by the inclusion of the extended prophecy from the prophet Ahijah in chapter 11 (vv. 29-39). Ahijah's prophecy is actually more anti-Solomonic than any other portion of the record of Solomon's reign. What is most telling is that Ahijah is identified as a Shilonite—the very city where the Elides ministered (cf. 11:29; 1 Samuel 1–4). It is likely that Ahijah was known to those from Anathoth due to this connection, and was the source used here. Why else would the author mention the prophet's association with Shiloh? Ahijah's prophecy concerning the giving of the northern tribes to Jeroboam would be fitting in light of Solomon's affront in ceding twenty northern cities to Hiram, several of which were Gershonite Levitical cities.[25] If these Levites were forced south to the Levitical cities where Abiathar's family lived, as suggested by Halpern, the anti-Solomonic rhetoric takes on even more force.[26] Moreover, Solomon's treatment of these Levites is even more stinging if the Ahimaaz, who was over Solomon's northern district of Naphtali, was the son of Zadok (4:15), Abiathar's replacement.[27] Thus Solomon's rule comes to a close with a strong negative assessment. Jonathan may have been the one to record these words, but even if he did not, one of his offspring could have.

It is also at this juncture that the regnal, death, burial, and succession formulae appear for only the second time in the DtrH (11:42-43). The formulae here are reversed as compared to their first appearance in 1 Kgs. 2:10-11. In the former case, the regnal formula appears before the death and burial formulae. In the latter, the death

---

25. Halpern, "Sectionalism and the Schism," 526. Halpern suggests that Ahijah was a Gershonite Levite displaced by Solomon's sale of the region of Kabul to Hiram.
26. Ibid., 519.
27. Ibid., 530.

and burial formulae precede the regnal formula. The only other place this latter order appears is with Jehu's death (2 Kgs. 10:35-36). It is possible that Jonathan initiated the ordering of 1 Kgs. 2:10-11, which was changed by a later author. Because a number of scholars have proposed that authorial implications can be deduced from the use of these formulae, a brief overview of select formulae may be helpful.

Formulae in Kings

By far, the books of Kings have the most formulae of any of the DtrH books. This may betray intentional annalistic-type editing/compilation. In the discussion that follows I will briefly examine five of the most notable formulae/catchphrases: (1) death notices; (2) the evaluation formula for kings; (3) the incomparability formula; (4) the editorial notation, "until those days"; and (5) the prophetic formula.

First, as previously noted with the death of David, we see the introduction of a new death formula for the kings of Judah and Israel (1 Kgs. 2:10). The formula follows the basic pattern, "And [X] slept with his fathers" (עם אבתיו [X] וישכב *wayyiškab* [X] *ʿim ʾăbōtāyw*).[28] This change may point to a different author or compiler of the material, at least from 1 Kgs. 2:10 onward, as opposed to the person who recorded the material in Joshua to 2 Samuel.[29] Now, to be sure, someone at a later date may have inserted these formulae but, as previously noted, one cannot rule out that Jonathan (or his father) may have started it and later authors picked it up. This may also be the reason why the evaluation formula (see immediately below) starts *after* Solomon's reign. The annalistic style of the DtrH clearly changes at this juncture.

---

28. This phrase appears twenty-three times in the DtrH and ten times in the Chronicler. The Chronicler appears to have borrowed it directly from the DtrH.
29. The notation of 1 Kgs. 2:11 parallels that of 2 Sam. 5:5. Although difficult to prove, the similarities in these regnal formulae may point to the same editor at this period in the DtrH editorial history.

Second, with the exception of Solomon and Rehoboam, every king, whether northern or southern, receives an evaluative notice about his reign. There seems to be some rhetorical intent behind the use of these formulae. For example, when assessing the regnal formulas of the northern kings, McKenzie notes,

> The first eight kings, Jeroboam through Joram, have the same basic evaluation (with Joram being somewhat transitional): they walk in the way of Jeroboam and provoke Yahweh to anger. The next eight, Jehu through Pekah, share a different pattern: they do not depart from the sin of Jeroboam. The last king, Hoshea, does evil but not like his predecessors. The entire list is well balanced and seems to convey a clear message. The first eight kings belong to the royal houses of Jeroboam, Baasha and Omri, which are all in turn targets of the familiar oracle of annihilation incorporating the curse, 'He who dies in the city the dogs will eat; he who dies in the country the birds will eat.' They are the true apostates, ending with the Omrides, the worst of the lot. Then comes the great reformer, Jehu. From him on, the Israelites kings are not so bad, but they perpetuate the sin of Jeroboam until the end. Hoshea stands alone as not so bad as the other kings (or the worst, if the Lucianic reading is correct). In either case, he alone is not to blame for Israel's demise; he is only the last in a long line of evil rulers.[30]

McKenzie sees in this type of rhetorical unity and symmetry the work of one hand—Dtr.[31] While this is indeed possible, this still does not rule out the possibility of the narrative content itself being compiled over time. Of course, the regnal formulae may have been added along the way as well and only later tweaked to suit the last author's rhetorical intent. For example, Halpern and Vanderhooft have presented a forceful argument that textual evidence in the DtrH,

---

30. McKenzie, "Books of Kings," 300. McKenzie here is actually giving a summation of Campbell's work *Of Prophets and Kings*, 139–57. See also comments by Campbell, *Of Prophets and Kings*, 157–68; Robert R. Wilson, "Unity and Diversity in the Book of Kings," in *'A Wise and Discerning Mind': Essays in Honor of Burke O. Long*, ed. Saul M. Olyan and Robert C. Culley, BJS 325 (Providence, RI: Brown University Press, 2000), 304–305; and Richard D. Nelson, *The Double Redaction of the Deuteronomistic History*, JSOTSup18 (Sheffield: JSOT, 1981), 29–42.

31. So, too, Mayes, *Story of Israel*, 107.

in relation to the Chronicler's work, shows that at given times the death formulas have changed—most specifically after the time of Hezekiah. [32] Similarly, Iain Provan has done extensive work on the judgment, succession, regnal, and death and burial formulae, along with the pro-David theme.[33] With such an array of possibilities, it is perhaps best not to overemphasize the value of these formulae when positing authorship.

Closely associated with this discussion is the formula, "[X] did evil in the eyes of YHWH" (עשה הרא בעיני יהוה 'āśāh hāra' b^eênê YHWH).[34] Interestingly, this phrase appears throughout the DtrH and three times in Jeremiah (Jer. 32:30; 52:2; 7:30)—the only place it appears in the prophets. Now, to be sure, this does favor Jeremiah as an editor; however, the fact that this phrase appears even in the Tetrateuch may suggest that it was a stock phrase used over a period of time. Moreover, its appearance in Deuteronomy may have been the basis for many authors to utilize it at either a late or early date, depending on one's dating of Deuteronomy.[35]

A third formula that appears only in Kings is what some scholars call the "incomparability" formula, namely, "no king has arisen before or after like [X]" (paraphrased). The use of this phrase evokes apparent conflicting notices about the reigns of Solomon, Hezekiah, and Josiah (cf. 1 Kgs. 3:12; 2 Kgs. 18:5; 23:25). This has caused some to suggest that the phrase betrays different periods of redaction

32. Halpern and Vanderhooft, "Editions of Kings," 189–90. See also the work of Helga Weippert, "Die 'deuteronomistischen' Beurteilungen der Könige von Israel und Juda und das Problem der Redaktion der Königsbücher," *Bib* 53, no. 3 (1972): 301–39.

33. Iain Provan, *Hezekiah and the Books of Kings: A Contribution to the Debate about the Composition of the Deuteronomistic History*, BZAW 172 (Berlin: de Gruyter, 1988), 33–143. See also the perspective of Campbell, *Of Prophets and Kings*, 139–202, regarding the two layers of tradition from northern and southern perspectives.

34. A variety of forms are used for the verb *'āśāh* ("to do").

35. Num. 32:13; Deut. 4:25; 9:18; 17:2; 31:29; Judg. 2:11; 3:7, 12; 4:1; 6:1; 10:6; 13:1; 1 Sam. 15:19; 1 Kgs. 11:6; 14:22; 15:26, 34; 16:19, 25, 30; 21:20, 25; 22:53; 2 Kgs. 3:2; 8:18, 27; 13:2, 11; 14:24; 15:9, 18, 24, 28; 17:2, 17; 21:2, 6, 16, 20; 23:32, 37; 24:9, 19.

connected to a given monarch.[36] In light of our ongoing thesis, it is possible that the authors from Anathoth, at key periods in Israel's history, edited the compiled DtrH up to a given era. Indeed, we know this to be the case with the book of Proverbs (Prov. 25:1). Nevertheless, McConville righty cautions that the "incomparability" clause may be no more than a stock phrase.[37] Similarly, Gary Knoppers points up that the formula may represent a particular trait of a given king that the author seeks to highlight. Thus, Solomon had wealth and wisdom (1 Kgs. 3:13, 28; 4:29–34; 5:7, 12; 10:21–29), Hezekiah was known for his trust in YHWH (2 Kgs. 18:5), and Josiah was the great reformer (2 Kgs. 23:25; cf. Deut. 6:5).[38] Therefore, caution must be taken when assigning redactional layers based upon this notation.

Next, much like our analysis of the phrase "until this day" in chapter 4 above, the fourth phrase "until those days" may shed light on the period when the material of Kings was finally redacted. While not a "formula" in the strictest sense, this phrase does appear in 1 Kgs. 3:2 and 2 Kgs. 18:4. In both cases, the author reflects back on a time, first in Solomon's day and then in Hezekiah's day, when cultic practices were not as refined as they were at a later period. Based upon its last appearance, this period could be anytime from Josiah's day until the destruction of the temple in 586 or thereafter. Closely connected to this phrase is also the notation "as it is today," which appears at select spots in the DtrH (Deut. 2:30; 4:20, 38; 6:24; 8:18; 10:15; 29:27 [Heb]; 1 Sam. 22:8, 13; 1 Kgs. 3:6; 8:24, 61). Interestingly, in keeping with our thesis, the latter phrase is also used frequently in the book of Jeremiah (cf. Jer. 11:5; 25:18; 32:20; 44:6,

---

36. Gary N. Knoppers, "'There Was None Like Him': Incomparability in the Book of Kings," *CBQ* 54, no. 3 (1992): 411–31, esp. 411–13.
37. McConville, "Old Testament Historical Books," 7.
38. Knoppers, "'There Was None Like Him,'" 413–14. Moses' incomparability is connected to his signs and wonders and for seeing YHWH face to face in Deut. 34:10-12.

22, 23).[39] In the former case, the phrase "until those days" fits well within the time period of Jeremiah—a priest who was focused on proper worship. In the latter case, while the use of "as it is today" *may* point to Jeremiah, it may have been a stock phrase used over a period of time or borrowed from Deuteronomy.

The fifth formula, often labeled the prophetic formula ("According to the word of YHWH which he spoke by the hand of [PN]"; cf. 1 Kgs. 13:26; 14:18; 15:29; 16:12; 17:16; 2 Kgs. 24:2), is another common phrase in Kings. A variation of the phrase that eliminates "by the hand of" appears as well (e.g., 2 Kgs. 1:17; 10:17; see also 1 Kgs. 22:38). Notice that the majority of the occurrences appear later in the DtrH and thus point to a later editor. However, unlike those who argue for a separate redactional layer assigned to an editor with a prophetic interest (e.g., DtrP of the Göttingen School), the priestly and prophetic elements could easily have been blended into one overarching presentation at a later date by someone like Jeremiah who embodied both ideals. As such, McCarter is correct in seeing the smooth integration of the prophetic voice in the DtrH.[40]

We can draw a few conclusions from our brief overview of these formulae. First, whoever used these formulae appears to have been responsible for at least the editing of Kings at a period close to the exile or shortly thereafter. Second, the individual(s) had access to a variety of sources, both from the north and south. In this vein, the priests who were displaced by the Assyrian invasion of 722 BCE no doubt brought the annals of the kings of Israel as well as priestly and

---

39. This phrase appears elsewhere in Genesis (39:11; 50:20), Daniel (9:7, 15), Ezra (9:7, 15), Chronicles (1 Chr. 28:7; 2 Chr. 6:15), and once in Nehemiah (9:10). In noting the conclusions of I. L. Seeligmann, "Aetiological Elements in Biblical Historiography," *Zion* 26 (1960–1961): 141–61, esp. 146, Moshe Weinfeld, *Deuteronomy and the Deuteronomistic School* (Oxford: Clarendon, 1972), 174–75, suggests that this phrase is most often connected to the "day of the author."

40. P. Kyle McCarter, *II Samuel: A New Translation with Introduction: Notes and Commentary*, AB 9 (Garden City, NY: Doubleday, 1984), 8.

prophetic accounts with them; a concept not at all foreign to the scholarly discussion. These priests would have settled in and around Jerusalem, Anathoth included (see more on this below). Third, it is very likely that the southern priests of Anathoth, so close to the royal city, kept a running history of their own. And, in keeping with Jewish tradition, Jeremiah—also from Anathoth—or Baruch could easily have supplemented this history from the royal archives and edited it into the form we have today. Their recorded history, stored outside of the city at Anathoth, thus explains why the DtrH survived the destruction of Jerusalem and other named sources did not.

Prophetic and Priestly Perspectives: 1 Kings 12–16

As noted in our discussions above, as with the priestly concerns, the prophetic perspective is inextricably intertwined throughout the DtrH, especially in Kings. Nowhere is this more pronounced than in 1 Kings 12–16, where the narrator consistently employs the prophecy-fulfillment motif (cf. 1 Kgs. 11:29-39//12:15; 12:22-24a//12:24b; 13:1-5//2 Kgs. 23:15; 14:12-13//ch. 18; 16:1-4//16:12; Josh. 6:26//1 Kgs. 16:34, etc.).[41] At the same time, the priestly perspective of 1 Kgs. 12:25-33 is not lost. It is obvious that the compiler wanted the reader to draw connections between Jeroboam's words in 1 Kgs. 12:28 and those of Aaron in Exod. 32:4. Other priestly concerns in 1 Kings 12 include: Jeroboam's recruitment of non-Levitical priests (12:31); alternate cultic centers (12:29); and new feast days (12:33)—all of which would have created a problem for an "orthodox" priestly *or* prophetic author. Now, to be sure, some may argue that no priestly author would disparage Aaron the high priest in this way by connecting him to Jeroboam. However, are we

---

41. A. Graeme Auld, *Kings without Privilege: David and Moses in the Story of the Bible's Kings* (Edinburgh: T&T Clark, 1994), 168, notes the central focus of prophecy in Kings and the book of Jeremiah, which in turn may point to authorship connections.

to think that priests could not be self-critical and evaluative? Not surprisingly, of all the priestly prophets, Jeremiah records the most oracles of judgment against priests (Jer. 1:18; 2:8, 26; 4:9; 5:31; 6:13; 8:1, 10; 13:13; 14:18; 18:18; 19:1-5; 20:1-6; 23:11, 33-36; 26:7-8, 16; 29:24-32; 32:32; 34:18-20; 52:24-27).

Also, when determining a date for the editing/compiling of this portion of Kings, one is faced with the problem of how to handle the prophecy of 1 Kgs. 13:2-5.[42] Verse 2 is the key: "And he [the unnamed prophet] proclaimed against the altar by the word of YHWH, 'O altar, O altar, thus says YHWH; A son will be born to the house of David, Josiah by name, and he will sacrifice upon you the priests of the high places, the ones who offer incense upon you, and the bones of men he will burn upon you.'" Here an unnamed prophet declares God's judgment on the syncretistic altar of Jeroboam by naming Josiah as the coming king who would desecrate it. Scholars are quick to proffer this text as the classic example of *vaticinium post eventum* ("prediction after the event"). Thus the redactional implications point to sometime during or after the reign of Josiah.[43] Now, apart from the clear presuppositional biases associated with such a conclusion, one is still left with the obvious discussion of whether or not YHWH would give a tenth-century prophet a specific name of a coming king some four centuries in the future. How one approaches this text is important for coming to a conclusion on how to understand the possible redaction history behind it. If someone refuses to believe that God uses the prophetic

---

42. For a unique handling of this text, see John Van Seters, "The Deuteronomistic History: Can It Avoid Death by Redaction?," in *The Future of the Deuteronomistic History*, ed. Thomas Römer (Leuven: Leuven University Press, 2000), 213–22.

43. See, for example, Jeffrey C. Geoghegan, *The Time, Place, and Purpose of the Deuteronomistic History: The Evidence of "Until This Day,"* BJS 347 (Providence, RI: Brown University Press, 2006), 121; Halpern and Vanderhooft, "Editions of Kings," 242; and Otto Eissfeldt, "Die Komposition von I Reg 16 29—II Reg 13 25," in *Das ferne und nahe Wort Festschrift Leonhard Rost*, BZAW 105 (Berlin: Topelmann, 1967), 49–58.

voice in such a manner, then Josiah's era for editing is a fitting conclusion. But then I would ask: What are we to do with Micah 5:2?[44] If, however, one holds to the possibility of a supernatural prophetic voice, then the majority opinion for the editing of this section of the DtrH falls by the wayside in favor of a date closer to the actual events.

Closely connected to this discussion is Dtr's writing style, which we discussed in chapter 2. The "prophetic speeches" recorded in Kings such as those found on the lips of Ahijah (1 Kgs. 11:31-39; 14:6-16) and the historical summary of 2 Kgs. 17:7-41 have been assigned to a late Dtr by some scholars.[45] The speech patterns in these prophetic utterances also have been linked to Jeremiah's style in particular (Jeremiah 7; 11).[46] This, according to Ronald E. Clements, is particularly apparent in parallels between 2 Kgs. 17:7-23 and Jeremiah 1–25.[47] He insists that the same hand that shaped Jeremiah 1–25 also shaped the exilic form of the DtrH c. 550 BCE.[48] He goes on to suggest that it was at this time that much of Jeremiah 26–52, which reflects differences in theological outlooks for the restoration of the nation, was added to the book of Jeremiah due to the "upheavals" that

---

44. The prophet Micah predicts, by name, Bethlehem as the birthplace of the Messiah. This was fulfilled almost eight centuries in the future.

45. Otto Plöger, "Speech and Prayer in the Deuteronomistic and the Chronicler's Histories," in Knoppers and McConville, eds., *Reconsidering Israel and Judah*, 34–35. For an overview of the redactional perspectives on ch. 17, see McKenzie, *Trouble with Kings*, 140–42.

46. Plöger, "Speech and Prayer," 34–35. Interestingly, in 2 Kings 17 the phrase "unto this day" actually appears three times (vv. 23, 34, 41; see ch. 4 above and our connections to Jeremiah's era).

47. Ronald E. Clements, "Jeremiah 1–25 and the Deuteronomistic History," in *Understanding Poets and Prophets: Essays in Honour of George Wishart Anderson*, ed. A. Graeme Auld, JSOT Sup 152 (Sheffield: Sheffield Academic Press, 1993), 94–96. Clements sees no fewer than four central themes to each block: "1. The Northern Kingdom of Israel had been disloyal to God, and this is proven by its idolatry. 2. Yahweh had warned of God's anger through the prophets, but the people rejected the prophetic warnings. 3. Israel was punished by being sent into exile, but Judah has also disobeyed God. 4. Disloyal kings, who followed the path of Jeroboam and disobeyed God's law, were primary causes of Israel's downfall" (95).

48. Ibid., 95–96.

took place at this time.[49] Of course, I would argue that this was done by either Jeremiah himself or Baruch!

These links to a prophetic voice should not be surprising in light of the desire of the authors of the DtrH to present a word, either spoken by YHWH or one of his servants, at the beginning of an account that is later fulfilled.[50] While prophecy and fulfillment may be found interwoven throughout the DtrH (e.g., Josh. 1:2-9; 3:13; 6:5; 8:1; 1 Sam. 1:17; 2:27-36, etc.), many times it is used as a structuring device to organize a given narrative (e.g. Joshua 3; 6; 8; 10; 11). [51] Thus, as Helga Weippert notes, YHWH becomes "the guarantor of an announcement of the future."[52] And, as noted immediately above, Jeremiah may have had a key role to play in this organizational technique; however, for pre-Solomonic narratives, Abiathar could just as easily have used this perspective, especially if he adopted it from someone like Samuel, Nathan, or Gad. It is likely that Abiathar, as a priest, would have understood the power of prophecy-fulfillment structures. On the other hand, not surprisingly, the tenor of the prophetic elements in the books of Kings, especially after the division of the kingdom in 930 BCE, takes on an ominous tone, often pointing to impending disaster.[53] Of course, this ominous tone also fits the period of Jeremiah and his message prior to the destruction of Jerusalem.[54]

49. Ibid., 110.
50. So, too, Hans Walter Wolff, "The Kerygma of the Deuteronomistic Historical Work," in Knoppers and McConville, eds., *Reconsidering Israel and Judah*, 64.
51. For a detailed list of these occurrences, see Helga Weippert, "'Histories' and 'History': Promise and Fulfillment in the Deuteronomistic Historical Work," in Knoppers and McConville, eds., *Reconsidering Israel and Judah*, 49–50. Wilson, "Unity and Diversity," 305–306, notes that the prophecy-fulfillment formula appears to be a structural device used up until the time of Jehu in the north and, in the south, to the time of Hezekiah. This, he posits, may be evidence of a Hezekian edition of the book of Kings.
52. Weippert, "'Histories' and 'History,'" 47–61, at 48.
53. Ibid., 58.
54. I am not trying to downplay the role of prophetic "doom," which does appear prior to 1 Kings (e.g., 1 Sam. 2:27-36; 3:11-14; 2 Samuel 12, etc.), rather, I am trying to point out the pervasive nature of the prophetic in this regard as it appears in the book of the Kings.

Nevertheless, one need not look immediately to Jeremiah as the source of all the prophetic content in the DtrH. As noted in our discussion of 1 Kings 11, the prophet Ahijah from Shiloh could easily have been the source for much of the narrative of 1 Kgs. 11:29–14:18. And, as already noted, his ties to Anathoth should not be overlooked.[55] Therefore, the *terminus ad quem* for the material in this block would be c. 908 BCE (930 minus the twenty-two-year reign of Jeroboam). The uniqueness of this material is bolstered by the fact that after 1 Kgs. 14:18 a new formula appears, which obtains for the rest of the DtrH. This formula, namely "Now the rest of the acts of [X] are they not written in the Chronicles of the kings of Israel/Judah," is first used in 14:19 and continues to be used until 2 Kgs. 24:5 (thirty-three times). Furthermore, the style of the narrative changes at 14:19 and becomes annalistic until the Elijah/Elisha narrative, after which time it resumes. It is possible that Jeremiah or the priests of Anathoth may have drawn from earlier written records in Anathoth and introduced the annalistic aspects of the text. This is not that farfetched in light of the subtle notes about the tribal region of Benjamin. For example, in 15:22 we find a note on the building of Mizpah and Geba; in 15:29, Ahijah the Shilonite is mentioned again; and the rebuilding of Jericho is noted in 16:34.

The Northern Perspective of 1 Kings 14–16

As touched on above, closely tied to the appearance of the Ahijah material is the northern perspective in Kings. Nowhere is this more pronounced than in 1 Kgs. 14:19–16:34. Even though the "northern" tribe of Benjamin, of which Anathoth was a part, allied itself with Judah against the remaining northern tribes after the split

---

55. The narrative of the unnamed prophet from Judah who goes to Bethel (1 Kings 13) may have been well known by Ahijah and those of Anathoth. Bethel was a key cult site from as early as the judges' period (cf. Judg. 20:18, 26; 21:2; 1 Sam. 7:16; 10:3).

of 930 BCE (1 Kgs. 12:21), the northerly perspective in the DtrH may be accounted for beyond this possible Benjaminite setting. Three key historical events would have forced devout northern priests southward: (1) Solomon's selling of the northern Levitical towns to Hiram (c. 950 BCE); (2) Jeroboam's initiation of syncretism and calf worship (c. 930–908 BCE); and (3) the catastrophe of the exile in 722 BCE.[56] The preponderance of northern perspective may easily be accounted for by these three events. If these priests and prophets moved to Anathoth and the surrounding cities, which one would certainly expect, then our theory obtains even in the period between the death of Abiathar and his sons and the later period of Jeremiah. Indeed, it is in this time period that the northern perspective predominates in the DtrH. This northerly perspective comes into full view in the Elijah-Elisha cycle.

The Elijah-Elisha Narrative: 1 Kings 17—2 Kings 13

There is no shortage of debate when dealing with the rhetorical purpose and the redaction history of the Elijah-Elisha narratives.[57] Questions arise, such as: Why did the author/compiler include this block? Why does it focus so heavily on the northern kings, especially those from Ahab's line? Or, why does it occupy the central portion of the book of Kings?[58] Furthermore, while scholars have often noted the apparent disconnect/unevenness between these chapters and the rest of the book of Kings, John Van Seters is no doubt correct in

---

56. See also comments by Mark Leuchter, *Samuel and the Shaping of Tradition* (New York: Oxford University Press, 2013), 16.

57. Marsha White, *The Elijah Legends and Jehu's Coup*, BJS 311 (Atlanta: Scholars, 1997), propounds that the accounts of Elijah are a fictitious literary construct written after the fact as propaganda for the coup of Jehu against the Omrides. However, one is left wondering why someone would go to such lengths to create an entire account with specific details just to propagate that the Omrides were evil and deserving of judgment?

58. If one includes the five chapters devoted to Jehu and his family, then the number of chapters totals nineteen.

noting that they are well integrated by Dtr.[59] Jeffery Geoghegan says it well when he asserts that ". . . 'unevenness' depends on one's perspective. . . . unevenness is in evidence throughout the DH as the result of Dtr's attempt to synchronize the lives of the northern and southern kings."[60] In light of these questions and concerns, I will attempt to show that many of these issues are more apparent than real, especially when the Elijah–Elisha cycle is placed within its rhetorical setting of Jeremiah's day in the town of Anathoth.

To begin, most would agree that the Elijah–Elisha tradition was recorded by northern prophets and carried south in 722 BCE.[61] It is also possible that the prophets of the border region such as the school of the prophets from Jericho (2 Kgs. 2:5, 15, 18; cf. also 1 Kgs. 20:35) or Bethel (2 Kgs. 2:3) may also have been responsible for this process. Not surprisingly, 2 Kgs. 2:18-22 pushes one in this direction especially with the comment about the water being purified in Jericho "unto this day" (see discussion in ch. 4 above). This block of material appears to have been woven into an already existing history by a later hand.[62] In this vein, it is possible that Jeremiah may have had a rhetorical purpose for including this block in his history. On more than one occasion we find narratives within the DtrH that bring to the forefront the conflict between prophet and king (e.g., Samuel and Saul; Nathan and David; the unnamed prophet and Jeroboam I).[63] However, none are as sustained and tense as we see

59. John Van Seters, *In Search of History: Historiography in the Ancient World and the Origins of Biblical History* (New Haven: Yale University Press, 1983; repr., Winona Lake, IN: Eisenbrauns, 1997), 305. Van Seters (306) does go on to suggest that the Elisha collection probably was not a part of the DtrH but was added later. For the opposite view, see McKenzie, *Trouble with Kings*, 97–98.

60. Geoghegan, *Time, Place, and Purpose*, 129.

61. Susanne Otto, "The Composition of the Elijah–Elisha Stories and the Deuteronomistic History," *JSOT* 27, no. 4 (2003): 502, suggests prophetic circles as the likely origin of the Elijah–Elisha cycle.

62. So, too, Geoghegan, *Time, Place, and Purpose*, 132.

63. Ibid., 139.

in the Elijah–Ahab/Ahaziah and the Elisha–Joram accounts. Jeremiah may have included the sustained Elijah-Elisha narrative as a central part of Kings in order to highlight his conflicts with Jehoiakim and Zedekiah.

At the macro level, the Northern Kingdom's idolatry and refusal to adhere to the words of the prophets had ushered in its destruction and exile (cf. 2 Kings 17). In his lifetime, Jeremiah was facing the same dilemma in Judah. Elijah's struggle with Ahab and Jezebel over the institution of Baal worship mirrored the rebellion and idolatry taking place in Jeremiah's era. The word of YHWH through Elijah and Elisha had come to pass regardless of Ahab's (and the kings who followed him) refusal to listen. Jeremiah's message echoed that of Elijah and Elisha.[64] Jeremiah's word would come to pass even though Jehoiakim and Zedekiah made every attempt to thwart it (e.g., Jer. 36:12-23). Other parallels between the Elijah-Elisha cycle[65] and Jeremiah include:

1. Idolatry/Baal worship permeated the culture: 1 Kgs. 16:31-32; 18:19-40; 21:26; 22:53; 2 Kgs. 3:2; 10:18-28; 11:18; 17:17; 21:3-5; cf. Jer. 2:8; 7:9; 11:13, 17; 12:16; 19:5; 23:13, 27; 32:29, 35.

2. The prophets' words came to pass: 1 Kgs. 17:14//17:16; 18:1//18:45; 20:13//20:21; 21:19//22:38; 1 Kgs. 21:21-22//2 Kgs. 9:25-26; 1 Kgs. 21:23//2 Kgs. 9:36-37; 2 Kgs. 1:4//1:17; 4:16//4:17; 4:43//4:44; 7:1-2//7:16-20; 8:1//8:3; 10:10, 17; 13:18//13:25; cf. Jer. 21:7//24:1; 28:15-16//28:17; 32:3-5//39:5-7; 21:10; 37:10; 38:18, 23//39:8.

3. Their lives were threatened: 1 Kgs. 18:10; 19:2, 10, 14; 2 Kgs. 6:31; cf. Jer. 11:21; 20:2; 26:8, 11; 37:15-20; 38:9.

---

64. We may include Micaiah here as well (1 Kings 22).
65. For a brief listing of the proposed redactional layers of the cycle, see Otto, "Composition," 489.

4. They struggled with rejection: 1 Kgs. 19:4; cf. Jer. 15:10-21 (cf. also Jer. 11:18—12:6; 17:12-18; 18:18-23; 20:7-18).

5. They had protégés: 1 Kgs. 19:16, 19, 21; 2 Kgs. 3:11; chs. 4–5; cf. Jeremiah 32; 36; 43; 45.

6. They ministered in cities under siege: 1 Kgs. 20:1;[66] 2 Kgs. 6:24; cf. Jer. 37:5; 39:1.

7. Cannibalism was a result of the siege: 2 Kgs. 6:28-29; cf. Jer. 19:9.

8. YHWH's control of his people is challenged: 1 Kgs. 18:21; 20:23, 28; 2 Kgs. 1:2-4, 16; cf. Jer. 7:18; 8:19; 14:22; ch. 44.

9. Kings took it upon themselves to disobey the law and word of the prophets: 1 Kgs. 20:35-42; cf. Jer. 34:8-22.

10. The curse of being devoured by beasts of the field and birds after death is frequent: 1 Kgs. 21:19, 23, 24; 22:38; 2 Kgs. 9:10, 36; cf. Jer. 7:33; 12:9; 15:3; 16:4; 19:7; 34:20.

11. False prophets opposed them: 1 Kgs. 18:19-22, 40; 22:6, 12-13, 22-23; 2 Kgs. 3:13; 10:19; cf. Jer. 5:13, 31; 14:14, 15; 23:13-31; 27:9-18; 29:8; 37:19.

12. Prophets were imprisoned for their message: 1 Kgs. 22:27; cf. Jer. 37:15-18.

13. Prophets tell of the destinies of kings and adversaries: 1 Kgs. 20:42; 21:21-23; 2 Kgs. 1:4, 9-12; 2:24; 5:27; 7:2; 8:13; cf. Jer. 20:6; 28:15-16; 29:21; 32:4-5; 42:21-22; 44:1-12, 27.

14. Foreigners honor the prophet and YHWH where Israel does not: 1 Kgs. 17:24; 2 Kgs. 5:15; 8:8-9; cf. Jer. 39:11-12.

15. The sons of the king die: 2 Kgs. 10:7; cf. Jer. 39:6.

16. A pit (בור bôr) is mentioned in the context of a usurper killing a group of people: 2 Kgs. 10:13-14; cf. Jer. 41:5-7.

---

66. In this case, the prophet is unnamed but may in fact be Elijah.

17. The Rechabites are presented as the ideal godly family: 2 Kgs. 10:15-16, 23; cf. Jeremiah 35.

Although this list is by no means exhaustive, it is striking how many parallels exist between the Elijah-Elisha cycle and the life/book of Jeremiah. Interestingly, the appearance of the Rechabites in the context of godly zeal appears only in these two places in the Bible! While one cannot be certain of the reason for the inclusion of the Elijah-Elisha cycle in the DtrH, connections such as these are tantalizingly close to the proverbial smoking gun needed to determine authorship, or at least the era of compilation.

Now, that is not to say that the entire Elijah-Elisha cycle was added en bloc; on the contrary, some portions appear to betray southern concerns as well. For example, the account of Joash's anointing by Jehoiada in 2 Kings 11 may have been added to the Elijah-Elisha narrative for the purpose of juxtaposing Jehu's purge of Baal worship in the north (2 Kings 10) with Jehoiada's purge of Baalism in the south. Both accounts tell of the slaughter of the offspring of Ahab and the priests of Baal, and the destruction of their temple. Further, 2 Kings 11 and 12 have a strong priestly overtone that focuses on Judah and the temple. Although one cannot be certain, these chapters may have derived from the priestly sources at Anathoth or Jerusalem. Also, any of the annalistic notations that do appear could have been added by Jeremiah at the time of the final compilation of the DtrH (e.g., 1 Kgs. 22:39-53; 2 Kgs. 8:16-29; 10:28-36; 12:1-3, 19-21; 13:1-13).[67] Finally, the dominant theme of the fulfillment of YHWH's word

---

67. Otto, "Composition," 487–508, proposes no less than a four-step process for the compilation of the cycle (i.e., 1 Kgs. 16:29–2 Kgs. 10:36) covering a 150-year period. Based upon the parallels with Jeremiah, the historical setting of each, and the unity of the cycle, there is no good reason to draw such a conclusion. Otto's propounded inconsistencies in the Elijah-Elisha cycle are not at all convincing (see 495–96). For example, are we to assume that Dtr would not want to show how, after a victory on Mt. Carmel, Elijah could face near-defeat? Or is it not possible that Baal worship prevailed even though Elijah killed 450 prophets of Baal? All one needs to do is look at the rapid retreat from Josiah's reforms after his death to see how quickly a nation can revert

through his prophets cannot be downplayed. Based upon parallel number 2 in our list above, clearly the author had a prophetic agenda and desired to present history through the prophecy-fulfillment grid.[68] The book of Jeremiah is no less forceful in this regard.

The Northern Kingdom's Slide into Exile: 2 Kings 14–17

Covering roughly seventy-four years (796–722 BCE), 2 Kings 14–17 connects the Elijah-Elisha narrative with the Hezekiah-Isaiah-Sennacherib account. The rapid rundown of the kings of this period and the Northern Kingdom's slide into exile is punctuated heavily with formulaic notations (e.g., 2 Kgs. 14:1-4; 15-29; 15:1-38; 16:1-2, 19-20; 17:1-2) and shows evidence of heavy reliance on the Chronicles of the kings of Judah and Israel, especially in chapter 15 (2 Kgs. 14:15, 18, 28; 15:6, 11, 15, 21, 26, 31, 36; 16:19). In this regard, the laconic nature of these chapters vis-à-vis the more detailed Elijah-Elisha cycle lends credence to the theory that the Elijah-Elisha narratives were woven into the history for rhetorical reasons. This is further supported by the presence of the so-called Dtr summary statement in 2 Kings 17, which offers a clear division between the cycle and the Hezekiah narratives that follow.

At the same time, one must not overlook the priestly and prophetic perspectives in the text. With the exception of 2 Kings 16, every chapter once again notes some type of prophetic fulfillment (i.e., 2 Kgs. 14:25 [Jonah is mentioned by name]; 15:12; 17:13). Chapter 16 betrays priestly concerns by focusing heavily on Ahaz's cultic malfeasance regarding his rearrangement of the temple altar and furniture (16:10-18 [Urijah the priest is mentioned]; see also 17:27-28, 32). Besides the typical prohibition of the high places (14:4;

---

to idolatry and paganism. Ancient history should not be measured by a twenty-first-century concept of what is "inconsistent."

68. So, too, ibid., 492.

15:4, 35; 16:4), twice we see notations about the law of Moses (2 Kgs. 14:6; 17:34-39 [intimated]) and the plundering of the temple treasury (2 Kgs. 14:14; 16:8).

Finally, while we have covered 2 Kings 17 in our discussions in chapter 4 above, suffice it to say that the Dtr summary speech here is slightly different than those found in Deuteronomy through Samuel. Here we find a historical summary by an unnamed author. Nevertheless, the perspective points to the work of a priest-prophet like Jeremiah: Israel's idolatry is pointed out (17:7-12, 16-17); they had rejected the prophetic word (17:13-14) and the law of God (17:15); and YHWH had vindicated the prophets' oracles (17:23). Finally, the author notes that a priest was brought from exile to live at Bethel to teach the new inhabitants of the Northern Kingdom about YHWH—to no avail (17:27-28). It is interesting that this tidbit of information is noted, along with the fact that the transplanted peoples of the Northern Kingdom continued, presently, as of the time of the author, to practice syncretism.[69] This seems to point to someone who may have lived in this area. Based upon our discussion in chapter 4, this chapter reflects a late seventh-century or an early sixth-century date of authorship, perhaps by Jeremiah who was from Anathoth—a city less than ten miles from Bethel. Therefore, one is not surprised to find in this chapter a sharp warning to Judah about the repercussions of continued cultic misbehavior (17:18-19)—the essence of Jeremiah's message (e.g., Jer. 8:19; 10:14, 22; 16:18).

Hezekiah and Sennacherib: 2 Kings 18–20

The much-disputed source-critical history of this block of the DtrH is beyond the scope of this present work.[70] The questions that need

---

69. For a similar conclusion, see Leuchter, *Samuel and the Shaping of Tradition*, 15.
70. For a detailed treatment of these chapters, see Paul Evans, *The Invasion of Sennacherib in the Book of Kings: A Source-Critical and Rhetorical Study of 2 Kings 18–19* (Leiden: Brill, 2009).

to be asked in light of our ongoing discussion are: (1) How does this block fit rhetorically in the DtrH? and (2) Who authored it? The "slowing down" of the narrative here in light of the rapid flow of chapters 14–16 must have served a particular function for the compiler. In stepping back from the narrative, the larger picture becomes evident. The message derived from the Hezekiah episode is one of trusting in YHWH and his word through his prophet. Hezekiah was a man who not only followed YHWH as David had but who also removed the high places. Yet, even in this era of reformation, Hezekiah had rebelled against his Assyrian overlord, Sennacherib, and had brought terrible devastation upon the land (2 Kgs. 18:7, 13-14). It was only when Sennacherib blasphemed YHWH that Isaiah delivered oracles of doom against the Assyrian king (2 Kgs. 19:5-7, 20-34). At this juncture, Hezekiah heeded the words of Isaiah and YHWH's blessings followed, at least for Jerusalem.

These motifs of international intrigue and obedience to prophetic oracles resonate with Jeremiah's day. Whereas the DtrH is silent on Isaiah's involvement in Hezekiah's original rebellion against Sennacherib, Jeremiah had pleaded with the kings of Judah not to rebel against Nebuchadnezzar but, rather, to go out to the Babylonians and save the city (Jer. 32:3-5; 38:2-3, 17-23).[71] Even though Hezekiah's political debacle was self-inflicted, YHWH honored him as a godly king who obeyed the word of his prophet, Isaiah. Conversely, even though Jehoiakim's and Zedekiah's political headaches were of their own making (2 Kgs. 24:1, 20), both had refused to hear the word of YHWH's prophet, Jeremiah. YHWH had sent Nebuchadnezzar as a means of punishing Judah for their many

---

71. Surprisingly, Ezekiel's message was not tempered with the hope of saving the city. For more on this, see Brian Peterson, *Ezekiel in Context: Ezekiel's Message Understood in its Historical Setting of Covenant Curses and Ancient Near Eastern Mythological Motifs*, PTMS 182 (Eugene, OR: Pickwick, 2012).

sins but the people refused to accept YHWH's correction; therefore, the city and people suffered destruction.

The content of these chapters also shows the author's clear intent to weave them into the greater history. Second Kings 17 records the exile of Israel, which reappears in chapter 18. Note in particular the list of cities of deportation in 17:6//18:11 and the breach of the covenant in 17:15//18:12. As is typical within Kings, annalistic notations appear at the beginning and end of the narrative (2 Kgs. 18:1-3; 20:20-21). Moreover, notations about Hezekiah's cult reforms (18:4) and observance of the Mosaic Law (18:6) help compare him to righteous kings who came before him. Some have also pointed out how Hezekiah's prayer (2 Kings 18) reflects the prayers of David and Solomon.[72] At the same time, the author also notes that Hezekiah is not perfect. He stripped the temple of its treasures to pay tribute to Assyria (18:15-16) and, in his pride, had flaunted his wealth to the Babylonians (20:13-19), thus drawing the ire of YHWH and Isaiah.

As for the question of who may have authored this block, Jeremiah could have easily borrowed historical material from Isaiah's work. The many verbatim parallels between Isaiah 36–39 and 2 Kings 18–20 is a given. Of course, the question has been which one came first.[73] It makes the most sense in this context to look to Jeremiah's use of the earlier prophet's work. For the most part, the DtrH follows a basic chronological pattern, but 2 Kings 18–20 follows closely to the inverted chronological ordering of Isaiah 36–39. The reworked chronological ordering of Isaiah 36–39 was apparently done for rhetorical reasons to introduce the Babylonian threat in Isaiah 40–55. In the case of the DtrH, this inverted order does not work to the same end. From Manasseh to Josiah, the Assyrians remain the dominant foe in 2 Kings 21–23. Also, Isaiah's ministry was to the kings of Judah

---

72. Knoppers, "'There Was None Like Him,'" 421–23.
73. Ibid., 423–24, argues that Isaiah's rebuke of Hezekiah in ch. 20 is from a later exilic editor.

(Isa. 1:1). As such, Isaiah no doubt lived in or near the city.[74] In light of Dtr's reliance on prophetic material from 2 Kings 11 onward, Jeremiah or Baruch could easily have accessed Isaiah's prophetic material if it was stored in Jerusalem.

Finally, as we saw in 2 Kgs. 14:25 with the appearance of Jonah, in 2 Kings 18–20 we have the only other reference to one of the writing prophets. While these appearances are unique in the DtrH, the lack of Dtr's mentioning of the other writing prophets should not be surprising. It is not because these books were not in existence (contra Noth[75]) but, rather, many of these prophets' works were already in existence and being used, no doubt even by Jeremiah. There was no need for Dtr to incorporate aspects of every prophetic book into the history of Israel when in fact these books had their own literary voice.[76]

Judah's Slide into Exile despite Josiah's Reforms: 2 Kings 21–25

Richard Nelson attributes 2 Kings 21–25 to a different author because of the "different character" of the work. This, indeed, may be the case if this was the first block of the DtrH contributed by Jeremiah in toto.[77] Although we cannot be certain, Jeremiah (c. 650 [?]–560 [?] BCE) may have been alive for the last few years of Manasseh's reign (687–642 BCE). As such, he would also have been an eyewitness to the reigns of the kings from Amon (642–640 BCE) to Zedekiah (597–586 BCE) noted in 2 Kings 21:18—25:26 (if Jeremiah did not

74. Tremper Longman III and Raymond Dillard, *An Introduction to the Old Testament*, 2d ed. (Grand Rapids: Zondervan, 2006), 311. Jewish tradition preserves the belief that Isaiah was a cousin of Uzziah (*Meg.* 10b).

75. Noth, *Deuteronomistic History*, 99.

76. So, too, Walter Dietrich, "Martin Noth and the Future of the Deuteronomistic History," in McKenzie and Graham, eds., *The History of Israel's Traditions*, 170 n.4.

77. Richard D. Nelson, "The Double Redaction of the Deuteronomistic History: The Case is Still Compelling," *JSOT* 29, no. 3 (2005): 320.

record the final notation of Jehoiachin's release in 2 Kgs. 25:27-30, Baruch certainly could have).

The fifty-seven years covered in 2 Kings 21 pushes forward this assertion. For example, in 2 Kgs. 21:10 the author again notes that YHWH had warned his people through the prophets. The unpacking of what the prophets had spoken follows in 21:12-15. Here the language of verses 12-15 has a number of parallels with the prophetic texts and other portions of the DtrH. Not surprisingly, it is with the book of Jeremiah where one finds the most parallels. These are as follows:

1. Ears tingling when people hear about YHWH's judgment: 21:12 = Jer. 19:3-9 (cf. also 1 Sam. 3:11).
2. Stretching a line and plummet over Jerusalem for judgment: 2 Kgs. 21:13 = Isa. 34:11; 28:17.
3. The remnant abandoned: 2 Kgs. 21:14 = Jer. 24:8.
4. Judah will be spoil and plunder: 2 Kgs. 21:14 = Ezek. 7:21.
5. They will be delivered into the hand of their enemies: 2 Kgs. 21:14 = Jer. 34:20, 21 (cf. also Josh. 21:44).
6. Judah provoked YHWH to anger: 2 Kgs. 21:15 = Jer. 7:18, 19, 30; 8:19; 11:17; 26:6, 7; 32:29, 30, 32; 44:3, 8 (cf. also Deut. 4:25; 9:18; 31:29; 32:16; 1 Kgs. 14:9, 15; 15:30; 16:2, 7, 13, 26, 33; 22:54; 2 Kgs. 17:11, 17; 21:6, 17; 23:19, 26).
7. Judah did evil in the sight of YHWH: 2 Kgs. 21:15, 20 = Jer. 7:30; 52:2 (cf. also Judg. 3:12; 2 Sam. 11:27; 1 Kgs. 11:6; 14:22; 2 Kgs. 8:18, 27; 15:9; 23:32, 37; 24:9, 19).

Beyond these connections in chapter 21, we also see almost verbatim content between 2 Kings 24–25 and the book of Jeremiah. These parallels include: 2 Kgs. 24:18—25:21 = Jer. 52:1-27; 2 Kgs. 25:27-30 = Jer. 52:31-34. Also, 2 Kgs. 25:22-26 summarizes the account of

Jeremiah 40–41.[78] These parallels no doubt helped solidify traditional Jewish understanding that Jeremiah wrote Kings. Now, to be sure, Jer. 51:64b causes one to suspect that Jeremiah 52 is a later addition, but this does not preclude the input of Baruch.

Also, the assessment of the faithfulness of the priests in 2 Kgs. 22:7 harks back to the days of Joash in 2 Kgs. 12:16—certainly Jeremiah as a priest would want to show that his generation (at least during Josiah's era) was no less faithful in matters of the temple. Sadly, Manasseh's sin was enough to bring about YHWH's judgment on Judah (23:26; 24:3-4), the hastening of which was brought on by the rebellion of both Jehoiakim and Zedekiah (24:1, 20). Not surprisingly, the author makes one final note that this judgment had been forewarned by the prophets (24:2).

Rhetorically, these final chapters of 2 Kings present a gloomy end to the long history of the kings of Judah. After the reign of Hezekiah, YHWH's promise to preserve Jerusalem and Judah for the "sake of David" no longer had currency (1 Kgs. 11:12-13, 34-36; 15:3-4; 2 Kgs. 8:19; 19:34; 20:6).[79] This may be telling of the ongoing authorship at this time. Having witnessed the destruction of the city of David, Jeremiah realized that, after the sin of Manasseh, YHWH had refused to save Jerusalem for David's sake any longer.

Finally, although many DtrH scholars hail the reign of Josiah, recorded in 2 Kings 22–23, as the moment when Dtr wrote his "first edition" of Israel's history, one nagging question still remains: Why would Dtr only record the equivalent of two chapters for the king who was supposed to be *the* defining king of Judah's history next

78. For example, Jer. 52:10b, 11c, 23, and 28-30 are not in 2 Kings 25; 2 Kgs. 25:8 has the "seventh" day as opposed to the "tenth" day in Jer. 52:12; the wording of 2 Kgs. 25:11 and Jer. 52:11 are slightly different, as are 2 Kgs. 25:15-17 and Jer. 52:19-21; 2 Kgs. 25:19 and Jer. 52:25.

79. Richard E. Friedman, *The Exile and Biblical Narrative: The Formation of the Deuteronomistic and Priestly Works*, HSM 22 (Chico, CA: Scholars, 1981), 3–5. See also the work of Nelson, *Double Redaction*, 99–118.

to David?[80] This is especially problematic in light of the extensive records of Joshua, the judges, Samuel, Saul, David, and Solomon—or, for that matter, Jeroboam I and Ahab. Perhaps the reason for the "final edition" of the DtrH was not so much to praise Josiah's reforms, and why they had failed, but simply to complete an ongoing history, which sadly ended in exile.

Furthermore, it is obvious that the compiler of Kings wanted his readers to realize that Manasseh's lengthy reign (even though it is literarily short in the DtrH) was responsible for enough sin in the land to override all the good done by his grandson Josiah (2 Kgs. 23:26). The final Dtr (i.e., Jeremiah or Baruch) makes it clear that judgment was coming for all the idolatry and sin practiced by Manasseh and his generation.[81] The finding of the law book, the religious reforms, and the putative policy of centralization were, in the end, futile efforts to stop the coming destruction on the land. The people's hearts were far from YHWH—a reality reflected in the rapid decline of the nation after the death of Josiah (2 Kgs. 23:31—25:26). Into this mêlée Jeremiah and his message fit well (cf. Jeremiah 44). The Josianic reforms, of which he was no doubt a part, were quickly set aside by those who succeeded Josiah. Jeremiah's prophetic pronouncements against Jehoiakim and Zedekiah in particular are ample evidence that Jeremiah's frustrations must have influenced the writing of these final chapters of Kings. Thus, it is possible to concur, to a degree, with Percy van Keulen when he avers that these closing chapters formed more of a warning than a message of hope[82]—a warning rooted in the message that the punishment for sustained idolatry and

---

80. Note Nelson, "Case Is Still Compelling," 320.
81. So, too, Halpern and Vanderhooft, "Editions of Kings," 244. Of course, neither scholar identifies Jeremiah or Baruch as the exilic Dtr.
82. Percy S. F. van Keulen, *Manasseh Through the Eyes of the Deuteronomists: The Manasseh Account (2 Kings 21:1–18) and the Final Chapters of the Deuteronomistic History* (Leiden: Brill, 1996). See also a similar assessment by McConville, "Narrative and Meaning," 44–46.

sinful practices like those of Manasseh would override any blessings associated with the short-term keeping of the law. Thus, van Keulen concludes, "Dtr could have ignored the information of the sources on Josiah, which did not fit in with the pessimistic account of Judah's end. Instead, he fully exploited his sources in order to warn his audience that the kind of sins Manasseh committed could never be blotted out."[83] Indeed, the authors of the DtrH had continually "exploited" their sources for rhetorical reasons even though they may not have always sounded a harmonious tune to the satisfaction of a twenty-first-century reader.

Conclusion

The southerly perspective of the final form of Kings is evident by the number of reasons posited for Judah's demise. Conversely, the Northern Kingdom went into exile for one main reason: they repeated the sins of Jeroboam the son of Nebat. For Judah, the reason for the exile varies depending on a given text. Thus, is the exile due to Hezekiah's pride in showing Babylon his wealth (2 Kgs. 20:16-19), or is it due to the sins of Manasseh (2 Kings 21)?[84] This disparity may reflect the combination of editors from the priests at Anathoth (Jeremiah included), who had different perspectives on what caused/would cause Judah to fall. At the same time, the unified theme against the Northern Kingdom may in fact reflect the animus of the priests of Anathoth and of northern priestly refugees toward Jeroboam on account of his abrogation of the Aaronic priesthood and his appropriating of non-Levitical priests for the service of the cult.[85]

---

83. Van Keulen, *Manasseh*, 203. Jon D. Levenson, "Who Inserted the Book of the Torah?," *HTR* 68 (1975): 231, proposes that this portion was added by Dtr2 in the exile.
84. Wilson, "Unity and Diversity," 306.
85. Campbell, *Of Prophets and Kings*, 204.

Of course, this would be of particular interest and importance for a priestly family from Benjamin, so close to Bethel.

Finally, in concluding this chapter, a few points need to be reiterated. First, the perspective of 1 Kings 1–11 points to that of Jonathan, Abiathar's son. Second, even though Jeremiah or Baruch may have lightly edited these earlier chapters, from 1 Kings 12 onward it is very likely that Jeremiah (and perhaps the priests of Anathoth) is responsible for bringing together blocks of prophetic and priestly traditions from Anathoth, the surrounding region, and Jerusalem. These prophetic interests, along with the priestly concerns, find harmony in a prophet and priest like Jeremiah. He compiled and edited these traditions in such a way as to show the downward spiral of Israel's and Judah's history and to draw parallels with his own day. Third, as an eyewitness to the final days of Jerusalem and Judah, Jeremiah's perspective fits the gloomy tone of 2 Kings 21–25. Whether Jeremiah survived to add the final comments of 2 Kgs. 25:27-30 is impossible to know for certain, but Baruch cannot be ruled out. From this perspective, Jewish tradition attributing the authorship of the book of Kings to Jeremiah may be more than fanciful "tradition." The prophet from Anathoth may in fact have had the last word when it came to the recording of the formal history of the nation that had rejected his message!

Conclusion

*Israel's was an historically oriented culture ... we may expect the records to
be as extensive as they are for any ancient culture. . . . That from the tenth
century to the seventh she should impose an historiographic moratorium on
herself is sufficiently improbable to command disbelief. In all likelihood, Israel
had a flourishing historiographic tradition. Scholars may or may not be able
to effect its recovery. But it is the duty of the historian to bear the possibility
into account—in his reconstructions, in his researches, and in his deliberations.
Treatments delinquent in this regard impoverish themselves, impoverishing the
society that is their subject.*[1]

Baruch Halpern's assessment is indeed the reality that we have sought
to reveal throughout our foregoing discussion. I have argued that the
authors of this long-running history are to be located in Anathoth,
beginning with the priest Abiathar, and continuing with his sons
and the priestly lineage, and ending with Jeremiah. Theories that
exclude, a priori, the possibility that large portions of the DtrH
may derive from antiquity serve only to hamstring open debate. As
we have shown, from the earliest periods of the monarchy authors
began recording Israel's history. This history, influenced by both
northern and southern priests and prophets, was recorded by those
living at Anathoth. Propagandistic, polemical, prophetic, and priestly

1. Baruch Halpern, "Sacred History and Ideology: Chronicles' Thematic Structure—Indications of
an Earlier Source," in *The Creation of Sacred Literature: Composition and Redaction of the Biblical
Text*, ed. Richard E. Friedman, NES 22 (Berkeley: University of California Press, 1981), 54.

agendas are intertwined in these accounts. Sometimes these agendas drive the narrative while at other times they are masterfully threaded throughout (e.g., Judges; 1 Samuel 13—2 Samuel 8; 2 Samuel 12–20; 1 Kings 17—2 Kings 13). As we have demonstrated, the best explanation for this diversity is to see the DtrH as a history preserved over a long period of time that was reworked some time shortly after the fall of Judah, with final notations added c. 560 BCE. To this end, Robert Wilson concludes, "The apparent contradictions in the text, then, may simply be an indication that history writing in Israel was not static but a continually developing, living art."[2]

Of course, we are still left with a canonical text that begs the question: What is the purpose of the DtrH? If the entire purpose of the DtrH is to explain the reason why the nation went into exile, then why, as Hans Walter Wolff comments, "does he [Dtr] keep his readers occupied with the ups and downs of events, concatenated through the centuries?"[3] To be certain, it is impossible to pigeonhole the entire DtrH into one neatly themed whole as was attempted in bygone eras.[4] Perhaps the author of the final form did, in some way, seek to present Israel's history as cyclical, much like the judges' period.[5] There is precedent for seeing the long recitation of Israel's history in this manner. According to Wolff, when Israel had rebelled in the past and then repented (i.e., "turned"; שוב *šûb*), YHWH was faithful to start afresh with YHWH's people.[6] To this end, Dietrich's

---

2. Robert R. Wilson, "Unity and Diversity in the Book of Kings," in 'A Wise and Discerning Mind': Essays in Honor of Burke O. Long, ed. Saul M. Olyan and Robert C. Culley, BJS 325 (Providence, RI: Brown University Press, 2000), 310.

3. Hans Walter Wolff, "The Kerygma of the Deuteronomistic Historical Work," in Reconsidering Israel and Judah: Recent Studies on the Deuteronomistic History, ed. Gary N. Knoppers and J. Gordon McConville (Winona Lake, IN: Eisenbrauns, 2000), 66.

4. Thus, the conclusion of Noth and others; see, for example, ibid., 62–78, esp. 64. Wolff lists the following verses as evidence of the overarching motif in the DtrH of the promise of God's judgment on the nation for idolatry: Deut. 4:25-28; Josh. 23:16; 1 Sam. 12:14-15, 25; 1 Kgs. 9:8-9; 2 Kgs. 17:23; 21:14-15.

5. So, too, J. Gordon McConville, "Narrative and Meaning in the Books of Kings," Bib 70, no. 1 (1989): 47.

theological assessment seems accurate, "The Deuteronomistic History presents YHWH as the one who was, is and remains turned toward Israel, whether in affection or in anger. For God's anger is nothing other than the form of God's turning toward Israel that is appropriate to Israel's turning away from God. Why should God not again be able to turn toward Israel in affection?"[7]

For an exilic audience reading this history, they would see that there is still hope if they repented.[8] Hope is also exemplified in the release of the Davidic king, Jehoiachin (2 Kgs. 25:27-30), but, more importantly, it is evinced in the prayer of Solomon and the words of Moses. Both had spoken of the very moment in which the exiles found themselves (cf. 1 Kgs. 8:46-53; Deut. 30:1-10).[9] Indeed, the prayer of Solomon marked the turning point in the DtrH when the nation's history began to take a marked shift toward exile (1 Kings 12; 2 Kings 17; 25).

Nevertheless, as Wolff criticized Martin Noth, in like manner Wolff's perspective may be challenged. In this vein, Gary Knoppers astutely critiques Wolff's theory by saying, "Why would a Deuteronomist, living during the Babylonian exile, write such an ambitious and laborious history, if his only message was a guarded

---

6. Wolff, "Kerygma," 69.

7. Walter Dietrich, "Martin Noth and the Future of the Deuteronomistic History," in *The History of Israel's Traditions: The Heritage of Martin Noth*, ed. Steven L. McKenzie and M. Patrick Graham, JSOTSup 182 (Sheffield: Sheffield Academic Press, 1994), 175.

8. McConville, "Narrative and Meaning," 47–48.

9. Wolff, "Kerygma," 70–71. Wolff (77) does not wish to impose upon Dtr the idea that "hope" was a part of his thinking. However, any time YHWH responds to the people's turning to YHWH, there is hope implicit in the action (note the period of the Judges). Indeed, the release of Jehoiachin would have evoked hope, to a degree, regardless of the projected timeframe for the end of the exile. See also comments by J. Gordon McConville, "1 Kings 8:46-53 and the Deuteronomic Hope," *VT* 42, no. 1 (1992): 67–79, esp. 67–71; and Gerhard von Rad, *Studies in Deuteronomy* (London: SCM, 1953), 74–91. On the other hand, Rainer Albertz, in his work "In Search of the Deuteronomists: A First Solution to a Historical Riddle," in *The Future of the Deuteronomistic History*, ed. Thomas Römer (Leuven: Leuven University Press, 2000), 7–8, suggests that Jer. 22:24-30 is evidence against the hope of Jehoiachin or his family coming back to Judah. This may be true in reality, but Jeremiah was not above changing his position if YHWH so deemed it (cf. Jeremiah 18).

expectation of divine compassion, predicated upon abject repentance?"[10]

Based upon these foregoing critiques, I have concluded that the DtrH is not monochromatic. There can be little doubt that portions of the DtrH had a prehistory and purpose far beyond what they now present as a unified whole.[11] And some of the rhetorical agendas noted in the preceding chapters reveal concepts and themes that push against an exilic context—agendas best assigned to Abiathar, his sons, and the priests of Anathoth.[12] Some portions were meant to be propaganda for David (Judges; 1 Samuel 13—2 Samuel 8) and the Davidic throne (2 Kgs. 18:5; 23:25).[13] At the same time, the authors of portions of the DtrH recoil from a certain type of kingship (1 Samuel 8 and 12; 1 Kings 12; 1 Kings 17—2 Kings 13; 21, etc.), while praising the ideal Davidic monarchy (2 Samuel 1–10; 2 Kings 18–20; 22–23).[14] Yet, as can be seen throughout, Dtr was not slavishly accountable to a king per se or his agendas. On the contrary, we see authors who were just as quick to point out the faults of a king, David included, as they were to praise him. Finally, some sections obviously were meant

10. Gary Knoppers, *Two Nations under God: The Reign of Solomon and the Rise of Jeroboam*, HSM 52 (Atlanta: Scholars, 1993), 25. Scholars are coming to recognize that Noth's assumption that Dtr had basically a singularity of purpose in his writing, which was predominantly negative, is no longer a tenable argument in light of the diversity of themes. See, for example, the work of Dietrich, "Martin Noth," 153–75, esp. 154–59.

11. On the unity of the DtrH, see Richard D. Nelson, "The Double Redaction of the Deuteronomistic History: The Case is Still Compelling," *JSOT* 29, no. 3 (2005): 320–23.

12. So, too, J. Gordon McConville, "The Old Testament Historical Books in Modern Scholarship," in *Them* 22, no. 3 (1997): 10–11.

13. Jeffrey C. Geoghegan, *The Time, Place, and Purpose of the Deuteronomistic History: The Evidence of "Until This Day,"* BJS 347 (Providence, RI: Brown University Press, 2006), 135, avers that "propaganda is an ill-suited term for the DH." He may be correct on the macro level but as we have demonstrated on the micro level, if an entire book can be classified as "micro," there is clear evidence of the presence of propaganda-type material.

14. See also the dominant use of the formula, "And [X/he] did evil in the sight of the Lord" in Kings (e.g., 1 Kgs. 11:6; 15:26, 34; 16:7, 19, etc.), which also appears to reflect this negative assessment. Of course, it is also possible for one to give a negative assessment without being "antimonarchic."

to sound a note of foreboding concerning the coming judgment of YHWH on the nation (2 Kgs. 23:29—25:26).

These concerns being noted, the authors still had one overarching goal as they recorded their history; yes, they may have had agendas at select periods of Israel's long history, but when all was said and done, they also wanted to record their history accurately from sources![15] Not just for their own purposes, but so that their children and grandchildren would know where they came from. They had been instructed to do just that (cf. Deut. 4:40; 12:25, 28; 17:18; 27:3, 8; 32:7; Josh. 4:6, 21, 22; 1 Sam. 8:9; 12:23; Hos. 4:6). Therefore, as the exile loomed ominously on the horizon and then became a reality, Jeremiah (and Baruch) set to work at drawing together the long history passed down to him from a variety of hands. As the fifteenth-century Jewish exegete Abravanel concluded,

> The prophet Jeremiah gathered together and combined these writings [DtrH] and set the books in order based upon their accounts. . . . It is [Jeremiah] who says "unto this day" and he was the one who wrote "previously in Israel," "for the prophet of today was previously called a seer," and the rest of the phrases that I have demonstrated indicate a later time—all of them are from the activity of the arranger and compiler.[16]

While Abravanel's conclusion focused on the use of select phrases in the DtrH such as "unto this day," his assertion that Jeremiah was responsible for the final ordering and compilation of the DtrH obtains in light of our working thesis. Jeremiah may not have written

---

15. So, too, the conclusion of Geoghegan, *Time, Place, and Purpose*, 136; and Steven L. McKenzie, *The Trouble with Kings: The Composition of the Book of Kings in the Deuteronomistic History*, VTSup 42 (Leiden: Brill, 1991), 150. Note the Book of Jashar (Josh. 10:13; 2 Sam. 1:18); the Book of the Acts of Solomon (1 Kgs. 11:41); and the Book of the Chronicles of the Kings of Israel (1 Kgs. 14:19; 15:31; 16:5, 14, 20; 16:27; 22:39; 2 Kgs. 1:18; 10:34; 13:8, 12; 14:15, 28; 15:11, 15, 21, 26, 31) and Judah (1 Kgs. 14:29; 15:7, 23; 22:45; 2 Kgs. 8:23; 12:19; 14:18; 15:6, 36; 16:19; 20:20; 21:17, 25; 23:28; 24:5).

16. Don Isaac Abravanel (1437–1508), as cited by Geoghegan, *Time, Place, and Purpose*, 164.

the entire DtrH, but he certainly could have completed and edited it as one of the final contributors from Anathoth.

Appendix: Character Parallels between Saul, Ishbosheth, and the Judges

Gideon	Saul
1. The account of Gideon starts with an introduction of his father, Joash (Judg. 6:11), and is followed by a story about Gideon and his father concerning the altar of Baal (Judg. 6:25-32).	1. The account of Saul starts with an introduction of his father, Kish (1 Sam. 9:1), and is followed by a story about Saul and his father concerning his father's lost donkeys (1 Sam. 9:3-21).
2. Gideon is directed by God in the altar of Baal event (Judg. 6:25).	2. Saul is directed by God through the prophet Samuel in the lost donkeys event (1 Sam. 9:20).
3. Gideon's name is changed to "Jerubbaal" (Judg. 6:32).	3. Saul has a new designation as being "among the prophets" (1 Sam. 10:12).
4. Gideon is chosen by God for the particular purpose of leading God's people from the hand of the Midianites (Judg. 6:11-14).	4. Saul is chosen by God for the purpose of leading God's people from the hand of the Philistines (1 Sam. 9:16).

5. Gideon protests his appointment by noting he is from the smallest family in Manasseh (Judg. 6:15).[1]	5. Saul protests his appointment by noting he is from the smallest family in Benjamin (1 Sam. 9:21).
6. Gideon receives three signs from God to prove that he is truly called (Judg. 6:17-24; 36-40).	6. Saul receives three signs from God to prove that he is truly called (1 Sam. 10:2-7).
7. The Spirit of the Lord comes upon Gideon for leading the people in the battle (Judg. 6:34).	7. The Spirit of the Lord comes upon Saul for leading the people in the battle (1 Sam. 10:10; 11:6).
8. Gideon's forces are reduced at the command of God (Judg. 7:4).	8. Saul's forces are reduced through fear at the sight of the enemy (1 Sam. 13:6).[2]
9. Gideon's battle plan includes dividing the people into three companies (Judg. 7:16).	9. Saul's battle plan includes dividing the people into three companies (1 Sam. 11:11).
10. Gideon ends up with 300 men with which he wins the battle without swords; rather, he uses pitchers, torches, and trumpets (Judg. 7:8-23).	10. Saul ends up with 600 men but the battle is postponed out of fear. Saul's men do not have swords or spears (1 Sam. 13:15-22).[3]
11. Gideon's leadership and ability to conquer the Midianites is questioned by the men of Succoth (Judg. 8:6), and after the victory he punishes them (Judg. 8:16).	11. Saul's leadership and ability to conquer the Ammonites is questioned by "evil men" (1 Sam. 10:27), but Saul refuses to punish them after the victory (1 Sam. 11:13).
12. After the victory, Gideon rejects kingship and tells the people to look to YHWH for leadership (Judg. 8:22, 23—a proper response).	12. After the victory, Saul accepts kingship despite Samuel's final reminder of the Lord's leadership in the past and God's anger against them for asking for a king (1 Samuel 12—an improper response).

13. Gideon's spiritual lapse in fashioning the ephod causes him, his household, and Israel to sin by worshiping the ephod (Judg. 8:27).	13. Saul's spiritual lapse in offering a burnt sacrifice causes him and Israel to suffer. Saul loses the kingship and Israel eventually loses to the Philistines (1 Samuel 13).
14. Gideon's spiritual lapse is directly related to the spoils of war (Judg. 8:24-27).	14. Saul's second spiritual lapse is directly related to the spoils of war (1 Samuel 15).
15. After Gideon's proper choice of allowing YHWH to be king, the story ends with peace for forty years (Judg. 8:28).	15. After the people's improper choice for a king, hardship follows. This account ends the way Gideon's had begun. The people are hiding in caves, pits, and cliffs (1 Sam. 13:6//Judg. 6:2).

1. For a discussion on the nuances between Saul's and Gideon's call, see Bruce Birch, "The Development of the Tradition on the Anointing of Saul in 1 Sam 9:1—10:16," *JBL* 90, no. 1 (1971): 61–64.
2. Sam Dragga, "In the Shadow of the Judges: The Failure of Saul," *JSOT* 38 (1987): 40.
3. Ibid., 41. Dragga posits that Saul was twice as blessed militarily as Gideon but only half as obedient.

Abimelech	Saul and Ishbosheth
1. Abimelech secures the throne with the aid of relatives—Shechemites (Judg. 9:1-3).	1. Ishbosheth secures the throne with the aid of relatives—Abner (2 Sam. 2:8-9).
2. Abimelech kills seventy innocent brothers, with one escaping—Jotham (Judg. 9:5). Abimelech has the help of "reckless fellows" (Judg. 9:4).	2. Saul kills eighty-five innocent priests, with one escaping—Abiathar. Saul has the help of Doeg the Edomite (1 Sam. 22:18-20).
3. Abimelech's kingship is denounced by Jotham (Judg. 9:7-20) and God fulfills the curse (Judg. 9:56-57).	3. Saul's kingship is denounced by Samuel (1 Sam. 13:14; 15:23; 28:17) and God fulfills the prophecy (1 Samuel 31; 2 Samuel 4).
4. God sends an evil spirit to drive a wedge between Abimelech and the Shechemites (Judg. 9:23).	4. God sends an evil spirit to trouble Saul (1 Sam. 16:14).
5. Abimelech reigns only a short period of three years (Judg. 9:22).	5. Ishbosheth reigns only a short period of two years (2 Sam. 2:10)
6. Abimelech wages war with his own people for their treachery (Judg. 9:34-57).	6. Ishbosheth wages war with his own people (2 Sam. 2:12-32), as did Saul (1 Sam. 22:18-19).[4]
7. An oracle is given concerning the negative outcome for Abimelech and the people of Shechem (Judg. 9:20).	7. An oracle is given concerning the negative outcome of Saul and his sons (1 Samuel 28).
8. After Abimelech is wounded in battle, he asks his armor bearer to kill him (Judg. 9:54).	8. After Saul is wounded in battle, he asks his armor bearer to kill him (1 Sam. 31:4).

4. Moshe Garsiel, *The First Book of Samuel: A Literary Study of Comparative Structures, Analogies and Parallels* (Israel: Revivim, 1985), 98, notes that Saul's destruction of Nob was for an act of "treachery" as was Abimelech's destruction of Shechem.

Jephthah	Saul and Ishbosheth
1. The elders of Gilead choose Jephthah for a selfish and immediate need for protection (Judg. 11:4-8).	1. The elders of Israel choose Saul for a selfish and immediate need for protection (1 Samuel 8).
2. Salvation of the Gileadites from the Ammonite attack inaugurates Jephthah's leadership (Judges 11).	2. Salvation of Jabesh-Gilead from the Ammonite attack inaugurates Saul's kingship (1 Samuel 11)
3. Unsavory men follow Jephthah (Judg. 11:3).	3. Unsavory men follow Saul (1 Sam. 22:18).
4. The people make Jephthah leader in a formal setting in the presence of YHWH at Mizpah before the battle is won (Judg. 11:11).	4. The people make Saul leader in a formal setting in the presence of YHWH at Mizpah before the battle is won (1 Sam. 10:17).
5. The Spirit of YHWH comes upon Jephthah for the battle at hand (Judg. 11:29).	5. The Spirit of YHWH comes upon Saul for the battle at hand (1 Sam. 11:6).
6. Jephthah makes a foolish vow that affects his only child—a daughter (Judg. 11:31).	6. Saul makes a foolish vow that affects his oldest child, Jonathan (1 Sam. 14:24).
7. Jephthah is remorseful for the vow (Judg. 11:35).	7. Saul is not remorseful for the vow (1 Sam. 14:44).
8. Jephthah's daughter is willing to allow the vow to be fulfilled (Judg. 11:37).	8. Jonathan is willing to allow the vow to be fulfilled (1 Sam. 14:43).
9. Jephthah fights his own people in a senseless battle (Judg. 12:1-6).	9. Ishbosheth fights his own people in a senseless battle for the throne (2 Samuel 2).

Samson	Saul
1. Samson begins the deliverance of Israel from the Philistines (Judg. 13:5), but his sin causes him to fall short (Judg. 16:21).	1. Saul begins the deliverance of Israel from the Philistines, but his sin causes him to fall short (1 Sam. 13; 15; 28; 31).
2. Samson's life is marked by a lack of self-control and a constant downward spiral spiritually (Judges 16)	2. Saul's life is marked by a lack of self-control and a constant downward spiral spiritually (1 Samuel 13; 15; 28)
3. The Philistines try to capture Samson in Gaza after the gates are closed, but God helps him escape (Judg. 16:1-3).	3. Saul tries to capture David in Keilah with "double gates," but God helps him escape (1 Sam. 23:7).
4. The Spirit departed from Samson (Judg. 16:20).	4. The Spirit departs from Saul (1 Sam. 18:12).
5. Samson's last interaction with a woman leads to his demise (Judg. 16:4-21).	5. Saul's last interaction with a woman foretells his demise (1 Samuel 28).
6. Samson kills himself in the presence of the Philistines (Judg. 16:30).	6. Saul kills himself in the presence of the Philistines (1 Sam. 31:4).
7. Samson's weapon (i.e., his body) becomes a trophy before the god Dagon (Judg. 16:23).	7. Saul's weapons and body become a trophy before the god Asherah (1 Sam. 31:10).
8. Samson's body is taken from the enemy and is buried by his family (Judg. 16:31).	8. Saul's body is taken from the enemy and buried is by family (1 Sam. 31:11-13).[5]

5. A. E. Cundall and L. Morris, *Judges and Ruth: An Introduction and Commentary* (London: Tyndale, 1968), 181; and Tammi J. Schneider, *Judges*, Berit Olam: Studies in Hebrew Narrative & Poetry (Collegeville, MN: Liturgical, 2000), xv, have also drawn this familial comparison between the story of Samson and the story of Saul. The fact that Saul was no doubt a descendant of marriages between the warriors of Benjamin and the virgins of Jabesh-gilead (Judges 21) may have been the reason for his quick action on their behalf and their act of kindness at his death.

Bibliography

Ackroyd, Peter R. *The First Book of Samuel*. Cambridge: Cambridge University Press, 1971.

Aharoni, Yohanan. *The Land of the Bible: A Historical Geography*. Trans. A. F. Rainey. Philadelphia: Westminster John Knox, 1967.

Albertz, Rainer. "In Search of the Deuteronomists: A First Solution to a Historical Riddle." In *The Future of the Deuteronomistic History*,1–17. Ed. Thomas Römer. Leuven: Leuven University Press, 2000.

Alexander, T. Desmond. *From Paradise to the Promised Land: An Introduction to the Pentateuch*. 3d ed. Grand Rapids: Baker Academic, 2012.

Amit, Yairah. *Hidden Polemics in Biblical Narrative*. Biblical Interpretation Series 25. Leiden: Brill, 2000.

Andersen, Francis I., and David Noel Freedman. *Hosea*. Anchor Bible 24. Garden City, NY: Doubleday, 1980.

Anderson, A. A. *2 Samuel*. Word Biblical Commentary 11. Dallas: Word, 1989.

Anderson, Greger. *Untamable Texts: Literary Studies and Narrative Theory in the Books of Samuel*. New York: T&T Clark, 2009.

Arnold, Patrick M. "Mizpah." In *The Anchor Bible Dictionary*, 4:879–81. Ed. David Noel Freedman. 6 vols. New York: Doubleday, 1992.

Auld, A. Graeme. *Kings without Privilege: David and Moses in the Story of the Bible's Kings*. Edinburgh: T&T Clark, 1994.

Avigad, Nahman. *Bullae and Seals from a Post-Exilic Judean Archive.* Qedem Monographs of the Institute of Archaeology 4. Jerusalem: Hebrew University Press, 1976.

_____. *Hebrew Bullae from the Time of Jeremiah: Remnants of a Burnt Archive.* Jerusalem: Israel Exploration Society, 1986.

Baldwin, Joyce. *1 and 2 Samuel.* Tyndale Old Testament Commentary. Downers Grove, IL: InterVarsity, 1988.

Baltzer, Klaus. *Das Bundesformular.* Neukirchen: Neukirchener, 1960. In English: *The Covenant Formulary.* Trans. David E. Green. Philadelphia: Fortress Press, 1971.

Barber, Cyril J. *A Narrative of God's Power: Judges.* Neptune, NJ: Loizeaux Brothers, 1990.

Barrett, Rob. "The Book of Deuteronomy." In *A Theological Introduction to the Pentateuch: Interpreting the Torah as Christian Scripture*, 145–76. Ed. Richard S. Briggs and Joel N. Lohr. Grand Rapids: Baker Academic, 2012.

Barthélem, Dominique, David Wooding, Johan Lust, and Emanuel Tov. *The Story of David and Goliath: Textual and Literary Criticism: Papers of a Joint Research Venture.* Orbis biblicus et orientalis 73. Göttingen: Vandenhoeck & Ruprecht, 1986.

Bartlett, J. R. "Edom." In of *The Anchor Bible Dictionary*, 2:287–95. Ed. David Noel Freedman. 6 vols. New York: Doubleday, 1992.

Bauer, G. L. *The Theology of the Old Testament: Or, a Biblical Sketch of the Religious Opinions of the Ancient Hebrews.* Extracted and translated by P. Harwood from *Theologie des Alten Testaments.* London: Charles Fox, 1838.

Beal, Richard H. "Hittite Military Organization." In *Civilizations of the Ancient Near East*, 1:545–54. Ed. Jack M. Sasson. 4 vols. New York: Scribner, 1995.

Becker, Uwe. *Richterzeit und Königtum: Redaktionsgeschichtliche Studien zum Richterbuch.* Beihefte zur Zeitschrift für die alttestamentliche Wissenschaft 192. Berlin: de Gruyter, 1990.

Benzinger, Immanuel. *Jahvist und Elohist in den Königsbüchern.* Beiträge zur Wissenschaft vom Alten und Neuen Testament 27. Berlin: Kohlhammer, 1921.

Birch, Bruce. "The Development of the Tradition on the Anointing of Saul in 1 Sam 9:1—10:16." *Journal of Biblical Literature* 90, no. 1 (1971): 55–68.

_____. *The Rise of the Israelite Monarchy: The Growth and Development of I Samuel 7–15.* Society of Biblical Literature Dissertation Series 27. Missoula: Scholars, 1976.

Blenkinsopp, Joseph. "Another Contribution to the Succession Narrative Debate (2 Samuel 11–20; 1 Kings 1–2)." *Journal for the Study of the Old Testament* 38, no. 1 (2013): 35–58.

Block, Daniel. *Judges, Ruth.* New American Commentary 6. Nashville: Broadman and Holman, 1999.

Boling, Robert G. *Judges: Introduction, Translation, and Commentary.* Anchor Bible 6A. New York: Doubleday, 1975.

_____. "Judges, Book of." In *The Anchor Bible Dictionary*, 3:1107–17. Ed. David Noel Freedman. 6 vols. New York: Doubleday, 1992.

Borgman, Paul. *David, Saul, & God: Discovering and Ancient Story.* New York: Oxford University Press, 2008.

Brensinger, Terry L. *Judges.* Scottdale, PA: Herald, 1999.

Brettler, Marc Zvi. "The Book of Judges: Literature as Politics." *Journal of Biblical Literature* 108, no. 3 (1989): 395–418.

_____. *The Book of Judges.* New York: Routledge, 2002.

Brichto, Herbert C. "Kin, Cult, Land, Afterlife: A Biblical Complex." *Hebrew Union College Annual* 44 (1973): 1–54.

Bright, John. *A History of Israel.* 4th ed. Philadelphia: Westminster, 2000.

Brueggemann, Walter. *David's Truth in Israel's Imagination & Memory*. Philadelphia: Fortress Press, 1985.

_____. *First and Second Samuel*. Interpretation. Louisville: John Knox, 1990.

Buber, Martin. *Kingship of God*. New York: Harper & Row, 1967.

Budde, D. Karl. *Das Buch der Richter*. Kurzer Hand-Commentar zum Alten Testament 7. Leipzig: J. C. B. Mohr, 1897.

_____. *Die Bücher Richter und Samuel, ihre Quellen und ihr Aufbau*. Giessen: Ricker, 1890.

_____. *Die Bücher Samuel erklärt*. Kurzer Hand-Commentar zum Alten Testament 8. Tübingen and Leipzig: J. C. B. Mohr, 1902.

Burney, C. F. *The Book of Judges with Introduction and Notes*. 2d ed. London: Rivingtons, 1920.

Bush, George. *Notes on Judges*. New York: Newman & Ivison, 1852. Repr.: Minneapolis: James & Klock, 1976.

Byrne, Ryan. "The Refuge of Scribalism in Iron I Palestine." *Bulletin of American Schools of Oriental Research* 345 (2007): 1–31.

Campbell, Antony F. *Of Prophets and Kings: A Late Ninth-Century Document (1 Samuel 1–2 Kings 10)*. Catholic Biblical Quarterly Monograph Series 17. Washington, DC: Catholic Biblical Association of America, 1986.

_____. "Martin Noth and the Deuteronomistic History." In *The History of Israel's Traditions: The Heritage of Martin Noth*, 31–62. Ed. Steven L. McKenzie and M. Patrick Graham. Journal for the Study of the Old Testament: Supplement Series 182. Sheffield: Sheffield Academic Press, 1994.

_____. *The Ark Narrative (1 Sam 4–6; 2 Sam 6): A Form-critical and Traditio-Historical Study*. Society of Biblical Literature Dissertation Series 16. Missoula: Scholars, 1975.

_____, and Mark A. O'Brien. *Unfolding the Deuteronomistic History: Origins, Upgrades, Present Text*. Minneapolis: Fortress Press, 2000.

Carr, David M. *Writing on the Tablet of the Heart: Origins of Scripture and Literature*. New York: Oxford University Press, 2005.

Carroll, Robert P. *Jeremiah: A Commentary*. Old Testament Library. Philadelphia: Westminster, 1986.

Cartledge, Tony W. *1 & 2 Samuel*. Macon, GA: Smyth & Helwys, 2001.

Chavel, Simeon. "Compositry and Creativity in 2 Samuel 21:1-14." *Journal of Biblical Literature* 122, no. 1 (2003): 23–52.

Childs, Brevard S. "A Study of the Formula, 'Until this Day.'" *Journal of Biblical Literature* 82, no. 3 (1963): 279–92.

————. *Introduction to the Old Testament*. Philadelphia: Fortress Press, 1979.

Christensen, Duane L. "A New Israel: The Righteous from among All Nations." In *Israel's Apostasy and Restoration: Essays in Honor of Roland K. Harrison*, 251–59. Ed. R. K. Harrison and Avraham Gileadi. Grand Rapids: Baker, 1987.

Clements, Ronald E. *Prophecy and Covenant*. Studies in Biblical Theology 43. London: SCM Press, 1965.

————. "Jeremiah 1–25 and the Deuteronomistic History." In *Understanding Poets and Prophets: Essays in Honour of George Wishart Anderson*, 93–113. Ed. A. Graeme Auld. Journal for the Study of the Old Testament: Supplement Series 152. Sheffield: Sheffield Academic Press, 1993.

Coggins, Richard. "Prophecy—True and False." In *Of Prophets' Visions and the Wisdom of Sages: Festschrift for R. N. Whybray*, 80–94. Ed. Heather A. McKay and David J. A. Clines. Journal for the Study of the Old Testament: Supplement Series 16. Sheffield: JSOT, 1993.

————. "What Does 'Deuteronomistic' Mean?" In *Those Elusive Deuteronomists: The Phenomenon of Pan-Deuteronomism*, 22–35. Ed. Linda S. Schearing and Steven L. McKenzie. Journal for the Study of the Old

Testament: Supplement Series 268. Sheffield: Sheffield Academic Press, 1999.

Collins, John J. *Daniel*. Hermeneia. Ed. Frank Moore Cross. Minneapolis: Fortress Press, 1993.

Cornill, Carl Heinrich. *Einleitung in das Alte Testament*. GTW 2/1. Freiburg: Mohr Siebeck, 1891.

Craigie, Peter. *Deuteronomy*. New International Commentary on the Old Testament. Grand Rapids: Eerdmans, 1976.

————. *The Old Testament: Its Background, Growth, and Content*. Nashville: Abingdon, 1986.

Cross, Frank Moore. *Canaanite Myth and Hebrew Epic: Essays in the History of the Religion of Israel*. Cambridge: Harvard University Press, 1973.

————. "Divine Warrior in Israel's Early Cult." In *Biblical Motifs: Origins and Transformations*, 11–30. Ed. Alexander Altmann. Cambridge: Harvard University Press, 1966.

————. "The Structure of the Deuteronomistic History." In *Perspectives in Jewish Learning*, 9–24. Ed. Judah M. Rosenthal. Annual of the College of Jewish Studies 3. Chicago: College of Jewish Studies, 1968.

Crüsemann, Frank. *Der Widerstand gegen das Konigtum: Die antikoniglichen Texte des alten Testamentes und der Kampf um den fruhen israelitischen* Staat. Wissenschaftliche Monographien zum Alten und Neuen Testament 49. Neukirchen-Vluyn: Neukirchener, 1978.

————. "Le Pentateuque, une Torah: Prolégomènes à l'interprétation de sa forme finale." In *La Pentateuque en question*, 339–60. Ed. Albert de Pury. Le Monde de la Bible. Geneva: Labor et Fides, 1991.

Cryer, Frederick H. "On the Recently-discovered 'House of David' Inscription. *Scandinavian Journal of the Old Testament* 8, no. 1 (1994): 3–19.

Cundall, Arthur E. "Judges—An Apology for the Monarchy?" *Expository Times* 81, no. 6 (1970): 178–81.

_____, and Leon Morris. *Judges and Ruth: An Introduction and Commentary*. London: Tyndale, 1968.

Davies, Philip R. "'House of David' Built on Sand: The Sins of the Biblical Maximizers." *Biblical Archaeology Review* 20, no. 4 (July/August 1994): 54–55.

_____. *In Search of "Ancient Israel."* Journal for the Study of the Old Testament: Supplement Series 148. Sheffield: JSOT, 1992.

Davis, D. R. "A Proposed Life-Setting for the Book of Judges." PhD diss., Southern Baptist Theological Seminary, 1978.

Davis, Ellen F. *Swallowing the Scroll*. Bible and Literature Series 21. Sheffield: Sheffield Academic Press, 1989.

Delekat, Lienhard. "Tendenz und Theologie der David-Salomo-Erzählung." In *Das ferne und nahe Wort Festschrift Leonhard Rost*, 26–36. Beihefte zur Zeitschrift für die alttestamentliche Wissenschaft 105. Berlin: Topelmann, 1967.

Demsky, Aaron. "Education." In *Encyclopaedia Judaica*, 6:381–98. Ed. Cecil Roth. 16 vols. Jerusalem: Encyclopedia Judaica, 1972.

_____. *Literacy in Ancient Israel* [Heb]. The Biblical Encyclopaedia Library. Jerusalem: Bialik Institute, 2012.

_____. "Literacy in Israel and Among Neighboring People in the Biblical Period." PhD diss., Hebrew University in Jerusalem, 1976.

De Wette, Wilhelm M. L. *Beiträger zur Einleitung in das Alte* Testament. 2 vols. Halle: Schimmelpfennig, 1806–1807.

Dietrich, Walter. *David, Saul und die Propheten: Das Verhältnis von Religion und Politik nach den prophetischen Überlieferungen vom frühesten Königtum in Israel*. Beiträge zur Wissenschaft vom Alten und Neuen Testament 122. Stuttgart: Kohlhammer, 1987.

_____. "Martin Noth and the Future of the Deuteronomistic History." In *The History of Israel's Traditions: The Heritage of Martin Noth*, 153–75. Ed. Steven L. McKenzie and M. Patrick Graham. Journal for the Study of the Old Testament: Supplement Series 182. Sheffield: Sheffield Academic Press, 1994.

_____. *Prophetie und Geschichte: Eine redaktionsgeschichtliche Unterschung zum deuteronomistischen Geschichtswerk.* Forschungen zur Religion und Literatur des Alten und Neuen Testaments 108. Göttingen: Vandenhoeck and Ruprecht, 1972.

_____, and Thomas Naumann. "The David–Saul Narrative." In *Reconsidering Israel and Judah: Recent Studies on the Deuteronomistic History,* 276–318. Ed. Gary N. Knoppers and J. Gordon McConville. Winona Lake, IN: Eisenbrauns, 2000.

Dillard, Raymond, and Tremper Longman III. *An Introduction to the Old Testament.* Grand Rapids: Zondervan, 1994.

Dragga, Samuel. "In the Shadow of the Judges: The Failure of Saul." *Journal for the Study of the Old Testament* 38 (1987): 39–46.

Driver, S. R. *A Critical and Exegetical Commentary on Deuteronomy.* Edinburgh: Clark, 1895.

_____. *An Introduction to the Literature of the OT.* Edinburgh: Clark, 1891.

_____. *Notes on the Hebrew Text and the Topography of the Books of Samuel.* 2d ed. Oxford: Clarendon, 1960.

Duhm, Bernhard. *Das Buch Jeremia.* Kurzer Hand-Commentar zum Alten Testament 11. Tübingen: J. C. B. Mohr, 1901.

Duhm, Hans. "Zur Geschichte der Alttestamentlichen Geschichtsschreibung." In *Festschrift für Theodor Plüss,* 118–63. Basel: Helbing & Lichtenhahn, 1905.

Dumbrell, William J. "'In Those Days There Was No King in Israel; Every Man Did What Was Right in His Own Eyes': The Purpose of the Book of Judges Reconsidered." *Journal for the Study of the Old Testament* 25 (1983): 23–33.

Dutcher-Walls, Patricia. "The Social Location of the Deuteronomists: A Sociological Study of Factional Politics in Late Pre-Exilic Judah." *Journal for the Study of the Old Testament* 52 (1991): 77–94.

Eissfeldt, Otto. *The Old Testament: An Introduction.* Trans. Peter R. Ackroyd. New York: Harper & Row, 1965.

————. "Die Komposition von I Reg 16 29—II Reg 13 25." In *Das ferne und nahe Wort Festschrift Leonhard Rost,* 49–58. Beihefte zur Zeitschrift für die alttestamentliche Wissenschaft 105. Berlin: Topelmann, 1967.

Eslinger, Lyle M. *Kingship of God in Crisis: A Close Reading of Samuel 1–12.* Bible and Literature Series 10. Decatur: Almond, 1985.

————. "Viewpoints and Points of View in Samuel 8–12." *Journal for the Study of the Old Testament* 26 (1983): 61–76.

Evans, Paul. *The Invasion of Sennacherib in the Book of Kings: A Source-Critical and Rhetorical Study of 2 Kings 18–19.* Leiden: Brill, 2009.

Ficker, R. "Komposition und Erzählung: Untersuchungen zur Ludeerzählung (1 S 4–6; 2 S 6) und zur Geschichte vom Aufstieg Davids (1 S 15–2 S 5)." ThD diss., University of Heidelberg, 1977.

Flanagan, James W. "Court History or Succession Document? A Study of 2 Samuel 9–20 and 1 Kings 1–2." *Journal of Biblical Literature* 91, no. 2 (1972): 172–81.

Fohrer, Georg. *Introduction to the Old Testament.* Trans. David Green. London: SPCK, 1970.

Fokkelman, J. P. *Narrative Art and Poetry in the Books of Samuel. A Full Interpretation Based on Stylistic and Structural Analysis I: King David (II Sam. 9–20 & I Kings 1–2).* Assen: Van Gorcum, 1981.

————. *Narrative Art and Poetry in the Books of Samuel. A Full Interpretation Based on Stylistic and Structural Analysis II: The Crossing Fates (1 Sam. 13–31 & 2 Sam. 1).* Assen: Van Gorcum, 1986.

_____. *Narrative Art and Poetry in the Books of Samuel. A Full Interpretation Based on Stylistic and Structural Analysis III: Throne and City (II Sam. 2–8 & 21–24).* Assen: Van Gorcum, 1990.

Friedman, Richard E. *The Exile and Biblical Narrative: The Formation of the Deuteronomistic and Priestly Works.* Harvard Semitic Monographs 22. Chico, CA: Scholars, 1981.

_____. *Who Wrote the Bible?* New York: Summit 1987.

Garrett, Duane. *Rethinking Genesis.* Great Britain: Christian Focus Publications, 2000.

Garsiel, Moshe. *The First Book of Samuel: A Literary Study of Comparative Structures, Analogies and Parallels.* Jerusalem: Revivim, 1985.

Geoghegan, Jeffrey C. "Additional Evidence for a Deuteronomistic Redaction of the Tetrateuch." *Catholic Biblical Quarterly* 67, no. 3 (2005): 405–21.

_____. *The Time, Place, and Purpose of the Deuteronomistic History: The Evidence of "Until This Day."* Brown Judaic Studies 347. Providence, RI: Brown University Press, 2006.

_____. "'Unto this Day' and the Preexilic Redaction of the Deuteronomistic History." *Journal of Biblical Literature* 122, no. 2 (2003): 201–27.

Gerbrandt, Gerald E. *Kingship According to the Deuteronomistic History.* Society of Biblical Literature Dissertation Series 87. Atlanta: Scholars, 1986.

Globe, Alexander. "Enemies Round About: Disintegrative Structure in the Book of Judges." In *Mappings of the Biblical Terrain*, 233–51. Ed. Vincent L. Tollers and John R. Maier. Lewisburg, PA: Bucknell University Press, 1990.

Gnuse, Robert Karl. *The Dream Theophany of Samuel: Its Structure in Relation to Ancient Near Eastern Dreams and Its Theological Significance.* Lanham, MD: University Press of America, 1984.

Gooding, D. W. "The Composition of the Book of Judges." In *Eretz-Israel, Archaeological Historical and Geographic Studies, Vol. 16: Harry M. Orlinsky Volume*, 70–79. Ed. B. A. Levine and A. Malamat. Jerusalem: Israel Exploration Society, 1982.

Gordon, Robert P. "David's Rise and Saul's Demise: Narrative Analogy in 1 Samuel 24–26." *Tyndale Bulletin* 31 (1980): 37–64.

Graf, Karl Heinrich. *Die geschichtlichen Bücher des Alten Testaments: Zwei historisch-kritische Untersuchungen*. Leipzig: Weigel, 1866.

Gray, John, ed. *Joshua, Judges and Ruth*. London: Thomas Nelson, 1967.

―――――. *Joshua, Judges, Ruth*. 2d ed. Basingstoke, UK/Grand Rapids: Morgan & Scott/Eerdmans, 1986.

Greenberg, Moshe. *Ezekiel 1–20*. Anchor Bible 22. Garden City, NY: Doubleday, 1983.

―――――. *Ezekiel 21–37*. Anchor Bible 22a. Garden City, NY: Doubleday, 1997.

Gressmann, Hugo. *Die Anfänge Israels (von 2. Mosis bis Richter und Ruth) übers., erklärt und mit Einleitungen versehen*. Göttingen: Vandenhoeck & Ruprecht, 1914.

Gunn, David M. "Narrative Patterns and Oral Tradition in Judges and Samuel." *Vetus Testamentum* 24, no. 3 (1974): 286–317.

―――――. *The Story of King David*. Journal for the Study of the Old Testament: Supplement Series 6. Sheffield: JSOT, 1982.

Halpern, Baruch. *David's Secret Demons: Messiah, Murderer, Traitor, King*. Grand Rapids: Eerdmans, 2001.

―――――. "Erasing History: The Minimalist Assault on Ancient Israel." *Bible Review* 11, no. 6 (1995): 26–35, 47.

―――――. "Sacred History and Ideology: Chronicles' Thematic Structure—Indications of an Earlier Source." In *The Creation of Sacred Literature: Composition and Redaction of the Biblical Text*, 35–54. Ed.

Richard E. Friedman. Near Eastern Studies 22. Berkeley: University of California Press, 1981.

_____. "Sectionalism and the Schism." *Journal of Biblical Literature* 93, no. 4 (1974): 519–32.

_____. "Shiloh." In *The Anchor Bible Dictionary*, 5:1213–15. Ed. David Noel Freedman. 6 vols. New York: Doubleday, 1992.

_____. *The Constitution of the Monarchy in Israel.* Harvard Semitic Monographs 25. Chico, CA: Scholars, 1981.

_____. "The Rise of Abimelek Ben-Jerubbaal." *Hebrew Annual Review* 2 (1978): 79–100.

_____, and David S. Vanderhooft. "The Editions of Kings in the 7th-6th Centuries B.C.E" *Hebrew Union College Annual* 62 (1991): 179–244.

Hamilton, Victor. *Handbook on the Historical Books.* Grand Rapids: Baker Academic, 2008.

_____. *Handbook on the Pentateuch.* 2d ed. Grand Rapids: Baker Academic, 2005.

Harrison, R. K. *Introduction to the Old Testament.* Grand Rapids: Eerdmans, 1969.

Harvey, Paul B., Jr., and Baruch Halpern. "W. M. L. de Wette's '*Dissertatio Critica . . .*': Context and Translation." *Zeitschrift für altorientaliche und biblische Rechtgeschichte* 14 (2008): 47–85.

Hayes, Christine. *Introduction to the Bible.* New Haven: Yale University Press, 2012.

Hengstenberg, E. W. *Dissertations on the Genuineness of the Pentateuch* I. Trans. J. E. Ryland. Edinburgh: John D. Lowe, 1847.

Hertzberg, Hans Wilhelm. *I & II Samuel.* Trans. John S. Bowden. Philadelphia: Westminster, 1964.

Hess, Richard. *Israelite Religions: An Archaeological and Biblical Survey.* Grand Rapids: Baker Academic, 2007.

Hill, Andrew, and John Walton. *A Survey of the Old Testament*. Grand Rapids: Zondervan, 1991.

Hoerth, Alfred J. *Archaeology and the Old Testament*. Grand Rapids: Baker Academic, 1998.

Hoffner, Harry A., Jr. "Propaganda and Political Justification in Hittite Historiography." In *Unity and Diversity: Essays in the History, Literature, and Religion of the Ancient Near East*, 49–62. Ed. Hans Goedicke and J. J. M. Roberts. Baltimore: Johns Hopkins University Press, 1975.

Holladay, John S., Jr. "The Day(s) the *Moon* Stood Still." *Journal of Biblical Literature* 87, no. 2 (1968): 166–78.

Hubbard, R. Pearce S. "The Topography of Ancient Jerusalem." *Palestine Exploration Quarterly* 98 (1966): 130–54.

Hutton, Jeremy. *The Transjordanian Palimpsest: The Overwritten Texts of Personal Exile and Transformation in the Deuteronomistic History*. Beihefte zur Zeitschrift für die alttestamentliche Wissenschaft 396. Berlin: de Gruyter, 2009.

Hyatt, J. Philip. "The Writing of an Old Testament Book." *Biblical Archaeologist* 6, no. 4 (1943): 71–80.

Irwin, Brian. "Not Just Any King: Abimelech, the Northern Monarchy, and the Final Form of Judges." *Journal of Biblical Literature* 131, no. 3 (2012): 443–54.

Ishida, Tomoo. "Adonijah the Son of Haggith and His Supporters: An Inquiry into Problems about History and Historiography." In *The Future of Biblical Studies—The Hebrew Scriptures*, 165–87. Ed. Richard Elliott Friedman and H. G. M. Williamson. Atlanta: Scholars, 1987.

_____. *History and Historical Writing in Ancient Israel: Studies in Biblical Historiography*. Leiden: Brill, 1999.

Jamieson-Drake, David W. *Scribes and Schools in Monarchic Judah: A Socio-Archaeological Approach*. Journal for the Study of the Old Testament: Supplement Series 109. Sheffield: Almond, 1991.

Jobling, David. *The Sense of Biblical Narrative: Three Structural Analyses in the Old Testament (1 Samuel 13–31, Numbers 11–12, 1 Kings 17–18)*. Journal for the Study of the Old Testament: Supplement Series 7. Sheffield: JSOT, 1978.

_____. "What, If Anything, Is 1 Samuel." *Scandinavian Journal of the Old Testament* 7, no. 1 (1993): 17–31.

_____. *1 Samuel*. Berit Olam. Collegeville, MN: Liturgical, 1998.

Jüngling, Hans-Winfried. *Richter 19–Ein Plädoyer für das Königtum*. Analecta biblica 84. Rome: Biblical Institute Press, 1981.

Kaiser, Otto. *Introduction to the Old Testament*. Oxford: Western Printing Services, 1975.

Kalland, Earl S. *Deuteronomy*. Expositor's Bible Commentary 3. Grand Rapids: Zondervan, 1992.

Kaufmann, Yehezkel. *The Biblical Account of the Conquest of Palestine*. Jerusalem: Magnes, 1953.

Keil, Carl Friedrich, and Franz Delitzsch. *Joshua, Judges, Ruth, 1 and 2 Samuel*. Commentary on the Old Testament 2. Edinburgh: T&T Clark, 1866–1891. Repr.: Peabody, MA: Hendrickson, 2001.

Keys, Gillian. *The Wages of Sin: A Reappraisal of the 'Succession Narrative.'* Journal for the Study of the Old Testament: Supplement Series 221. Sheffield: Sheffield Academic Press, 1996.

Kitchen, Kenneth A. *On the Reliability of the Old Testament*. Grand Rapids: Eerdmans, 2003.

Kline, Meredith G. *Treaty of the Great King: The Covenant Structure of Deuteronomy*. Grand Rapids: Eerdmans, 1963.

Klostermann, A. *Die Bücher Samuelis und der Könige*. Kurzgefasster Kommentar zu den heiligen Schriften Alten und Neuen Testaments 3. Nördlingen: Beck, 1887.

Knight, Douglas A. "Deuteronomy and the Deuteronomists." In *Old Testament Interpretation Past, Present, and Future: Essays in Honour of Gene*

M. Tucker, 61–79. Ed. James Luther Mays, David L. Petersen, and Kent Harold Richards. Edinburgh: T&T Clark, 1995.

Knoppers, Gary N. "Is There a Future for the Deuteronomistic History?" In *The Future of the Deuteronomistic History*, 119–34. Ed. Thomas Römer. Leuven: Leuven University Press, 2000.

_____. "Prayer and Propaganda: Solomon's Dedication of the Temple and the Deuteronomist's Program." *Catholic Biblical Quarterly* 57, no. 2 (1995): 229–54.

_____. "Rethinking the Relationship between Deuteronomy and the Deuteronomistic History: The Case of Kings." *Catholic Biblical Quarterly* 63, no. 3 (2001): 393–415.

_____. "'There Was None Like Him': Incomparability in the Book of Kings." *Catholic Biblical Quarterly* 54, no. 3 (1992): 411–31.

_____. *Two Nations under God: The Reign of Solomon and the Rise of Jeroboam*. Harvard Semitic Monographs 52. Atlanta: Scholars, 1993.

_____. *Two Nations under God: The Deuteronomistic History of Solomon and the Dual Monarchies*. Harvard Semitic Monographs 53. Atlanta: Scholars, 1994.

Kratz, Reinhard G. *The Composition of the Narrative Books of the Old Testament*. Trans. John Bowden. London: T&T Clark, 2005.

Kraus, Hans-Joachim. "Gilgal: A Contribution to the History of Worship in Israel." In *Reconsidering Israel and Judah: Recent Studies on the Deuteronomistic History*, 163–78. Ed. Gary N. Knoppers and J. Gordon McConville. Winona Lake, IN: Eisenbrauns, 2000. In German: "Gilgal: Ein Beitrag zur Kultusgeschichte Israels." *Vetus Testamentum* 1, no. 3 (1951): 181–99.

Kuenen, Abraham. *Het onstaan van de Historische Boeken des Ouden Verbonds*. Vol. 1 of *Historisch-kritisch onderzoek naar het ontstaan en de verzameling van de boeken des Ouden Verbonds*. 3 vols. Leiden: Engels, 1861.

_____. *Historisch-kritische Einleitung in die Bücher des Alten Testaments.* Trans. T. Weber. Vol. 1. Leipzig: Otto Schulze, 1887.

Langlamet, F. "Les récits de l'institution de la royauté (I Samuel, VII–XII): De Wellhausen aux travaux récents." *Revue Biblique* 77, no. 2 (1970): 161–200.

Lasor, William, David Hubbard, and Frederic Bush. 2d ed. *Old Testament Survey.* Grand Rapids: Eerdmans, 1996.

Laurie, S. S. "The History of Early Education: The Semitic Races." *The School Review* 1, no. 8 (1893): 482–90.

Legrand, Lucien. *The Bible on Culture.* Maryknoll, NY: Orbis, 2000.

Lemche, Niels Peter. "David's Rise." *Journal for the Study of the Old Testament* 10 (1978): 2–25.

_____. *The Israelites in History and Tradition.* Louisville: Westminster John Knox, 1998.

_____. "The Old Testament—A Hellenistic Book?" *Scandinavian Journal of the Old Testament* 7, no. 2 (1993): 163–93.

Leuchter, Mark. *Samuel and the Shaping of Tradition.* New York: Oxford University Press, 2013.

Levenson, Jon D. "Who Inserted the Book of the Torah?" *Harvard Theological Review* 68 (1975): 203–33.

_____. "1 Samuel 25 as Literature and as History." *Catholic Biblical Quarterly* 40, no. 1 (1978): 11–28.

Lilley, J. P. U. "A Literary Appreciation of the Book of Judges." *Tyndale Bulletin* 18 (1967): 94–102.

Lohfink, Norbert. "Culture Shock and Theology." *Biblical Theology Bulletin* 7, no. 1 (1977): 12–21.

Longman, Tremper, III, and Raymond Dillard. *An Introduction to the Old Testament.* 2d ed. Grand Rapids: Zondervan, 2006.

López, F. García. *Le Deutéronome: Une Loi prêchée. Cahiers évangile* 63. Paris: Cerf, 1988.

Malamat, Abraham, ed. *The World History of the Jewish People. Vol. 4, Part 1: The Age of the Monarchies: Political History.* Jerusalem: Masada, 1979.

Maly, Eugene H. "The Jotham Fable—Anti-Monarchical?" *Catholic Biblical Quarterly* 22, no. 3 (1960): 299–305.

Manley, G. T. *The Book of the Law: Studies in the Date of Deuteronomy.* Grand Rapids: Eerdmans, 1957.

Margalit, Baruch. "The Day the Sun Did Not Stand Still: A New Look at Joshua x 8–15." *Vetus Testamentum* 42, no. 4 (1992): 466–91.

Martin, James D. *The Book of Judges.* Cambridge: Cambridge University Press, 1975.

Matthews, Victor H. *Judges & Ruth.* Cambridge: Cambridge University Press, 2004.

Mayes, A. D. H. "Deuteronomistic Royal Ideology in Judges 17–21." *Biblical Interpretation* 9, no. 3 (2001): 241–58.

————. *Judges.* Sheffield: JSOT, 1985.

————. *The Story of Israel Between Settlement and Exile: A Redactional Study of the Deuteronomistic History.* London: SCM, 1983.

Mazar, Benjamin. "The Military Élite of King David." *Vetus Testamentum* 13, no. 3 (1963): 310–20.

McCann, J. Clinton. *Judges.* Interpretation. Louisville: Westminster John Knox, 2002.

McCarter, P. Kyle. "Plots, True or False:" The Succession Narrative as Court Apologetic." *Interpretation* 35, no. 4 (1981): 355–67.

————. "The Apology of David." *Journal of Biblical Literature* 99, no. 4 (1980): 489–504.

————. "The Books of Samuel." In *The History of Israel's Traditions: The Heritage of Martin Noth*, 260–80. Ed. Steven L. McKenzie and M. Patrick Graham. Journal for the Study of the Old Testament: Supplement Series 182. Sheffield: Sheffield Academic Press, 1994.

_____. *I Samuel: A New Translation with Introduction: Notes and Commentary*. Anchor Bible 8. Garden City, NY: Doubleday, 1980.

_____. *II Samuel: A New Translation with Introduction: Notes and Commentary*. Anchor Bible 9. Garden City, NY: Doubleday, 1984.

McCarthy, Dennis J. *Old Testament Covenant: A Survey of Opinions*. Richmond: John Knox, 1972.

_____. *Treaty and Covenant*. Rome: Pontifical Biblical Institute, 1963.

McConville, J. Gordon. "Narrative and Meaning in the Books of Kings." *Biblica* 70, no. 1 (1989): 31–49.

_____. "Restoration in Deuteronomy and the Deuteronomic Literature." In *Restoration: Old Testament, Jewish, and Christian Perspectives*, 11–40. Ed. James M. Scott. Journal for the Study of Judaism in the Persian, Hellenistic, and Roman Periods Supplement Series 72. Leiden: Brill, 2001.

_____. "The Old Testament Historical Books in Modern Scholarship." *Themelios* 22, no. 3 (1997): 3–13.

_____. "1 Kings 8:46-53 and the Deuteronomic Hope." *Vetus Testamentum* 42, no. 1 (1992): 67–79.

McKenzie, Steven L. *King David: A Biography*. New York: Oxford University Press, 2000.

_____. "Postscript: The Laws of Physics and Pan-Deuteronomism." In *Those Elusive Deuteronomists: The Phenomenon of Pan-Deuteronomism*, 262–71. Ed. Linda S. Schearing and Steven L. McKenzie. Journal for the Study of the Old Testament: Supplement Series 268. Sheffield: Sheffield Academic Press, 1999.

_____. "The Books of Kings in the Deuteronomistic History." In *The History of Israel's Traditions: The Heritage of Martin Noth*, 281–307. Ed. Steven L. McKenzie and M. Patrick Graham. Journal for the Study of the Old Testament: Supplement Series 182. Sheffield: Sheffield Academic Press, 1994.

_____. *The Chronicler's Use of the Deuteronomistic History*. Harvard Semitic Monographs 33. Atlanta: Scholars, 1984.

_____. "The Divided Kingdom in the Deuteronomistic History and in Scholarship on It." In *The Future of the Deuteronomistic History*, 135–45. Ed. Thomas Römer. Leuven: Leuven University Press, 2000

_____. "The Trouble with Kingship." In *Israel Constructs Its History: Deuteronomistic Historiography in Recent Research*, 286–314. Ed. Albert de Pury, Thomas Römer, and Jean-Daniel Macchi. Journal for the Study of the Old Testament: Supplement Series 306. Sheffield: JSOT, 1994.

_____. *The Trouble with Kings: The Composition of the Book of Kings in the Deuteronomistic History*. Supplements to Vetus Testamentum 42. Leiden: Brill, 1991.

_____, and M. Patrick Graham, eds. *The History of Israel's Traditions: The Heritage of Martin Noth*. Journal for the Study of the Old Testament: Supplement Series 182. Sheffield: Sheffield Academic Press, 1994.

Mendelsohn, Isaac. "Samuel's Denunciation of Kingship in the Light of the Akkadian Documents from Ugarit." *Bulletin of American Schools of Oriental Research* 143 (1956): 17–22.

Mendenhall, George. "Covenant Forms in Israelite Tradition." *Biblical Archaeologist* 17, no. 3 (1954): 50–76.

Merrill, Eugene. "Deuteronomy and de Wette: A Fresh Look at a Fallacious Premise." *Journal for the Evangelical Study of the Old Testament* 1, no. 1 (2012): 25–42.

_____. *Kingdom of Priests: A History of Old Testament Israel*. 2d ed. Grand Rapids: Baker Academic, 2008.

Miller, J. Maxwell, and John H. Hayes. *A History of Ancient Israel and Judah*. London: SCM, 1986.

Miller, Patrick D., Jr. *Deuteronomy*. Interpretation. Louisville: Westminster John Knox, 1990.

Miscall, Peter. *The Workings of Old Testament Narrative*. Society of Biblical Literature Semeia Studies. Philadelphia: Fortress Press, 1983.

Montgomery, J. A. "Archival Data in the Book of Kings." *Journal of Biblical Literature* 53, no. 1 (1934): 46–52.

Moore, George F. *A Critical and Exegetical Commentary on Judges*. Edinburgh: Clark, 1895.

Mowinckel, Sigmund. *Zur Komposition des Buches Jeremia*. Kristiania: Jacob Dybwad, 1914.

Muilenburg, James. "Baruch the Scribe." In *Proclamation and Presence: Essays in Honour of G. Henton Davies*, 215–38. Ed. John I. Durham and J. R. Porter. Richmond: John Knox, 1970.

Murphy, Francesca Aran. *1 Samuel*. Grand Rapids: Brazos, 2010.

Na'aman, Nadav. "The Law of the Altar in Deuteronomy and the Cultic Site Near Shechem." In *Rethinking the Foundations: Historiography in the Ancient World and in the Bible: Essays in Honour of John Van Seters*, 141–61. Ed. Steven L. McKenzie, Thomas Römer, and Hans Heinrich Schmid. Berlin: Walter de Gruyter, 2000.

_____. "The Pre-Deuteronomistic Story of Saul and Its Historical Significance." *Catholic Biblical Quarterly* 54, no. 4 (1992): 638–58.

Naveh, Joseph. "A Paleographic Note on the Distribution of the Hebrew Script." *Harvard Theological Review* 61, no. 1 (1968): 68–74.

Nelson, Richard D. "Josiah in the Book of Joshua." *Journal of Biblical Literature* 100, no. 4 (1981): 531–40.

_____. "The Altar of Ahaz: A Revisionist View." *Hebrew Annual Review* 10 (1986): 267–76.

_____. *The Double Redaction of the Deuteronomistic History*. Journal for the Study of the Old Testament: Supplement Series 18. Sheffield: JSOT, 1981.

_____. "The Double Redaction of the Deuteronomistic History: The Case Is Still Compelling." *Journal for the Study of the Old Testament* 29, no. 3 (2005): 319–37.

_____. "The Role of the Priesthood in the Deuteronomistic History." In *Reconsidering Israel and Judah: Recent Studies on the Deuteronomistic History*, 179–93. Ed. Gary N. Knoppers and J. Gordon McConville. Winona Lake, IN: Eisenbrauns, 2000.

Newman, Murray L., Jr. *The People of the Covenant: A Study of Israel from Moses to the Monarchy.* New York: Abingdon, 1962.

Nicholson, Ernest W. *Deuteronomy and Tradition.* Philadelphia: Fortress Press, 1967.

_____. *Jeremiah 1–25.* Cambridge Bible Commentary. Cambridge: Cambridge University Press, 1973.

Niditch, Susan. *Judges: A Commentary.* Old Testament Library. Louisville: Westminster John Knox, 2008.

Noll, Kurt L. "Deuteronomistic History or Deuteronomic Debate? (A Thought Experiment)." *Journal for the Study of the Old Testament* 31, no. 3 (2007): 311–45.

_____. "Presumptuous Prophets Participating in a Deuteronomic Debate." In *Prophets, Prophecy, and Ancient Israelite Historiography,* 125–42. Ed. Mark J. Boda and Lissa M. Wray Beal. Winona Lake, IN: Eisenbrauns, 2013.

Noth, Martin. *Das Buch Joshua.* 2d ed. Handbuch zum Alten Testament 7. Tübingen: Mohr, 1953.

_____. "Remarks on the Sixth Volume of the Mari Texts." *Journal of Semitic Studies* 1, no. 4 (1956): 322–33.

_____. *The Deuteronomistic History.* Journal for the Study of the Old Testament: Supplement Series 15. Sheffield: JSOT, 1981.

_____. "The Jerusalem Catastrophe of 587 B.C. and Its Significance for Israel." In *The Laws in the Pentateuch and Other Studies,* 260–80. Trans. D. R. Ap-Thomas. London: Oliver & Boyd, 1966.

O'Brien, Mark A. "Judges and the Deuteronomistic History." In *The History of Israel's Traditions: The Heritage of Martin Noth*, 235–59. Ed. Steven L. McKenzie and M. Patrick Graham. Journal for the Study of the Old Testament: Supplement Series 182. Sheffield: Sheffield Academic Press, 1994.

O'Connell, Robert H. *The Rhetoric of the Book of Judges*. Supplements to Vetus Testamentum 63. Leiden: Brill, 1996.

Oeste, Gordon. "Butchered Brothers and Betrayed Families: Degenerating Kinship Structures in the Book of Judges." *Journal for the Study of the Old Testament* 35, no. 3 (2011): 295–316.

————. *Legitimacy, Illegitimacy, and the Right to Rule: Windows on Abimelech's Rise and Demise in Judges 9*. New York: T&T Clark, 2011.

————. "The Shaping of a Prophet: Joshua in the Deuteronomistic History." In *Prophets, Prophecy, and Ancient Israelite Historiography*, 23–41. Ed. Mark J. Boda and Lissa M. Wray Beal. Winona Lake, IN: Eisenbrauns, 2013.

Otto, Susanne. "The Composition of the Elijah-Elisha Stories and the Deuteronomistic History." *Journal for the Study of the Old Testament* 27, no. 4 (2003): 487–508.

Peckham, Brian. "The Composition of Joshua 3–4." *Catholic Biblical Quarterly* 46, no. 3 (1984): 413–31.

————. *The Composition of the Deuteronomistic History*. Harvard Semitic Monographs 35. Atlanta: Scholars, 1985.

————. "The Deuteronomistic History of Saul and David." *Zeitschrift für alttestamentliche Wissenschaft* 97, no. 2 (1985): 190–209.

————. "The Significance of the Book of Joshua in Noth's Theory of the Deuteronomistic History." In *The History of Israel's Traditions: The Heritage of Martin Noth*, 213–34. Ed. Steven L. McKenzie and M. Patrick Graham. Journal for the Study of the Old Testament: Supplement Series 182. Sheffield: Sheffield Academic Press, 1994.

Perdue, Leo G. "Is There Anyone Left of the House of Saul . . . ? Ambiguity and the Characterization of David in the Succession Narrative." *Journal for the Study of the Old Testament* 30 (1984): 67–84.

Perlitt, Lothar. *Bundestheologie im Alien Testament.* Wissenschaftliche Monographien zum Alten und Neuen Testament 36. Neukirchen-Vluyn: Neukirchener, 1969.

Person, Raymond F., Jr. *The Deuteronomistic School: History, Social Setting, and Literature.* Society of Biblical Literature Studies in Biblical Literature 2. Atlanta: SBL, 2002.

Peterson, Brian. *Ezekiel in Context: Ezekiel's Message Understood in its Historical Setting of Covenant Curses and Ancient Near Eastern Mythological Motifs.* Princeton Theological Monograph Series 182. Eugene, OR: Pickwick, 2012.

_____. "Could Abiathar, the Priest, Be the Author of Judges?" *Bibliotheca Sacra* 170, no. 680 (2013): 432–52.

_____. "The Gibeonite Revenge of 2 Sam 21:1-14: Another Example of David's Darker Side or a Picture of a Shrewd Monarch?" *Journal for the Evangelical Study of the Old Testament* 1, no. 2 (2012): 201–22.

Plöger, Otto. "Speech and Prayer in the Deuteronomistic and the Chronicler's Histories." In *Reconsidering Israel and Judah: Recent Studies on the Deuteronomistic History*, 31–46. Ed. Gary N. Knoppers and J. Gordon McConville. Winona Lake, IN: Eisenbrauns, 2000. In German: "Reden und Gebete im deuteronomistischen und chronistischen Geschichtswerk." In *Festschrift für Günther Dehn zum 75. Geburtstag*, 35–49. Ed. W. Schneemelcher. Neukirchen-Vluyn: Neukirchener, 1957.

Polzin, Robert. *Moses and the Deuteronomist: A Literary Study of the Deuteronomistic History I. Deuteronomy, Joshua, Judges.* Bloomington: Indiana University Press, 1993.

_____. *Samuel and the Deuteronomist: A Literary Study of the Deuteronomistic History II: 1 Samuel.* San Francisco: Harper & Row, 1989.

Porter, J. Roy. "The Succession of Joshua." In *Reconsidering Israel and Judah: Recent Studies on the Deuteronomistic History*, 139–62. Ed. Gary N. Knoppers and J. Gordon McConville. Winona Lake, IN: Eisenbrauns, 2000.

Pritchard, James B., ed. *Ancient Near Eastern Texts Relating to the Old Testament*. 3d ed. Princeton: Princeton University Press, 1969.

Provan, Iain. *Hezekiah and the Books of Kings: A Contribution to the Debate about the Composition of the Deuteronomistic History*. Beihefte zur Zeitschrift für die alttestamentliche Wissenschaft 172. Berlin: de Gruyter, 1988.

Pusey, E. W. *The Minor Prophets with a Commentary*. London: Smith, 1883.

Rabin, Chaim. "Discourse Analysis and the Dating of Deuteronomy." In *Interpreting the Hebrew Bible: Essays in Honour of E. I. J. Rosenthal*, 171–77. Ed. J. A. Emerton and Stefan C. Reif. Cambridge: Cambridge University Press, 1982.

Rabinowitz, Rabbi Chaim Dov. *Commentary on the Books of Yehoshua Shoftim; Da'ath Sofrim Torah, Prophets, Sacred Writings*. Trans. Rabbi S. Carmel. New York/Jerusalem: H. Vagshal, 2004.

Rainey, A. F. "Mizpah." In *The International Standard Bible Encyclopedia*, 3:387–88. Ed. by Geoffrey W. Bromiley. 4 vols. Grand Rapids: Eerdmans, 1986.

Reiner, Erica. "Fortune-Telling in Mesopotamia." *Journal of Near Eastern Studies* 19, no. 1 (1960): 23–35.

Rendsburg, Gary A. "A New Look at Pentateuchal *HW*." *Biblica* 63, no. 3 (1982): 351–69.

Richter, S. L. "Deuteronomistic History." In *Dictionary of the Old Testament: Historical Books*, 219–30. Ed. Bill T. Arnold and H. G. M. Williamson. Downers Grove, IL: InterVarsity, 2005.

Richter, Wolfgang. *Die Bearbeitungen des 'Retterbuches' in der deuteronomischen Epoche*. Bonn: P. Hanstein, 1964.

_____. *Traditionsgeschichtliche Untersuchungen zum Richterbuch.* Bonner Biblische Beiträge 18. Bonn: P. Hanstein, 1963.

Riehm, Eduard. *Die Gesetzgebung Mosis im Lande Moab.* Gotha: Friedrich Andreas Perthes, 1854.

Robinson, Henry Wheeler. *Corporate Personality in Ancient Israel.* Philadelphia: Fortress Press, 1967.

Robson, James. "The Literary Composition of Deuteronomy." In *Interpreting Deuteronomy: Issues and Approaches*, 19–59. Ed. David G. Firth and Philip S. Johnston. Downers Grove, IL: IVP Academic, 2012.

Rofé, Alexander. *Deuteronomy: Issues and Interpretation.* London: T&T Clark, 2002.

_____. "Ephraimite Versus Deuteronomistic History." In *Reconsidering Israel and Judah: Recent Studies on the Deuteronomistic History*, 462–74. Ed. Gary N. Knoppers and J. Gordon McConville. Winona Lake, IN: Eisenbrauns, 2000.

Rollston, Christopher A. "Scribal Education in Ancient Israel: The Old Hebrew Epigraphic Evidence." *Bulletin of American Schools of Oriental Research* 344 (2006): 47–74.

Römer, Thomas. "Book-Endings in Joshua and the Question of the So-Called Deuteronomistic History." In *Raising Up a Faithful Exegete*, 85–99. Ed. Kurt L. Noll and Brooks Schramm. Winona Lake, IN: Eisenbrauns, 2010.

_____. "Deuteronomy in Search of Origins." In *Reconsidering Israel and Judah: Recent Studies on the Deuteronomistic History*, 112–38. Ed. Gary N. Knoppers and J. Gordon McConville. Winona Lake, IN: Eisenbrauns, 2000.

_____. "How Did Jeremiah Become a Convert to Deuteronomistic Ideology." In *Those Elusive Deuteronomists: The Phenomenon of Pan-Deuteronomism*, 189–99. Ed. Linda S. Schearing and Steven L. McKenzie.

Journal for the Study of the Old Testament: Supplement Series 268. Sheffield: Sheffield Academic Press, 1999.

_____. "L'école deutéronomiste et la formation de la Bible hébraïque." In *The Future of the Deuteronomistic History*, 179–93. Ed. Thomas Römer. Leuven: Leuven University Press, 2000.

_____. "The Book of Deuteronomy." In *The History of Israel's Traditions: The Heritage of Martin Noth*, 178–212. Ed. Steven L. McKenzie and M. Patrick Graham. Journal for the Study of the Old Testament: Supplement Series 182. Sheffield: Sheffield Academic Press, 1994.

_____. *The So-called Deuteronomistic History: A Sociological, Historical, and Literary Introduction.* London: T & T Clark, 2005.

_____, and A. de Pury. "Deuteronomistic Historiography (DH): History of Research and Debated Issues." In *Israel Constructs Its History: Deuteronomistic Historiography in Recent Research*, 24–141. Ed. Albert de Pury, Thomas Römer, and Jean-Daniel Macchi. Journal for the Study of the Old Testament: Supplement Series 306. Sheffield: Sheffield Academic Press, 2000.

Rösel, Hartmut N. "Does a Comprehensive 'Leitmotiv' Exist in the Deuteronomistic History?" In *The Future of the Deuteronomistic History*, 195–211. Ed. Thomas Römer. Leuven: Leuven University Press, 2000.

Rost, Leonhard. *Die Überlieferung von der Thronnachfolge Davids.* Beiträge zur Wissenschaft vom Alten und Neuen Testament 3/6. Stuttgart: Kohlhammer, 1926. In English: *The Succession to the Throne of David.* Trans. Michael D. Rutter and David M. Gunn. Sheffield: Almond, 1982.

Sanders, Seth L. "Writing and Early Iron Age Israel: Before National Scripts, Beyond Nations and States." In *Literate Culture and Tenth-Century Canaan: The Tel Zayit Abecedary in Context*, 97–112. Ed. Ron E. Tappy and P. Kyle McCarter Jr. Winona Lake, IN: Eisenbrauns, 2008.

Schmid, H. H. *Der sogenannte Jahwist: Beobachtungen und Fragen zur Pentateuchforschung.* Zurich: Theologischer, 1976.

Schneider, Tammi J. *Judges*. Berit Olam: Studies in Hebrew Narrative & Poetry. Collegeville, MN: Liturgical, 2000.

Schnittjer, Gary Edward. *The Torah Story: An Apprenticeship on the Pentateuch*. Grand Rapids: Zondervan, 2006.

Schultz, Samuel J. *Deuteronomy*. Everyman's Bible Commentary. Chicago: Moody, 1971.

Seeligmann, I. L. "Aetiological Elements in Biblical Historiography." *Zion* 26 (1960–1961): 141–61 [Heb].

Sellin, Ernst. *Introduction to the Old Testament*. Trans. W. Montgomery. London: Hodder & Stoughton, 1923. In German: *Einleitung in das Alte Testament*. ETB 2. Leipzig: Quelle & Meyer, 1910.

Smend, Rudolf. *Die Entstehung des Alten Testaments*. Stuttgart: Kohlhammer, 1978.

————. "The Law and the Nations: A Contribution to Deuteronomistic Tradition History." In *Reconsidering Israel and Judah: Recent Studies on the Deuteronomistic History*, 95–110. Ed. Gary N. Knoppers and J. Gordon McConville. Winona Lake, IN: Eisenbrauns, 2000. In German: "Das Gesetz und die Völker: Ein Beitrag zur deuteronomistischen Redacktionsgeschichte." In *Probleme biblischer Theologie: Festschrift Gerhard von Rad zum 70. Geburtstag*, 494–509. Ed. Hans Walter Wolff. Munich: Kaiser, 1971.

Smith, Mark. *The Early History of God*. 2d ed. Grand Rapids: Eerdmans, 2002.

Soggin, Alberto. *Judges*. Trans. John Bowden. Old Testament Library. Philadelphia: Westminster, 1981.

Sperling, S. David. "Joshua 24 Re-examined." *Hebrew Union College Annual* 58 (1987): 119–36.

Steinberg, Naomi. "Social Scientific Criticism: Judges 9 and Issues of Kinship." In *Judges and Method*, 45–64. Ed. Gale Yee. Minneapolis: Fortress Press, 1995.

Stuart, Douglas K. "The Old Testament Prophets' Self Understanding of Their Prophecy." *Themelios* 6, no. 1 (1980): 9–14.

Sturtevant, Edgar H., and George Bechtel. *A Hittite Chrestomathy*. Special Publications of the Linguistic Society of America. William Dwight Whitney Linguistics Series. Philadelphia: University of Pennsylvania, 1935.

Sweeney, Marvin. "Davidic Polemic in the Book of Judges." *Vetus Testamentum* 47, no. 4 (1997): 517–29.

Tappy, Ron E., and P. Kyle McCarter Jr., eds. *Literate Culture and Tenth-Century Canaan: The Tel Zayit Abecedary in Context*. Winona Lake, IN: Eisenbrauns, 2008.

Tetlow, Elisabeth Meier. *Women, Crime, and Punishment in Ancient Law and Society*. 2 vols. New York: Continuum, 2005.

Thompson, J. A. *Deuteronomy: An Introduction and Commentary*. Tyndale Old Testament Commentary Series. Downers Grove, IL: InterVarsity, 1978.

Thompson, Thomas. "Martin Noth and the History of Israel." In *The History of Israel's Traditions: The Heritage of Martin Noth*, 81–90. Ed. Steven L. McKenzie and M. Patrick Graham. Journal for the Study of the Old Testament: Supplement Series 182. Sheffield: Sheffield Academic Press, 1994.

————. *The Early History of the Israelite People: From the Written and Archaeological Sources*. Leiden: Brill, 1994.

Thornton, T. C. G. "Solomonic Apologetic in Samuel and Kings." *Church Quarterly Review* 169, no. 371 (1968): 159–66.

Tigay, Jeffrey. *The Evolution of the Gilgamesh Epic*. Philadelphia: University of Pennsylvania Press, 1982.

————. "The Significance of the End of Deuteronomy (Deuteronomy 34:10–12)." In *Texts, Temples, and Traditions: A Tribute to Menahem Haran*, 137–43. Ed. Michael Fox, Victor Hurowitz, Avi Hurvitz, Michael Klein, Baruch Schwartz, and Nili Shupak. Winona Lake, IN: Eisenbrauns, 1996.

Uitti, Roger W. "Hilkiah." In *The Anchor Bible Dictionary*, 3:200–201. Ed. David Noel Freedman. 6 vols. New York: Doubleday, 1992.

VanderKam, James A. "Davidic Complicity in the Deaths of Abner and Eshbaal: A Historical and Redactional Study." *Journal of Biblical Literature* 99, no. 4 (1980): 521–39.

Van der Toorn, Karel. *Scribal Culture and the Making of the Hebrew Bible*. Cambridge: Harvard University Press, 2007.

Van Keulen, Percy S. F. *Manasseh Through the Eyes of the Deuteronomists: The Manasseh Account (2 Kings 21:1–18) and the Final Chapters of the Deuteronomistic History*. Leiden: Brill, 1996.

————. *Two Versions of the Solomon Narrative: An Inquiry into the Relationship between MT 1 Kgs. 2–11 and LXX 3 Reg. 2–11*. Leiden: Brill, 2005.

Van Seters, John. *In Search of History: Historiography in the Ancient World and the Origins of Biblical History*. New Haven: Yale University Press, 1983. Repr.: Winona Lake, IN: Eisenbrauns, 1997.

————. "Joshua 24 and the Problem of Tradition in the Old Testament." In *In the Shelter of Elyon: Essays on Ancient Palestinian Life and Literature in Honor of G. W. Ahlström*, 139–58. Journal for the Study of the Old Testament: Supplement Series 31. Sheffield: JSOT, 1984.

————. *The Biblical Saga of King David*. Winona Lake, IN: Eisenbrauns, 2009.

————. "The Deuteronomistic History: Can It Avoid Death by Redaction?" In *The Future of the Deuteronomistic History*, 213–22. Ed. Thomas Römer. Leuven: Leuven University Press, 2000.

Vater, Johann Severin. *Commentar über den Pentateuch*. 3 vols. Halle: Waisenhaus Buchhandlung, 1802–1805.

Veijola, Timo. *Die ewige Dynastie: David und die Entstehung seiner Dynastie nach der deuteronomistischen Darstellung*. Annales Academiae Scientiarum Fennicae B/193. Helsinki: Suomalainen Tiede-akatemia, 1975.

_____. *Historiographie: Eine redaktionsgeschichtliche Untersuchung.* Annales Academiae Scientiarum Fennicae B/198. Helsinki: Suomalainen Tiede-akatemia, 1977.

_____. "Solomon: Bathsheba's Firstborn." In *Reconsidering Israel and Judah: Recent Studies on the Deuteronomistic History*, 340–57. Ed. Gary N. Knoppers and J. Gordon McConville. Winona Lake, IN: Eisenbrauns, 2000.

_____. *Verheissung in der Krise: Studien zur Literatur und Theologie der Exilszeit anhand des 89. Psalms.* Annales Academiae Scientiarum Fennicae B/220. Helsinki: Suomalainen Tiede-akatemia, 1982.

Vincent, Albert. *Le Livre des Juges, Le Livre de Ruth.* Paris: Les Editions du Cerf, 1952.

Von Rad, Gerhard. *Studies in Deuteronomy.* London: SCM, 1953.

_____. *The Problem of the Hexateuch and Other Essays.* Trans. E. W. Trueman Dicken. London: Oliver and Boyd, 1966.

Wallace, H. "Hilkiah." In *The International Standard Bible Encyclopedia*, 2:713. Ed. Geoffrey W. Bromiley. 4 vols. Grand Rapids: Eerdmans, 1986.

Walton, John. *Ancient Near Eastern Thought and the Old Testament.* Grand Rapids: Baker Academic, 2006.

Webb, Barry. *The Book of Judges: An Integrated Reading.* Journal for the Study of the Old Testament: Supplement Series 46. Sheffield: JSOT, 1987.

Weinfeld, Moshe. *Deuteronomy and the Deuteronomistic School.* Oxford: Clarendon, 1972.

_____. *Deuteronomy 1–11.* Anchor Bible 5. New York: Doubleday, 1991.

Weippert, Helga. "Die Ätiologie des Nordreiches und seines Königshauses (I Reg 11 29–40)." *Zeitschrift für alttestamentliche Wissenschaft* 95, no. 3 (1983): 344–75.

_____. "Die 'deuteronomistischen' Beurteilungen der Könige von Israel und Juda und das Problem der Redaktion der Königsbücher." *Biblica* 53, no. 3 (1972): 301–39.

_____. "'Histories' and 'History': Promise and Fulfillment in the Deuteronomistic Historical Work." In *Reconsidering Israel and Judah: Recent Studies on the Deuteronomistic History*, 47–61. Ed. Gary N. Knoppers and J. Gordon McConville. Winona Lake, IN: Eisenbrauns, 2000.

Weiser, Artur. "Die Legitimation des Königs David: Zur Eigenart und Entstehung der sogen Geschichte von Davids Aufstieg." *Vetus Testamentum* 16, no. 3 (1966): 325–54.

_____. *Einleitung in das Alte Testament.* Göttingen: Vandenhoeck & Ruprecht, 1963.

Wellhausen, Julius. Die *Composition des Hexateuchs und der historischen Bucher des Alten Testaments.* 3d ed. Berlin: Georg Reimer, 1899.

_____. *Prolegomena to the History of Ancient Israel.* Edinburgh: A&C Black, 1885. Repr.: Gloucester, MA: Peter Smith, 1973.

Wenham, Gordon. "The Date of Deuteronomy: Linch-pin of Old Testament Criticism. Part One." *Themelios* 10, no. 3 (1985): 15–20.

_____. "The Deuteronomic Theology of the Book of Joshua." *Journal of Biblical Literature* 90, no. 2 (1971): 140–48.

_____. "Were David's Sons Priests?" *Zeitschrift für alttestamentliche Wissenschaft* 87 (1975): 79–82.

Westermann, Claus. Die *Geschichtsbücher des Alten Testaments: gab es ein deuteronomistisches Geschichtewerk?.* Kaiser: Gütersloher, 1994.

White, Marsha. *The Elijah Legends and Jehu's Coup.* Brown Judaic Studies 311. Atlanta: Scholars, 1997.

_____. "'The History of Saul's Rise': Saulide State Propaganda in 1 Samuel 1–14." In *'A Wise and Discerning Mind': Essays in Honor of Burke*

O. *Long*, 283–91. Ed. Saul M. Olyan and Robert C. Culley. Brown Judaic Studies 325. Providence, RI: Brown University Press, 2000.

Whitelam, Keith. "The Defence of David." *Journal for the Study of the Old Testament* 29 (1984): 61–87.

Whybray, R. Norman. *The Succession Narrative: A Study of II Samuel 9–20; I Kings 1 and 2*. Studies in Biblical Theology 9. London: SCM, 1968.

Widengren, Geo. "King and Covenant." *Journal of Semitic Studies* 2, no. 1 (1957): 1–32.

Wilcoxen, Jay A. "Narrative Structure and Cult Legend: A Study of Joshua 1–6." In *Transitions in Biblical Scholarship*, 43–70. Ed. J. C. Rylaarsdam. Chicago: University of Chicago Press, 1968.

Wilson, Robert R. "Unity and Diversity in the Book of Kings." In *'A Wise and Discerning Mind': Essays in Honor of Burke O. Long*, 293–310. Ed. Saul M. Olyan and Robert C. Culley. Brown Judaic Studies 325. Providence, RI: Brown University Press, 2000.

_____. "Who Was the Deuteronomist? (Who Was not the Deuteronomist?): Reflections on Pan-Deuteronomism." In *Those Elusive Deuteronomists: The Phenomenon of Pan-Deuteronomism*, 67–82. Ed. Linda S. Schearing and Steven L. McKenzie. Journal for the Study of the Old Testament: Supplement Series 268. Sheffield: Sheffield Academic Press, 1999.

Winther-Nielson, Nicolai. "The Miraculous Grammar of Joshua 3–4." In *Biblical Hebrew and Discourse Linguistics*, 300–319. Ed. Robert D. Berger. Winona Lake, IN: Eisenbrauns, 1994.

Wiseman, D. J. "The Vassal Treaties of Esarhaddon." *Iraq* 20, no. 1 (1958): 1–99.

Wolf, Herbert. *Judges*. Expositor's Bible Commentary 3. Grand Rapids: Zondervan, 1992.

Wolff, Hans Walter. "The Kerygma of the Deuteronomistic Historical Work." In *Reconsidering Israel and Judah: Recent Studies on the*

Deuteronomistic History, 62–78. Ed. Gary N. Knoppers and J. Gordon McConville. Winona Lake, IN: Eisenbrauns, 2000. In German: "Das Kerygma des deuteronomistischen Geschichtswerks." *Zeitschrift für alttestamentliche Wissenschaft* 73, no. 2 (1961): 171–86.

Wong, Gregory T. K. *Compositional Strategy of the Book of Judges: An Inductive, Rhetorical Study*. Supplements to Vetus Testamentum 111. Leiden: Brill, 2006.

Wood, Bryant. "The Search for Joshua's Ai." In *Critical Issues in Early Israelite History*, 205–40. Ed. Richard S. Hess, Gerald A. Klingbeil, and Paul J. Ray Jr. Winona Lake, IN: Eisenbrauns, 2008.

Yee, Gale. "Ideological Criticism: Judges 17–21 and the Dismembered Body." In *Judges and Method: New Approaches in Biblical Studies*, 146–70. Ed. Gale Yee. Minneapolis: Fortress Press, 1995.

_____. "Introduction: Why Judges?" In *Judges & Method: New Approaches in Biblical Studies*, 1–16. Ed. Gale Yee. Minneapolis: Fortress Press, 1995.

Yeivin, S. "Social, Religious and Cultural Trends in Jerusalem under the Davidic Dynasty." *Vetus Testamentum* 3, no. 2 (1953): 149–66.

Young, Edward J. *An Introduction to the Old Testament*. 3d ed. Grand Rapids: Eerdmans, 1965.

Young, Ian. "Israelite Literacy: Interpreting the Evidence: Part I." *Vetus Testamentum* 48, no. 2 (1998): 239–53.

_____. "Israelite Literacy: Interpreting the Evidence: Part II." *Vetus Testamentum* 48, no. 3 (1998): 408–22.

Index of Subjects and Authors

Index of Scripture References

Judges